Confronting Jim Crow

ROBERT COHEN

Confronting Jim Crow
Race, Memory, and the
University of Georgia in the
Twentieth Century

The University of North Carolina Press *Chapel Hill*

This book was published with the assistance of the Fred W. Morrison Fund of the University of North Carolina Press.

© 2024 Robert Cohen
All rights reserved
Set in Arno Pro by Westchester Publishing Services
Manufactured in the United States of America

Library of Congress Cataloging-in-Publication Data
Names: Cohen, Robert, 1955 May 21– author.
Title: Confronting Jim Crow : race, memory, and the University of Georgia in the twentieth century / Robert Cohen.
Description: Chapel Hill : University of North Carolina Press, [2024] | Includes bibliographical references and index.
Identifiers: LCCN 2024020858 | ISBN 9781469681399 (cloth ; alk. paper) | ISBN 9781469681405 (paperback ; alk. paper) | ISBN 9781469681412 (epub) | ISBN 9781469681429 (pdf)
Subjects: LCSH: University of Georgia—History—20th century. | College integration—Georgia—History—20th century. | African Americans—Segregation—Georgia. | Racism against Black people—Georgia—History—20th century. | Georgia—Race relations. | BISAC: SOCIAL SCIENCE / Ethnic Studies / American / African American & Black Studies | EDUCATION / History
Classification: LCC LD1983 .C58 2024 | DDC 378.1/982996073075818—dc23/eng/20240604
LC record available at https://lccn.loc.gov/2024020858

Covert art courtesy of Alvin Levert Hood and Hargrett Rare Book and Manuscript Library, University of Georgia Libraries.

Chapters 2 and 3 were previously published in a different form. Chapter 2 was published as "'Two, Four, Six, Eight, We Don't Want to Integrate': White Student Attitudes toward the University of Georgia's Desegregation," *Georgia Historical Quarterly* (Fall 1996): 616–45. Chapter 3 was published as "G-Men in Georgia: The FBI and the Segregationist Riot at the University of Georgia, 1961," *Georgia Historical Quarterly* (Fall 1999): 508–38. Both are republished with the permission of the Georgia Historical Society.

In Memory of Walter Stovall
(1938–2018)

Bob, that was the same sort of thing I heard when the Nazis were coming to power.

—Sigmund Cohn, UGA professor of international law, refugee from Nazi Germany, as he exited the campus chapel after hearing a Georgia gubernatorial candidate's white supremacist speech advocating militant resistance to integration in the streets, the courts, and the legislature. UGA's Law Day event, in the wake of the *Brown* decision (1954), From Robert Ayers, *Memoirs of a Southern Liberal*

NIGGER GO HOME!!!

—Words on the banner wielded by segregationist students as they marched, chanted racist slogans, and rioted outside Charlayne Hunter's dormitory the night of January 11, 1961, after she and Hamilton Holmes became the first African American students to attend UGA.

"Two words, Athens and Georgia, represent all of the arrogance of the white western world—a tradition of wrongness and injustice and certainly nothing black." He added, almost as a footnote, that small groups of blacks would be invited onto white campuses in "little trickling dabs of black."

—Vincent Harding, director, Institute of the Black World, opening speaker for Black Awareness Week, UGA, Athens, Georgia, *Red and Black*, May 14, 1970

A Black student on this campus quickly learns to assume everyone is "against him until proven otherwise." Blacks "presume" discrimination from police, teachers, white students, and others. . . . The communications breakdown is from your side. Communications isn't a foot shuffle or a head scratch. When you clear up some of the things black students have to presume around here, then communication can start.

—Dwight Thomas, speaker at the Black student ceremony honoring Martin Luther King Jr.'s birthday, UGA, Athens, Georgia, *Red and Black*, January 19, 1971

Racism is still here—it has become more subtle in some ways, but when racism becomes subtle, it becomes harder to fight.

—Hamilton Holmes, speaking to UGA students following the Martin Luther King Jr. Remembrance March, Athens, Georgia, *Red and Black*, January 12, 1990

Our greatest challenge in the years ahead is overcoming ignorance and intolerance.

—Charlayne Hunter-Gault, fiftieth anniversary commemoration of UGA's desegregation, Athens, Georgia, January 9, 2011

Contents

Author's Note on Derogatory Language ix

Preface xi

Introduction: Race, Memory, and the University of Georgia in the Twentieth Century 1

CHAPTER ONE
Leading and Misleading Georgia: University of Georgia and Jim Crow Georgia's Education and Political Power Elite 19

CHAPTER TWO
Two, Four, Six, Eight, We Don't Want to Integrate: White Student Attitudes toward the University of Georgia's Desegregation, 1961 52

Postscript to Chapter Two 71

CHAPTER THREE
G-Men in Georgia: The FBI and the Segregationist Riot at the University of Georgia, 1961 86

Postscript to Chapter Three 105

CHAPTER FOUR
Black Memory and University of Georgia's Desegregation Struggle 141

CHAPTER FIVE
Freedom Dreams and Segregationist Nightmares: Charlayne Hunter, Walter Stovall, and University of Georgia's First Interracial Marriage 175

CHAPTER SIX
Decades of Desegregation: The Slow Death and Afterlife of Jim Crow at University of Georgia, 1963–1989 205

CHAPTER SEVEN
New Day or Old South? Late 1990s University of Georgia Student Reflections on Campus Race Relations in Their Time vs. 1961 242

Coda: Commemorations 265

Acknowledgments 281

Notes 285

Index 335

A gallery of images follows page 124.

Author's Note on Derogatory Language

Confronting Jim Crow is more than simply the title of this book; it is a demanding task, and at times an unpleasant one. It involves reading vulgar racist words and viewing bigoted images that offend our humane and egalitarian sensibilities. Difficult as it is, we need to read, hear, and see these racist expressions to grasp fully how harmful and demeaning they were during the Jim Crow era and remain so in the years that follow. When quoting even the most hateful words, I have done so verbatim rather than censor, abbreviate, or sugarcoat them. The N-word, for example, is spelled out in full, in all its crudity. The photos of, and drawings by, racist individuals shown in this book are presented to illustrate the dangerous ideology of white supremacy and how this belief system warped the minds of many members of the college-trained elite in the Jim Crow South.

I admire and agree with those who seek to banish the bigotry that produces hate speech in the United States, specifically, and the world, generally. In this book, I seek to provide the twentieth-century context for bigoted language and to deconstruct the antidemocratic social order in which such bigotry flourished. My hope is that by teaching about that context and exposing that social order's inhumanity, this book will contribute to the ongoing struggle against racism and the rise of a more humane and egalitarian world in which racist expression becomes extinct.

My approach to the difficult matter of how best to handle offensive language was strongly influenced by one of the preeminent voices for racial justice at the University of Georgia (UGA), Charlayne Hunter-Gault. In 2005, at the Center-Myers dormitory on UGA's campus where Hunter-Gault resided as a student in 1961, a display was erected in acknowledgment of her having been the first African American woman to attend the university. The display featured a photo of Hunter-Gault, accompanied by the vulgar quote, "Make way for the nigger," which had been yelled at her by racist students as she entered the campus for the first time.[1] In response to student criticism, the quote was covered over.[2] Responding to the matter, Hunter-Gault, in a letter to UGA's student newspaper, wrote that she was gratified to learn that UGA students had been offended by the racial slur that had been directed at her, since this showed that they were carrying on the struggle against racism that she and fellow classmate Hamilton Holmes had pioneered at the university decades earlier. But Hunter-Gault opposed removing or covering up the quote, arguing that "those words ... [should] stand as a reminder, however painful, that ... students of color ... are the heirs to a legacy of struggle, but also of victory over bigotry and that it is through their knowledge and understanding of the past that they fight with every fiber of their being to defend that victory and keep it real. Rigorous, righteous debate is a part of doing so. And I would hope that their white classmates will join them in defense of decency and human rights."[3] Instead of removing the quote, Hunter-Gault advocated that it be contextualized within the display.[4] Hunter-Gault's statement regarding "knowledge and understanding of the past" eloquently expresses that delving into the history of Jim Crow, including its most unsettling aspects, can empower us by equipping us to confront and address the enduring legacy of bigotry in our present-day struggles.

Preface

Sometimes it is the silences in history that are the most revealing. This is surely the case with the literary output of those who in the 1950s and 1960s were the southern university students most vehemently opposed to racial integration. At their white supremacist rallies, segregationist student militants at the University of Alabama (1956), the University of Georgia (1961), and the University of Mississippi (1962) raised their voices in ugly racist chants and ended up rioting in their attempts to halt their schools' court-ordered desegregation. But though these rallies and riots involved masses of rowdy white students (as well as adult allies), these participants later grew silent. Not one of the rioters has published a memoir seeking to explain, justify, or apologize for this racist violence. The silence of these Jim Crow alumni has been deafening.

This is quite a contrast to the few intrepid Black students who braved both this violence and what today we would call the racist microaggressions that followed, as resentful white students tried to make as unpleasant and lonely as possible the college experience of these Black students who had dared to challenge the university color line. The University of Mississippi's trailblazer of integration, James Meredith, in 1966 published the first book-length Black memoir of the campus integration struggle, *Three Years in Mississippi*, and more recently came out with a second memoir, *A Mission from God: A Memoir and Challenge for America* (2016). An equally powerful memoir, *In My Place* (1992) came from Charlayne Hunter-Gault, recounting her experience as the University of Georgia's first Black female student. Hunter-Gault also brought back into print her articles on those UGA years and their aftermath in her recent anthology *My People: Five Decades of Writing About Black Lives* (2022). The most recent book length retrospective on Georgia's integration struggle came in 2021 from Mary Frances Early, the African American student who broke UGA's graduate school color line, a story told in her inspiring memoir, *The Quiet Trailblazer: My Journey as the First Black Graduate of the University of Georgia*.

These integrationist memoirs narrate the triumphant struggles of antiracist Black students prevailing over Jim Crow.[1] They are in essence creation stories, heralding the rebirth of these universities as institutions finally forced to begin making their admissions decisions based on merit rather than skin color. And like most births, these involved some pain as whites resisted this shift away from racial discrimination and regional parochialism.

Alumni who had been segregationist militants or sympathizers had no such triumphant stories to tell. Not only had they been defeated as their universities integrated, but their cause—preserving Jim Crowism—was thoroughly discredited as 1960s America buried the Jim Crow system thanks to the civil rights movement, President Lyndon Johnson, and Congress, culminating with the Civil Rights Act of 1964 and the Voting Rights Act the following year. If being history's losers was not enough to discourage segregationist student memoirs, there was also the fact that racist militants had violently broken laws during their campus riots, and none have proven eager or willing to own up to their criminality.

So the few published memoirs by white alumni that discussed the violent response to the integration of their Deep South universities came not from the ranks of militant racist students who rallied and rioted but rather from their nonviolent classmates. These did not appear until the twenty-first century and came from University of Mississippi alums who, as student journalists in 1962, covered and editorialized their campus's deadly segregationist riot. Especially memorable is Sidna Brower Mitchell's short, dramatic account, written on the occasion of the sixtieth anniversary of the University of Mississippi's desegregation. In 1962 Mitchell had been editor of the student newspaper, the *Daily Mississippian*. Her editorials criticizing the riot and other misconduct by segregationist militants—including the ransacking of the rooms of seven students who had dared to dine with James Meredith, Ole Miss's first Black student—led to her being nominated for the Pulitzer Prize.[2]

Given the strongly racist atmosphere of Mississippi in 1962, Mitchell's public opposition to segregationist violence at the University of Mississippi was courageous. And yet, as she acknowledged in her memoir, her editorials were actually quite moderate. Though privately sympathetic to integration, which she linked to the influence of her unusually egalitarian father, Mitchell never wrote an editorial championing the end of Jim Crowism at the University of Mississippi since she felt that doing so "would only create more chaos, and possibly severely hurt my father's business and any relationship with my mother's Mississippi relatives."[3] Even so, her criticism of racist violence on campus aroused fierce opposition, with the student senate voting overwhelmingly to censure her, which she "found ... to be the most hurtful experience of this difficult year."[4] The Kappa Alpha fraternity started a petition drive to impeach her. Two of her own sorority sisters "who lived at the top of the stairs" of her sorority house would "often spit on" Mitchell and call her names.⁵ For Mitchell, even writing a brief chapter reviewing these painful experiences sixty years later proved difficult and "brought back tears and depression."⁶ So it is not surprising that she did not probe the roots of the racist student culture at Ole Miss that had yielded such segregationist animus from her classmates. Nor did she discuss the failure of the university's academic classes, administration, and faculty to uproot such racism, or the role the university had played in upholding the discriminatory social order of Jim Crow Mississippi.

This same lack of analysis is found in the visually powerful photo book *Riot: Witness to Anger and Change* (2015) compiled by Edwin E. Meek, a white University of Mississippi alumnus, who, as a graduate student working for the university's office of public information, photographed the riot and its aftermath.⁷ Meek's photos did catch Mississippi students rallying for segregation, but his few pages of personal reflection do not tell us anything about how or why the university served as a vehicle for such racism. Nor does the introduction to Meek's book by Curtis Wilkie, his fellow journalism alumnus from the riot year, illuminate the reader. Wilkie appropriately termed it "appalling" that during desegregation, the University of Mississippi's "greatest crisis" since the Civil War, "the university administration abdicated its responsibility to the [state's intransigent segregationist] politicians, the champions of 'Never [will we integrate].'" But he offered no explanation for this abdication.⁸

Aside from his photographs, Meek takes us closest to the racist realities of the University of Mississippi in the Jim Crow era not when he discusses the university but when he reflects on his own roots on the white side of the Mississippi color line. "Having grown up a native son of Tallahatchie County, where segregation was an accepted way of life, I brought these prejudices with me to Ole Miss." Even though aware that President Kennedy had sent in troops to halt further racial violence on campus, Meek recalled feeling "suspended between compromise and conscience" and "as conflicted as" the Mississippi National Guardsmen who "hung Rebel flags on their trucks even as they upheld their federal duty" to restore order.⁹ It was nothing Meek had learned in his classes at Ole Miss, and not even the campus riot itself, that led him to reject his racist past. That rejection came more than a year after the riot, with President Kennedy's assassination. Meek was working in the dark room developing photos at the university when he heard "some fool" shout "'Thank God that sonofabitch is dead.'" The shock of this led a tearful Meek to reflect on "how warped my thinking had been" and to feel remorseful "for having resented the Kennedys and having accepted segregation and racial injustice as the status quo."¹⁰

No such candor or introspection is to be found in the memoir of Trent Lott, the most famous of the University of Mississippi's white alums from the era of integration. Lott, the former US senate majority leader, discussed his Ole Miss days in a chapter of his *Herding Cats: A Life in Politics* (2005). Lott had been a student leader at the university. Lott discussed his experiences as a law-abiding fraternity officer at Mississippi at the time of the segregationist campus riot. While convincing in asserting that he had no involvement in this racist violence, his Ole Miss chapter's overall treatment of race amounts to an often disingenuous exercise in denial, as might be expected since he wrote the memoir shortly after stepping down as majority leader because of the furor ignited by his nostalgic remarks—widely regarded as racist—praising the Jim Crow leadership of Strom Thurmond on the occasion of the South Carolina senator's one-hundredth birthday.

In *Herding Cats*, Lott claims that in his student years at the University of Mississippi he was not a segregationist, but he offers no evidence of ever having opposed segregation either publicly or privately. He claims that he and the fraternity he led played no role in the riot, yet he wrote nothing about the role that students from other fraternities played in the racist resistance to integration, including Kappa Alpha's attempt to impeach Mitchell for her editorializing against segregationist campus violence. Lott was also mute on the Jim Crow loyalties and racist attitudes that pervaded the racially exclusive fraternity system, the larger student body, and the university's leadership. Though Lott was the University of Mississippi's head cheerleader, he never mentions that at a pep rally the day before Meredith came to campus, the racist cheer "hotty toddy, we want a body" went up.[11] Lott noted with pride Ole Miss's role in training the state's political elite and that "in the 1950s all of the governors and statewide officials were graduates of the University of Mississippi," but he avoids discussing the shared racism of these leaders, that Ole Miss–trained political figures were among the South's most intransigent segregationists, including Mississippi governor Ross Barnett and senator James Eastland.[12] Lott mentions the rise of an extremist anti-integration student organization at the University of Mississippi and Barnett's incendiary half-time segregationist speech at an Ole Miss football game at the height of the desegregation crisis but never tells us why neither he nor any of his classmates publicly opposed such racism. Lott notes that on the night of the riot he spotted many cars with out-of-state license plates—suggesting that outside agitators caused the racist bloodshed—but says nothing about the students' role in the riot or in the segregationist rallies leading up to it. This is quite a contrast to more candid contemporary accounts of segregationist student violence during the University of Mississippi's integration crisis, like that of Ole Miss history professor James W. Silver, an eyewitness to the riot scene, who noted with dismay racist students cursing, threatening, and assaulting federal marshals, leaving Silver pondering "how eighteen- and nineteen-year-old students had suddenly been turned into wild animals."[13] Nor did Lott include even a sentence discussing what he and his fraternity brothers thought of Meredith or whether they interacted with him or any other African American at Ole Miss in the days and months after the riot. Nor do we learn whether the white students' and white Mississippi's racial hatred and resentment, which helped pave the way for the riot, ever abated in his college years.

The most candid observation Lott offered on race in his University of Mississippi chapter came in its closing passage where he acknowledged feeling "anger in my heart over the way the federal government had invaded Ole Miss to accomplish something that could have been handled peacefully and administratively."[14] Here at last was the genuine voice of the resentful student body at Ole Miss, where these white youths viewed themselves rather than Meredith as the victims of the desegregation crisis. Lott, like his fellow students, expressed anger not over Meredith's life having been threatened by a mob of armed racists who rampaged for more than two hours, but over what he viewed as a Yankee invasion, which in reality consisted of the Kennedy administration's belated and reluctant use of federal marshals and troops to protect Meredith, a dangerous task that ended up with almost 40 percent of the more than 500 marshals being injured, a reporter being fatally shot by someone in the mob, and the death of an onlooker.[15] In the wake of Governor Barnett's reckless incitement, which summoned violent bigots from across the state and region to the campus, Lott's claim that this crisis could have been "handled peacefully" was perhaps the most brazen form of denial in a chapter filled with it.

Lott's evasions and denials on race, much like the literary silence of his riotous classmates and their counterparts at the universities of Georgia and Alabama, speak to a refusal to engage critically with the racist past. Nor has the public ever been pushed to confront these universities' historic roles as bulwarks of the Jim Crow social system. This is an old story, but lately it has gotten a new twist. This kind of refusal has recently extended far beyond the South, currently serving as standard operating procedure for the Trumpified version of conservatism across red state America, where Republican lawmakers have outlawed as "divisive" classroom discussion of the history and legacy of American racism—demonizing and banning Critical Race Theory and the

1619 Project educational curriculum project on slavery, leading to the intimidation of history educators and the firing of teachers who dared to explore this controversial history. It is this alarming and spreading trend toward censoring the history of racism that spurred me to return to this work I had begun three decades ago on the intersection between that history and the history of the University of Georgia, especially that of the anti-Black thought and action of its students and alumni in the Jim Crow era.

I came to realize that the public faced—and still faces—this outbreak of historical censorship without an understanding of how damaging it could be to drive the history of racism from schools and classrooms. I realized that right wing politicians were, in effect, turning the clock back from the rich multicultural education of the twenty-first century to a narrow monocultural education reminiscent of the Jim Crow era, whose impact on Georgia students I had studied. Much of red state America today fails to understand that rather than making "America great again," such censorship threatens to make today's American students ignorant on race, as the Jim Crow generations of white students had been across Georgia, with a curriculum that largely ignores the civil rights movement, Blacks, and historical sources that could teach whites anything meaningful about African Americans, racial tension, inequality, and conflict—or prod them to raise any question at all about racial discrimination and injustice.[16] So a key reason for this book, with its evidence on the educational and intellectual history of Jim Crow Georgia, is to serve as a kind of warning about the dangers of offering youths a truncated education, miseducation, or no formal education at all on the history of racism in America.

This study is also designed to offset the paucity of memoirs by students who resisted integration at UGA. Archived writings of those students and FBI files on their riot enable us to see with great clarity what UGA's first Black students were up against as they interacted with white classmates whose thinking about race had been shaped by their upbringing in Jim Crow Georgia. The African American experience at UGA during and after the initial desegregation struggle is explored on these pages, as is the way later generations of UGA students compared race relations at the end of the twentieth century with those in the first year of desegregation, 1961. At the risk of sounding unduly pessimistic, much evidence herein indicates that despite the demise of the color line, Jim Crow had a considerable afterlife at UGA. This study speaks to the debate about whether the social function of higher education has been to promote opportunity or to reproduce social inequality. For in Jim Crow Georgia, UGA, as this study documents, reinforced the state's white supremacist system and its political and social power elite. And though changing such a baked-in social function is possible, the UGA experience indicates, to put it mildly, that this did not happen overnight.

Why Georgia? Initially I chose to study Georgia because I saw its history of racism as neither unique nor typical. I made that choice because, in the 1990s, I spent almost a decade on the faculty of the University of Georgia and realized that everything from the names of campus buildings to the nature of the campus administration to the attitudes of my students and colleagues was impacted by UGA's racial history. So if I wanted to understand the mostly white university environment in which I worked, I had to grapple with this history. I quickly learned, however, that though not unique, UGA and only two other Deep South universities—the University of Mississippi and the University of Alabama—had greeted desegregation with racist riots. And UGA had been one of the slowest universities to desegregate its faculty, administration, and athletic teams. So if one was interested in understanding collegiate racism, UGA was, and is, a rich site for study since racism was so strong and enduring there.

I certainly was not singular in my concern about the problem of racial injustice, past and present, during my UGA years. In fact, it was African American faculty and students who did the most to challenge racial inequality there. And talented Black UGA colleagues Robert A. Pratt of the Department of History and Maurice Daniels of the School of Social Work began their work on the historical struggle against Jim Crowism at UGA at about the same time as I started my research on UGA student racism in the Jim Crow era.

All this ran parallel to an impressive movement in UGA's history department in the 1990s on behalf of a kind of antiracist public history, symbolized by the *Georgia Historical Quarterly*'s emergence, under the editorship of John Inscoe, as one of the most iconoclastic history journals in the South. Georgia's preeminent segregationist politician, Senator Richard Russell, must have been turning over in his grave as funds from the endowed chair named for him at UGA were used to promote such public history, thanks to the late William S. McFeely, the Pulitzer Prize–winning historian who held that chair. Bill, who would crusade against capital punishment and document its racist tendencies, helped to fund and organize a major conference at UGA in 1996 with help from Pratt, Inscoe, and other UGA faculty (including me): Civil Rights in Small Places explored the successes and failures of the civil rights movement to end racial discrimination in the small towns of Georgia. One of those small towns was Athens, and the conference featured not only a session on UGA's desegregation but also a speech by Judge Horace T. Ward, who—at our invitation—made his first appearance at UGA since 1961. Ward, who in

1950 sought to become the first Black student at UGA, was blocked by the color line and rejected by the law school but later served as part of the legal team that helped slay Jim Crow by winning the admission to UGA of Charlayne Hunter and Hamilton Holmes in the court case *Holmes v. Danner* in 1961. So it is fair to say the critical history of Jim Crow UGA you are reading here reflects not just my own historical perspective but a larger movement among dissenting Georgia faculty to rethink the state's history and to promote a dialogue on this, and not just on campus.

My interest in the history and legacy of racism began long before I set foot in Georgia and had led me to work in graduate school at UC Berkeley on studies of African American history with Leon Litwack, and to use my National Academy of Education postdoctoral fellowship to explore both the upsurge of racist incidents on American campuses in the Reagan era and the history of the movement to end racial discrimination in the University of California's fraternities and sororities in the 1950s and 1960s. At Berkeley in the 1980s, I was part of a generation of student activists who struggled to end the university's investments in companies that did business with South Africa's apartheid regime, promote the hiring of a racially diverse faculty and recruitment of students of color, and elect Berkeley's first African American student government president. I helped organize the twentieth anniversary commemoration of the Free Speech Movement and through that work met and interviewed that movement's famed orator, Mario Savio, whose memorable discussion of his organizing experience in Mississippi Freedom Summer drew me to the history of the freedom struggle in the Deep South (a quarter century later I would become Savio's biographer). Racism struck me then, as it does now, as a central historical and contemporary affliction whose roots, meaning, and impact need to be critically assessed, and whose legacy needs to be confronted.

My interest in the history of bigotry and the struggle against it has deep autobiographical roots dating back to my childhood and the terrifying stories my grandmother told me of her life-threatening experiences as a young Jewish girl in a pogrom in Poland, and her explaining that the reason I never met the great uncle for whom I am named (in Hebrew) was because "Hitler killed him." I am not sure she realized how much her words upset me as a child, and I doubt either of us realized back then how much they would shape my historical and political sensibilities. This part of my upbringing made the history of racism and its legacy feel deeply personal since the very name I carried was a reminder of just how deadly bigotry could be. Raised in a family where the memories of pogroms and the Holocaust were conveyed so powerfully,

I could not help but notice, study, and push back against the ways white Georgians (like much of the white South and white America) tend to bury the memory of their racist past.

Taken together, then, in Georgia I was an outsider by background and yet an insider in that I was a UGA faculty member when I started this research. I point all this out both to explain my focus and outlook and to suggest that though the topic of this book is race, racism, and their legacy in a Deep South state and its leading public university, I have no illusion (nor should you) that racism and bigotry were and are merely southern problems; they afflict our whole nation and all too much of the world.

Confronting Jim Crow

Introduction
Race, Memory, and the University of Georgia in the Twentieth Century

Asked to explain why she planned to vote for Georgia governor Brian Kemp's reelection, on the eve of the state's Republican gubernatorial primary in May 2022, Linda Reeves, a Trump-supporting retiree, told a *New York Times* reporter that Kemp had proven his conservative bona fides by signing a law limiting discussion of race in schools.[1] That law, known as the Protect Students First Act, bars the teaching of "divisive concepts," most notably the apparently heretical idea that "the United States of America is fundamentally racist."[2] It is fitting that a white conservative Georgia governor with deep ties to the University of Georgia—Kemp is a fourth generation UGA graduate, whose forebear was a member of the board of trustees that founded the university—should sign into law a ban on candid classroom discussion of American racism.[3] After all, UGA spent more than a century and a half refusing to confront its long history of racism as it promoted two doomed white supremacist social systems, first the slavery regime of the Old South and then the Jim Crow South's apartheid regime. It was not until decades after a federal court order forced the desegregation of UGA's student body in 1961—enabling Hamilton Holmes and Charlayne Hunter to become UGA's first African American students since the university's founding in 1785—that the University of Georgia began, haltingly and superficially, to acknowledge the racism of its segregated past. And not until the second decade of the twenty-first century would a scandal over the UGA administration's removal of the remains of enslaved African Americans from the campus grounds finally force UGA to begin to face up to its historic connections to slavery.[4]

UGA's problem with historical amnesia regarding its racist past struck me with considerable force on the very first day I set foot on the campus back in 1991. I had come to UGA interviewing for a history professorship in its College of Education. Before traveling to Georgia I read up on the university's history and on the plane had finished *New Yorker* staff writer Calvin Trillin's classic account of the assault on the campus color line, *An Education in Georgia: Hamilton Holmes, Charlayne Hunter, and the Integration of the University of Georgia* (1964). Among the most memorable events described in Trillin's book occurred during the UGA desegregation court case *Holmes v. Danner*, in which UGA's president O. C. Aderhold lied under oath in open court as part of UGA's attempt to preserve the segregated status quo by preventing the admission of Holmes and Hunter: Despite the fact that no Blacks had ever been admitted to UGA, Aderhold testified that in all his years as UGA's president (dating back to 1950), it had not been "the policy of the University of Georgia to exclude students on account of their race of color."[5] He falsely claimed that Black and white applicants to UGA were considered "on exactly the same basis."[6]

Aderhold prevaricated here because he knew that if he admitted that UGA excluded qualified Black applicants, the university would lose its legal case since the *Brown* decision outlawed such discrimination. Aderhold's lies were refuted quickly and convincingly with evidence offered by Constance Baker Motley and Donald Hollowell, attorneys for Holmes and Hunter, who showed that lily white UGA had indeed excluded these two highly qualified applicants on account of their race, leading US district court Judge William Bootle to order their admission as UGA's first Black students in January 1961.[7] With this history in mind, it came as a shock that the itinerary given to me indicated that part of my day of interviews at UGA in 1991 would occur in Aderhold Hall, which was, of course, named in honor of former president O. C. Aderhold. That was where I was scheduled to meet the education school dean, whose office was housed in Aderhold.

In my meeting that day with the dean, I had a hard time focusing on his job-related questions. Try as I might to put them aside, I just could not rid myself of the questions that troubled me. Didn't anyone here know the history of Jim Crow Georgia and Aderhold's role in attempting to preserve the campus color line? Didn't they understand how inappropriate it was to name a university building after Aderhold, especially one that housed much of UGA's education school, honoring a man who had perjured himself in a futile, even absurd, attempt to cover up the university's anti-Black admissions policies? My interview with the dean must have gone well since I got the job—and would spend almost a decade as a UGA faculty member— but even a few minutes after that meeting the whole conversation was just a blur to me, since Aderhold loomed so much larger to me than what I said or what the dean said in our meeting. This experience convinced me I would have to devote historical research to probing UGA's racist history and why it seemed so little remembered.

In retrospect I can see how naïve I was about such blindness to the racist past. I had not come to grips yet with Faulkner's admonition, "The past is never dead. It's not even past." Nor had most Americans, north or south, back in 1991. It took the national wave of the Black Lives Matters protest following the police murder of George Floyd in our current century to push America to confront its tradition of idealizing and commemorating historical figures while ignoring their white supremacist beliefs and acts. Whether it was Yale's Calhoun College, whose name for years honored the proslavery racist leader John C. Calhoun; New York City honoring Columbus with a heroic statue and ignoring his abuse and enslavement of Indigenous people; the US Army bases named for Confederates who had taken up arms against the United States in the service of a proslavery rebellion; or UGA's Aderhold Hall, whitewashing public history was a *national* problem. So back in the 1990s, my UGA years, I misunderstood as distinctly Georgian and Southern a process of racial evasion that I now realize differed only in degree in Georgia from such evasions in every region of the United States. Today, moreover, it is evident that such evasiveness lives on and has taken the form of a right wing backlash. Both in and beyond the South, right wing legislatures and governors of one red state after another in the past few years have sought to end such iconoclasm by enacting laws and educational policies that have banned candid teaching about America's racist past and present—especially Critical Race Theory and the 1619 Project on slavery—from public schools, equating such teaching with "wokeism," left wing intolerance, and anti-Americanism.

I HAD NO WAY OF KNOWING BACK in 1991 that thirty years later any initiative to rename buildings whose existing names honored segregationists like Aderhold (or slave owners or Indian killers) would be banned by law from succeeding in Georgia and thus forbidden by the University of Georgia Regents.[8] This was consistent with the Georgia legislature's dismal civil rights record when it enacted law after law to resist desegregation even after the *Brown* decision. A state in which it took a civil war to end slavery and multiple federal court orders to end de jure segregation now has a legislature preventing its citizens from ending its tradition of honoring racists. You would have to be sleepwalking though history not to see this is a brazen historical (or ahistorical) cover-up. This ban on name changing is in its own way an act of silencing. However one feels about renaming buildings, there is no doubt that by rendering futile movements initiated to remove the names of buildings that honored segregationists (or slave owners or Indian killers), the state government and regents cut off public discussion of the racist past. By outlawing name changes (or removal of Confederate statues) we lose that engagement with public history that accompanies name changing initiatives.[9]

So unless that law is repealed, UGA's education school will forever honor a segregationist perjurer, and most people will not know enough Georgia history even to understand this, to grasp who Aderhold was, or how and why his behavior in defense of white supremacy was so shameful.

The reason this more than half-century-old history of Jim Crowism needs public recognition and critical discussion is that white supremacy did not die with de jure segregation back in the Long 1960s; it lives on—as we saw at Charlottesville in 2017 and the US capitol on January 6, 2021—and its ugly history and legacy cannot be overcome unless it is exposed and confronted. Consider, for example, the persistent racial homogeneity of fraternities and sororities on Deep South campuses (and the many students who enter college after attending schools that are de facto segregated), and ponder the impact it might have if white students in these exclusive organizations were exposed to the great *Life* magazine photographer Joe Scherschel's haunting photos taken during the UGA desegregation crisis of 1961. Scherschel captured the crude, callous, hateful racism of UGA's frat row. The first of these photographs is of a well-dressed UGA fraternity member smiling broadly while publicly dangling a Black puppet hanging from a noose. This shot would appear with the story *Life* ran on the segregationist riot that erupted outside Charlayne Hunter's dormitory on January 11, 1961, after her and Hamilton Holmes's first day of classes.[10] What *Life* did not include in its story were the ugly words this racist student uttered, referring to Hunter, the first African American student housed on campus, as he dangled this Black doll in front of news cameras: "This is what I'm going to do to that goddamn nigger."[11] Scherschel took a second shot of this same student (though it went unpublished for more than four decades), and in this photo the racist student is not alone: He is seen parading his lynched Black puppet before his UGA fraternity brothers, who were smiling and chuckling over this racist display.[12] This shot is even more chilling than the one that appeared in *Life* since it attests that there was an appreciative fraternity audience for this kind of display, evoking the racist student culture of the whites-only Greek system—which also manifested itself in the fraternity role in helping to plan UGA's segregationist riot.

Such white supremacist "humor" persists in some corners of America's fraternity system into our own century. As recently as 2015 a major scandal ensued when fraternity members at the University of Oklahoma were caught reciting a racist chant that there would "never be a nigger" in their fraternity house.[13] This was the same chant used by UGA students as they protested the court-ordered desegregation of their university by holding a segregationist march in downtown Athens in January 1961. The only difference was that in 1961 UGA students did their racist chanting in public while their twenty-first century Oklahoma counterparts did it in private—on a bus chartered by fraternity members—but were caught on an iPhone video that was somehow leaked to the media.[14]

Racism in UGA's fraternity system endured long beyond the University of Georgia years of Hunter and Holmes in the early 1960s. In fact, it surfaced not long after I joined UGA's faculty almost three decades later. This was the Pi Kappa Phi scandal involving the pledge pamphlet given to its new members in September 1992 setting down the fraternity's rules and traditions. The pamphlet included the words "no niggers" in the house. The only difference between this racist incident and the one captured in Scherschel's photo back in 1961 was that back then the racism had been expressed openly—by the student parading his lynched puppet in front of reporters and photographers—while in 1992 the racism was displayed privately in a pamphlet that was supposed to stay in-house and be available only to fraternity members. The local chapter of the National Association for the Advancement of Colored People responded by circulating a petition, with more than a thousand signatures, urging that UGA president Charles Knapp respond firmly to this racist display by suspending the fraternity for three years.[15]

Having completed a study of the attempt in the 1950s and 1960s to desegregate UC Berkeley's fraternities and sororities, as part of my National Academy of Education postdoctoral fellowship, I was, in 1992, taken aback by how archaic conditions seemed on UGA's frat row. Here were organizations that, decades after the university admitted its first Black students, still remained segregated. From my study of California I knew that that state's attorney general had ruled way back in 1959 that racially exclusive fraternities and sororities affiliated with state universities were unconstitutional since, as residential houses linked to public educational institutions, they barred nonwhites from equal access to housing, a violation of the Fourteenth Amendment.[16] So it seemed long past time for UGA to bar such discrimination. This understanding shaped the letter I sent to UGA President Knapp amid this fraternity scandal. Though praising him for his public statement chastising Pi Kappa Phi for its racist pledge pamphlet, I objected to his refusal to take a tough stance against the fraternity system's racial segregation.[17]

Citing Knapp's quote in the student newspaper that he was "encouraging" the "Greeks to integrate" and that "the final decision on Greek diversity rests with the Greeks themselves,"[18] I criticized this weak language, writing Knapp that "as a historian who has studied this issue on other campuses, I very much doubt that our Greek system is capable of reforming itself. Though it has been more than three decades since fraternities and sororities nationally began to desegregate ... the Greeks still maintain a color line here in Athens.... Instead of merely 'encouraging' desegregation, why not require it?"[19] I reminded Knapp that "as President you can set deadlines by which the houses must have taken steps towards non-discrimination."[20] I urged him to put teeth in such a nondiscrimination policy by declaring that houses that refuse to comply with the policy "will lose their University recognition—and with it their access to UGA facilities and other campus resources." Such policies, I stressed, had been used on other campuses to promote Greek system desegregation back in the 1950s and 1960s, "and since in this area we are decades behind the times, it makes sense to employ these old remedies."[21]

Knapp wrote me an appreciative letter in reply and offered to meet to discuss the Pi Kappa Phi scandal.[22] We did meet. But it was disappointing to find Knapp—a relatively liberal president—unwilling to confront the history and legacy of Jim Crow on frat row. He said he would not mandate fraternity desegregation because it would "tear this campus apart." Knapp was correct that there would likely be considerable resistance to such a desegregation initiative. In fact, the late Clark Kerr, who as president of the University of California (UC) presided over the attempt to desegregate the frat rows at UC Berkeley and UCLA, told me that influential alumni active in the Greek system were outraged by his desegregation order. This included members of the UC Board of Regents, who never forgave Kerr, and he viewed their alienation as a key reason they went along with California Governor Ronald Reagan's firing of him in 1967.[23] Still, Knapp's timidity reflected another way in which the meaning and legacy of Jim Crow at UGA were neither understood nor confronted. Here was a lost opportunity to move toward completing the desegregation of student life that had bogged down on frat row. And Georgia's Pi Kappa Phi fraternity chapter was not even suspended over this ugly racist incident.[24] Thus segregation in fraternity life would endure at UGA into the twenty-first century, making possible such scandals as that of its Lambda Chi Alpha fraternity chapter, which was suspended in 2020 in response to a particularly ugly display of anti-Black racism.[25]

While researching and publishing articles in the 1990s on the history of racism at UGA and its desegregation crisis, I encountered other forms of denial and evasion when it came to acknowledging UGA's racist past and its consequences. After some newspaper articles appeared on my study of UGA's segregationist riot of January 11, 1961, I received letters from UGA alumni, some of whom sought to blame the riot on outside agitators, most notably, crude blue collar racists in the Ku Klux Klan. This was a popular rationalization that dated back to 1961, when the white public in Georgia, especially UGA alums, refused to believe that educated UGA students could foment racist violence, and so they scapegoated the Klan.[26] The FBI documents from its investigation of the riot and press reports do confirm a KKK presence at the riot but make it clear that it was UGA law students and hard-core segregationist undergraduates who organized the riot outside of Charlayne Hunter's dormitory.[27] Thus it would be a mistake, a form of denial, and a failure to recognize the centrality of racism to UGA student culture if we fell into this stereotyped view of racists—critiqued so brilliantly by civil rights historian Charles Payne—as "stupid, vulgar, and one-dimensional." Such stereotyping was "a device by which ... [evasive observers] certify their own enlightened status by distancing themselves from the grossest expressions of racism, thus giving racism the face of the ignorant, the pot-bellied, and the tobacco chewing, an image with which almost no one can identify and which easily supplants more complex and realistic images of racism."[28]

A second form of denial I encountered from UGA alumni and a few of their children (who were among my students when I taught at UGA) was that the segregationist riot at UGA in 1961 was a spontaneous outburst of youthful frustration rather than an expression of deep-seated collegiate racism. The argument there was that since the riot followed a close, overtime basketball loss to hated rival Georgia Tech, it was the foul mood from that loss that explains the formation of an ugly mob that descended on Charlayne Hunter's dormitory.[29] But the FBI investigation of the riot and press coverage of the riot's origins showed that the violence had been planned before that basketball game. And where is the logic anyway of this claim that the outcome of a rivalry between two all-white basketball teams would lead a white mob to besiege the dormitory of a Black student? Tellingly, when I made these points in response to a UGA alumnus who had written me and who had been present at both that basketball game and the riot, he never replied to my letter or responded to my invitation to discuss all this in an oral history interview.[30]

From a senior faculty colleague at UGA in 1998, I encountered a form of denial that brings to mind the recent backlash by conservative politicians against candid discussion of racism in schools, which by 2022 had led to the adoption or introduction of laws and policies that "restrict teaching about race and racism ... in at least 36 states."[31] The idea was that it is somehow overly emotional and potentially emotionally damaging to probe the history of racism. This colleague objected to the illustration on the flyer I used to publicize a discussion of my article (a revised version of which appears as chapter 2 of this book) on the white student response to UGA's desegregation in 1961. That illustration was a critical political cartoon that the *Baltimore Sun* ran soon after the riot, featuring a hooded KKK "fanatical elder" holding a book opened to pages that read, "The 3 R's: Rabble Rousing, Race Hatred, Rioting."[32] This racist elder is depicted in the cartoon directing a "University of Georgia student mob" to hurl bricks (apparently at the dorm of Charlayne Hunter), and the "University of Georgia student mob" is pictured following that direction and throwing bricks. The cartoon was headed with an antiracist quotation from the musical *South Pacific* that "you have to be carefully taught to hate." My colleague objected, stating that this political cartoon was not compatible with the ideal of education as "rational process" but struck him instead "as appealing to base emotions as well as ideological positions. It does not invite an objective consideration of alternative positions.... [It] does not encourage ... free inquiry."[33] He sent these objections in a letter to my boss, Russell Yeany, the education school dean at UGA, and announced in his letter that he was so offended by my use of this cartoon that he was resigning from the College of Education's Task Force for Multicultural Education because it was listed on the flyer as the sponsor of my talk.[34]

This idea that using a political cartoon somehow foreclosed rational analysis struck me as bizarre at the time. I saw this in part as a reflection of my colleague's lack of familiarity (he was not a historian) with the way historians critically interrogate primary sources; that is, just because a historian finds a political cartoon thought provoking and useful for a talk flyer, a book cover, or a conversation starter does not mean the historian agrees with the cartoon or all of its implications. I wrote the dean that while, of course, the cartoonist had created "images that had a good deal of emotional power" to mock the segregationist rioters at UGA, the whole point of the cartoon was "to provoke critical thought."[35] The cartoon, I explained, could be used to raise many important historical questions about both the riot itself and its representation in this work of art. These included, "Why are the students throwing bricks? Is the cartoon fair in implying that all UGA students were rioters? What about its suggestion that the teachings of 'fanatical elders' were responsible for the racial violence? Is that suggestion well grounded in historical reality? How, in fact, did Georgians learn about race in 1961? And the KKK image implies Klan involvement in the riot. Was there Klan involvement? What political biases are reflected in the cartoon? What alternative views are there in interpreting the riot? What does the cartoon tell us about the national response to the UGA desegregation crisis?"[36]

This concern my colleague expressed about emotion and rationality seemed to me at the time and in retrospect not well thought out and more an expression of his discomfort with the subject matter. Much like those who ban Critical Race Theory today, he seemed to think that putting racism under the microscope was not a genuine or open intellectual project but instead reflected some radical "ideological" agenda. Perhaps this is why in the three decades since UGA's desegregation, neither he nor any of the senior faculty of the college of education had written a word about UGA's desegregation crisis or, apparently, given a second thought to having their departments housed in a building named for O. C. Aderhold.

The most personal form of denial that I witnessed in my work on desegregation at UGA concerned the question of individual guilt for involvement in the segregationist riot. After an article appeared in a Georgia newspaper about my study of the FBI investigation of this riot—and stating that I had obtained, through the Freedom of Information Act, the FBI files from that investigation—I was contacted in 1997 by Phil Campbell, who, back in 1961 had been a high-ranking member of the Georgia state government as the agriculture commissioner in the Vandiver administration. He had contacted me concerning a key question about the riot: what role had Georgia state government leaders played in encouraging students to resist violently the desegregation of the university? Campbell, or some other state officials, did play such a role—as we shall explore in more depth in chapter 3—by letting segregationist student militants know that they approved of their resistance to UGA's desegregation and implying that the Georgia State Patrol would not show up promptly to suppress their segregationist mob violence (and the state patrol would, in fact, turn out to be AWOL, not showing up at the riot scene for almost two hours even though the patrol had an office near the Athens campus). Campbell wanted me to interview him so he could give his side of the story. He seemed to have a guilty conscience and used our interview to deny he had been involved in any such collusion with the students who planned the riot.[37] It was almost as if he knew in advance of our meeting that the FBI files showed that he was the one state official named by a student rioter as being involved in that collusion (in that rioter's FBI interview).

Campbell clearly did not want to go down in history being implicated in nasty criminal activity associated with a segregationist riot, all the more so because by the time we met in 1997, segregation itself had long since been discredited both in Georgia and nationally. But Campbell could not explain why a rioter in 1961 would name him in his interview with the FBI.[38] Still, though there is no way to determine definitively if Campbell lied to me, it is significant that either the governor of Georgia or someone close to him, or perhaps both, were so angry about UGA's court-ordered desegregation that they would use their power to encourage violent resistance to that court order and commit the potentially dangerous act of emboldening the riot planners by implying that the state patrol would not show up on time to suppress that violence.

Though the FBI would—as we shall see in chapter 3—prove useful in disproving some of the myths about the riot, it did not offer an intensive probe that could settle who within the student body and the state government did what in the planning and execution of UGA's segregationist riot. Nor did the UGA administration's belated disciplinary actions against the rioters (initially UGA suspended Hunter and Holmes rather than the racist students who had rioted to protest their matriculation at UGA) do much to illuminate the making of this riot. The UGA administration's files do not even indicate which students had broken the law by committing violent acts at the riot scene.[39] This lack of accountability and the impossibility of offering a definitive account of the riot added to the tendency of white Georgians to avoid facing up to the depth and lawlessness of intransigent segregationism both on the Athens campus and among top state officials in Atlanta. Nor was there any reflection on the part of the UGA administration on how the way its students were educated (or miseducated) on race in their homes, dorms, frat houses, debating societies, and classes paved the way for the riot, and how the university's curriculum and extracurricular life might be changed so as to foster more humane and democratic race relations.

A different, and one might say more subtle, form of denial regarding such segregationist extremism arises in connection with the surprising outcome of the UGA desegregation crisis. I am referring here to Georgia governor Ernest Vandiver's belated recognition after UGA's court-ordered desegregation that Georgia's legislature had to repeal the massive resistance law that he had supported in the recent past (including in his segregationist 1958 gubernatorial campaign) mandating that UGA—or any educational institution in the state—be denied state funds and close down rather than be desegregated. With the governor's support that law was repealed in January 1961, allowing UGA's limited integration (just two Black students in a UGA student population of more than 7,000) to proceed. In other words, it was a rejection of the massive resistance position that it was better to close the university than to see it desegregated.

Thus, in the story of UGA, 1961 became in part Georgia's retreat from the brink, the beginning of the end of massive resistance against racial integration and the triumph of Holmes, Hunter, and the National Association for the Advancement of Colored People in removing UGA's color line. Moreover, no one was killed in the riot at Athens in 1961, unlike the deadly racist rebellion during the University of Mississippi desegregation crisis in 1962, and Governor Vandiver did not, at UGA in January 1961, go in for the symbolic neo-Confederate posturing that Governor George Wallace orchestrated with his stand at the schoolhouse door at the University of Alabama in 1963.[40] This made it possible for white Georgians to feel as if their leaders had been more reasonable than their counterparts in Mississippi and Alabama. All this is true, but it removes from the spotlight the intransigent segregationism that had prevailed in Georgia for generations. It has yielded a lack of attention to the important role that UGA had long played in upholding the state's segregationist regime and the university's consistent refusal and its inability to intervene in a way that might end its role in producing many of the state's most powerful, intransigent, and provincial segregationist leaders.

More recently, what has happened both in the historical memory and in the historical writing about race at twentieth-century UGA is that the university's most important story is not that of its long years of segregationism but rather the triumphant overthrow of its color line. This makes good sense, of course, since UGA was reborn, or one might even say it began to emerge finally as a true university in 1961. This was in a real sense a new University of Georgia, which for the first time could start to make admissions and hiring decisions based on merit rather than having such decisions marred and corrupted by racial discrimination. So it is certainly fitting that historians of UGA and the UGA administration from the mid-1980s onward—myself included—have focused on the triumphant story of the origins of this new University of Georgia. Excellent books narrating this story have been published by journalist Calvin Trillin, historian Robert Pratt, and biographer Maurice Daniels, along with memoirs by UGA's first female African American undergraduate, Charlayne Hunter-Gault, and first Black graduate student, Mary Frances Early.[41] These books all stress the courage, intelligence, and determination that led to the triumph of these first Black UGA students and their supporters over the forces of segregation. And the Foot Soldier Project, initiated by Maurice Daniels, produced documentary films that valorized not only Holmes, Hunter, and Early, but also the first Black applicant to UGA, Horace Ward, whose earlier and unsuccessful attempt to integrate UGA's law school in 1950 was less well known, and the role of pioneering Black civil rights attorney Donald Hollowell in the struggle to desegregate UGA.[42] Similarly, and much to its credit, UGA has in highly significant acts of symbolic commemoration in this century named a campus building for

Charlayne Hunter-Gault and Hamilton Holmes and named UGA's school of education the Mary Frances Early College of Education, along with other gestures to honor its pioneers of integration.[43]

Admirable as all this is, the heroic narrative of antiracism offered in these books, the photos on their covers, UGA's commemorations of desegregation, and the Foot Soldiers documentary films is so attractive that it can distract us from focusing on the genesis and longevity of racism in UGA's history. The heroic narrative invites us to think of these civil rights icons when we think about race, memory, and the history of UGA. Certainly, these heroes of multiracial democracy deserve all this attention and admiration. But it is also true that, as will be discussed in chapter 1, UGA's larger and longer-term record on race, much like the state that subsidized it, was the opposite of heroic. UGA had for decades served as a kind of leadership academy for Jim Crow Georgia. UGA graduates ranked among the state's most influential segregationists, including Eugene Talmadge, arguably the state's most effective racist demagogue, who rose to the governorship of Georgia; his white supremacist son Herman Talmadge, who also served as governor and then US senator—and who authored one of the South's most widely circulated books defending segregation; Roy Harris, known as the "kingmaker" for governors in Jim Crow Georgia, who published the state's most racist newspaper while serving on Georgia's Board of Regents; and Richard Russell, Georgia's long-serving US senator, who was the key strategist and leader of that body's white Southern segregationist caucus and for years used the filibuster to make the US Senate the graveyard of civil rights legislation. He coauthored the Southern Manifesto, the defiant Congressional statement against the *Brown* decision, which helped rally whites across the South to resist racial integration.[44]

UGA graduates and faculty also figured prominently among white supremacist intellectuals who helped to produce and promote racist myths about the history of Georgia and the South that served as a key part of the ideological foundation of the Jim Crow regime, as we will see in chapter 1. For example, U. B. Phillips, who took both his bachelor's and master's degrees at UGA, was the most influential historian of slavery in the United States during the opening decades of the twentieth century; he depicted slavery as a benign institution that served as a schoolhouse of civilization for benighted Africans.[45] And E. Merton Coulter, the long-time chair of UGA's history department, published influential white supremacist works that through the mid-twentieth century promoted the idea that the post–Civil War Reconstruction era had been a tragic era in which a vengeful North forced upon the South Black enfranchisement, leaving the South poorly governed by ignorant, corrupt African Americans and their sinister carpetbagger and scalawag puppeteers.[46] The lesson of such works, polluted by racist assumptions and biases, was that Blacks ought never again be accorded voting rights, one of the central tenets of Jim Crow Georgia.

And beyond such political leaders and intellectuals, if we are to understand the damage done by Jim Crow ideas and traditions, we need to look closely at their impact upon ordinary UGA students up to and during the university's desegregation crisis. This I do in chapter 2 by probing the essays written by a class of UGA calculus students about their views on race, integration, education, and violence a week after the campus segregationist riot in January 1961. These essays reveal what a challenge it would be to crack the campus's segregationist consensus, even in the aftermath of a federal court order and a racist riot that drew scathing criticism from the national news media.

Though I began this work on UGA's racism during my years on its faculty in the late twentieth century, my current thinking about how to contextualize this research has been influenced by the new historiography on the connections between slavery and universities that began to be written in the first decades of the twenty-first century.[47] This scholarship revealed that America's oldest universities had deep connections to the slave regime, enslaved African Americans, and the slave trade. The physical plants of such universities, especially in the South, had been built with enslaved labor, university and college endowments had been enriched by profits from slavery, and enslaved labor did much of the physical work required to keep these institutions functioning.[48] These connections to slavery, however, had been largely neglected by historians prior to the twenty-first century due to a combination of racial parochialism and inattention to the fact that university history ought to encompass not merely the academic work of all-white student bodies, faculty, and administrators but the labor and social history of African Americans who worked and in some cases even lived on campuses that benefitted from their labor while excluding them from the university's academic life.[49]

This new historiography has also explored the ideological role that the university played in upholding the slavery regime across the Old South. This included not only contributing to the class formation of a slaveholding elite but publishing and promoting proslavery arguments and ideas that helped to shape both the politics and the legal doctrines of the slavocracy.[50] When considered in this light, one can see striking parallels and continuities between antebellum UGA as a stronghold of the slavocracy and UGA as a bulwark of segregation and white supremacy in the Jim Crow era. As we have seen, UGA functioned as a leadership academy for Georgia's Jim Crow regime. But this role in rendering Georgia and the Jim Crow South "an authoritarian enclave"—a term introduced by political theorist Robert Mickey to denote the Deep Southern states' status as provinces where "components of democracy (free and fair elections, universal suffrage, independent and responsive institutions) are absent" —was not new for UGA.[51] The university had done much to legitimate racial tyranny for the slavocracy. Consider, for example, the role that John Henry Lumpkin, founder of UGA's law school and the first chief justice of the Supreme Court of Georgia, played in creating legal doctrines that codified racist authoritarianism, subordinating enslaved African Americans legally by denying them all citizenship rights, making the law an instrument of racial injustice.[52] Consider too the impact of Lumpkin's protégé and son-in law Thomas R. R. Cobb, a UGA graduate, whose classic work *An Inquiry into the Law of Negro Slavery in the United States* (1858) promoted and affirmed these laws of racial tyranny and offered a virtual encyclopedia of proslavery arguments.[53] And then of course there was Alexander Stephens, the slavocracy's most famed UGA graduate. Stephens not only helped to lead the slave South's antidemocratic revolt as vice president of the Confederate States of America but articulated the most powerful statement of its proslavery raison d'être, his "Cornerstone Address." Here he cited racial slavery, belief in Black inferiority, and slave-owning as a sacrosanct property right as constituting the cornerstones of the Confederacy.[54] It would be difficult to find another university that contributed more to the Confederate ideology affirming this "pro-slavery and anti-democratic state dedicated to the principle that all men were not created equal."[55]

These UGA contributions to the racist regime of the slave South by Lumpkin, Cobb, and Stephens parallel the contributions UGA made to the racist regime of the Jim Crow South by the Talmadges, Russell, Harris, Phillips, and Coulter. This is why when we think of race, memory, and the University of Georgia, we have to keep in mind this antidemocratic tradition of the old UGA along with the heroic African Americans and the federal court judges who forced the university to finally and reluctantly embrace multiracial democracy and academic meritocracy. And one should also bear in mind that the old antidemocratic UGA endured from its chartering in 1785 through its desegregation in 1961—and if one goes beyond student admissions and considers that the color line on UGA's athletic fields and faculty hires took another decade to fall, the old UGA actually lasted for at least 176 years whereas the new racially integrated UGA is only 63 years young. This means that a comprehensive history of UGA needs to devote at least as much attention to the old UGA as to the new. But all of the recent books published on UGA's history highlight the new, which inadvertently freed the university and Georgia from an accounting for their much longer racist past, a history that, judging by the recent law signed by Governor Kemp, will be almost impossible to discuss in the state's schools.

Fortunately, a new generation of historians at UGA, led by Chana Kai Lee and Scott Nesbit, has initiated a project devoted to unearthing the connections between slavery and UGA. Lee has already published an insightful article on this history, and Nesbit narrated a short, illuminating documentary film on slavery at UGA, and a book is in the works.[56] This work began in 2015 as part of the faculty reaction to the scandalous way the UGA administration handled the discovery of the remains of enslaved people on the campus—causing outrage on campus and in the Black community of Athens by reinterring these remains without consulting that community. The scholarship is ending the whites-only history of old UGA, documenting the role that enslaved laborers played in the construction and functioning of UGA when Georgia was a slave state. And it links UGA with a larger national effort. Pioneered by Brown University and Ruth Simmons, its first African American president, (as well as Yale University) two decades ago, Brown set a standard for serious exploration of the ways in which its university was connected to slavery, which has been emulated by a score of universities.[57] I see my work on twentieth-century UGA as aligned with this new scholarship and its insistence on a candid accounting of the university's racist past.

Historian Chana Kai Lee's candor in discussing the way that contemporary UGA politics impacted her in writing a critical history of race and slavery at the university struck me as both refreshing and revealing.[58] Her experience, like mine, reflects the difficulties involved in airing aspects of the university's past involving bigotry and oppression, a history that has long since been buried and that boosters of the university would prefer to remain forgotten. Her writing led me to see that my own encounters with denial, hesitancy, and unwillingness to face a racist past among UGA alumni, senior faculty, and administrators back in my own UGA years in the 1990s were part of the legacy of the history I have been studying, and so I have chosen to follow her lead in sharing these experiences in these pages.

In stressing the need to confront UGA's racist past, I do not mean to diminish the significance of the achievements of those who challenged and finally overcame the color line at the university or to dismiss the fine books, chapters, articles, and commemorations that have spotlighted this antiracist struggle.[59] In fact a fuller understanding of the depth, strength, and endurance of racism at UGA and in Georgia during the Jim Crow era enables us to better understand what foes of the color line were up against and so to better appreciate their courage and resourcefulness in defying the bigoted norms of that society. One can see this struggle between racism and antiracism play out even within a family in chapter 5 as I examine the controversy ignited by the interracial marriage of UGA students Charlayne Hunter and Walter Stovall in 1963.

The transition from the provincialism of Jim Crow Georgia to a more cosmopolitan university was not an easy one, nor was it quick—and some would argue that it is still incomplete. Chapter 6 explores this transition through the end of the Long 1960s and beyond as UGA struggled to become a genuine research university whose academic and extracurricular lives were truly diverse and racially integrated—and as UGA and Athens together became a more culturally liberal site in a state whose legislature and electoral politics leaned conservative far more often than not.

I am aware, of course, that the historical portrait I am drawing of the University of Georgia is not pretty. Having spent one of the happiest decades of my life at UGA—my son was born in Athens less than two miles from the campus—I am well aware that when most alums think about UGA, what comes to mind, along with the prowess of its football team (and the chants "GO DAWGS" that rumble through Sanford Stadium every autumn), is the beauty of its north campus, the lush garden created by one of America's first garden clubs, the elegant old buildings, the arch, and the walkways shaded by tall trees, all surrounded by manicured lawns. That beauty is the focus of attractive coffee table books, such as historian F. N. Boney's *A Pictorial History of the University of Georgia* (2000); legendary football coach Vince Dooley's *History and Reminiscences of the University of Georgia* (2011), illustrated with the striking paintings of Steve Penley; and UGA alumnus Garson Hart's *The University of Georgia: Images and Recollections* (2009). But none of these authors stopped to think that some of this beauty and the oldest buildings were created by enslaved laborers. Nor do they reflect on the university's service to white supremacy and its social function in support of slavery and Jim Crow: how its doors were closed to the greatest social scientist and historian ever to teach in Georgia, W. E. B. Du Bois, to the most inspiring democratic protest leader ever produced by the "Peach State," Martin Luther King Jr., to the famed jazz quartet of Dave Brubeck because it was integrated with white and Black musicians, and to northern football teams unless they benched their African American athletes.

Yes, I know UGA is beautiful, but much of its history is not. If we are to understand that history, we need to move beyond nostalgia and defy those who would inhibit serious and critical discussion of that history, the politicians who would ban it from classrooms or dismiss it as "woke" without daring to grapple with the historical evidence that demands our attention. This evidence should lead us to apply to UGA's history the words that James Baldwin left us with regarding our nation's past as he noted that "American history is longer, larger, more various, more beautiful, and more terrible than anything anyone has ever said about it."[60]

Baldwin's words beckon us to confront what was terrible in UGA's twentieth-century history: Jim Crowism, with its racism, cruelty, dishonesty, and its corruption of the university so that it served to undermine rather than promote equal opportunity. What was beautiful was largely confined to the Black side of the color line, where intrepid students, their lawyers, and families worked diligently and sacrificed much to challenge that line—championing a most un-UGA-like vision of multiracial democracy and a university where merit rather than skin color determined admission. How many whites at UGA shared and acted on this vision in the Jim Crow era and in the early days of desegregation? Walter Stovall, one such Georgia-born antiracist, told me that in his undergraduate years at UGA in the early 1960s there were very few like him, that if you had gathered them together you could fit them in a "small room and they wouldn't be bunking into each other," which was why he so disliked the university.[61] So we need to understand why there would be so few in that room but also what enabled those few to stand up for democracy in an antidemocratic state and university.

RATHER THAN A COMPREHENSIVE ACCOUNT of race, memory, and the University of Georgia, this book brings together essays that in their chronological focus explore select but also key events, figures, and ideas in UGA's troubled racial history. These essays span the early-twentieth-century era of Jim Crow, the UGA desegregation crisis of 1961, its aftermath in the mid and late 1960s and early 1970s, and reflections from the 1990s on that crisis and what had and had not changed in Black-white relations on campus since the 1960s. The vintage of these essays varies. The oldest, which I first published as articles in the *Georgia Historical Quarterly* nearly three decades ago, reflect—as indicated earlier in this introduction—my interest in UGA's desegregation crisis, which is what first drew me to the study of Georgia history. These articles, the first on white UGA student attitudes toward the university's desegregation in 1961 (chapter 2) and the second on the FBI investigation of UGA's racist riot during the desegregation crisis (chapter 3), both brought major new sources to light that illuminated those turbulent times. Though

I have updated the notes and added a few important points in adapting these articles for this book, I have resisted the temptation to make major revisions since historians have found them useful in their original form. But with both of these articles I have included postscripts that allow for greater contextualization, enabling me both to supplement and to reflect on the limitations of the sources I used and some of the conclusions I reached in those articles.

As indicated earlier in this introduction, I have recently come to see that the singular focus on UGA's desegregation by myself and other writers has led to a neglect of the university's role in sustaining Georgia's segregationist order in the Jim Crow era. And so to illuminate this earlier history, the book opens with a chapter on UGA's service as a kind of white leadership academy for Jim Crow Georgia's power elite. It is a depressing story but a necessary one if we are to understand just how provincial and bigoted UGA and many of its most powerful alumni were, and to appreciate how resistant they were to democratic change. The same can be said about their disdain for interracial marriage, discussed in chapter 5, so that even though we have in this chapter moved into 1963, after UGA had officially desegregated, Jim Crow ideas and prejudices were still going strong.

Recognizing that desegregation is best understood as not a brief event but as a protracted process, I have sought in several parts of this book to broaden the focus on that process beyond the desegregation crisis of 1961 and the early 1960s college years of UGA's first generation of Black students (though I do explore in chapter 4 Black memories of that crisis). In this I have been influenced by Charlayne Hunter-Gault, who in returning to UGA in 1969 as a *New York Times* reporter wrote with great insight on what she learned after interviewing Black and white UGA students about the progress and obstacles to progress that a later generation than hers experienced in the struggle for a university committed to racial integration and equity. This is the subject I explore concerning UGA's students, faculty, and administration from 1963 through the 1980s in chapter 6, and with my own UGA students in the late 1990s in chapter 7. The book ends with a coda on twenty-first century Georgia historical memory, as reflected in UGA's fortieth anniversary commemoration in 2001 (echoed in the fiftieth and sixtieth anniversary commemorations in 2011 and 2021) of its desegregation. I hope this work helps open the door to more in-depth explorations of desegregation as a multigenerational process that yielded struggles not merely to have Black student admissions accelerate but to desegregate the faculty, the curriculum, the administration, and the university's social and cultural life.

CHAPTER ONE

Leading and Misleading Georgia
University of Georgia and Jim Crow Georgia's Educational and Political Power Elite

At their best, universities serve as centers of scholarship where professors and students engage in the pursuit of truth and research generates new forms of knowledge. The University of Georgia's top officials in the Jim Crow era, however, had been so corrupted by racism that at times they barely resembled leaders of a genuine university, going to court in December 1960, wielding one lie after another in the *Holmes v. Danner* case attempting to preserve UGA's status as a racially segregated institution by arguing that the university's refusal to admit two highly qualified Black applicants, Charlayne Hunter and Hamilton Holmes, had not been caused by racial discrimination.[1]

UGA officials sought to justify rejecting Charlayne Hunter by testifying in court that the university was so overcrowded there was no room for any new students in the dormitories.[2] With Hamilton Holmes, the "no room in the dorm" rationale would not work because with transfer students only women were required to live on campus. So UGA dishonestly claimed that Holmes was rejected because he had been evasive in his required admissions interview.[3]

These lies quickly fell apart, however, when the lawyers for Hunter and Holmes showed that white students had been allowed to transfer to UGA and that the supposed campus housing crisis had not stopped one of the university's deans from traveling to New York to recruit white students.[4] And the alleged evasiveness of Holmes in his UGA interview centered on his answering (truthfully) that he had never been arrested, which his white interviewers sought to depict as dishonest on the grounds that he admitted to getting a speeding ticket.[5]

Judge W. A. Bootle refused to follow UGA's lead in equating a minor traffic violation with an arrest or finding any evasiveness in Holmes's interview on the basis of this spurious equation, or on any other responses that UGA officials cited in their absurd allegations of evasiveness.[6] And the admissions interview, which UGA sought to present as an important part of the admissions process, was given to some white UGA students "*after* they were already attending the University."[7] University records revealed that some white students had no such interview at all.[8]

The UGA administration's hypocrisy concerning the Holmes interview was striking and did not go unnoticed by Judge Bootle. Here was UGA claiming that Holmes had been evasive in the interview when the interview process itself was dishonest, conducted, as the judge put it, "with the purpose in mind of finding a basis for rejecting Holmes."[9] No other UGA student was grilled, as Holmes was, by three UGA officials for a solid hour. And Holmes was confronted with personal and political questions, which, as Bootle noted, "had probably never been asked of any applicant before."[10]

The interview questions posed to Holmes had no relevance to his academic qualifications to attend UGA (which is supposedly what an admissions interview is meant to ascertain), but they do tell us a good deal about the segregationist mindset of the UGA administrators who designed and posed them: first, that Holmes was a troublemaker ("Have you been arrested?") and a radical agitator ("Have you ever participated... [in] the student sit-in movement?" "Give some insights into the working of the student sit-in movement in Atlanta") who had applied to UGA not for his own educational goals but rather to serve the NAACP's school integration agenda ("What is your opinion concerning the [school] integration crises in New Orleans and in Atlanta?" "Since you are interested in a premedical course, why have you not applied to Emory University since it is in Atlanta?"). Then there were the insulting questions linked to segregationist assumptions about Black sexuality ("Have you ever attended houses of prostitution?" "Do you know about the red light district in Athens?" "Have you ever attended... Beatnik places in Atlanta?"). Finally, they tried to imply that the ultimate goal of Holmes and the NAACP was not the schoolhouse door but white bedrooms ("Have you ever attended inter-racial parties?").[11]

Thanks to the able job done by Holmes's attorneys, Bootle recognized not only that UGA was misusing the interview process to serve its racially discriminatory agenda but that it was a repeat offender in this regard. UGA had used a similarly biased and insulting interview back in 1951 to label Horace Ward as "evasive" and to reject on that basis this first Black applicant's futile attempt to gain admission to UGA's law school. In that interview, as the judge noted, UGA officials had said "almost the same thing" about Ward that they "said about Holmes in this case."[12] Seeing through such blatant dissembling and unfairness, Bootle concluded, "It is evident... that the interview of Holmes was not conducted as the interview of white applicants, and from the evidence as a whole and particularly from Holmes' appearance at the trial, it is also evident that, had the interview of Holmes been conducted in the same manner as the interviews of white applicants, Holmes would have been found 'to be an acceptable candidate for admission to the University.'"[13]

Though at times in the trial UGA's dishonesty about its dealing with Black applicants could be infuriating—as with this bogus interview process—there were other moments when the lying was so ham-handed that it could seem comical. This was the case when, as we have seen, President Aderhold gave the absurd testimony that UGA's admissions policies—which had excluded Blacks for generations—were not racially discriminatory.[14] And Aderhold was not the only high ranking UGA official to prevaricate. UGA registrar Walter Danner too tied himself up like a pretzel on the witness stand trying to avoid coming off as discriminatory so as not to get caught on the wrong side of the *Brown v. Board of Education* precedent and lose the case. Danner even claimed he had no objection to admitting to UGA qualified African American students, even though the admissions process he administered had just shut the door on two such qualified applicants.[15]

Struck by the humor in such absurd testimony, journalist Calvin Trillin, who covered the trial for *Time* magazine, later asked Constance Baker Motley, the eminent NAACP civil rights lawyer, about it. Baker Motley, who questioned these UGA officials at the trial, and who had similar encounters with officials at the University of Mississippi and with white Southern registrars in voting rights cases, explained,

> it's not funny, really. The [judicial] system is based on people getting on the stand and telling the truth. But people who talk about their respect for tradition and integrity and the Constitution get involved in one lie after another. They're willing to break down the system to keep a Negro out. In Mississippi, university officials got up on the stand and said they never even discussed the [James] Meredith case [in which the University of Mississippi in 1962 sought to prevent his admission as its first Black student]. They do the same kind of thing in voting [rights] cases. People are denied the right to vote [these disingenuous segregationist officials claim] not because they're Negroes but because they don't dot an "I" or interpret the Constitution correctly. This is one of the most serious byproducts of segregation. The people get a disregard for the law. They see supposedly important people get up day after day on the stand and lie. The reason the whole thing seems funny to watch is that you spend all that time proving something everybody knows [i.e., that Jim Crow universities discriminate against Black applicants].[16]

But what Trillin and Baker Motley did not explain here is why winning this court case and preserving the segregationist status quo at UGA was so important to white Georgians and university leaders that those leaders, from the very top—President Aderhold—on down were willing to perjure themselves for this cause. Since their testimony in court was evasive by design, one can find no direct evidence there to answer this question. With Aderhold, his biography helps to explain this willingness to battle to preserve segregation. He was born in rural Georgia in 1899, the son of a farmer, and prospered on the white side of the state's segregated educational system, graduating from UGA in 1923 and serving first as the principal of a white high school and then as a county school superintendent before becoming a professor of rural education at segregated UGA in 1929, then rising to the education school deanship in 1946 and UGA's presidency in 1950. Having headed UGA when it doctored its admissions process to bar its first Black applicant—Horace Ward (requiring for the first time endorsements by a local judge and UGA alum, using a slanted admissions interview, etc.)—and battled successfully in court to keep Ward out of UGA, Aderhold performed as expected in doing all he could to keep Holmes and Hunter from gaining admission to UGA.[17]

Aderhold's case makes it evident that to be a university administrator in Jim Crow Georgia meant towing the segregationist line. If you wanted to hold high office in the educational world, you not only defended the Jim Crow university from attempts to integrate it but acted as a good company man (or woman), deferring to those above you in the segregationist educational and political establishments. Thus when asked by a reporter in May 1954 for his response to the historic Supreme Court ruling *Brown v. Board of Education* declaring segregated education unconstitutional, Aderhold simply deferred to the state's board of regents. As to whether the ruling would prompt any change at UGA, Aderhold came off more like a clerk than an intellectual or educational leader, simply reminding the reporter that "we operate under the Board of Regents. They formulate policies and programs. I don't know of any immediate change contemplated by the Board at this time."[18]

William Tate, UGA dean of men, who worked closely with Aderhold and knew him well, remembered him sentimentally as perfectly suited to lead the university in and beyond the Jim Crow era. Like Tate, his life's work had been serving in Georgia's whites-only educational establishment, and Aderhold was, according to Tate, "very knowledgeable about the state of Georgia, born and raised a segregationist. He knew nigras 'in their place,' as we say in the South" and was "perfectly conscious of how Georgia [white] people felt."[19] Tate thought Aderhold was more aware than the state's political leadership that, given the Supreme Court's support of integration, Jim Crow's days were numbered, but he never said so publicly and in fact spoke "very firmly against integration" since he was convinced that "Georgia was not ready for integration."[20] Tate characterized Aderhold as "an organization man, who could take orders" and would never risk "bucking the state" political leadership, "which, after all, was in control of us." That segregationist leadership has mandated that "we could not get any [state] funds" if the university integrated. "President Aderhold was very conscious of that. He also felt that . . . we had to live with the State Legislature, the Board of Regents, and the laws of [Jim Crow] Georgia."[21]

Aderhold was not merely loyal to the state's leading segregationist politicians, but he had no scruples about publicly serving as a cheerleader for them. For example, in 1952 when Richard B. Russell, Georgia's senatorial champion of Jim Crow, announced his presidential candidacy, Aderhold declared that "the University is proud of the senator and considers him one of its most distinguished sons. . . . He is a great leader and would bring honor to the University and the state as president. He has always been loyal as an alumnus of this institution to the institution and its purposes."[22]

The best evidence of the mindset and racial attitudes that characterized UGA's leaders in the Jim Crow era is found in their private correspondence, where they were most candid in expressing their racism and provincialism. This can be seen in a letter Robert O. Arnold, chairman of the Board of Regents of the University System of Georgia, sent to UGA law school dean J. Alton Hosch amid the battle to bar Ward from UGA in 1952.[23] Close to Aderhold, Hosch had been selected by UGA's president to serve on that white supremacist committee that interviewed Horace Ward, treating him (a future federal judge) as if he was a fraud or some alien life form.[24] In September 1951 Hosch wrote the report of the interview recommending that Ward's application to the law school be rejected—which of course Aderhold welcomed and affirmed—in order to prevent the law school's desegregation.[25] A little over five months after this, dean Hosch sent regent chair Arnold an article from the *Red and Black*, UGA's student newspaper, featuring interviews with eight UGA students on how they felt about "an Atlanta Negro [Horace Ward] seeking entrance to the University law school." The overwhelming consensus of these students, with only one exception, was, as the headline indicated, "Students Turn Thumbs Down on Negro Seeking Entrance."[26]

Arnold's letter back to Hosch indicated that what concerned him about the interviews in this news story was not the seven (white male) students who expressed opposition to desegregating UGA's law school but the one

UGA student interviewee who expressed support for integration. This integrationist student, Helen Cannon, apparently the only northerner interviewed for the article, was an education major from Ohio. She told the reporter, "I think that as long as the Negroes meet the same standard of education and personal traits required of white students they should be allowed to attend the University. It will soon be the custom to educate the two peoples together."[27]

Arnold was an intransigent segregationist. In fact, he opened his letter to Hosch noting that Ward's attempt to desegregate UGA's law school "caused me considerable anxiety." But having used the interview process to reject Ward, Arnold noted happily that "our handling" of Ward's application "has been wise or lucky—maybe both."[28] So it is not surprising that he viewed Helen Cannon's integrationist sentiments as ignorant and misguided. Noting that she was from Cleveland, Arnold wrote that "this sounds more like Ohio than Georgia. I wonder what she could know about the personal traits of negroes, and if B.O. [body odor] could come under the heading of traits with this young lady."[29] So here we have a top leader of the University of Georgia privately expressing the bigoted notion that Blacks are unclean and so carry a bad odor, and invoking the regional conceit that only Southern whites were familiar with Black people's negative traits and so were best able to recognize their inferiority.

Arnold went on to write something extraordinarily revealing about his views on the social function of education, informing Hosch that this northern student's racial egalitarianism suggests "that her education is lacking somewhere, although she is a candidate for major in education. With her thinking, she had best be careful to locate above the Mason & Dixon line."[30] This suggests that part of Arnold's definition of a well-educated person is one who believes in racial segregation and inequality and that there is no place below the Mason-Dixon Line for a teacher with Cannon's integrationist mindset. So educational institutions, in this Jim Crow vision, existed to support the segregationist status quo in the South rather than to foster or even allow questioning of it. The fact that Arnold felt free to share these reactionary, bigoted views with UGA's law school dean, and that he in turn was close to Aderhold, suggests that such thinking was widespread among UGA's leadership cadre.

The implications of Arnold's words about education aligning with and supporting the segregated status quo in the Jim Crow South call to mind one of the most scathing and revealing passages from Charlayne Hunter-Gault's memoir, *In My Place* (1992), about the white side of the Georgia color line.

Hunter-Gault was reflecting upon what she had learned in her UGA years from her future husband, Walter Stovall, a UGA student, about what it had been like growing up white and middle class in Douglas, a small south Georgia town, in the Jim Crow era. Stovall had described it as "a stultifying society that in its own way kept whites in their place—self-centered, socially homogenous puritans, whose worldview was restricted to the Protestant Church on Sunday and a limited range of weekday activities that included running small businesses or farming, regular bridge parties, the occasional round of golf at the country club, and Friday night football. Everybody wrapped himself in the Confederate flag but the Black citizens who washed and ironed it. Except for their value as manual labor, they were hardly regarded at all."[31] As to education's place in this social order, Stovall provided Hunter-Gault with "a window into small-town white public education: it was designed to teach you to read, write, and do your sums, and prepare you to go to a non-threatening, non-challenging place like the University of Georgia, where you would be educated to take your place in that little world, thrive in it, and see to it that it continued in perpetuity as it was."[32]

The *Red and Black* interviews (that Arnold and Hosch corresponded about) with Southern UGA students offering their responses to the prospect of the university desegregating in 1952 confirm what Hunter-Gault wrote about the university as a "non-challenging place." This was certainly so with regard to race. There is no indication that any of these interviewees had learned a thing at UGA that inclined them to oppose or even question the segregated social order in which they had been raised.

In fact, these responses mostly recycled hoary rhetoric about supporting separate but equal education for Blacks when in actuality the funding of schools for African American students in Georgia lagged far behind white schools, as did Black higher educational opportunity in the state.[33] Some blindly clung to Jim Crowism because that was how they were raised. As Lamar Harris, an engineering student from Taylorsville, Georgia, told the *Red and Black*, "No, I don't believe they [Blacks] should be admitted." Segregation is "a Southern tradition.... My father and his father were against ... [integration], and that is why I am against it."[34]

Though none of these UGA students had contact with Horace Ward or offered evidence of any familiarity with Black college students, several claimed to know, as Jack Leverett, a UGA freshman pharmacy student put it, that "negroes ... do not want to attend the University of Georgia ... or to break down segregation."[35] They just wanted to get a college education at their own Black institutions. This meant, of course, that Blacks like Horace

Ward, who applied to UGA's law school, did so not out of genuine educational interest but were rather—in the words of interviewee Donald Lee, a veterinary medicine student—sent to UGA by "a group in Atlanta who are simply agitators."[36]

The year of these overwhelmingly segregationist interviews was 1952, but the sentiments students expressed could as easily have been found dominating UGA in 1942, 1932, 1922, 1912, 1902, or any time in the Jim Crow era. Indeed, what is striking when one reads student publications and other UGA student sources is how pervasive and unchanging white racial parochialism and bigotry were on campus. The casual racism of the place cropped up year after year, whether it was UGA student newspaper photos of students in blackface in 1950 frolicking in their "primitive Africa" Arty Party; the 1932 UGA yearbook cartoon depicting armed UGA students in the Reconstruction era enjoying "a day of real sport" and having "fun" chasing formerly enslaved African Americans (represented via racist caricatures) from campus to "enlighten" them that they would never be allowed to matriculate at UGA; the racist caricatures and derisive humor of the UGA yearbook in 1914; or the front page 1941 student newspaper story "Racial Equality Poster Found on University Bulletin Board" reflecting the outraged reaction to a Rosenwald Fund recruitment poster on campus publicizing scholarships for those who wanted to do Black education–related work, which students disdained as designed to "entice Southern students to the damn-yankee north and teach them to be 'nigger lovers' before they return home."[37] This atmosphere both reflected and reinforced the racism most UGA students had imbibed in their hometowns during the Jim Crow era; and UGA's administration never and the faculty rarely publicly pushed back against it. So in this sense the university was very much complicit in this informal yet powerful form of racial miseducation. This may be what the famed poet Karl Shapiro was referring to in the opening line of "University," his scathing poem published in 1946 reflecting on the Jim Crow university (though in his case it was his alma mater, the University of Virginia, rather than UGA): "To hurt the Negro and avoid the Jew is the curriculum."[38]

While more work needs to be done to fully understand how exactly the faculty of Jim Crow era Southern institutions of higher education like UGA could be rendered virtually mute when it came to challenging or rebuking students for their crude racism, as expressed in their publications and elsewhere, it seems a natural outcome of the way their campus administrations used favoritism and fear to secure a segregationist consensus. The favoritism came into play with regard to faculty hiring, which at UGA tended to be disproportionately skewed toward Southerners (all white, of course). They would either support racial segregation or, understanding how risky it would be to express any kind of dissent from the Jim Crow social order, avoid any such dissent even if they had an inclination to express it. As UGA sociology professor John C. Belcher recalled, in the Jim Crow era, at UGA and other white

> universities and colleges of the South . . . there was a conscious attempt . . . to employ individuals who shared [white] Southern values. It was very difficult, in fact impossible in some schools and departments, for a person to be employed if he did not clearly qualify for Southern heritage. One born outside the South or, if born in the South and educated in the North, had to proclaim his adherence to the life patterns of the South. One of the best ways to accomplish this, and without any personal commitment to a value system, was to express, "My granddaddy fought for the Confederates during the War for Southern Independence." If the individual said "Civil War," he was suspect.[39]

This favoritism toward white Southern faculty in hiring left much of the UGA professoriate during the Jim Crow era mired in a parochial elitism that was not compatible with racial egalitarianism. This is what business professor Robert Dince was referring to when he recalled that to those who, like him,

> came from the North, it seemed . . . that the old University of Georgia was very much like keeping the concept of the French aristocracy. To become a professor at the University was an honored profession for a man of good family to do. There were a lot of faculty here that were of the upper class of Georgia, which did not mean necessarily money in those days, it mean[t] social standing and prestige, and we sure had our share of them, who expressed extremely benign attitudes towards Negroes, as long as they maintained a given [subordinate] position in society.[40]

So when as a new faculty member he would interact with veteran faculty, not only from his own but from other departments, he would hear "what were to me amazing statements" of white racial elitism, especially from colleagues "in the English department, and also the History department." This was, as Dince explained, a kind of genteel racism that he distinguished from a crude Klan type of racism: "I didn't know many violently racist faculty here. They had violently conservative political views, and they certainly were anti-activist black movements, such as the ones that [Martin Luther] King and others led, but I never heard that many strong statements against blacks, except by one man ... in the Sociology department."[41] Their elitist sensibility of wanting to "keep the colored in their place" meant that much of the faculty would not be inclined to intervene intellectually or politically to challenge the white supremacist assumptions and expression of their students either in person or in print during the Jim Crow era.

As to fear, this was generated by powerful Georgia state government officials and the UGA administration's intolerance of integrationism, which made it evident that criticism of racial segregation would lead to all kinds of negative consequences. Robert Ayers, who had served as UGA's chaplain in the 1940s, recalled the kind of retribution racially egalitarian faculty faced. Ayers detailed the case of two philosophy professors, Paul Pfuetze and Rubin Gotesky, who were so harassed by their dean after they wrote articles favoring racial integration that they ended up leaving UGA. The more senior of the two, Pfuetze, was not only tenured but had been department head. Yet his senior faculty status could not protect him from his segregationist dean who was furious at him not only because he had advocated integration in print but had written an admiring letter to the African American congressman Adam Clayton Powell. As Ayers recalled,

> Adam Clayton Powell was opposed to universal military conscription, and Paul, being a Quaker, accepted that position. So, he wrote a letter to Adam Clayton Powell indicating that he supported him on that position, and then also stated (I think it was a footnote to his letter) that he was opposed to the Southern way of segregation. Well, Adam Clayton Powell read the letter on the floor of the House, and it got in the Congressional Record. From that time on, Fitzie and Gotesky began to have all sorts of problems here at the University.... They were badgered [by the dean]; pressure was put on them in all sorts of little, piddling ways, their salaries were not raised, and there was an attempt to get rid of them ... [even though] they couldn't fire them because they had tenure.... So, Martin [the dean] took every opportunity to badger him [Pfuetze]. For example, if grades happened to be late, he'd call and put all sorts of pressure on him, and talk to him in ways that were not dignified; you just do not talk to another human being like that. Well, the upshot of it was that Paul finally had enough of it, and had a good offer from Vassar and went to Vassar.... And then Gotesky left a couple of years later, [after he] ... suffered from ... persecution ... from the Administration. As for example, delaying of promotion when he had the credentials and should have been promoted to full professor long before. Well, he left.[42]

In a 1955 letter to famed Southern liberal writer Lillian Smith, Pfuetze offered what is perhaps the most evocative and chilling account of the political repression prointegration professors faced at UGA during the Jim Crow era. He wrote Smith that "we are in deep trouble again.... The roof fell in" on him and Gotesky. "We were both called into the Dean's office and read the riot act. The general impression was that we were "personae non-grata" and that we could expect no increase in rank or salary, nor further support for our department unless we resigned, or kept silent, or rolled over and played dead. They even threatened to abolish the philosophy department if they could not get rid of us in other ways." Pfuetze speculated that "someone high up in the State government or the University administration must have been 'riding' him [the dean], and he passed on the pressure to us instead of defending us." Pfuetze, a northerner with a doctorate from Yale Divinity School, suspected that segregationist politics, plus the temperament of his "thin skinned" dean, "a deep-dyed southerner" whom he "feared shared some of the attitudes of the men [militant segregationist politicians] in Atlanta," was making it impossible for critics of Jim Crow to survive at UGA. "We have become, for some here, a kind of 'symbol' and 'scapegoat' for all these tensions and pressures, hostilities and grievances. Our very being here is a kind of standing rebuke to these frightened and desperate men who are fighting with their own consciences."[43]

The dean would in fact abort Pfuetze's term as department chair in philosophy by combining that department with religious studies and making Ayers chair of the new department, a role which Ayers took on reluctantly since he was close to Pfuetze.[44] In his years as UGA chaplain, Ayers had had his own problems with the administration on race. He encountered friction when he brought in prominent scholars of religion, such as Paul Tillich, whose remarks included criticism of Jim Crow, since this "upset the administration." His dean was "very upset" when Ayers brought in a friend who had helped build libraries in Black communities because this invited speaker taught at Paine College, one of Georgia's historically Black colleges.[45] The dean was in a panic when he saw the notice of this talk in UGA's student newspaper, fearing that Ayers had done something beyond the pale—inviting a Black educator to speak on campus. But since the speaker was white, the event was allowed to occur. Ultimately, the UGA administration found an institutional mechanism to put an end to this influx of chaplain-invited speakers critical of Jim Crow by severing UGA's connection to such religious liberalism. As Ayers explained, "When I left the Chaplain's Office, they abandoned the whole office because they didn't want that program going on."[46]

Other than Pfuetze (who left for Vassar in 1959), of the many UGA faculty, student, and administration sources I have read, I have encountered only *one* example of a professor who indicated that in his instructional work in the classroom he dared to challenge racial segregation during the Jim Crow era, and this came near the end of that era. This was political scientist Pete Range, who recalled that in the late 1950s he had been "speaking in favor of integration in classes, arguing that it wouldn't destroy the University, that they wouldn't pollute the students or the culture or the society if we had Negroes in the classrooms."[47] Conveying integrationist ideas in the classroom at UGA was so unusual that offended students saw it as a form of professional misconduct, and so, as Range explained, they went "home with complaints, and then the parents had gotten on somebody connected with the University or in the Legislature and complained about me."[48] Range was then "called in by the Dean ... to be asked if I were a Communist or something of that kind." Similarly, when Range had arranged a debate with a member of the Georgia state legislature about segregation, he heard from the UGA president's office that this "unwise" act had "upset" President Aderhold, who viewed Range as risking antagonizing the legislature.[49]

Range's earlier experience with similar pressure at his prior job, at Abraham Baldwin Agricultural College in Tifton, Georgia, attests that UGA was quite typical of the state's higher education institutions in its intolerance of dissent against Jim Crow. Back in the early 1940s, Range had gotten into hot water not because of his teaching but rather because he had published "a column for the local newspaper complaining about how some Negroes had been treated by the ice and coal company down there. The Governor [the militant segregationist Eugene Talmadge] got a copy of that, and we had a member of the Board of Regents in our town, and I got a called into the President's Office about putting such things into the newspaper." Range was "really put on the carpet" and warned by the college president "that if I irritated the Governor and Board of Regents member in that town, he would be helpless to protect me ... [if they] decided ... to get rid of me."[50]

At UGA this repressive political atmosphere meant that most students never had their minds open when the idea of racial integration came up. As Chappelle Matthews, UGA class of 1933, who later became a leading champion of public education in the Georgia state legislature, noted in an oral history interview four decades later, in his college years "in no way" would UGA faculty have even "instigated" a discussion of the possible integration of the university. And had anyone actually tried to integrate UGA back when he was at the university, the vast majority of students, in Matthews's words, "just flat wouldn't have allowed it. They'd have stopped it [even] if they had to use force at that time."⁵¹

As will be discussed in chapter 2, where a class full of UGA student essays on integration in January 1961 are analyzed, none of the students in that class mentioned their white supremacist assumptions being challenged or their minds changed about race by any professor or reading that they were assigned at UGA in the Jim Crow era (one essayist mentioned those assumptions being challenged by a social science study but did not indicate this reading had been done at UGA or for a class at the university). The oral histories John C. Belcher did with UGA students and faculty turned up only one example of a teacher who (while using racist language) had such an antiracist impact on a student, but this occurred at a community college before this student transferred to the University of Georgia. At that "junior college" Roger Thomas recalled he had a teacher

> in a Biology class, he was a very down-home kind of fellow, he was an ex-coach who was teaching Introductory Biology, chewed tobacco and so forth—he would frequently attack prejudices of many kinds, he would frequently point out certain kinds of myths—like—well, let me get right on to the racial thing here. One day, in his very gruff kind of way, he said, "There ain't no difference between niggers and whites. A lot of people say they smell different, they [Blacks] smell bad. But when they take a bath, there's no difference." Now that seems like a small, little thing, but that was the first time I really began to confront these myths that I had accepted all of my life, that there was something terrible about a black person's smell. By this time, it was 1957 and I was eighteen years old. That was an awakening.⁵²

Since we have so little record of what UGA faculty said about race in their classrooms during the Jim Crow era, we ought not assume a *complete* absence of racial egalitarianism. Let us assume for the moment—though I have found precious little evidence of this (since open dissenters such as Pfuetze, Gotesky, and Range were so rare and so at risk)—that the university over the long course of the Jim Crow era taught *something* in its social science and humanities course work that might lead students to question their white supremacist assumptions.⁵³ Such learning would be decisively undermined and overwhelmed by the all-white extracurricular world and living arrangements of the university, which reinforced white supremacist habits of mind. In this case we might think of UGA's racial politics, racial education, and miseducation, as a totally uneven match between the university's extracurricular life and anything that might be remotely racially egalitarian in its academic curriculum. You can best experience this today by immersing yourself in decades of UGA student yearbooks (all titled the *Pandora*) from the Jim Crow era, each with hundreds of pages of photos of white social and academic clubs, athletic teams, campus military units, fraternities, and sororities, and where Blacks appear in photos only as servants or objects of racist ridicule and as caricatured comic figures in cartoons and sketches. When Blacks, who assisted in the Greek houses and with the athletic teams, do appear in *Pandora* photographs, their names were rarely provided, and if a name appeared at all it was rendered condescendingly with just the first or a nickname.[54] Black servants in the fraternities, typically photographed in white waiter's jackets, were known as "house boys" even when they were adults.[55]

The only time UGA students encountered Blacks in their campus world, then, was with those who waited on them, cooked for them, and cleaned up after them. This all just reinforced assumptions about white superiority, since never was a Black academic, college student, lawyer, or civil rights leader invited to campus in the Jim Crow era; it was as if the African American professional class did not exist, and Blacks existed only to serve, be ordered about, and serve as the butt of racist humor. So racial inequality was almost literally in the air that UGA students breathed in their Jim Crow campus world. This being the case, even if a professor briefly challenged racist assumption in an academic classroom setting (and, as we have seen, such challenges were very rare), this would be no match for the twenty-four/seven white supremacist experience of living as the dominant race at UGA.

A SKEPTIC GLANCING at the *Red and Black* interviews with UGA students in 1952—that the law school dean and regent chair corresponded about—might agree that they do attest to the university's failure to educate its students about race, equality, and civil rights, but might see these interviews as having little consequence. After all, these were only undergraduates. But this misses the significance of UGA in the social order of Georgia in the Jim Crow era (and even today). The university served as the launching pad for many members of the educational, political, and economic elite of Georgia. So some of those who matriculated as UGA students in the first third of the twentieth century, and who were as poorly educated on race as their counterparts interviewed by the *Red and Black* in 1952, would go on to lead the state and help to shape the white response to the NAACP's desegregation cases in the 1950s and 1960s. In fact, this is precisely what happened with regard to UGA's culminating desegregation case, *Holmes v. Danner*, and the subsequent political crisis. We have already seen that one UGA graduate, O. C. Aderhold, as president of UGA, mobilized his administration to battle against integration. Important as was his role in the courtoom phase of UGA's desegregation crisis, Aderhold was not the most influential UGA graduate to impact this crisis. That role would be played by Georgia's governor Ernest Vandiver.

Much like those Southern UGA students interviewed by the *Red and Black* in 1952, Vandiver graduated from the University of Georgia without having learned to question the segregationist social order in which he had been raised. He entered UGA in 1936 and would take both his BA and his law degree there.[56] Even before his college years, Vandiver was strongly drawn to white supremacist politics, mentored by his father who was an enthusiastic supporter of Georgia's leading segregationist politicians, Eugene Talmadge and Richard Russell.[57] Vandiver would emerge as a major figure in the Talmadge faction of Georgia state politics. Talmadge was a racist demagogue who battled to preserve the white primary and made race-baiting and intransigent segregationism a regular feature of his successful campaigns for the Georgia governorship—a position he held from 1933 to 1937 and 1941 to 1943.[58] Talmadge had, as historian Thomas Dyer aptly put it, built his political "career through skillful manipulation of the [white] rural masses in Georgia ... combining a strong populist appeal with anti-urbanism, anti-intellectualism, and racism."[59] Typical of Talmadge was his remark that "I like the nigger in his place, and his place is at the back door with his hat in his hand."[60]

Vandiver remained loyal to Governor Talmadge even after he damaged UGA in one of Talmadge's most unethical race-baiting attacks. This was the Cocking affair, in which Talmadge falsely charged Walter Cocking, dean of UGA's education school, with being an integrationist and got him fired in 1941 on that basis. The firing would lead to UGA losing its accreditation, causing outrage that would ultimately yield a rare Talmadge defeat in his re-election campaign. This looks all the worse when you consider that Talmadge too was a UGA alumnus. But then again for Talmadge, any threat to UGA loyally serving the segregationist social order had to be eliminated even if the threat was imaginary.[61] Vandiver would, as a loyal Talmadgeite, be elected lieutenant governor in 1954 and governor in 1958.[62]

If one thinks that the social function of higher education is to preserve the existing social order no matter how unjust, then one could see UGA as a smashing success in helping to produce such powerful segregationist public officials. But on the other hand, if one is concerned with human rights, progress, and morality, the ascendance of such racist politicians can be seen as a tragedy, reflecting the failure of the university to educate leaders who aspired toward a more humane and democratic world, free of racism.

As a teenage undergraduate at Morehouse College in Atlanta, Martin Luther King Jr. displayed a keen awareness of these issues, and in one of his first published articles, which appeared in the Morehouse student newspaper in 1947, offered the kind of critical read of Talmadge that Vandiver, weighed down by political ambition and bigotry, proved incapable of providing. The young King wrote that

> the function of education ... is to teach one to think intensively and to think critically. But education which stops with efficiency may prove the greatest menace to society. The most dangerous criminal may be the man gifted with reason, but with no morals.... Eugene Talmadge ... possessed one of the better minds of Georgia.... He wore the Phi Beta Kappa key.... Mr. Talmadge could think critically and intensively; yet he contends that I am an inferior being. Are those the types of men we call educated? ... Intelligence is not enough. Intelligence plus character—that is the goal of true education ... [which] gives one not only power of concentration, but worthy objectives upon which to concentrate. The broad education will, therefore, transmit to one not only ... accumulated knowledge ... but also the accumulated experience of social living. If we are not careful, our colleges will produce a group of close-minded, unscientific, illogical propagandists, consumed with immoral acts.... Be careful, teachers![63]

Close-minded is a good way to describe Vandiver on race as he ascended to high elective office in Georgia in the 1950s. If anything, his UGA education—or rather his miseducation on Southern history—as a history major made him simply more intransigent as a white supremacist. Having learned the mythical, anti-Black version of Radical Reconstruction, in which post–Civil War Black enfranchisement and officeholding were viewed as horrific impositions on, and punishment of, the South by a vindictive North, Vandiver cited this as proof that it was a tragic error for the federal government to again seek to force the South to democratize race relations via civil rights legislation. It was on this basis that Vandiver opposed as "dangerous" the civil rights act being considered by Congress in 1959, claiming that it resembled Reconstruction laws "so base that no man can read them now without a sense of shame."[64]

As lieutenant governor serving with the late Eugene Talmadge's white supremacist son Herman, who occupied the governor's chair, Vandiver joined the chorus of leading Georgia politicians who denounced the *Brown* decision. Vandiver called the historic school desegregation decision "a judicial monstrosity fabricated upon sociology... a Swedish textbook of sociology... and psychology rather than legal precedents."[65] This hostility to social science is another reflection of the poor education Vandiver got at UGA as an undergraduate. Though his undergraduate years coincided with the pathbreaking scholarship of such social scientists as Otto Klineberg—whose analysis of IQ test data of Blacks who had migrated out of the South refuted traditional racist assumptions about whites having superior and Blacks inferior intelligence—Vandiver seemed ignorant of this scholarship and so claimed social science research had no place in courts of law as they ruled on racial matters.[66] This was a common refrain among segregationists.

Vandiver not only criticized the *Brown* decision but joined Governor Talmadge in pushing for a constitutional amendment that would enable the state to close down its public schools if the federal courts ordered their integration. And when President Dwight D. Eisenhower sent federal troops to Little Rock in 1957 to enforce court-ordered school desegregation, which was being blocked by violent racist mobs, Vandiver demanded that the president be impeached.[67] Vandiver pandered to white supremacist sexual anxieties and fears of racial amalgamation, pointing out that most Brazilians had intermarried with Blacks, "an example of what could happen in the event of integration in this country."[68]

So Vandiver's hard-line segregationist campaign for Georgia's governorship in 1958 was totally in keeping with his long reactionary record on race. He drew upon white Georgia's fears in the wake of the *Brown* decision and NAACP integrationist lawsuits, assuring the state's segregationist majority that he would lead the battle against integration. Indeed, the most famous words he uttered during the campaign were defiantly segregationist, pledging all-out resistance to school desegregation: "As long as Ernest Vandiver is your governor there will be no mixed schools or college classrooms in this state—no not a single one!"[69] Initially true to his word, Vandiver started his term of office getting the legislature to pass five out of the six bills he proposed to block the integration of educational institutions, including laws that affirmed the closing of integrating schools and defunding desegregated schools.[70]

To his credit, Vandiver, facing the court-ordered integration of the University of Georgia in January 1961, and realizing that UGA's many alumni and college parents in the state were opposed to closing down or defunding the university, finally saw that Georgia's extremist law mandating the closing of UGA and other desegregating educational institutions was not viable. So, after the school-closing law was ruled unconstitutional in federal court by Judge Bootle, Vandiver used his influence to get that law repealed. This was a major retreat from massive resistance to integration, and usually Vandiver is credited with showing some political courage in making this shift.[71]

There is some truth in this. But on the other hand, Vandiver made this move grudgingly, while denouncing the integrationist federal court order as a violation of states' rights, and while also supporting local options for communities to opt out of school integration[72] So he did nothing to quell white resentment of court-ordered integration, and his angry rhetoric during the UGA desegregation crisis helped sustain this ugly mood by feeding into the myth that whites were the victims of overbearing judges. This helped to pave the way for the segregationist riot at UGA.

While, of course, it was a plus that Vandiver proved unwilling to close UGA because its color line fell, one can also see this as being more about white self-interest than justice or Black rights. Segregation existed to privilege whites, but now that the federal court had forced integration, whites were for the first time having to choose whether they were willing to sacrifice their privilege, having UGA as their accessible public university, or closing it out of segregationist principle. They chose, out of self-interest, to preserve their university and the opportunities it afforded them but, like their governor, made no admission that ending Jim Crowism at UGA was the democratic, moral, and right thing to do. It also needs to be kept in mind that the extremism Vandiver had finally and reluctantly decided to abandon was in part his creation as well as that of the whole Talmadge faction of which he was a part as they mobilized white Georgians against integration throughout the 1950s.

The Talmadge faction's resistance to desegregation also had a literary dimension. Herman Talmadge, who would serve as Georgia's governor for two terms and as one of Georgia's US senators for almost a quarter century, also found the time to publish a book that offered a passionate defense of segregation, *You and Segregation* (1955).[73] Talmadge had served a term as president of the UGA Alumni Society and was a graduate of UGA's law school, and so we can credit him with producing his university's most elaborate, and certainly its longest (eighty pages) published brief on behalf of segregation, which was simultaneously a UGA alum's most extensive attack on racial integration.[74] Indeed, while this book was the work of one person, it represented Jim Crow UGA's and Jim Crow Georgia's predominant white views on race, the civil rights movement, and segregation in the 1950s, displaying the racism, fear of change, and disdain for social equality that ran rampant in Georgia's world of legally ordained racial segregation.

Predictably and eloquently, northern liberal critics denounced Talmadge's book as a narrow-minded, bigoted polemic. Paul Mayhew of the *New Republic* wrote that he had looked "in vain for something to lift the heart, something which reveals a philosophy of government rising above prejudice, something to indicate that law had a social significance, that states' rights are not what they were before the Civil War, that there are some things in heaven and earth which a Talmadge can object to without the resort to the cry of Communism. In this pamphlet, Talmadge takes his place alongside men like [Mississippi segregationist James] Eastland and [red-baiting senator Joseph] McCarthy, who denounce Chief Justice [Earl] Warren as a fellow-traveler [of the Communist Party]."[75] Mayhew was correct to stress the way that Talmadge's book combined red-baiting and race-baiting, that in an era of Cold War tension, Talmadge was quick to dismiss all foes of segregation by demonizing them as either subversive Communists or their fellow traveling dupes. But Mayhew's narrow focus on Talmadge's demagoguery misses the deeper questions about the social and intellectual roots of his bigotry, the role of the University of Georgia in fostering Talmadge's racial ignorance and hatred, and why such a polemic would prove so popular on the white side of Jim Crow Georgia's color line.

On the matter of popularity, Talmadge had already proven his appeal and expertise in aligning with white majority sentiment as a two-term governor of Georgia. And the timing of *You and Segregation* was significant, coming as Talmadge had begun his campaign that would win him his first term in a US Senate career that would span nearly a quarter century. In lieu of a campaign biography, Talmadge realized that at a time of Cold War tension and surging white Georgian anxiety about the threat the *Brown* decision represented to its segregated world, his polemical book on behalf of segregation would enhance his electability. It would assure white Georgia (as if the son of Gene Talmadge needed to provide such assurance) that he was prepared to take his place as one of the filibustering Southern Senate caucus's leading voices of opposition to the civil rights movement.

Though much more elaborately expressed than those brief *Red and Black* interviews with UGA students in 1952 about why they opposed the integration of the university, *You and Segregation* displayed the same parochialism. Talmadge had just completed two terms as governor of Georgia, but his book evidenced the same ignorance of Black aspirations that we saw with those UGA undergraduates. In fact, Talmadge's book does not mention by name a single African American from the state he had been serving so long as governor. The shared racial parochialism of UGA undergraduates and Talmadge as a UGA graduate attests that on race in the Jim Crow era, the university was not providing a *higher education* but rather a continuation of the racial isolation and miseducation that white Georgians had experienced in secondary and primary school.

It would be unfair and inaccurate to argue that Talmadge learned nothing at UGA. After all, he did earn a law degree at the university, and so almost half of the sixteen chapters in *You and Segregation* focus on legal issues that he could discuss competently, though his polemical inclinations often prevented this—as when he made such wild claims as that "the NAACP . . . would destroy the Bill of Rights and our American way of life."[76]

His view of the law with regard to race was reactionary, focusing on the Tenth Amendment and states' rights and arguing that the *Plessy* precedent was virtually transhistorical and must never be challenged, seeing such precedents as permanently binding and so able to preserve the segregated world that he cherished. His legal arguments were most strained when it came to his critique of the Supreme Court's use of social science in the *Brown* decision in ruling that segregation was discriminatory and damaging to Black children. Talmadge acted as if the use of such studies in a legal proceeding was a horrendous and radical break with the history of the Supreme Court when in fact such use of social science evidence dated back to the "Brandeis Brief" of the early twentieth century when as an attorney Louis Brandeis used it to make the case for protective labor legislation for women.[77]

Lacking the social science background to challenge the sociological and psychological scholarship used by the Warren court in *Brown*, Talmadge instead stooped to red-baiting the scholars who produced such scholarship. Thus Talmadge denounced Gunnar Myrdal, author of *An American Dilemma* (a classic study of American race relations) as a Communist–sympathizing Swedish socialist, and he similarly slandered Black sociologist E. Franklin Frazier and Black psychologist Kenneth Clark as fellow travelers of the Communist Party.[78] But this approach did nothing to refute the idea that in the half century since *Plessy*, social science scholarship had advanced understanding of the harmful impact of segregation way beyond where it had been back when *Plessy* was decided, necessitating a revisiting and ultimately a rejection of *Plessy*.

Much like the UGA student interviews in the *Red and Black*, Talmadge in *You and Segregation* made claims about segregation's benign impact that were vague and ahistorical. He would cite increased expenditures for Black education and social services that he claimed occurred during his governorship without even mentioning how poorly funded these had been for a half-century, so that such increases still did not even come close to bringing equity between state funding of the needs of Blacks and whites.[79] He wanted to make the case that separate had been equal without an honest accounting of the vast inequality that separated white from Black social services in Jim Crow Georgia.

Dressed up as it was with states' rights rhetoric and constitutional references, *You and Segregation* tended to avoid the crude racist discourse of the sort that Herman Talmadge's father had used earlier in the century in his years as a gubernatorial candidate and Georgia governor. But in *You and Segregation*'s chapter "Intermingling and Intermarriage" Talmadge could not disguise his racism.[80] This is because at some point white segregationists have to deal with the question of why they think it so important to separate Blacks and whites. And that almost inevitably leads to articulating a racialized, white supremacist view of history, assumptions about racial purity, superiority, inferiority, and fears of interracial sex. All of this was present in Talmadge's "Intermingling and Intermarriage" chapter, where after quoting Disraeli that "the principle of Race . . . [is] the key to history," Talmadge asserts,

> history teaches that when two separate races, living in the same country, do not follow a pattern of segregation, an amalgamation of the races occurs which ultimately results in [the] destruction of each individual race. . . . The decline and fall of the Roman Empire came after years of intermarriage with other races. Spain was toppled as a world power as a result of amalgamation of the races. In Cuba, in Mexico, and in the South American countries, segregation has never been practiced. As a result the races have intermarried and become a mongrel race in which the strongest and best features of both have been destroyed. . . . History shows that nations composed of a mongrel race lose their strength and become weak, lazy, and indifferent.[81]

Talmadge further contended that "God advocates segregation." God "did not intend" races "to be mixed" or he "would not have separated or segregated them" as "different" and distinct races.[82]

For Talmadge a key reason the NAACP was such a threat was that "its ultimate aim . . . is the complete amalgamation of the races." Talmadge cited NAACP leader Walter White's marriage to a white woman as proof of this.[83] Actually, the NAACP, wary of stirring such sexual fears, tended to avoid antimiscegenation work, which is why the key US Supreme Court case that in 1967 outlawed bans on interracial marriage (*Loving v. Virginia*) was argued by the ACLU, not the NAACP.[84]

There was nothing original about any aspect of the segregationist case Talmadge made in his book. He simply elaborated on and offered a legalistic veneer to what had by 1955 become the common segregationist assumptions of Jim Crow Georgia. But to have a former governor, prominent UGA alum, and soon-to-be US senator making these arguments likely enhanced their legitimacy in Georgia.

Though Talmadge's *You and Segregation* was the longest, most elaborate defense of segregation written by a UGA alum, it was not the most influential. That dubious distinction belongs to *The Southern Manifesto*, which UGA alum Richard Russell, Georgia's senior senator, coauthored with other leading Senate segregationists in 1956.[85] The statement, pledging opposition to the *Brown* decision and racial integration, was signed by almost the entire congressional leadership cadre of ex-Confederate states, including nineteen senators and eighty-two members of the House of Representatives. It denounced the *Brown* decision as "a clear abuse of judicial power" by the Supreme Court, a violation of states' rights, and a trampling of decades of judicial precedents—dating back to *Plessy*—which by undermining segregationist traditions was "destroying the amicable relations between the white and Negro races that have been created though 90 years of patient effort by the good people of both races. It has planted hatred and suspicion where there had heretofore been friendship and understanding." The manifesto pledged the use of "all lawful means" to resist desegregation and reverse *Brown*.[86] This statement, signed by so many Southern political leaders, lent powerful legitimation to anti-integration organizing, state legislatures legislating to preserve segregation, and the entire massive resistance movement seeking to negate *Brown*'s edict across the South.

Russell hailed from an elite Georgia family. His father was not only a UGA graduate but had served on the university's board of trustees.[87] How parochial the social atmosphere was when Russell entered UGA's law school in 1915 is suggested by the fact that all forty-five new law students in his class were Georgians. Russell explicitly linked his white supremacist views to his Georgia lineage, explaining in 1935 that "as one who was born and reared in the atmosphere of the Old South, with six generations of my forbears now resting beneath Southern soil, I am willing to go as far and make as great a sacrifice to preserve and insure white supremacy in the social and economic and political life of our state as any man who lives within her borders."[88]

Whether it was the bill to abolish the poll tax or the proposal for an antilynching act, Russell saw them, and all civil rights legislation, as part of a "nefarious movement of the Communist Party" and its allies to "destroy white civilization in the South."[89] An expert in Senate procedure, Russell from the 1930s to the 1960s helped orchestrate segregationist filibusters that killed most civil rights legislation. Russell, who to this day has a library and an endowed chair in history named after him at UGA, according to his biographer Gilbert C. Fite,

> held the elitist, paternalistic view of blacks so common among upper class whites in the South during [the Jim Crow era].... He believed that white and black societies must be strictly segregated and that blacks should make progress within their own social, economic, and political communities. He vigorously opposed any kind of integration, which he saw as a step toward mongrelization of the races. Social and educational contacts with each other, he believed, would ruin both races. Russell's attitudes and beliefs came more from inheritance and southern tradition than from any rational examination of race relations. His contact with blacks was entirely with servants or with those who were not pressing for equality and held basically a second class position in society.[90]

So whether it was Georgia educational leaders like Aderhold, or members of the state's political elite, such as Russell or Vandiver or the Talmadges, these UGA alumni went through their university years without the kind of educational intervention that could have pushed them to question their white supremacist assumptions. And, in fact, to the extent that educational institutions did intervene on race, they tended to move in the opposite direction—reinforcing inherited Jim Crow attitudes and traditions. This can be seen, for example, in some revealing correspondence in 1958 between students in a white Savannah high school's English class (of eleventh-grade students), their teacher, and Russell when he was Georgia's senior senator.

The ostensible rationale for this correspondence, explained Harold Davenport, an English teacher in Savannah's Jenkins High School, was to teach his class "formal letter writing." But despite this claim, whatever writing skills were cultivated by this class project were in the service of loyalty to the segregationist social system in which the students had been raised. The students' letter was focused on the controversial initiation of Supreme Court–ordered school desegregation in several Southern states (and related attempts at racial integration), which the students opposed and wrote to solicit Senator Russell's views about. In explaining this writing project to Russell, Davenport asserted that the students' letter "is solely the work of the class as a whole. All ideas and the finished product are the result of class discussion and synthesizing of ideas and suggestions. The project was, of course, under the guidance of the teacher."[91]

There is no way of knowing how much of the "guidance" the teacher provided this class of high school juniors shaped the strongly segregationist bias of the class letter to Russell. Let us for the moment take the teacher at his word that "all ideas" in the letter came from the students. This still leaves unanswered the question of who came up with the idea of sending this letter to Russell. That was likely the teacher's idea, but even if it was the students' (or someone else's), it was sure to yield a writing project in which students' minds were being closed rather than opened. If this letter writing was directed to opening these white Georgia students to consider the other side of the controversy over desegregation, they would have written to a critic or opponent of segregation instead of to Russell, who ranked among the South's most prominent segregationist leaders. Or if the class wanted to approach the issue in a debate format, it could have written both to Russell and to an integrationist civil rights leader, such as Martin Luther King Jr. It is doubtful, however, that this kind of debate was even possible in a white Georgia high school classroom in 1958, where it seems likely that a teacher who initiated such a debate or correspondence with a civil rights leader would be putting that teacher's job at risk. On the other hand, the class project Davenport initiated seemed sure to confirm and strengthen the class's segregationist views, and that is exactly what happened.

Their letter to Russell reflects the students' idealized views of segregation and of their senior senator; it also evidences their living in a segregationist bubble. The letter opens by expressing the students' "sincere hope" for "understanding and compromise in racial relations," expressing to Russell their confidence that "you are exerting your utmost efforts in this direction." But, in fact, Russell was doing nothing of the sort. He had spent decades in the Senate opposing and obstructing civil rights legislation, not promoting compromise and understanding in race relations. This misguided praise for Russell was followed by an expression of student devotion to racial segregation, which was grounded in faith, not facts:

> Segregation is a cherished way of life for all of us. We believe its continuation will be in the best interests of both Negroes and white people in the South. We realize, of course, that in some cases segregation has spawned evil, but we feel that this has resulted, not from the general will, but from the unscrupulous activities of a few individuals who would find another way to persecute their fellow men if segregation did not exist. We know

that as a rule the Negro in the South has equality before the law and is not considered an inferior by the general population. But we also know that Negroes and white people are different racially, and we feel that social integration and intermarriage would bring on the land an era of racial discrimination inconceivable to present-day minds.[92]

This statement, of course, ignores the exclusion of Blacks in the Jim Crow South from juries and voting rolls and the pervasiveness of racial discrimination in employment, housing, law enforcement, education, and health care. Its claim that eliminating the Jim Crow system, which was grounded in racial discrimination, would yield unprecedented levels of such discrimination is ludicrous. All of this reflects a lack of contact with civil rights organizers or any awareness of the critical Black perspective on the Jim Crow system; it embodies the racial parochialism that predominated on the white side of the color line.

The class's letter closes with two paragraphs on the *Brown* decision, stressing how unfair it was for "nine members of the Supreme Court who we did not elect" to overturn the system of segregation. This violated what "our schools every day" stress "over and over . . . the meaning and importance of majority rule." Such crucial matters in race relations ought to be handled "the democratic way" via "legislation at the hands of our elected representatives" rather than by Supreme Court justices who were "out of step with . . . a majority of the American people."[93] Here the students, in their white majoritarian enthusiasm, were ignoring the whole issue of minority rights and the court's role in protecting those rights from bigoted and abusive majorities.

Less than a week after receiving what he characterized as the students' "very fine letter," Russell responded with an extensive four-page, single-spaced letter to the class. His letter affirmed the students' segregationist faith, denounced all attempts by the federal government to undermine the Jim Crow system, and gave the high school juniors a white supremacist history lesson on what he took to be the evils of interracial marriage: "Segregation does not necessarily mean discrimination, certainly not before the law. . . . The right of a man to choose his associates, associates of his children, from among those of his own kind, is as inalienable a right as any an American can possess. I fail to understand why the finger of scorn should be pointed at those of us who have pride of race. I have been a student of history for many years and I have never found a case where people of mixed blood ever developed their civilization when miscegenation was completed."[94] In his letter, Russell not only concurred with the student criticism of the Warren court and its *Brown* decision but did so quite vitriolically. He praised the "real judges and lawyers" who, since *Plessy*, had made the "separate but equal" doctrine "a fundamental part of the law of our land." And then he contrasted them with "the political opportunists and amateurs [sic] sociologists who now serve on the [Supreme] Court" and who overturned *Plessy*. The Warren court, Russell charged, "was composed of weak men" who chief justice Earl Warren could dominate. Though Warren "is no part a lawyer, and without a day of judicial experience ... the assortment of political hacks and college professors he found on the Court have followed him meekly. The court's decision in the school cases is completely contrary to every constitutional principle this country had ever recognized ... and ... threaten[s] our great Constitutional system."[95] Note that as with Talmadge's *You and Segregation*, Russell here derided the use of social science by the court but could not refute the social science evidence against the segregationist system and so took refuge in ad hominem and even anti-intellectual attacks on the justices as "amateur sociologists" and timid "college professors."

Russell also agreed with and extended the students' critique of the *Brown* decision and the Supreme Court as antidemocratic and added personal detail to this white Southern sense of victimhood. He narrated the struggle that he and his besieged fellow Southern senators had waged against civil rights legislation they viewed as unconstitutional—these could be and were stopped by the filibuster, but "we had no means of circumventing Executive Orders ... [and] the decision by the Supreme Court in the School cases." So, much like the students, Russell depicted not Black but white Southerners as the oppressed minority: "Those of us in the Congress who seek to uphold Constitutional Government and States rights are pitifully few in number and the odds against us are staggering."[96]

While Russell provided a lesson in white supremacy, Southern chauvinism, and segregationism to this class of white students, other UGA alumni and faculty provided similar lessons to much larger groups of students. These were Georgia textbook authors whose work was used inside and out of the state's schools, promoting the idea that slavery had been a positive good (civilizing Africans, providing needed labor to build the white South), valorizing the Confederacy as a noble cause (the "Lost Cause" myth), demonizing Radical Reconstruction and the very idea of Black enfranchisement and election to public office. Indeed, from the late nineteenth century through the long Jim Crow era in the twentieth century, UGA alumni dominated this branch of Georgia history education, producing such white supremacist works as *A School History of Georgia as a Colony and State* (1893) by Charles Henry Smith (a.k.a. Bill Arp); *A History of Georgia for Use in the Schools* (1898) and *First Lessons in Georgia History* (1913), both by Lawton B. Evans; and *History of Georgia* (1913) by Robert Preston Brooks.[97] And at the college level similar lessons were conveyed through the white supremacist writings of eminent Old South historian U. B. Phillips, another UGA alum, and UGA history department chair E. Merton Coulter, whose racist-inflected view of slavery and Radical Reconstruction dominated both the writing and teaching of Georgia history until the 1960s.[98]

This reading of history by UGA textbook authors and historians left generations of white students in Jim Crow Georgia ill-equipped to think of Black people as anything but inferiors who could not be trusted with political power or integrated into white educational institutions. Indeed, African Americans were so marginalized in this history that they often appeared as mere afterthoughts, barely mentioned at all. The idea that African Americans could equal or even surpass whites in intellectual attainment or political vision was never even considered in these textbooks and "scholarly" works, which were written in such a way as to dismiss the very idea of Black historical agency.

Arguably the most dramatic educational interventions on behalf of segregationist orthodoxy by UGA alumni in Jim Crow Georgia were those involving blatant, and even headline-making, violations of academic freedom and free speech. The most famous of these—mentioned earlier in connection with the political career of Gene Talmadge—occurred in 1941 when Governor Talmadge fired Walter Cocking, dean of UGA's College of Education, on the grounds that he was championing racial integration in education. Actually, Talmadge's depiction of Cocking as an integrationist was false. All Cocking had done was issue a report—at the request of the regents—on the state of Black education in Georgia, which advocated better funding for Black schools. But Cocking had gotten on the wrong side of a teacher fired from her position in a school connected to UGA, which initiated this false accusation and to great effect because she had ties with Talmadge, and Cocking was a northerner.[99] It is true that eventually this termination of Cocking backfired politically on Talmadge, who lost reelection due to the electorate's anger that the governor's heavy-handed political interference in the university had led to its loss of accreditation. But the firing had a chilling effect on dissent at UGA. If a dean could be fired for even being suspected of integrationist sympathies, what chance would a professor or a student have to survive at UGA if one dared to question the Jim Crow system? And even top UGA officials who supported Cocking did so not on the grounds that he had the right to support integration but rather that he offered no such support and had been falsely accused of integrationist sympathies.[100] Similarly, in the petition UGA students wrote and submitted to the governor in October 1941 opposing his actions in the Cocking affair, a petition promoted on the front page of UGA's student newspaper, students "representing every county in our beloved state" refuted Talmadge's charge "that racial equality has been taught and practiced on the University of Georgia campus.... We honestly state to the Governor and to the state that no racial equality has been taught, advocated, or practiced on this campus.... Students and faculty harbor no such ideals of racial equality."[101]

It is hard to say what is more pitiful, the fact that Cocking was fired or that UGA students who came to Cocking's defense did so on the basis that neither he nor they were integrationists, and that the students even boasted—as we saw above—about their never having been taught about racial equality at their university. The idea that deans, professors, and students ought to be free to debate or even advocate racially integrated education (and to confront the best scholarship on integrated education) seems never to have occurred to these UGA students. This is a striking testament to the racially bound parochialism of UGA in the Jim Crow era. In their whites-only world, UGA students would never come into contact with the much more illuminating and deeply critical perspective on the Cocking affair offered at this time by the state's most profound critic of Jim Crowism, W. E. B. Du Bois, housed at Georgia's leading center of African American higher education, Atlanta University. Du Bois observed that "what really is happening . . . is the attempt to deny to any person, even a dean at the University of Georgia, any right to express an opinion . . . simply because that opinion is opposed to the majority of opinion of white folk of the state. There lies the kernel of intolerance and despotism. The white people of Georgia are not being educated by their leaders in modern social thought.... White Georgians are being deliberately misled along the lines of their prejudices; and just as long as the intelligent social leadership of the South permits this denial of freedom of thought and opinion . . . the South is going to continue to be the major social problem of this land."[102]

Twelve years after the Cocking affair, UGA students witnessed a similar act of suppression in the service of segregationist orthodoxy, this time trampling free speech and freedom of the student press. This suppression came at the hands of Roy Harris, a regent of the university system, founder of the militantly segregationist *Augusta Courier*, and one of the most influential leaders in the Talmadge faction of Georgia state politics. Harris had received his UGA BA in 1917 and earned his law degree in 1919 from UGA; his vision of UGA did not include the right of students to challenge segregation.[103] So in 1953 when Bill Shipp, a crusading student editor of UGA's student newspaper, used the pages of the *Red and Black* to support Horace Ward's bid to desegregate UGA's law school and to oppose Governor Talmadge's segregationist policies, Harris lashed out. He used his connection with the board of regents to have the board inform UGA's administration that the student newspaper could not continue to publish unless such integrationist editorials ceased. Harris also got the state legislature to introduce a resolution demanding that Shipp and his fellow editors resign. This pressure led President Aderhold and the dean of UGA's journalism school to require all future *Red and Black* editorials to be cleared with a faculty advisor. Refusing to go along with this censorship, Shipp and his fellow editor, Walter A. Lundy, resigned their editorships after being told by a UGA journalism professor that they would be fired if they did not resign. It is symptomatic of the dire state of free speech at UGA that though a number of faculty members privately expressed to Shipp their agreement with him, none dared to say so publicly.[104]

To say that Shipp and Lundy were unusual in the UGA of the Jim Crow era is an understatement. Most students at the university were far too conformist, owing to their segregationist outlook and deference to the campus consensus in favor of Jim Crow, to ever dare to openly defy the reigning racial orthodoxy. Among the most striking examples of such conformity and timidity involved UGA's Jazz Club, which in 1959 invited the Dave Brubeck Quartet to play at the university without realizing that the quartet's bass player, Eugene Wright, was Black. When the Jazz Club president found out that Brubeck's quartet was racially integrated, he promptly disinvited the band since UGA policy barred interracial musical groups.[105] This drew a stinging rebuke from Ralph Gleason, the *San Francisco Chronicle*'s eminent jazz critic, who wrote, "Maybe we better get busy and send a couple of cultural missions, some interpreters and maybe even an ambassador down to Georgia. . . . Jazz music is the music of democracy and it just might be that it's too good for the students of Georgia. The jazz club president was a 'sociology senior,' the news stories said. What a recommendation for the University of Georgia as center for the study of social sciences. I would like to see all jazz musicians refuse to play at the University of Georgia. . . . Who do they think plays jazz, Herman Talmadge?"[106] Gleason went on to urge the members of UGA's Jazz Club to resign: "It's the least they can do, since apparently they haven't got the guts to go ahead and hold their concert somewhere else." No such resignations occurred. The Jazz Club's president offered only the most timid dissent, petitioning the student government, but when it refused to act to challenge the interracial band ban, he dropped the whole matter.[107]

Intolerance of dissent against segregation, then, was not merely an imposition on UGA students by Georgia politicians and university administrators. The segregationist ethos was so pervasive within the student body that its most influential social institutions, UGA's fraternities and sororities, insisted on conformity to segregationist norms. In fact, this ethos continued even after the campus color line had been breached in 1961 as the federal court order forced the admission to UGA of Hunter and Holmes. For the simple, humane act of walking Charlayne Hunter across the campus, a sorority member reported that she had been ostracized by her fellow sorority members.[108]

Nor was such pressure confined to the Greek houses. In her memoir, Charlayne Hunter-Gault told the story of Tony, a UGA student from Long Island who had befriended her, told her he was raised to be free of racism, and even chose her to manage his campaign to help lead a campus organization. But before long, he dissolved their friendship, explaining that the Southern students in his dormitory "were putting lots of pressure" on him to stop talking to her. "It was getting to him, he said, because the threats were escalating. It would be different if there were other guys like him, but he was the only one."[109]

Being a good UGA undergraduate in 1961 still meant, for all but a few members of the white student body, conforming to segregationist norms even after court-ordered desegregation had begun. On January 14, 1961, three days after the segregationist riot outside Charlayne Hunter's dormitory—and while she was still suspended from UGA "for her own safety"—interviews with all but 10 of the 163 students who lived in that dormitory (Center-Myers) voiced a preference "for segregation, but an acceptance of the fact that desegregation is mandatory."[110] The last thing these students wanted was for anyone to think they were happy to be living in the same dormitory as the first African American student to be housed on the UGA campus. As the interviewer recorded, among the students' "predominant sentiments" was "the desire that no publicity be given their views as expressed in the interviews and that these interviews not be used to make it appear that the dormitory would welcome Charlayne 'with open arms.' (The attitude was more that they would tolerate her)."[111]

And it wasn't only the students who clung to the old segregationist mode of thinking even after UGA's desegregation had begun. For several years the UGA administration housed the few Black students on campus together and refused to allow them to invite African American guests to campus social events despite the complaints of Black students.¹¹² UGA would not even consider allowing Holmes, a high school football star, to play for its team, and UGA football would not desegregate until 1971, eight years after he graduated.¹¹³ And months after Judge Bootle had ruled that UGA had corrupted its admission process via its biased interview with Holmes, UGA engaged in similar shenanigans with Mary Frances Early when she applied to be the first Black graduate student at the university. During her interview, university administrators had the gall to ask Early, a soft-spoken music teacher, insulting personal questions that she found "quite unpleasant" and seemed designed to provoke her to come off as belligerent so as to keep her out of UGA. As Early recalled recently in her memoir, *The Quiet Trailblazer* (2021),

> I was asked if I had ever visited a house of prostitution. I responded in the negative, telling them that I was a teacher, a professional, and had no reason or desire to visit a house of prostitution. This question still rings in my head as an utterly disingenuous and insulting attempt to undermine my self-esteem and dignity. . . . Even as a 24 year old, I realized that [UGA's registrar] Mr. Danner was hoping that I would become confrontational in response to some of his questions and comments. Having read the account of how Danner had characterized Hamilton Holmes' interview as "evasive" . . . I wanted to maintain my composure and not give him any indication of disrespect. . . . Though I succeeded in remaining calm, I left the interview feeling very disconcerted, but still determined to follow through on my quest for admission.
>
> It is the nature of insults and slights that they can crawl into our psyches and poison our self-worth; what these men tried to do to me was unconscionable, and I am glad I was able to focus my energy on the higher purpose, which was to make the UGA a place for *all* Georgians.¹¹⁴

The insulting interview was, however, only the most overt way in which UGA clung to its Jim Crow past. Behind the scenes, the University System of Georgia regents and UGA's admissions office had not—despite the court-ordered admission of Holmes and Hunter—changed the circuitous admissions process that had been designed to make that process lengthier and more difficult for African American applicants. As registrar Walter Danner explained in a 1975 oral history interview, "The Board of Regents" back in the Jim Crow era "had a committee at that time that we were supposed to submit all names of black race [applicants] to be acted on; we had no authority to act upon them without their approval." When asked whether the regents dropped this supervision of Black applications to the university after its first African

American students were admitted, Danner replied, "No, no, no, no, no." The regents "kept a tight hand on it for at least another year. Those two students [Holmes and Hunter] were well qualified." But the regents "used tactics to delay, delay, delay. Any other black applicants we had, we had to keep submitting" to the regents. We did—I know the list got as long as a couple of dozen or maybe more names that had applications, but you couldn't accept one without their approval. And that continued for at least a year."[115] While there is no way to know for certain without access to the applications, Danner's words strongly suggest that though *Holmes v. Danner* made it impossible for UGA to keep all Black students out, the regents were still doing all they could a year or two later to keep the number of Black admits to UGA as low as possible.

ONE COULD ARGUE THAT there is nothing surprising about any of this, that we should expect a historically segregated university and its alumni to support the racially segregationist society that produced it, just as one would expect the universities of a communist society to support communism or those in a capitalist society to support capitalism. But the fact is that universities in societies with democratic political cultures tend quite often to be pluralistic places where contradictions abound, different ideologies clash, and debates and disagreement surface among students and faculty, where university and societal conditions get criticized and challenged. After all, the same universities, among them Columbia, Wisconsin at Madison, and MIT, whose faculty did extensive research for the Pentagon, gave rise to antiwar student movements. Universities that excluded women, including Yale, gave rise to student movements demanding the admission of female students. Universities and colleges from Amherst to UC Berkeley that supported racially discriminatory fraternity and sorority houses got challenged by progressive students who demanded and won an end to such discrimination. Universities that serviced big business or deferred to rich benefactors, such as Stanford, got criticized by faculty and students who were socially democratic or even further left in their politics.

But, as we noted earlier, Jim Crow Georgia was not a democratic society. It was, to use Robert Mickey's term, an "authoritarian enclave" in which key components of democracy—"free and fair elections, universal suffrage, and responsive institutions"—were absent.[116] And this authoritarian enclave was supported by UGA, which was committed to maintaining the one-party South's antidemocratic white supremacist regime. As such UGA, like Jim Crow Georgia, was incapable of reforming itself or promoting multiracial democracy, meritocracy, and equal opportunity. Such reform and democratization had to come from outside UGA, Jim Crow Georgia's white leadership academy, and so was initiated by none of the famous UGA alumni who back then led Georgia's political and educational institutions. Reform and democratization were initiated by African American civil rights activists and attorneys, some of the best and brightest students in Atlanta's Black community, who dared to apply to UGA to challenge its color line, and federal courts committed to equal justice under law. And this move toward democratization, as we shall see in chapter 2, was not welcomed but resented by most white Georgia students. With them the old cliché about the fruit not falling far from the tree applies, and in this case the fruit was bitter.

CHAPTER TWO

Two, Four, Six, Eight, We Don't Want to Integrate
White Student Attitudes toward the University of Georgia's Desegregation, 1961

On January 13, 1961, two days after a segregationist riot on the campus of the University of Georgia (UGA), NBC "Today" show host David Garroway told his national television audience that he was "especially concerned" that college students had embraced racial violence. "If they had been ignorant, untutored," he stated, "you could probably understand why they deployed this action, but they are not an ignorant group. They're intelligent, educated, and they took an action that even an ignorant savage could understand any place in the world: brutal mob rule. And they won. In this country. But we speak of democracy, freedom, and the pursuit of happiness."[1]

Even before the incident that sparked Garroway's comments, the whole world seemed to be watching the University of Georgia, where on January 6, US district court judge William A. Bootle ordered the admission of Georgia's first African-American students, Hamilton Holmes and Charlayne Hunter. Print, radio, and television journalists besieged the Athens campus to see how students would react to the integration of their university. Optimistic observers, such as columnist Ralph McGill of the *Atlanta Constitution*, voiced hope that Georgia students would "save the honor of the South and warm the hearts of good people everywhere" by welcoming their first Black classmates. This sentiment was also expressed by one of the more progressive columnists for UGA's student newspaper, the *Red and Black*, who urged his classmates to treat Holmes and Hunter with "the proper respect they deserve" and thereby "show the rest of the United States that we in Georgia are the true leaders of the new South." Even Hamilton Holmes initially voiced some optimism about Georgia students, telling a reporter that "I have faith that they won't turn to violence."[2]

The UGA student body quickly proved itself unworthy of such hope and optimism. The first student demonstration on the Athens campus came on Friday evening, January 6, only a few hours after Judge Bootle issued his integration order; it showed that at least a vocal minority of the UGA student body had no interest in building a new South, choosing instead to defend the old South and its segregationist traditions. That night a crowd of some 150 to 200 students gathered by the historic archway entrance to the campus and hung a blackfaced effigy of Hamilton Holmes. The students "serenaded the effigy with choruses of Dixie" and sang "there'll never be a nigger in the [fraternity] house," whose various names they inserted. They also chanted, "Two, four, six, eight, we don't want to integrate." Later that night, students sought to burn a fifteen-foot-high cross in front of the home of UGA president O. C. Aderhold but were prevented from doing so by campus officials.[3]

These initial segregationist protests paled in comparison to the violent demonstration that erupted outside of Center-Myers, Charlayne Hunter's dormitory, five nights later on the evening of January 11, less than thirteen hours after Hunter and Holmes attended their first classes on campus. Hoisting a "Nigger Go Home" banner, a "howling, cursing mob" numbering between 500 and 2,000 "laid siege" on Center-Myers. Rioters set fires in the woods near Hunter's dormitory, threw bricks and other missiles at the dorm windows, tossed rocks and firecrackers at reporters, and scuffled with police. It took well over an hour for police and campus officials to restore order. Fire hoses and tear gas were needed to disperse the angry mob, whose fists injured a police officer and dean of men William Tate, and whose rocks hurt a student inside Center-Myers and shattered dozens of windows in Hunter's dormitory. Also shattered was UGA's reputation, since the riot was front page and prime time news. The national media denounced the student rioters as bullies, racists, and ignoramuses.[4] The administration on campus compounded the damage to the university's reputation by appearing to capitulate to the mob, suspending Hunter and Holmes, allegedly "for their own safety," rather than the rioters. The image of Charlayne Hunter's forced and tearful exit from the campus in the wake of the riot and her own suspension, captured in news photos published from coast to coast, was not one that would soon be forgotten or lived down.[5]

This was not the first time that white college students captured the national spotlight through violent resistance to desegregation of higher education in the Deep South. Five years before the crisis in Athens, white students at the University of Alabama had rioted when Autherine Lucy sought to become their campus's first African American student. Thousands of Alabama students, joined by outsiders, formed a roving racist mob, which threatened Lucy's life and literally drove her off the campus in February 1956.[6] Student riot leaders at UGA in 1961, such as Thomas Cochran from Butler County, spoke of being inspired by that mob action at the University of

Alabama. Cochran told the press that the UGA students' use of mob violence was aimed at achieving "the same sort of situation that prevails in Alabama. "They're integrated . . . legally. But there are no niggers going to school there" because of the segregationist riot and expulsion of Lucy.[7] The year after the UGA riot, white Southern students would have a hand in the most violent of all campus anti-integration riots: the bloody battle at the University of Mississippi in September 1962, which left two dead and twenty-eight federal marshals wounded by gunshot during furious protests against the admission of James Meredith to Ole Miss.[8]

Despite the prominent role white students played in these crucial battles against integration, historians have devoted little attention to Southern student bodies. Even the best accounts of desegregation on Deep South campuses published in the three decades after the integration crises —most notably Thomas Dyer's chapter on the University of Georgia, David Sansing's chapters on the University of Mississippi, and E. Culpepper Clark's book on the University of Alabama—have tended to be top-down political and legal histories. They focus primarily upon the tactical maneuvering of Southern governors, university presidents, regents, and civil rights attorneys rather than upon the mindset of Southern students, even though these students had far more direct and daily impact upon the college lives of the first African Americans to attend desegregating universities.[9]

Consequently, to this day we know almost nothing about the racial ideas that prevailed among white students (or their teachers) at Southern campuses during the era of desegregation and massive resistance. We know even less about where those ideas originated and why universities, supposedly centers of teaching and learning, served as launching pads for racist mob violence. If we are to understand what desegregation meant on the campuses where it occurred, we need to remember that the civil rights conflicts of the 1950s and 1960s were struggles not only about power but also about ideas—and in particular ideas about race, integration, and violence. These ideas shaped the reception that Black students received from their white counterparts on Southern campuses and made their college years a very trying time.[10]

The best place to start to reconstruct the mindset of white Southern students as the university color line fell is with the words of the students themselves. Fortunately, the archives of the University of Georgia include a set of student essays that shed considerable light on that mindset. They were written by thirty-five UGA students on January 17, 1961, during the final stage of the integration crisis. The authors, who were enrolled in a calculus class (Math 254), wrote their essays during a class session in response to a request by their professor, Thomas Brahana, that they explain their views on racial integration. Brahana asked the students to write the essays in place of a scheduled calculus test, which he realized they were—owing to the riot and the integration controversy—too upset to take.[11]

As sources of student opinion on the desegregation crisis, the Math 254 essays are by far the richest that have survived. While UGA students were quoted in local and national press coverage of that crisis, most of those quotations were very brief. So were the student statements to TV reporters, which usually amounted to little more than soundbites. The Math 254 essays offer far more extensive student commentary, with some running as long as three handwritten pages. Since students wrote these essays in a sedate and pensive classroom setting, they were free of the posturing that sometimes shaded the public statements that UGA students made to the media; as such these writings may be a more accurate reflection of student opinion.[12]

This is not to say, however, that the essays offer a perfect window for viewing the students' reactions to the desegregation crisis. There is a problem with the timing of the essays. They were written in the aftermath of the riot, following the flood of local and national criticism of this mob scene, and the day after the court-ordered reinstatement of Hunter and Holmes, which proved that the riot had failed to save the color line and had done nothing but damage UGA's reputation. The essays' authors obviously had more of an inducement to condemn segregationist violence than they would have had they written the essays a week earlier. Another possible inducement for the essayists to sound more moderate than the overall UGA student body came from the political dynamics of the class itself. At the time the students wrote their papers, they thought that, like other classwork submitted, these would be read by their professor. And since Brahana, as president of the campus chapter of the American Association of University Professors, had been a prominent critic of the riot and advocate of the reinstatement of Hunter and Holmes, the students almost certainly knew that he was far more progressive on racial issues than they were. Given the power realities that operate within college courses—where professors award and undergraduates worry about grades—students had reason to play up to Brahana by toning down their segregationism. But few, if any, of the students did so. Indeed, their willingness to take the risk of alienating their professor by candidly expressing their views makes the almost uniformly segregationist essays seem all the more credible and heartfelt.[13]

We will never know for certain whether all the views expressed in the Math 254 essays were typical of the entire student body. Nor do we even know whether these math students were similar intellectually to most UGA students. Certainly the fact that they were taking calculus differentiates them from many UGA students who were less advanced in their mathematical training and abilities—and this suggests at least the possibility that academically they were better-than-average students. But in one very important respect this class closely resembled most UGA students. All but one of the essayists were Southerners, and most were Georgians. This was much like the profile of the larger student body. Of 1,745 UGA freshmen in 1961, 1,501 (86 percent) were Georgians, and no northern state had more than 16 students in that freshman class.[14] Thus demographically at least, the Math 254 students were eminently qualified to represent the UGA student body.

MANY OF THE MATH 254 ESSAYS INVERT what today would be our understanding of just who were the victims and who were the aggressors in the UGA integration crisis. When the Math 254 students mentioned those victimized by force, most were referring to themselves rather than to Holmes and Hunter. These white students felt that the most egregious use of force in the desegregation crisis came not from the white mob's assault on Charlayne Hunter's dormitory but from the federal government coercing the state and University of Georgia to integrate. As one student explained,

> many students, parents, and Georgians feel hurt because our federal government . . . has shown us that it (fed. govern.) can force people to do things which we dislike. I feel as many students do at the University of Georgia that we as citizens should have a right to go to segregated schools. It seems to me the federal government has gotten too powerful or perhaps has always been for was it not partly the issue of state's rights that caused the Civil War? Why doesn't Congress question the almighty power of the Supreme Court, after all I thought the U.S. government was set up on a check-and-balance system. Perhaps in another hundred years integration would have come about voluntarily in the South but why must something we resent be crammed down our throats?[15]

The logic of white dissent and segregationist resistance was expressed by these students in terms of not only states' rights but also Americanism and God's will. They believed that the court-ordered integration of the university was un-American and violated their own and their state's rights. "I feel as many students here at the University of Georgia that we as citizens should have a right to go to segregated schools . . . because it is our American heritage and God-given right."[16] "I am mad," wrote another student, that an integrationist "federal judge took away state's rights" so that "the governor, the legislature, and school officials have no authority pertaining to the integration problem faced at Georgia.... This is wrong and does not make up a democracy, which is the belief that founded America and the way America is suppose[d] to be today."[17]

Having defined segregation as a God-given right and the option of choosing segregation as a fundamental American freedom, it followed that integrationists who challenged this right—particularly the leaders of the National Association for the Advancement of Colored People (NAACP)—were un-American. Several Math 254 students equated the NAACP with subversion. Their charges had a McCarthyite tinge and tapped into powerful emotions in the tense Cold War atmosphere of 1961: "If the NAACP is not Communist infiltrated, and I strongly believe it is, it is a perfect situation for the communists to use. They have a plan worked out where they know almost exactly when they can take over the U.S.... They have men specially trained in knowing how to incite riots and cause other types of trouble. What better situation could they ask for than this? If they are not controlling the NAACP, they are certainly using it. Americans must wake up."[18] Another student who saw the NAACP's integrationist efforts as part of a Communist plot "to break up the United States" concluded that the NAACP's name "should be changed to the National Association for the Advancement of the Communist Party."[19]

Less extreme foes of integration in the class echoed the "separate but equal" doctrine established in the historic *Plessy v. Ferguson* (1896) decision (though none knew enough history to cite the case itself). These students professed to have a benign attitude toward Blacks. They argued that Blacks should have educational opportunities equal to those of whites, but these should come through separate Black schools since this was traditional in the South—and since forced integration would evoke racial tensions and disrupt Southern education for both races. The students refused to see how underfunded Jim Crow Georgia's Black schools were in relation to the white schools, but at least they claimed to aspire toward educational equality.[20]

This contrasted with the most ardent segregationists in the class, who relied less on "separate but equal" clichés than on blatant appeals to racial prejudice. These reactionaries did not even pretend to care about securing equal educational opportunity between the races; they thought Blacks were inferior and unfit for such opportunity. As one student explained,

> the main reason I say I do not want integration is that I believe the Negroid race is inferior to the Caucasian race.... The Negro has an average

of one eighth more bone thickness on his skull. This leads one to believe that the Negro has not come as far through evolution as the "White" man. It is virtually impossible to remove someone or a race from a most primitive culture and replace him in one that has advanced over fifteen hundred years above his and expect him within two hundred fifty years to adjust himself to the new culture as well as the descendants of the founders of the old culture have.... The Negro is shiftless and undependable. Why does the average Negro have almost double the rhythm of a "white" man if he has become equal to the white man in his culture. This leads me to believe it is still the "jungle instinct."[21]

A sexual subtext frequently accompanied these racist passages. The most vehement critics of both integration and the NAACP among the student essayists were convinced that though civil rights activists had begun their quest for Black rights at the schoolhouse door, their real destination was white bedrooms: "I do not wish our ... social affairs integrated.... This is the point I feel most strongly about.... In college I feel that the women will be protected better if they don't have to dodge colored boys in the course of a day."[22] A female classmate worried that if school integration proceeded, it would yield so much interracial sex that by "the year 2061 A.D. there will be little left of a distinct Negro or white race; a hybrid race will be well on its way here in America." God too favored racial homogeneity, according to one student who wrote, "I am definitely a strong segregationist.... Mixing of the White and Negro races will only result in dissention [sic].... Negroes ... deserve a chance to better themselves. I do not favor this betterment by intermarriage.... I cannot understand why God would have bother[ed] to create varied races if he had not wanted us to remain as such."[23]

Stereotypes of Black inferiority pervaded the most strongly segregationist essays. "The Negro has a lack of ambition. He does not have the desire to work and better himself but is only concerned with having enough to eat. Ambition and drive are what has made this country strong. Secondly the Negro does not have the morals we have in Meriwether County. This is easily backed by the number of illegal children. The Negro also is not as physically clean as whites."[24] Another student noted, "I personally do not desire to associate with persons of low moral character.... Southern Negroes have a lower moral standard in general than I care to associate with. This is shown by 1 their brand new Cadillac standing in the yard of their one room tenant home (neither paid for yet), 2 the statistical percentage of taxes paid by Negroes as compared to Whites 3 The frequent number of court cases involving

Negroe [sic] stabbings, wife beating, driving drunk and disorderly, etc. 4 Lack of trust among themselves 5 General sanitation."[25]

No one familiar with the extreme segregationist rhetoric circulating in the South in 1961 will be surprised by these statements. But the fact that college students, among the state's best-educated youths, expressed with such seriousness absurd ideas about Black skull size, jungle rhythm, and shiftlessness should give us pause to consider the sources of these ideas and the nature of Georgian and Southern education—or more precisely miseducation—about race.

The most striking feature of this racial education was its informality. Only two out of the thirty-five essays made any mention of a formal educational institution influencing student thought about race. In almost every essay where there is an allusion to learning about race, segregation, or integration, the cited source of that learning is not a school, a campus, a text, an author, a teacher, or an academic discipline. Students learned about race from their families, friends, and communities; these were the primary sources of their racial education.[26]

UGA students did not have to be taught about segregation in school; they learned about segregation and were indoctrinated in white supremacy by merely living on the white side of the color line. Thus as the Math 254 essayists explained their support of segregation, they frequently invoked their Southern and Georgian upbringing and heritage. They believed in segregation because of their roots in and love for the Jim Crow South and the way of life in which they had been raised. This strong sense of place and its determinative power appears repeatedly in the essays. Typically, a student explained, "I believe strongly in segregation . . . because I have been reared in a section of the world where there was no form of integration." He then went on to spell out his belief in Black inferiority and proudly justified this belief in terms of his Southern lineage: "This belief was inherited from me [sic] by my ancestors who gave their lives [in the Civil War] that the Southern way of life would live." Another student wrote of personal opposition to school integration evolving out of his having been "born and raised in southwest Georgia, where the white man dominates the colored people."[27]

Growing up as a white Georgian often carried with it an exposure to only the segregationist side of the debate over civil rights. Thus some of the students' essays indicated that they were swayed by segregationist arguments because this was all they had heard in their hometowns: "I was born here in Athens, Georgia in 1940," wrote one. "Since that time I have heard nothing but talk in favor of segregation down to the last minute detail. Therefore, because of this I believe in segregation." "I am," another student wrote, "from a small south Georgia town.... All my life I have been told that segregation is right, it has been and always will be in effect." "Ever since I can remember while growing up in south Georgia," a third student recalled, "I have been told it is not right socially to have integration in our schools."[28]

These students neither admitted nor even suspected that growing up under and viewing the Jim Crow system from the white side of the color line limited their vision or understanding of the South's racial problems. Displaying no sense at all of their own provincialism, Brahana's students tended to assume that their background as white Southerners gave them special knowledge and insight into Black life, culture, and thought. Thus one student wrote, "I have worked with and lived around Negroes all my life. I was ~~raised by a~~ looked after by a Negro woman 10 hours of the day every day for 12 years. I pretty well know what the colored people want and don't want.... I know the majority of colored people in Georgia do not want to mix with the white people."[29] Another student noted that as a Southerner who had "worked with negro[e]s before and talked to many," he knew that the "majority of the negro[e]s do not want to go to school with us, but the naacp ... talk these negro[e]s into going to white schools. They tell the negro he is being done an injustice and feed them all sorts of balon[e]y."[30] These young whites felt that their Southern roots also gave them an empirical basis for their spurious claims about Black inferiority. They seemed to think that they were proving their racist statements when they attached to them such lines as "I am a southerner and have lived among Negroes all my life," "I know and understand the Negroes around my home town," and "Anyone who has lived around small southern towns will tell you."[31]

In discussing race, the student essayists invoked family and hometown observations and assumptions so frequently and their formal education so rarely that they leave us wondering what—if any—discussion of race relations occurred in white Southern schools. Why did the formal curriculums of grade school and college leave so little impression upon student thought about race? Although it would take a thorough study of high school and college course content in Georgia and the Jim Crow South to answer this question definitively, the Math 254 essays—along with my interviews with students and faculty who were at UGA in 1961— suggest that most teachers tended to stay away from contemporary racial issues. Even at the college level, discussions of race, and especially the civil rights movement, seem to have been rare. Pete McCommons, a leading moderate student at UGA in 1961, could not remember "any [UGA] teacher in a class talking about segregation or integration."[32] Professor Brahana, who as head of UGA's chapter of the American Association of University Professors in 1961 was in a good position to know about the state of academic freedom at that time, recalled that faculty tended to stay away from controversial issues regarding race and integration out of fear for their jobs: "Back then it wasn't a subject that was taught. It had been dangerous if you were a professor and talked about it [desegregation] too much." According to Brahana, memories were long, and the faculty remembered only too well when back in 1941 governor Eugene Talmadge attacked and fired a dean "for just hinting that one day integration would come to the South. So everybody just stayed off that topic."[33]

Learning about race appears to have been at least as sparse in Georgia's white primary, middle, and secondary schools as it was at UGA. The Georgia public school curriculum evaded all of the tough questions about race and did nothing to teach students to think critically about relations between whites and Blacks in the South. Most UGA students in 1961 would likely have experienced the very same evasions on race in their precollege schooling as those recalled by *Foxfire* magazine founder Eliot Wigginton:

> When I was in elementary and junior high school in Athens, Georgia ... I am positive that there was not a single instance—not one—when any of the teachers initiated, even allowed, a discussion about racism. In that nine year period, it was not even mentioned, and that was in a town ... [with] separate, clearly marked water fountains for whites and blacks, separate bathrooms in the downtown five-and-dime ... separate waiting rooms in the ... bus station, a separate ticket window and balcony for blacks at the movie theatre ... and absolute and total separation of blacks and whites in terms of schools, neighborhoods, and so on. And because it was never talked about, my classmates and I really never asked ourselves why the town was set up that way. That was just the way things were, had always been, and would always be. It would have done just as much good to ask why there was grass or why there were mocking birds. There just were.[34]

The textbooks used in Georgia public schools seem to have only reinforced its weaknesses on race. For example, in the late 1950s one of the Georgia public schools' most widely used social studies books, *Georgia: Government and History*, written by UGA political science professor Albert B. Saye, was 438 pages long but never mentioned the words "civil rights movement," the NAACP, or a single Black leader. Saye offered a brief, uncritical discussion of segregation, which he praised as "natural in many areas of life."[35] Saye's text, which was used in their precollege years by the generation of students who attended UGA during its desegregation crisis, suggests that en route to college these students heard very little in their classes about race or segregation, and what they did hear simply confirmed the dominant prejudices and social arrangements of the region.

Among the most penetrating critics of Georgia educators for failing to teach about race was Bruce M. Galphin of the *Atlanta Constitution*. In February 1961, Galphin took the UGA faculty to task for their failure to challenge the white supremacist notions that their students brought with them to college. Though Galphin praised UGA's professors for signing their historic petition condemning the riot and calling for the reinstatement of Holmes and Hunter, he also thought that if the faculty had been more forthright in their teaching about race, the riot might have been averted:

> One wonders what they [the students] have been studying at the university. Thus far, their only tutors in political science appear to have been the extremist politicians; they keep spewing up such cliches as "judicial tyranny," "federalism" or "socialism." (The prize was the complaint that "the long arm of federal tyranny is crushing us under the heel of its boot.") Perhaps the faculty, now that theory has turned into reality, and now that more than two-thirds of them have signed a petition supporting acceptance of the Negroes, will find the courage to cure this defect in their students' education.[36]

Galphin believed that a more intellectually rigorous and politically courageous faculty could have profoundly altered the way students thought about race and reacted to the desegregation of their university. There are reasons to doubt whether the UGA faculty (or any Deep South faculty)—even if they were so inclined—were free enough and sufficiently influential to reverse, in a few short years of classes, a lifetime of miseducation that their students had received about race in their Southern hometowns. Indeed, at first glance, Galphin's faith in the power and freedom of teachers and formal educational institutions may even seem naive. After all, this was a society organized around segregationist principles, and educational systems historically have more often reinforced than challenged existing social systems and their ideological foundations. But, on the other hand, had they chosen to use them, the UGA faculty could have tapped into a vast array of scholarly sources—the best scholarship in sociology, anthropology, and psychology—to prod students into questioning the racist doctrines upon which they had been raised. Even short-term exposure to the modern social science of Melville J. Herskovits, Gunnar Myrdal, John Dollard, Franz Boas, Kenneth B. Clark, and Otto Klineberg might have at least given students the opportunity to transcend their prejudices.[37]

There is evidence in one of the Math 254 essays that at least some students at UGA in 1961 were capable of embracing that opportunity. In this case it was exposure to psychological scholarship that led a student to question racial segregation. This undergraduate noted that white supremacist ideas had

> been hammered into my head for the entire time of my life and, yet, I cannot seem to reconcile myself to it. During my years in formal schooling I have seen printed evidence, as compiled by psychologists, that the men of the white and black race have equal potential to accomplish intellectually. This knowledge has served to open and broaden my mind somewhat. Therefore after considering this situation called integration I have arrived at the following conclusion: There is a disparity between the black and white races, but this disparity is not inherited, it is learned. The Negro has been downtrodden and debased.... In conclusion, and I must admit that this is a statement that is quite hard to write, I believe that the only way the Negro will be able to climb up from the hole that we have thrown him in is by his being permitted to secure an education which is exactly that of the white men.[38]

Comments such as these suggest that though segregationism predominated, it was not universal among UGA students in 1961. A small dissident minority in the Math 254 class (three out of the thirty-five students in that class) wrote essays that condemned Jim Crow. Attesting that not all white Southerners thought alike, one of these dissidents pointed out that he "was born and raised in Georgia ... my father was born in Georgia, and therefore I am no Yankee," and then went on to complain that it was

> hard to understand why integration is being fought against so violently because 9 out of 10 of the southern people have been practically integrated with the Negroes all their lives.... Most of us have been brought up by colored women while our mothers worked. When I was small I had a friend that was colored and we did almost everything together, and I bet if a role [roll] was taken almost every person in this room had a colored friend sometimes during his life that he would do almost anything for. What I can't understand is why we don't mind eating with Negroes in the kitchen but we wouldn't want to eat with them in the dining room.[39]

The strongest indictment of segregation in Math 254 came from a student who coupled his antipathy toward Southern racism with a sense of Southern nationalism, arguing that only when it was free of segregation would the South realize its great potential:

> My personal belief is that integration is right. There is no possible way to sanely defend segregation.... I, being a south Georgian, have heard the cry. "Do you want your daughter to marry a Nigger?" and "The Supreme Court is trying to kill the white race in the south" and the other usual statements until it makes me sick. The south has the potential to become the most prosperous region in the United States. Indeed, it should already be so. However, the segregation problem is going to hold us back until we straighten it out.[40]

If such indictments of segregation were rare in this math classroom, they were rarer still in the public expressions made by UGA student leaders during the integration crisis. The combination of racism, ideological solidarity, regional tradition, and peer pressure left UGA student leaders unwilling to voice in public the type of integrationist views that the two students above had shared privately with their liberal professor. In January 1961 the biggest conflict within the white student community at UGA was not between integrationists and segregationists (since virtually all students who spoke up said they preferred segregation) but between moderate and extreme segregationists. The moderates wanted UGA to remain segregated but were unwilling to sanction the use of violence or school closing toward that end. These students organized a large meeting in the UGA chapel on January 8, where they put together a petition, ultimately signed by 2,700 students urging that the university stay open—at a time when state law mandated that the legislature cut off funding to UGA should it become integrated. Prior to the riot of January 11, moderate newspaper columnists for the *Red and Black* and other student leaders also made statements in the campus paper urging that students remain calm and avoid violence.[41]

These calls for nonviolence failed because of a fundamental weakness in the moderates' position. That position was basically one of resignation, a grudging acceptance of the fact that federal law made inevitable the presence of the two Black students —something that had to be accepted not because this was the right or democratic thing to do but because there was no way to defy the Supreme Court. The moderates' cold logic obviously lacked the emotional punch of extreme segregationists passionately committed to using any means necessary (including violence) to maintain the "southern way of life." The moral fervor that one associates with the civil rights movement itself, which taught people that integration was desirable because it was more humane, liberal, and Christian than segregation, was simply not visible among UGA's white student leaders in January 1961. None of these whites would publicly associate themselves with the compelling integrationist position that an interracial university would be stronger intellectually because it could, for the first time, be truly meritocratic—open to the best students and faculty rather than just to whites, and better able to perform its service mission since it would now be more representative of a multiracial state and nation. With no students publicly challenging the morality of segregation, the overwhelmingly segregationist student body at the start of the desegregation crisis would prove susceptible to the appeals of the cross burners and effigy hangers, who, in effect, asked why if a community believes in a segregationist educational system its members should not fight to preserve that system.[42]

So the extremists had their day—or more precisely, their riotous night—on January 11 during the height of the desegregation crisis. But the riot's implications with regard to majority student opinion on campus have always been murky. Immediately after the riot, prominent Georgians, including newspaper editors, the mayor of Athens, and UGA alumni, who were appalled by the mob scene, defended the student body's reputation by blaming the riot on outside agitators, focusing on the few Ku Klux Klan members present at the riot. Adding to the confusion about how representative the rioters were of the student body were the conflicting reports about the size of the mob. Press estimates of the mob's size varied from 500 to 2,000. If the violent crowd approached the larger figure, this would obviously represent a significant percentage of UGA's overall student population of 7,100.[43] Finally, the fact that the mob that marched on Hunter's dormitory formed out of a basketball crowd, which had just watched a close overtime loss to hated rival Georgia Tech, was interpreted by some observers to mean that the riot was spontaneous and was as much a result of youthful anger about this athletic defeat as it was an expression of racial animosity.[44]

The Federal Bureau of Investigation (FBI) reports on the riot—which will be discussed in depth in chapter 3—and the work of the best journalists on the scene can clear up some, but not all of this ambiguity. Federal agents had infiltrated the KKK, and their undercover reports do not support the claim that the Klan organized the riot. FBI and police reports attest that the riot was not a spontaneous post–basketball game development but rather an event planned well in advance by extreme segregationists within the UGA student body.[45]

The crowd size issue will never be fully resolved, since in 1961, when mass student protests were almost unknown, few journalists had the kind of experience needed to make reliable crowd estimates. Given the divergence of such estimates, then, it is impossible to use quantitative measures to determine precisely how representative the mob was of the entire student body. What the Math 254 essays suggest, however, is that the level of racial bias, ignorance, and hatred among the student body was so high that it created a "poisonous" atmosphere that nurtured racial violence.[46] If you believe, as some of Brahana's students did, that the subversive NAACP together with a dictatorial federal government were victimizing white Southerners by forcing them to integrate with members of an inferior race, there is a logic to rioting against such oppression. And there was more than logic here. There was anger: anger that two Black outsiders imagined to be on the NAACP payroll were disrupting their educations and threatening their way of life. The Math 254 essays suggest that even a week after the riot, this anger toward Holmes and Hunter lingered: "Personally I would like to choke both of them to death," wrote one student, though she quickly indicated that she would "never do such a thing."[47] Integration, another student warned, "will build up so much friction in the south that there will be an outright war over race. We know that the NAACP will go all the way on getting the negro in all of the white schools. Then Hell will break loose, and the University of Georgia riot will simply be a little party compared to what will happen."[48]

Although these essays attest that a chilling degree of racial animosity and anger endured among UGA students well after the riot, they also show that the riot and its aftermath had taught students that translating this anger into violence was self-destructive. The riot had demonstrated that the moderates had been right. No matter how strong or violent it was, student opposition to integration—along with its segregationist allies in the state legislature—would fail to stop the federal courts from enforcing the law and desegregating the university. Two days after the riot, Judge Bootle ordered the reinstatement of Holmes and Hunter, negating both the university's suspension of them and the mob's efforts to drive them off. The Math 254 students could see, then, that further segregationist agitation and violence would be futile. As one student argued in his essay, despite his opposition to integration, the events of the past week had convinced him that "all these plans for riots and the riot last Wednesday aren't going to do any good because I doubt if they'll cause the Supreme Court to change its decision. Just a lot of people get hurt and the university gets a bad name. I just wish everybody would leave us alone so things could calm down and we could do some studying." And an equally segregationist classmate warned that not only was it impossible to resist the federal court's integration order, but such resistance might lead to a humiliating Little Rock–style occupation of Athens by federal troops: "If there are more riots or disturbances it will only tighten the federal courts hold over our school."[49]

The ugliness of the riot itself also had an effect on the student body. Prior to the riot, Professor Brahana recalled, "There were a lot of students who were sort of enjoying" the desegregation crisis. "They would get dates to watch media coverage of the events." But the glare of the spotlight came to burn when, in the wake of the riot, the national media heaped scorn upon UGA. The front page coverage of students throwing rocks and rallying behind the crude "Nigger Go Home" banner, the *Life* magazine photo of a grinning UGA student symbolically lynching a black puppet, the NBC "Today" show host's on-the-air denunciation of the Center-Myers mob, and the political cartoons lampooning UGA students (in northern as well as some Southern newspapers) as brick-throwing bullies and rednecks yielded genuine embarrassment.[50] And for some students this was a matter that went beyond bad publicity. According to Brahana, the violence of January 11 forced students "to decide whether they wanted to live in a world where riots were the way things were decided. And this was not a trivial question." Reflecting on this question, one of Brahana's students wrote, "Even if I had strong feelings about integration what is there I could do about it.[?] Play caveman and throw rocks. No!!!" Such sentiments left some of the math students resenting the activists on both sides of the barricades: "I do not hate these two illustrious members of the Negroid race who are now going to school with me. I do hate the ugly violence, the unstrung nerves, the many rules limiting our rights in order to protect theirs that they have so unconcernedly brought about."[51]

Militant segregationism wilted at UGA as students came to realize that segregation could no longer be maintained without the payment of a very high price. No longer did students and the state have the luxury of viewing segregated education as a cost-free tradition. Much as they valued that tradition, in the wake of Bootle's integration order they realized it could be maintained only (and fleetingly at best) by closing the university itself—as the proponents of massive resistance had advocated. Students had to ask themselves whether they were willing to sacrifice their educations and close their university rather than see it integrated. The answer to this question was ultimately self-evident, for educational segregation had existed to privilege whites, and when in 1961 its continuation not only ceased to confer such privilege but instead began to threaten the very existence of public higher education, it quickly became expendable: "I cannot see giving up our public schools which we have worked so hard for just to keep the Negroes from having equal opportunity."⁵² Putting this tradeoff in economic terms, another student wrote,

> I believe in segregation. But I come from a family of very modest means. I had to work for a year after graduating high school before I had enough money even to enter college. Now I work afternoons to make money to go to school. Because I live off a limited budget, the University of Georgia is the only place I can afford to attend to further my education. . . . My whole future depends on it. My situation being thus, I am for the University staying open, integrated or not. . . . My segregationist views and thoughts have given way considerably to the fact that I want a college education more than anything else in the world.⁵³

The racial arithmetic involved in the crisis at UGA in 1961 made it easier to give up the battle against integration with the matriculation of only two— obviously gifted— Black students in a university with some 7,100 white students. "Like almost all southerners," one student wrote, "I don't want integration. But when it comes to closing the schools I'm willing to accept *token* integration to get an education." "Let me put it this way," a classmate concluded. "If the Negro wants to come here as 1 or 2 in 7,000 let him come. It's not going to bother me."⁵⁴

The Math 254 essays leave us, then, with a complex story rife with contradictions. They show us a student body longing to hold on to segregation but beginning to realize that Jim Crow's days were numbered; Southern students loyal to their region and its state rights and white supremacist creed but even more loyal to their educational self-interest; and a minority whose loathing for integration might have led to further violence, coupled with a larger group uncomfortable with violence and resentful of the riot organizers for damaging UGA's reputation.

Since no further student violence of any consequence (after the January 11 riot) hit Holmes and Hunter during the two years leading to their graduation from UGA, they were affected less by the various student statements about rioting than by the white students' striking silence on questions of humanity and friendship. It would probably be unrealistic to expect that at such a time— when, as Charlayne Hunter-Gault put it, Georgia's "white sons and daughters [were] facing their most apocalyptic moment since Sherman marched to the sea"—they would pause at all to think of how it felt to be on the receiving end of the mobs, effigy hangers, and racial epithets.⁵⁵ Perhaps one should expect that owing to their youth, these white students would be self-absorbed and see a crisis of this sort exclusively in terms of how it affected them. Thus it comes as no surprise that not one of the thirty-five student essayists spoke with any compassion about the difficult situation Holmes and Hunter would face matriculating in a 99-percent white, overwhelmingly segregationist student body in a postriot environment amid a segregated college town. Nor did a single one of Brahana's students write of offering a hand of friendship to Georgia's first Black students. Indeed, the one essay alluding to friendship in connection with Hunter and Holmes did so only to suggest that the withholding of such friendship could be a valuable weapon for breaking down their morale: "We should try to avoid the negroes in hopes that by doing so they might be psychologically affected and will eventually drop out of school."[56]

Expressions such as these suggest that resentful UGA students were holding on to something that the federal courts could not take away from them: the right to be unfriendly, and in so doing making UGA a personally unpleasant place for the two students who had had the effrontery to tear down white Georgia's beloved educational color line. These aloof white students had abandoned unlawful and violent massive resistance for a lawful and yet inhumane form of passive resistance. Of course displays of unfriendliness did not have to occur in such a calculated manner. Some students just naturally shunned Hunter and Holmes because they could not stomach interacting with members of a pariah race, especially two accused of being puppets of the subversive NAACP. Others—as journalist Calvin Trillin's interviews on fraternity row suggest—stayed away from Holmes and Hunter because of peer pressure, which would have rendered as outcasts whites who displayed any signs of interracial friendliness.[57] But whatever the specific rationale for it, the determination to be unfriendly was widespread, and it manifested itself under the very roof where Hunter slept. The dean of women's survey taken of the residents (which covered 153 of the 163 students) in Hunter's dormitory three days after the riot found these "predominant sentiments . . . expressed":

1. The great desire for no more violence;
2. The desire for conditions conducive to study and sleep;
3. A preverance [sic] for segregation, but an acceptance of the fact that desegregation is mandatory;
4. The desire that no publicity be given to their views as expressed in these interviews and that these interviews not be used to make it appear that the dormitory would welcome Charlayne "with open arms." (The attitude was more that they would tolerate her.)[58]

This ethic of indifference and unfriendliness affected even prominent moderate students, such as Pete McCommons, who had led the petition drive to prevent the segregationist legislature from closing down the university. McCommons recalled that

> the last time I saw Hamilton Holmes I was headed up Ag Hill and saw him coming from the opposite direction. I turned off to the right, down the sidewalk, out of his path. He knew me and saw me, but I didn't meet his eyes. Though I hesitated before turning, I told myself that I had been representing all those students who wanted the University kept open, whether or not they welcomed Hamilton Holmes. I'd better stay neutral towards Hamilton personally. It was easy to think like that in 1961. I was a Student Leader . . . but such hypocrisy hurt Holmes and Hunter like hell.[59]

Looking back upon the desegregation battle at UGA, Brahana concluded that "the university was lucky. . . . We were truly lucky that no one was killed."[60] Indeed, compared to the charred and bloody battlefield that the University of Mississippi became when it underwent desegregation the year after UGA, the ugly scene at Center-Myers may seem almost tame. But it is also true that once the initial violence ended, Hunter and Holmes at UGA, much like James Meredith at Mississippi, matriculated in an environment characterized by white resentment, coldness, and hostility. Given the white supremacist tradition, values, and thought, articulated so clearly and frequently in the Math 254 essays, it could hardly have been otherwise, as students responded to an unwelcome and unexpected challenge to their Southern way of life. The change was accepted but accepted grudgingly and in ways that violated the Southern student body's own norms of gentility and even civility. This is what Pete McCommons had in mind when, in recalling his days at UGA in 1961, he drew a personal conclusion but one applicable to most of his classmates during that turbulent time: "It was all a tricky business, and even most of those who tried to overcome their segregated upbringing and accept this momentous change didn't carry it off with much class."[61]

Postscript to Chapter Two

I am not sure what amazed me most, that the Math 254 essays had been written and deposited at the University of Georgia's library or that nobody had published a word about them. As soon as I began reading these essays, written amid the UGA desegregation crisis by all the students in a calculus class, it was evident that these offered the deepest and most extensive commentary by white UGA students on how most viewed that crisis and its relation to their own history and educational careers. They were a gold mine of information on student thinking about race, Jim Crow Georgia, violence, segregationist militancy, and the university. It is rare to encounter such rich sources, and so my article "Two, Four, Six, Eight, We Don't Want to Integrate," published in the *Georgia Historical Quarterly* (with the help of its brilliant editor, John Inscoe), focused on mining them to illuminate the intellectual and political worlds of these student authors and the segregationist student majority at UGA that they so clearly represented. But all sources, no matter how rich, have their limitations. And though the Math 254 essays illuminate the thinking of the segregationist majority, they are less useful for understanding UGA's few dissenters, most notably those guided by religious principles toward more liberal racial views.

Since few of the Math 254 essays stressed religious themes or seem to have been written by students active in campus religious organizations, religion barely appeared in my study of their essays on UGA's desegregation crisis. This reflected the fact that students active in those organizations constituted only a small minority of UGA students in 1961—so that it was to be expected that they would not figure prominently among the thirty-five Math 254 essay authors. But while not represented among those essayists, and only a small minority on the UGA campus, the most socially conscious among these religious organization activists did make a difference in the university's desegregation crisis.

We need to be careful here not to exaggerate. When we think of religion at its most egalitarian regarding race, the first images that come to mind are of the Black church and such religiously inspired African American civil rights leaders as Martin Luther King Jr. and John Lewis, who put their lives on the line for racial equality and social justice. No white student at UGA, either in the Jim Crow era or at the time when the color line was collapsing at the university in the early 1960s, displayed that level of activism. None publicly made the moral case that segregation was evil, that UGA could never become a great university until it ceased practicing racial discrimination. But some of these religiously affiliated students did at least implicitly challenge the racism of the larger campus culture of UGA by advocating that Holmes and Hunter be welcomed, not shunned, by the student body. Students affiliated with Westminster House, UGA's Presbyterian organization, established an organization called Students for Constructive Action, which posted signs promoting the Golden Rule in campus buildings when UGA desegregated and had members accompany Hunter and Holmes when they crossed the campus in the early days of desegregation.[1] Members of Westminster House had open discussions of race relations, and as late as 1963—the year of Holmes and Hunter's graduation—as Calvin Trillin reported, "Westminster was still the only place [at UGA] where a Negro was accepted without question."[2] Members of Students for Constructive Action and Westminster House were prominent among those dissident students who befriended Charlayne Hunter.

One such friend, Joan Zitzelman, was, like Charlayne Hunter, a UGA journalism major. It was through her affiliation with Westminster House that Zitzelman began to question the racist social order of Jim Crow Georgia. As Zitzelman recalled,

> although quietly and without public display, my personal convictions were forming to believe strongly that I wanted to work toward racial equality. The major outlet for exploring and building these convictions was a Presbyterian student organization on campus. As civil rights activities occurred throughout the South in the late fifties and early sixties, our organization invited students from northern colleges to visit and talk with us about these issues. We went to Atlanta . . . and met with the leaders of the Student Non-Violent Coordinating Committee, the NAACP, liberal journalists such as Ralph McGill . . . and . . . author Lillian Smith. . . . In 1960 . . . about a dozen of us went to Paine College in Augusta for a weekend conference on civil rights . . . mingling among hundreds of students in an all-black college. The hospitality and friendship extended to us . . . was amazing. Three of the students I met were from Athens and had graduated from the all-black high school in town. Until this meeting I had never realized there was an all-black high school in Athens, less than a mile from my own all-white high school. The intellectual results of the weekend made an impact that lasts to this day. My emotional reactions

went even deeper. A curtain had been parted, and I suddenly understood that I had been living in a segregated society since the age of seven, and I had been unable or unwilling to see the reality of it.[3]

Zitzelman was candid about how difficult she found it in segregated Athens, Georgia, to act publicly on what were for her these new racially egalitarian ideas. Though she befriended Charlayne Hunter, in retrospect she wished she had been a more caring friend who had inquired more and been more aware of and helpful to Hunter in facing the difficulties of living on an unfriendly white campus. And Zitzelman found it all but impossible to discuss her critical view of segregation with her mother, whose attitude, as a New Jersey transplant to Athens, was that it was best to defer to the local customs of Jim Crow Georgia. So Zitzelman was not at UGA an open advocate of integration but nonetheless acted on those integrationist values as when on the first day of class, arriving before Charlayne, she erased the racist "Nigger Go Home" insult that a bigoted classmate had scribbled on the blackboard.[4]

The racial egalitarianism of Westminster House was due in large part to its liberal minister, Corky King, who was one of the very few vocal advocates of integration on the UGA campus in 1961. Indeed, King's integrationism was so unusual for anyone at UGA back then that his days at the university were numbered. As Trillin noted, he was the only person at UGA to lose his job for being too progressive during the desegregation crisis, purged by the Presbyterian board and replaced with a less outspoken successor.[5] Yet even after King's firing, Westminster House's racial egalitarianism lived on. Several of its white student members invited Harold Black, one of UGA's second small class of African American students, to join them at the services held at the all-white Presbyterian church downtown, a venture that seemed to go well initially but was shut down by resistance from racist members of that church.[6]

At times, however, the racial liberalism of white students in UGA's religious organizations came across as shallow or phony. For example, Hamilton Holmes noticed that the same students who were so friendly to him when he visited Canterbury House, UGA's Episcopal organization, acted as if they did not know him when he ran into them on campus. Disgusted by this, Holmes stopped going to Canterbury House.[7] And Charlayne Hunter was similarly disillusioned when one of her fellow Catholic students whom she had met at the campus Newman House acted cowardly, cutting off their friendship after being pressured to do so by segregationist students in his dormitory.[8]

While it is evident that these religious organizations at UGA could not get all of their members to live up to the ideal of interracial fellowship, the mere fact that such interracialism was even an aspiration for these organizations is itself of great significance. Here we need to keep in mind the compelling argument David L. Chappell made about religion and the battle over desegregation in the Jim Crow South in his important book *A Stone of Hope: Prophetic Religion and the Death of Jim Crow* (2004). Chappell stressed that a key reason for Jim Crow's demise was that most Southern white churches refused to side with the forces of massive resistance to integration and refused to find any Biblical justification for segregation and its preservation.[9] However reluctant or unwilling such churches might have been about enlisting on the side of the Black Freedom movement, the crucial fact was that they did not use their influence against that movement. This contrasted dramatically with the Black churches, which united so effectively on behalf of the movement to liberate Blacks by toppling the Jim Crow system.[10] Applied to UGA in 1961, we can see, then, that the crucial fact is that none of the campus religious organizations sided with the segregationist militants but instead urged their student members to respond peacefully to desegregation and apply the Golden Rule, treating UGA's first Black students the same way as they would want to be treated by their fellow students.

THERE IS NO GETTING AWAY from the fact that at the height of UGA's desegregation crisis it was not these religious students and their Golden Rule that prevailed but rather the campus's violent segregationist extremists whose racist riot so damaged UGA's reputation. At the outset of the crisis such an outcome did not seem inevitable. Within days of the integration order on Friday, January 6, a significant number of UGA students had been upset about the prospect that the Georgia legislature and governor would invoke the state's 1956 (massive resistance) law barring racially integrated public education and mandating that an integrated school would lose state funding, which in UGA's case would mean closing the university rather than see it integrated. For many UGA students eager to complete their college educations, this threatened closing of their university seemed a dangerous act of demagoguery: posturing politicians with no real chance to preserve segregation in the face of a federal court order were playing politics with the state's leading public university and placing the future of its students in jeopardy. On Sunday night, these students—who in relation to UGA's violent segregationists can be termed moderates—held a meeting in the campus chapel to organize a petition drive demanding that the legislature not close the university. Within a day, some 2,700 students had signed these petitions. This represented more than a third of the UGA student body and was larger even than the racist mob—of 1,000 to 2,000—that would besiege Charlayne Hunter's dormitory in the disgraceful riot of January 11. And this was a rejection of massive resistance, a rejection that Georgia's governor and legislature would finally and reluctantly come to embrace once Judge Bootle ruled unconstitutional the Georgia law mandating that UGA be closed if it integrated.

Given the impressive number of signatures they gathered on their petitions against closing UGA, which constituted a dissent against a massive resistance law, it may seem odd that moderate students lost out to the massive resistance forces on campus, whose segregationist protests and racist mob violence made headlines and dominated the student political scene during the desegregation crisis. This was because despite their significant numbers, the moderates suffered from political and moral ambiguity and timidity. The cause of keeping UGA open was not even necessarily a moderate one on campus, as the most intransigent and bellicose segregationist students wanted to keep UGA open too (and so did not oppose the petition drive) since they did not want the legislature to mandate UGA's closing, but hoped their acts of resistance—including violence—could lead to the university being kept open on a segregated basis. But the moderates' main weakness derived from the fact that publicly they took issue only with the tactics (threats of violence) and not the segregationist goals of their extremist classmates. No moderate student leader would openly denounce segregation itself. In fact, most moderates prefaced their calls for nonviolence and open schools with statements voicing their preference for a racially segregated university.

Despite their tactical differences, then, the unity that moderate and extremist students displayed in expressing reverence for segregation made it difficult at times to distinguish between these two groups during the desegregation crisis. Indeed, through the early stages of the crisis—until the riot of January 11—moderates and extremists had no difficulty working together politically, as when both supported the open university petition drive. As the extremist student (and soon-to-be riot) leader Thomas Cochran told a reporter, the "open school petition signed by some 2,500 students had been misrepresented by the press. He said the petition did not call for 'open schools regardless,' but simply for open schools. 'I want the school to stay open.' He said, 'but I want it to be segregated.' He indicated the petition was worded in such a way that students who felt the same way he did could sign it."[11] Pete McCommons, a moderate student leader who spearheaded the petition drive, agreed with Cochran on this. The petitions were phrased to indicate support for UGA staying open, and since they did not even hint that the battle against integration ought to be halted, the petition could draw support from moderate students as well as those who were segregationist militants.[12]

The line between moderates and extremists was also difficult to discern on the occasion of the UGA student protest on the night of January 9, which to that point was the largest prior to the segregationist riot of January 11. The January 9 march drew about 1,000 students and was sparked by reports that Governor Vandiver was going to implement the state's massive resistance law to defund and close their integrating university. Though one might think this was therefore a demonstration by moderates against the state's intransigent segregationist politicians, in fact, whatever moderates were in the crowd marched side by side with extremists, whose target was not Vandiver but integration itself. Demonstrators burned a cross, and then "a segregation chant filled the night air and the crowd grew." The marchers took to the streets of downtown Athens "following a hoisted Confederate flag, [and] the students became a running, shouting, fire-cracker shooting gang. . . . Somebody shouted derisively as a crowd of Negroes . . . drove past. . . . The demonstration was a segregationist movement only in the nucleus of its beginning: hundreds of students ordinarily considered 'moderate' on the subject joined in the exuberance of the moment and marched along."[13] Thus the gap between segregationist militants and moderates at times seemed so slight that they could both petition and march together.

During the early stages of the desegregation crisis, the pages of UGA's student newspaper, the *Red and Black*, attest to how ineffective and muddled was the campus's moderate student position. In an effort to promote a peaceful response to the admission of Hunter and Holmes, the paper's moderate editors gathered a series of quotations from prominent students under the heading "Campus Leaders Ask Students to Follow Non-Violent Course."[14] Since four of the ten quoted student leaders coupled their calls for nonviolence with statements opposing integration, the article left one with a feeling that UGA was being wronged by the federal courts and that something should be done about it. The line between moderation and segregationist extremism was so thin that the editor of this article failed to note that among the leaders quoted were at least two who ranked among the most militant segregationists, including the president of the Demonsthenian Society, who did not even come close to advocating nonviolence in his quote. Instead, he egged on students toward escalating resistance to integration, arguing that "I know that the people of Georgia and the students want this university segregated; I have deep faith in the legislature and its ability to maintain for us both segregation and open doors. I hope every student will express his disappointment in the federal decision and support the legislature," which at that point was still committed to massive resistance against integration. The

Interfraternity Council president, quoted in this same story, echoed these sentiments.[15]

Since moderates at UGA—in the student body or the administration—refused to advocate or even express sympathy with integration, this meant than no one with any significant degree of influence at the university was, in the crucial first week of the desegregation crisis, prepared to challenge the campus's traditional racist consensus on behalf of segregation. This failure manifested itself in something historians tend to overlook as they discuss the site of UGA's segregationist riot: what did *not* happen. Students at the riot scene were characterized as either rioters or onlookers. What none of them were was *counterdemonstrators*, who would dare to raise their voices or a banner, or anything at all, objecting to the racist rioting by their fellow students. As much as the riot itself, this deafening silence and inaction on the night of the riot, the apparent absence of vocal student foes of racism and racist violence, attests to the failure of UGA as an educational institution to teach its students about the oppressive racism and racial violence inherent in the Jim Crow system.

SINCE THE MATH 254 ESSAYS were written by UGA students amid the university's desegregation crisis and offer the most extensive archival evidence of their response to that crisis, it was natural that students took center stage in my study of those essays. But it is also true that those essays would never have been written or preserved were it not for their professor, Thomas Brahana, who asked his students to write the essays and then deposited their writings in the university library, where they have been preserved. Of course, when researching and writing about those essays, I realized Brahana's importance to the story of the Math 254 essays, which is why I conducted an oral history interview with him and wrote about him in my "Two, Four, Six, Eight" article. But there was no space in that article to offer much reflection on what Brahana represented, which was a large segment of the UGA faculty, who in the wake of the segregationist riot had finally dared to take a public stance against the massive resistance movement's extremist defense of Jim Crow. Brahana, as head of the university's American Association of University Professors chapter, had convened a faculty meeting in the university chapel after the riot, which had resulted in a strong statement signed by 406 UGA faculty members—about two-thirds of the university's faculty—with resolutions condemning the riot, demanding the reinstatement of Holmes and Hunter and the return of law and order so the university could conduct its educational work.[16]

On a number of levels this was a remarkable act by the faculty. In the previous Deep South university educational crisis that had resulted in a segregationist riot, the University of Alabama's in 1956 over the admission of Autherine Lucy, the Alabama faculty had never spoken out as UGA's faculty would in January 1961. Nor would the University of Mississippi's faculty in 1962 take the public stance en masse as UGA's faculty had, even though the James Meredith admission crisis had resulted in a riot much bloodier than that seen at UGA.[17] The UGA faculty statement was also unprecedented in the context of UGA's own history, in which such mass dissent against the Jim Crow regime seemed, for almost a century, a virtual impossibility given the lack of academic freedom on campus and the conservatism of many professors, especially those born and raised in the Jim Crow South. How then did the impossible suddenly become not just possible but political reality?

There were several interrelated developments that made such mass dissent possible. First, there was *Holmes v. Danner* itself, which in the history of UGA faculty politics represented a revolutionary event. Here the political weight of the federal government had been deployed to challenge and almost certainly to topple the Jim Crow regime on campus. To those who had never liked that regime, this was empowering as it opened up the possibility that one could express one's dissent without courting repression. And so, faculty liberals, like Brahana, could seize the moment and organize a professorial protest. While it is true that the most militant segregationists in Georgia's state legislature advocated the firing of UGA faculty who had signed the statement on behalf of Hunter and Holmes, and that some faculty worried that they had put their jobs on the line by signing the statement, such fears were overcome by the numbers involved: it would have been impossible for the legislature to purge so many professors.

Yet faculty liberals were a small minority of the UGA faculty. What enabled the hundreds of less progressive faculty to endorse the resolutions? One key point to note is that even though the resolutions culminated with a call for the reinstatement of Holmes and Hunter, they did not constitute an integrationist manifesto. Nowhere did the faculty statement say that racially integrated education was intellectually or morally superior to segregated education. Rather, it condemned the "lawless demonstrations" and the failure of state officials to "protect the rights and property of the university," warning that further campus violence could "destroy the prestige of the university, result in loss of faculty and depress the student body."[18] This reflected the tone of the chapel meeting where the faculty resolutions were adopted, which centered on the university's institutional stability rather than on a revolution in race relations. As UGA journalism professor George Abney, who attended that meeting, recalled, "I don't know how the faculty felt about integration, but it seemed to me that the emphasis at the meeting was on education, seeing that education was not disrupted in the state of Georgia and particularly at the University of Georgia, and the faculty go on record as backing the law of the land. Those seemed to be emphasized more than integrating the University."[19] Similarly, UGA history professor Kenneth Coleman, who was another key organizer of the faculty resolutions, later explained, "I'm sure that a lot of people signed who probably did not in practice believe in integration." They were motivated to sign because "they had gotten unhappy about the treatment of the University" by militantly segregationist politicians like Roy Harris, who had been denouncing UGA and its leaders for not closing down the university rather than complying with the court-ordered integration, and the resolutions represented a way to defend UGA and insist that it stay open.[20]

Given the court-ordered admission of Holmes and Hunter to UGA, the administration's suspension of them came off to many faculty as delaying the inevitable, and such delay risked another, and even more damaging, round of segregationist violence on campus. This too made it possible for even conservative faculty to sign the statement urging Holmes and Hunter's reinstatement since this seemed the surest way to end the crisis, ensure the return of law and order, and keep the university functioning as an educational institution; it was, in other words, a path toward peace and was consistent with the Constitution. As UGA economics professor Nick Beadle recalled, faculty who signed the statement "felt that you couldn't solve the problem by removing Hamilton Holmes and Charlayne Hunter from the student body, that the way to solve the problem was, if they're qualified, to let 'em into the university and treat 'em like any other student." Beadle also claimed that by 1961, as the color line headed for extinction, "most of the faculty—yeah they were Southern, but most of the faculty on this side have lived in other places and know perfectly well that color is not the determinant of brainpower and so forth . . . and . . . it was a vote in favor of supporting the Constitution and the Supreme Court decision."[21]

Lawlessness mattered in that the riot infuriated the faculty and helped motivate those who had supported the resolution endorsing Holmes and Hunter's reinstatement, seeing it as a rejection and an explicit condemnation of mob violence. They viewed the riot as a disgraceful event that badly damaged UGA's reputation. And some liberal faculty went beyond the statement itself, bringing this critical perspective into their classrooms, which also represents a sharp break with the Jim Crow past, when faculty shied away from teaching about civil rights and racism. Brahana, it will be recalled, asked his Math 254 students to write those essays to show that they could express their views on integration in a nonviolent way, which was in itself an implicit criticism of the riot. Much more explicitly critical was professor Joseph Parks, a liberal faculty member who chaired the history department. In fact, for Roger Thomas, whose senior year at UGA coincided with the desegregation crisis, the single most memorable hour for him during the crisis was in Parks's Civil War history course, the class session the morning after the riot. Parks was, in Thomas's words, "extremely outraged" that there had been a segregationist riot. He

> was very upset, and made it very clear that that kind of behavior was barbaric and completely unacceptable.... He spoke for the full hour just on the subject of how detrimental our behavior and whole racist attitude would be to the students of the University of Georgia.... He put it right down to what it meant to each student in that classroom personally. The way in which he did that was to point out to them how worthless their degrees were going to be if the University's reputation was badly damaged in this matter, particularly if the University was to close down over the acceptance of these two students.... He pointed out, for example, that they were trying to build a decent History department, and that they had been fortunate to attract some good young professors; but with this kind of behavior there was no way they were going to be able to keep those professors.... That this being 1961 and the South being what it was at that time, it was already difficult enough to recruit good professors from other regions of the country into the South; the South had such a questionable image. It was difficult enough prior to the actions at the riot, but did we think he would have any chance at all recruiting anyone to come in and teach at a school that tolerated and encouraged that kind of behavior? ... He was supporting integration, tolerance.[22]

Speech professor James E. Popovich's reflections on the integration crisis attest to how liberating it was politically for him as one of the few UGA faculty who had a record of public opposition to massive resistance. Even he, as a northerner, had, however, avoided discussing civil rights in his classes prior to that crisis, "having been long enough in Athens to have been cautious about what I said in my classes."[23] But now that the Jim Crow regime was on the verge of collapsing, he and other liberal faculty seized the opportunity to push for a more egalitarian campus climate. "For one thing ... any language which was either foul or aggressive was immediately—and different faculty got with it in different ways—basically you couldn't say some of the things that you had, with no problem, said a few years before, in that a faculty member was there to make you behave like a civilized human being."[24] Applied to his own discipline, when one of the students in Popovich's speech class "would say 'nigger' in a speech, everyone was going through the critique session afterwards, and I would write 'Negro' phonetically on the board, and I would write it phonetically 'nigra' and then 'nigger.' And I'd say 'Now this is substandard, this is a kind of regionalism, and this is correct.' And I think in a way, although I didn't like to do that, because it seemed to me to be baiting my students, I thought... they ought to be exposed to the fact that one doesn't talk like that of other human beings."[25]

Throwing caution to the wind, Popovich did not hesitate in class to urge his students to welcome Hunter and Holmes back to UGA on the day they were reinstated. He told them, "We are gentlemen and we are ladies. But we are human beings first.... And if you can think of anything else we are, I'd like to know, because on both those grounds we've got to act like civilized human beings, and have compassion." Popovich reached out to both Hunter and Holmes, befriending both and serving as a mentor to students in the campus Episcopal organization in an attempt promote an atmosphere of friendliness to the first Black students. His activism surprised some of his students, given his prior caution, and did lead to some harassment, as when his car door was inscribed with the words "Nigger Lover." But what impressed Popovich was that with regard to the administration, the response to antiracist dissent had changed in 1961. "At any other time," prior to integration, that response would have been "Jim, you're acting like some damn yankee, don't do it."[26] This time neither his activism nor the faculty resolutions against the riot and demanding Hunter and Holmes's reinstatement drew that kind of response from UGA's administration.

In Popovich's view, it was not his own surging activism but the faculty resolutions themselves that seemed almost earth-shattering. This was because instead of being an expression of a few and mostly northern-born faculty dissenters like him, those resolutions were signed by a majority of UGA's very Southern professoriate. He thought this made it a potentially powerful tool to challenge the white supremacist culture of the student body, explaining that "the very fact, the image of that night when over two-thirds of the faculty signed that petition was an overwhelming thing. If you were a Southerner and were aware that your professor, who was also a Southerner, had signed that petition, it may be right! Has my Dad been right, all these years, down in Oakus [Oak] Grove, Georgia, saying some of the [racist] things he's been saying? I think for the first time, we gave a kind of dignity to ideas that were" at odds with the Jim Crow regime.[27]

Given that this was the first time that UGA faculty members had collectively defied the university's Jim Crow tradition, it is understandable, and even touching, that they look back with pride on their stance in favor of Holmes and Hunter. That sense of pride shone through in my interview with Brahana and was evident when he discussed not only his role in initiating the chapel meeting where the faculty dissent was organized but also his service in the faculty patrol, guarding the campus through the nights against further racist violence in that tense week or so after the riot. Much like Brahana, his liberal UGA colleague Robert Ayers, a professor of religion, in his memoir depicted that faculty patrol and his participation in it as a manifestation of a heroic antiracist liberalism,

> riding around Athens, Georgia with a few other progressive and determined liberal UGA faculty members, protecting the first two African American students from being beaten or murdered. Charlayne Hunter and Hamilton Holmes were pioneers, two brave teenagers wading into a mob of white resentment fueled by restrictive conservative ideology. We open-minded liberals wanted to prove to the world that even the Deep South could overcome decades of prejudice and segregation. In order to do that, we had to keep them alive. They were living every minute of every day under the very real threat of murder. Ignorance is not an easy enemy to defeat.[28]

This same sense of pride was also visible in the pioneering oral history work that sociologist John C. Belcher did in the mid-1970s as the first UGA faculty member to devote any scholarly attention to the university's desegregation crisis. Belcher did a disproportionate number of oral history interviews with faculty involved in the chapel meeting and faculty patrol, leaving one with the impression that to him this faculty activism was central to the integration story, overshadowing even Holmes, Hunter, and the Black organizers and lawyers who launched the desegregation struggle—none of whom he interviewed. Similarly, back in 1995, when I interviewed Horace Montgomery, the UGA history professor who helped initiate and write the faculty statement, he still had in his Athens home hanging over his desk a framed letter from a racist detractor who—because of his role in penning the faculty statement—accused him of being a "Judas" who had sold out the white race.

And yet it also needs to be said that—admirable as it was—this faculty dissent was quite belated. Where was the faculty in the 1950s when the UGA administration spent more than half the decade preventing Horace Ward from becoming the first Black student to attend the university? Why had the faculty been mute regarding *Holmes v. Danner* and not organized a pro-integration statement when that decision came down ordering UGA's integration? Why had it taken an ugly and embarrassing riot, and Holmes and Hunter's suspension, to finally motivate the faculty to mobilize on behalf of integration? This seems, in part, a matter of old habits being hard to break, and in this case that meant the habit of deference to the Jim Crow regime. But it is nonetheless striking that in the days before the riot, when the state's political establishment suggested it might close the university rather than see it integrated, the faculty did not rise up *en masse* to defend the university.

The other issue that went unaddressed by even the dissenting faculty was curricular. While it is significant that the faculty statement condemned the segregationist riot, the faculty never got around to exploring the university's and their own educational failure that had made that riot possible. After all, the riot was not the act of outsiders. This was violence by *their* students. How is it that the university's coursework had failed to challenge their students' racist assumptions and segregationism? Didn't this failure suggest that by their negligence or curricular and political cowardice the faculty was at least indirectly complicit in the racial violence outside Charlayne Hunter's dormitory? How might the university curriculum be improved so that it would provide academic intervention challenging the widespread white supremacist assumptions and segregationist habits of mind of the university's—mostly Georgian—student body? And how promptly and smoothly could UGA be expected to adapt to integration when some 200 of the university's faculty members did not sign the statement in support of the reinstatement of Holmes and Hunter? These were the kinds of questions the faculty needed to consider were it to organize to take the university beyond token integration and toward a larger vision of university transformed by a large-scale and expeditious integration process. But UGA's faculty lacked the organization or vision for that. The best it could do was help UGA survive its integration crisis in 1961, and given the history of the university and its faculty in the Jim Crow era, this was likely the most one could hope for or expect.

In the aftermath of the integration crisis, UGA's faculty, which had yet to desegregate its own ranks, was a house divided. There were within its ranks conservative Southerners who had done nothing to bring about the university's integration and remained uncomfortable with it. These were the professors Charlayne Hunter-Gault looked back on scornfully, who over the course of a semester never even acknowledged that she was in their classes.[29] But there were also progressive faculty whom Hunter-Gault paid tribute to in her memoir, who befriended her, invited her into their homes, enhanced her educational experience at UGA, and made up somewhat for the coldness of many of her classmates.[30]

Pete Range's memories of his experience as a professor teaching Hamilton Holmes's introductory course in political science in spring 1961 attested to this same division. Range, who had a reputation as a liberal, had been asked by his department head if he would be willing to have Holmes in his class. This was, as Range explained it, part of "special efforts being made in those days to get both of them [Holmes and Hunter] in classes with instructors who would be acceptable," meaning that they were not put in a class with a "redneck [instructor who] might have made their life ... miserable."[31]

And it was a good thing Range agreed to teach this course with Holmes, because the very first day of class he witnessed what the ideas articulated in the Math 254 essays about waging psychological warfare against UGA's first Black students (isolating them in the hopes that they would drop out) meant when white students enacted them. The class had thirty students in a classroom that had space for sixty. Holmes sat in a front row seat on one side of the room. And all of the white students sat on the other side and toward the back of the room. Not one would sit anywhere near Holmes. Range was shocked by this, "awfully embarrassed, and I didn't know what to do. . . . Fearing that I might have a riot on my hands there," he just went through his typical first-day-of-class routine, introducing the course, thinking all the while, "well, I'll figure this out overnight."[32] That night, this situation had Range so upset he got no sleep as he was "trying to figure out what to do with those students to make some sit on the other side of the room and get them all near the front," where Holmes was sitting. Range hit upon the idea that since the students had been conditioned all through their twelve years of schooling "to do what the teacher tells them to do," he could get the students to dissolve the Jim Crow line they had created in his classroom by firmly ordering them to adhere to a new classroom seating arrangement.[33]

So the next day, "trembling a bit" as he came into the classroom, Range told the students, "Now, the last four rows of students there, move to the other side as I'm going to use just the first five rows of these two section[s]."[34] Though Range said this firmly, he still "had to say it two or three times" before the students finally moved. Still, none would sit directly next to Holmes, but at least he was no longer rows and rows apart from the rest of the class, across a de facto Jim Crow line.

Range later observed that the white supremacist assumptions that led to such students' disdain for Holmes were refuted by Holmes's academic performance. Holmes "was really the only student in the class who prepared every day. I think I had only two A's in that class, and one of them was his."[35]

SINCE THE MATH 254 ESSAYS SPEAK to the way race was thought about in Georgia and UGA and help us better understand white students' response to integration, I used them in my article to illuminate the UGA desegregation crisis. But the essays, and the desegregation crisis to which they responded, have relevance to more than just this Georgia history. If we shift our focus from the microhistory of UGA to the larger history of 1960s America and place both these sources and UGA's stormy desegregation into national perspective, they can challenge the popular understanding of the 1960s as a decade whose politics leaned toward liberalism off campus and leaned left (New Left) on campus—where students mobilized against racism and war.

UGA in 1961 offers us a very different vantage point on both student politics and the larger trajectory of American politics in the 1960s. Here the first campus violence came from UGA's racist Right, not the northern student Left. Indeed, if we use the broader chronological frame common to historians of the 1960s and speak of "the Long 1960s," extending back from the Montgomery bus boycott of 1955 onward, we could also include the segregationist student riot that prevented Autherine Lucy from becoming the first African American to matriculate at the University of Alabama in 1956. Thus it was old racism, not New Leftism, that made the earliest mark on American college campuses in the Long 1960s. It was not such New Left hotbeds as UC Berkeley and Columbia but the Universities of Alabama and Georgia that erupted first in ugly student riots. Similarly, the racist ideas, fear of change, and provincialism found in many of the Math 254 essays suggest that it is one-sided and naive to see the 1960s generation as simply a bulwark of progressive social change. The 1960s opened with the Eisenhower presidency and ended with Nixon in the White House and Nixon's Southern strategy built on the same kind of racial resentment we saw in many of the Math 254 essays and in UGA's segregationist riot. The point here is not to erase the New Left or 1960s liberalism but rather to acknowledge that the forces of liberalism and the Left always had to battle the politics of bigotry and fear articulated in the Math 254 essays, and those battles were not always successful. The distance between the narrow-mindedness and hatred at UGA in 1961, 'Bama in 1956, and that seen in Mar-a-Lago and Donald Trump's George Wallace–style rallies today and over the past eight years seems mighty small.

CHAPTER THREE

G-Men in Georgia
The FBI and the Segregationist Riot at the University of Georgia, 1961

A segregationist riot rocked the University of Georgia on the evening of January 11, 1961, when a large, angry crowd of students marching behind a "Nigger Go Home" banner shattered windows in the dormitory of Charlayne Hunter, who along with Hamilton Holmes had just broken the color line at UGA. Only hours before the riot, Hunter and Holmes had completed their opening day of classes as Georgia's first African American students. For two hours or so the rioters used bricks, firecrackers, beer bottles, matches, and their fists to vent their violent opposition to racial integration. Order was restored after police threw tear gas bombs and firefighters hosed the mob in a scene more reminiscent of a battlefield than a dignified college campus. A federal district court judge, W. A. Bootle, had ordered the admission of Hunter and Holmes, and so the white student attack upon the desegregation process occasioned a federal response. A crucial part of that response came the day after the riot when attorney general William P. Rogers of the Eisenhower administration announced the launching of a Federal Bureau of Investigation (FBI) probe designed to ascertain "whether or not federal law violations occurred" at UGA. Rogers referred specifically to the possibility that the rioters had violated "the provisions of Title I of the 1960 Civil Rights Act making it a criminal offense to impede or obstruct, or to attempt to obstruct federal court orders, such as the order of the federal court requiring admission of Negro students to the University of Georgia."[1]

The quick action in the Athens case by Attorney General Rogers was out of character with the Eisenhower administration's overall civil rights record. Under Ike, the Justice Department usually displayed great reluctance to use federal force or police power on behalf of court-mandated integration—preferring, as did the president himself, to leave state and local authorities with the responsibility to enforce the law and maintain order. Thus in 1956, when University of Alabama students (in the closest campus parallel to UGA's desegregation in 1961) rioted to drive Autherine Lucy, their university's first Black student, from campus, the Eisenhower administration refused to intervene—despite requests university officials made for federal marshals.

It was not until fall 1957 that the brazen defiance of federal authority by Arkansas governor Orval Faubus and a segregationist mob at Little Rock Central High compelled a very reluctant president to at last use his executive powers, in this case ordering in troops to enforce a federal court order on behalf of school integration. The political fallout from Little Rock led to the passage of the Civil Rights Act of 1960, a measure that, though largely symbolic, did set new penalties for those found guilty of obstructing federal court orders.[2]

Rogers may have been seeking to use the FBI probe in Georgia to prove that he was serious about enforcing the 1960 act. He may also have hoped that this quick action would prevent events at UGA from getting out of hand so that Eisenhower, whose term expired in less than two weeks, would not leave office beneath a cloud of racial conflict. It is equally possible that with the elections over and the Republicans on the way out, Rogers was, at last, willing to act quickly and forcefully on civil rights because he knew that at this late date neither he nor his boss could be made to pay a political price for such action.

Since there is not much of a justice department paper trail to explain Rogers's action, one can speculate endlessly about his motivations. Actually, the most direct evidence available suggests that the key to the decision to move quickly on the Athens riot may have rested less with Rogers himself than with his subordinate, Harold R. Tyler Jr., the assistant attorney general who headed the US Department of Justice's Civil Rights Division. Tyler held that position during the last six months of the second Eisenhower administration. A former federal prosecutor in New York, he was young, dynamic, and far more determined to enforce the civil rights laws than were his predecessors. Tyler had initiated voter and other antidiscrimination suits in four Southern states. He recalled the FBI investigation as arising because "I raised the issue of responding to the matter at the University of Georgia with the Attorney General of the United States, William P. Rogers. He reacted immediately and affirmatively, in part because the [US] Department [of Justice] and the attorney general had pressed hard to get the relevant investigative section of the 1960 Civil Rights Act passed by Congress.... Our initial goal was to use the weight of the federal government to discourage violence on college campuses and other communities. In addition, however, I am sure that I had in my mind at least the possibility of a prosecution, depending on the nature and extent of the facts developed."[3]

The FBI files on the riot investigation illuminate some of the key issues concerning the riot's origins, character, and political implications. These files were obtained via my request under the Freedom of Information Act. Unfortunately, many of the 256 pages in the FBI files on UGA's segregationist riot are incomplete since the FBI released these files with a substantial amount of excisions, and the bureau—citing the need to keep its sources confidential—turned down my appeal to release these deleted materials.[4] Incomplete though they are, the FBI files settle some old questions and raise some new ones regarding the riot itself and the role that local, state, and federal law enforcement officials played in responding to this mob violence.

Although there is no historical literature on the Athens FBI probe, there is a national historiographical context to consider. Over the past half century, historians have explored the role that FBI director J. Edgar Hoover and the bureau played in civil rights struggles across the South and nationally and have cast both in a very negative light. Such leading historians as David J. Garrow, Kenneth O'Reilly, and Athan Theoharis have argued that Hoover's social and political conservatism, segregationist preferences, obsessive anti-Communism, and racism led the FBI to undermine the civil rights movement. Hoover had his agents spy on and use dirty tricks to harass civil rights leaders, including Martin Luther King Jr. The FBI director sought to convince several of the presidents he served that the civil rights movement and some of its leaders included dangerous subversives, and he showed virtually no interest in meeting the bureau's legal obligation to protect movement activists from unlawful, violent, racist attacks. Indeed, if one classic image emerges from this historiography, it is that of the callous FBI agent in the Deep South, who stood around watching and taking notes while, right before his eyes, segregationist thugs beat up voter registration workers.[5]

The FBI's dismal historical reputation with regard to the civil rights struggle would lead one to expect very little from the bureau's investigation of the Athens riot. Indeed, in his landmark study *"Racial Matters": The FBI's Secret File on Black America, 1960–1972*, Kenneth O'Reilly's estimate of the value of such FBI investigations could not have been lower:

> Bureau agents investigated thousands of skirmishes between movement troops and the segregationist resistance and to describe one of these investigations is to convey a sense of them all. Federal agents stood by, to all appearances allied through their own studied neutrality, with the enemies of black people rather than with those who risked their lives to demand justice, dignity, and a fair share of the democracy that white America always seemed to be celebrating.... Federal policemen seemed to encourage [segregationist] brutalities by their refusal to protect [civil rights workers] in the first place or pursue justice after the fact.[6]

Even had FBI agents on the scene wanted to mount a tough-minded and thorough investigation of racist violence, these agents, according to O'Reilly, would have been handicapped by Hoover's policies on such investigations. Most notable among these was what O'Reilly terms the FBI's "disclaimer policy," a standing directive to FBI agents that before beginning a civil rights investigation they inform the public that they were launching their investigation "not because they wanted to but because they were told to." This contrasted, of course, with the image of FBI agents as superefficient G-men who relentlessly tracked down bank robbers and kidnappers. As O'Reilly put it, the Justice Department's "Civil Rights Division wanted G-men" to hunt down violent racists, but instead "Hoover sent over clock punchers who [because of the bureau's disclaimer policy] apologized before asking any white person a question in a voting rights or other civil rights case."[7]

The weight of the evidence that historians such as O'Reilly have arrayed against Hoover and the FBI is so formidable that the bureau's record on civil rights is really beyond redemption. The history of the FBI's investigation in Athens cannot even begin to rehabilitate Hoover or his bureau's reputation with regard to civil rights. Nonetheless the politics of that investigation suggest that historians such as O'Reilly, who focus upon FBI policy and the bureau's internal history and national impact, have not been sufficiently sensitive to the way an FBI investigation into racial violence might look to people in a small Southern town. He may thus have underestimated the deterrent effect that such an investigation could have on whites who might otherwise have been inclined toward continuing acts of racial violence.

Chronology is of critical importance in understanding the Athens case and why the FBI investigation there does not fit neatly into O'Reilly's interpretative framework. If segregationists in Athens in 1961 knew what we now know about FBI director J. Edgar Hoover's hostility to the civil rights movement, they would not have felt at all threatened by the FBI's riot probe. But January 1961 was still such an early time in civil rights history that the militant opponents of integration in Georgia did not yet know that for them the FBI was more friend than foe. The FBI probe at UGA preceded all those events that familiarized the American public with the FBI director's (and many of his agents') antipathy toward the civil rights movement. FBI agents came down to investigate the riot on the Athens campus months before the freedom rides and voter registration drives of the Kennedy years in which FBI failure to protect civil rights workers became a public issue; three years before Hoover publicly feuded with Martin Luther King Jr.; and more than a decade before the full range of the FBI's spying and dirty tricks against King and other civil rights leaders and organizations became public information.[8]

With respect to public perceptions of the FBI, then, Athens students, like most Americans—both Black and white—still lived in an age of innocence in January 1961. It was early enough for both segregationists and integrationists alike to be awed by the FBI's old G-men image: the heroic government agents who "would engage gun-toting gangsters [and] search out every detail needed to make a case against" lawbreakers.[9] Since UGA's segregationist rioters had broken the law, it was natural for them to worry that an agency famed for enforcing the law would bring them to justice and that these expert federal spies and investigators were watching their every move. This was an assumption shared by civil rights partisans, such as the *Richmond Afro-American*, whose account of the FBI's arrival at UGA made it sound as if the cavalry had come to the rescue: "Waves of FBI agents swarmed over the campus questioning segregationist leaders" and restoring "calm" to a riot-torn campus by "put[ting] the fear of God in" the segregationist students.[10]

The specter of FBI agents coming to their university town was sufficiently haunting to make an immediate impression on UGA students. The *Red and Black*, UGA's student newspaper, quickly took note of the G-men, reporting that they had begun to "comb the campus seeking information on any anti-integration demonstration." The student paper also ran an editorial cartoon depicting two male students being snooped on by spies hiding in garbage cans and trees and peeking out windows. The FBI's presence signaled at least the possibility that segregationist rioting (past or future) might yield federal prosecution. Having been questioned by agents, key student leaders who opposed integration knew that they could be held personally accountable for their role in rowdyism on campus. This had a chilling effect on segregationist organizing, which helped to prevent any renewal of mob violence at UGA when the federal court reinstated Hunter and Holmes as Georgia students in mid-January.[11]

The political significance of the FBI probe was compounded by the way the university administration responded to it. Chastened by the riot and upset by the damage it had done to the university's reputation, the administration banned segregationist demonstrations, threatening to suspend or expel individual students or student organizations that participated in any such protests—whether violent or not. In the midst of this new hard-line policy, UGA officials welcomed the FBI probe as part of the crackdown on lawlessness; they helped to relay to students the impression that the federal agents were hot on the trail of the riot's ringleaders and that the FBI presence made it impossible for militants to get away with any more rowdyism. For example, one UGA official told the press that "the FBI intends to prosecute students who have been making inflammatory statements 'inciting to riot.'" In a postriot statement to the press, dean of students Joseph Williams made it sound as if the FBI was investigating not only the riot but any ongoing segregationist activity, and would question "any student making inflammatory statements" (which unbeknown to the students was an exaggeration since the federal probe was focusing almost exclusively on the riot).[12] In short, student perceptions of the FBI probe were shaped not only by what the agency said and did but also by the way local authorities interpreted that probe—and they chose to take it very seriously indeed.

The impact of the FBI probe in Athens was all the more intense because of the way it contrasted with the initial response of state police authority to the segregationist turmoil on campus. The leaders of the riot had told their fellow students that they could resist integration without fear of reprisals from state law enforcement officials; they claimed that they had obtained assurances from high-ranking Georgia political leaders that the state patrol would not be mobilized against segregationist protesters. And in fact, this turned out to be no idle boast. Despite their proximity to the Athens campus, Georgia State Patrol officers failed to arrive at the riot scene until the disorder was over, leaving it to the understaffed Athens police and UGA officials to battle the rioters. The attorney general's quick announcement of the FBI probe, and the arrival immediately thereafter of FBI agents on the scene, signaled that the laxness and neglect of duty that had characterized the politicized state patrol—and that had emboldened student rioters—could no longer assure immunity for student agitators since the feds apparently could not be controlled by local or state politics. Once the FBI had come to Athens, one heard no more talk of student immunity from prosecution.[13]

Contrary to O'Reilly's claims, neither the FBI reports nor the press coverage of its investigation in Athens left the impression that bureau agents were apologizing in any public way for their riot probe. It is true that Hoover instructed FBI agents to tell the press that the Athens investigation had come at the request of the Justice Department, but this neither sounded nor was it perceived in Georgia as apologetic. Indeed, the student riot leaders felt they got no sympathy from the FBI agents who interviewed them.[14] To the contrary, the dominant note in those interviews was fear, as students—worried about federal prosecution—made defensive statements, obscuring their unlawful behavior wherever possible, and tensed up in the face of the intimidating presence of these inquisitive federal agents. These FBI interviews began with the agents issuing not an apology but rather a warning that anything the students said could be used against them in a court of law. As one student explained, "They don't tell you too much. They ask you all of the questions."[15]

Had it been Hoover's idea, the prompt announcement of an FBI probe into the Athens riot might lead one, at least in this one case, to reverse O'Reilly's negative assessment of J. Edgar Hoover's civil rights record. But the FBI director played no role in the decision to launch the investigation of racial violence at UGA. That decision came from the US Department of Justice's Civil Rights Division and from the attorney general. Hoover "was otherwise occupied on that day" when the Athens investigation was launched.[16]

On the other hand, in the Athens case, the FBI director did not come across as the kind of relentless foe of the civil rights movement that O'Reilly portrays and that Hoover certainly would become as the movement took to more daring direct-action campaigns and mass mobilizations by the end of the Kennedy administration. Assistant attorney general Harold R. Tyler, head of the Civil Rights Division at the time of the Athens investigation, recalled that the FBI director "reacted favorably to our request" for that probe. In the FBI files, Hoover did not appear to be dragging his feet about allowing the FBI to mount an investigation into the riot. In fact, his initial instructions to his agents in Georgia implied that this could be a serious and careful probe of the racial violence in Athens. Hoover ordered the "interviewing of city officials, police authorities, and officials of UGA for information as to those responsible for the mob action on January 11, 1961 . . . as well as tracing the origin of Klan-type literature that was distributed. Interviews should be conducted to determine the individuals directing the students and to determine the identities of the Klan or other officials who were responsible for the adults' participation in the demonstration. Interviews should be conducted with . . . the two colored students . . . for any information they have as to the identities of any persons who had endeavored to intimidate, threaten, or assault them to prevent their exercising a right to attend school under the order of a Federal Court."[17]

According to Tyler, by the end of the Eisenhower administration Hoover and the FBI showed a real dedication to bringing to justice those who provoked and perpetrated racist violence: "Contrary to views of many persons . . . the FBI had come around particularly in 1960 . . . to responding quickly and vigorously to civil rights confrontations or crises. In 1960 there had been a number of confrontations, particularly in Georgia, Louisiana, and Mississippi. The FBI had come to realize that these matters were serious and, as part of their jurisdiction under federal law, matters which they had to address with alacrity and diligence."[18]

Since Tyler headed the Civil Rights Division, his positive assessment of Hoover and the FBI deserves a respectful hearing. However, in light of Hoover and the FBI's overall performance in other civil rights cases as well as in the Athens case, Tyler (perhaps to compensate for their relentlessly negative depiction by revisionist historians) does seem to have exaggerated their interest and quality of work in these cases. John Doar, who succeeded Tyler as head of the Civil Rights Division, and who was involved in many more civil rights cases than Tyler, coauthored a study, "Performance of the FBI in Investigating Violations of Federal Laws Protecting the Right to Vote—1960–1967," which was far more critical of Hoover and the FBI on civil rights. Doar's study was more nuanced than O'Reilly's in that it acknowledged that at times the FBI did good work. However, Doar found that "sometimes the [FBI] interviews would be uneven and it appeared to us that little supervision of the individual agents' work was being done in Washington." Doar reported that since Hoover and FBI headquarters failed to push agents to ask the toughest questions and follow the appropriate leads in civil rights cases, the US Department of Justice's Civil Rights Division had to step in and do so: "We devised a guarantee of good performance standards in conducting the interviews. We became very careful in drafting FBI memos and requesting interviews with white witnesses."[19]

Doar's assessment of the FBI's overall civil rights record has great relevance to the Athens case. The FBI investigation of the riot was prompt and serious enough to scare segregationist student militants and thus deter further racial violence at UGA. FBI agents interviewed more than fifty witnesses and participants in the riot, including Athens police officers, segregationist student organizers, faculty, reporters, and Klansmen. But the FBI probe did not receive the type of attention and supervision from Hoover or FBI headquarters that would have been necessary to yield sufficient evidence for federal prosecution. For example, the agents' interviews with witnesses from the riot scene suggested that high-ranking Georgia politicians had promised student militants that they would keep the state patrol away from the riot and provide students with bail should they be arrested by local police. Yet the agents did not follow up these leads by promptly questioning officials in the political establishment about their alleged collusion with the rioters. Nor did Hoover or any other FBI supervisor push the agents to explore these important questions. It was left to John Doar himself to oversee the Athens case. A month after the preliminary investigation, Doar, who had recently (in the opening days of the Kennedy administration) become the acting head of the Civil Rights Division, sent the FBI a memo pressing for further investigation of why the state patrol had not come to the riot scene and who had promised and delivered bond for the rioters. It then took Hoover almost three weeks to provide his agents with appropriate, though not particularly penetrating or comprehensive, instructions for this follow-up work.[20]

As Doar's action suggests, the FBI's preliminary probe had turned up several pieces of evidence indicating that state politicians had encouraged lawless behavior by segregationist students. One eyewitness told the FBI that as the disturbance began outside Hunter's dormitory, protest organizers shouted, "Don't worry about getting into trouble with the University. We have word from Atlanta that they can't touch you and the State Patrol isn't going to help." Other rioters had heard protest leaders assert that "if they were expelled from the University or arrested by the local police department that politicians in Atlanta, Georgia would take care of the situation." A student who had attended a planning meeting for the mobbing of Hunter's dormitory went so far as to name names, informing the FBI that "one of the top leaders of the students in opposition to integration . . . stated 'I've been to Watkinsville and spoke to [Georgia agriculture department commissioner] Phil Campbell, who informed me that people taking part in the demonstration would not be punished.'"[21]

Perhaps the most startling evidence concerning the relations between student agitators and segregationist political leaders came as riot leader John Thomas Cochran, under the strain of FBI questioning, gave away just how close that relationship had been. Cochran, the most forceful public spokesman among student rioters, turned out to have been in contact with one of the state's top segregationist politicians (whose name was deleted by an FBI censor) in the weeks before and after the riot. Cochran "admitted he made several such calls" to this man. Later in his interview he "finally said that he had been in contact with" him every day of the week leading up to the riot and had even talked with him just before his FBI interview on January 14.[22] Cochran tried to make these daily phone calls sound innocent and denied that he was getting advised as to how to resist desegregation. But it strains credulity to think that the student leader wasn't at least receiving daily encouragement from this off-campus source for the militant protest that he was helping to organize.

Had the FBI dug harder for corroborating evidence, it seems entirely possible that the kind of collusion and incitement to riot suggested in the FBI report could have led to prosecution. But the follow-up report that the FBI made at Doar's request was superficial; it consisted of little more than denials by state officials of any such collusion—reflecting what was almost certainly a Georgia cover-up that the federal investigators lacked either the skills or the will to overcome. Of course, Doar could have sent the FBI back to Georgia for a third investigation. It is not entirely clear why this was not done. Perhaps with the riot over and no further campus violence in succeeding months, neither Doar nor anyone else in the Kennedy administration saw the need to stir things up via a controversial prosecution just as the situation was calming down in Georgia.

To this day, no state official has come forward to detail either the collusion with student militants or the political shenanigans that led to the failure of the state patrol to arrive in a timely fashion at the riot scene. To the contrary, in my oral history interview with Phil Campbell, he vehemently denied rendering any assistance to the rioters. The former agriculture commissioner insisted that he counseled student foes of integration to obey the law and that he knew nothing about any decision within the Vandiver administration to keep the state patrol away from the riot scene. Campbell could not explain, however, why the student who named him would have lied to the FBI.[23] Even if we accept Campbell's denial, we are left with a mystery: If all the Georgia officials were telling the truth, and no one colluded to keep state patrolmen away, then why did they go AWOL when the riot erupted? This was a crime that the FBI could not solve, and whose perpetrator (or perpetrators) went unpunished.

Although never used by prosecutors, the files generated by the FBI investigation are of historical value because they contain evidence that calls into question some of the self-serving myths that arose in the wake of the riot outside Charlayne Hunter's dormitory. Several have become a part of the folklore of white Georgia, as the local culture sought to explain away this ugly racist riot. To understand the origins of these myths one must first recognize the enormous embarrassment and humiliation that the riot caused for Georgia students, alumni, and local officials. The riot was front page news from coast to coast, and it was covered extensively on network news. Political cartoonists, newspaper editorial writers, and TV and radio news commentators denounced the incident and depicted the riotous students as uncouth, racist bullies. Bad as the riot itself was, the negative press over it was compounded by the national wire service photos of a tearful Charlayne Hunter, clutching her statue of the Madonna and being led away from campus by police after being suspended from UGA, allegedly for her own safety. Here was Hunter, the target of racial violence, being suspended, while her racist tormentors (at least initially) went unpunished. The injustice of the situation was so transparent that it elicited scorching condemnation. In the face of this hostile response, many UGA students, alumni, and friends of the university sought to free Georgia students from responsibility for the riot and blamed instead either outside agitators or spontaneous emotion (as opposed to a criminal student conspiracy) for the violence.[24]

The outside agitators most frequently cited in this kind of blame-shifting were racist nonstudents, particularly Ku Klux Klan (KKK) members. One popular line of thought was that one should not blame Georgia students for the riot since this violence was the result of a KKK plot in which UGA students were mere pawns. The FBI files attest that the presence of a handful of Klansmen and other nonstudents at the riot scene made a bad situation worse, but they do not imply that the KKK planned or led the riot. In their FBI interviews, Athens police at the scene implicated students as the source of most of the violence that night. Several officers were able to name specific students as leaders in the riot. But obviously the presence of these adult hate mongers added to the tension. The police told the FBI that the difficulty of handling the riot scene was compounded by the presence of nonstudents in the mob. A few of the police officers seemed to believe that had the crowd on January 11 been exclusively students—as it had been in nonviolent demonstrations earlier in the desegregation crisis—that it would have shown some deference toward police and university authorities. Campus officials might have been better able to calm students down if the rioters had not been egged on by nonstudents. And several policemen reported that one of the heaviest bombardments of rocks and other objects came from the area in which the Klansmen congregated.[25]

Although the FBI documents on the KKK's involvement have been heavily censored, most suggest that the Klan only joined in already-organized student resistance to integration at UGA and did not itself mastermind that resistance. One FBI source advised that "U.S. Klan officials had nothing to do with planning [the violent] demonstration" at UGA.[26] The bureau did have one unconfirmed report that a Klansman had appeared in a UGA fraternity house prior to the riot to encourage segregationist student activism, but there was nothing specific about a KKK role in actually organizing the riot.[27] The few segregationist student leaders who admitted Klan contacts prior to the riot portrayed those connections as superficial: in one case this consisted merely of being notified by telephone that the KKK planned to join the students in their January 11 demonstration; in others it consisted of obtaining and observing the distribution of Klan and other white supremacist literature in a local restaurant.[28]

Such testimony carries added weight when one considers that it would have been in the interests of students facing FBI questioning to shift the blame for the violence to a nonstudent group such as the KKK, and yet they did not do so. Even the strongest indication of Klan connections to segregationist students in the FBI files suggests that a student activist from UGA had invited Klan involvement in the Athens demonstration—requesting that both white supremacist state board of regents member Roy Harris and "an unknown representative of the Ku Klux Klan come to Athens *to assist them* [i.e. UGA students] in fighting desegregation of the University."[29] [emphasis added] The point here is that it was university students who led and initiated the resistance to integration in Athens, and any KKK role took the form of assistance to students already determined to act.

In the riot's aftermath the KKK thought it was in its own best political interests to boast publicly and claim a leadership role in the riot.[30] But despite the Klan's public bragging about such leadership, a KKK informant's report to the FBI attests that in its own meetings the Klan did not credit itself with orchestrating the riot. In this report, C. F. Craig, the grand dragon of the Klan, was depicted discussing the "situation at the state university, Athens, Georgia," where six Klansmen had been arrested "as a result of trying to stop the integration of this school." Craig contemplated a possible "underground" role at UGA and other schools in which the Klan would secretly funnel money to segregationist picketers. But he gave no indication that students had yet acted or would in the future agree to serve as this type of "good front" for the Klan in its drive "to keep the 'niggers' out of the schools and eating places." This report is especially chilling in its discussion of violence and suggests that Klan-led actions against desegregation would have been far bloodier than the student-led riot of January 11. Craig said that if integration proceeded at UGA and other educational institutions, "the only alternative is to kill the 'niggers,' starting with the students going to the schools and then the parents."[31]

The FBI documents also undermine the white Georgia myth of the riot as a wholly spontaneous event that evolved not out of a criminal conspiracy but rather out of youthful emotions of the moment. This might best be dubbed the basketball myth because it builds upon the fact that the rioters began to gather after a loss on the basketball court to Georgia Tech and then laid siege on Charlayne Hunter's dormitory. This view of the riot was presented to me at some length in a letter from a UGA alumnus who had been at the riot scene in 1961:

> There was a basketball game in old Woodruff Hall that night, and it was against the hated Georgia Tech team, which was heavily favored. Georgia played a great game, and was ahead by one point with only one second remaining and with Tech having the ball at the opposite end of the floor.

When time resumed, Tech threw the ball just short of mid-court to the great Roger Kaiser, who tossed the ball upward while on his knee—and it went in, giving Tech a one point victory. There was a stunned silence, and then someone said "Let's go get the ("N"-word)"! Everybody stormed out and up the hill to the dorm where Charlayne Hunter was to be housed. Most of us just went along to see what would happen and because it was an exciting event. Of course it turned ugly, with bricks thrown and police tear-gassing the students, which made them madder than before and caused some bystanders to join in. My point is that I do not believe to this day that the riot would have occurred if not for the basketball game. If Georgia had won, it would not have happened.[32]

Even without the benefit of the FBI files, one can see some logical problems with this explanation of the riot's origins. Why, for example, should a close loss in an athletic contest between two all-white teams lead anyone to participate in a racist march on a Black student's dormitory? But let us assume for the moment that the basketball loss contributed to the ugly mood on campus and accept that some rank-and-file students went to the riot scene spontaneously out of fury over the fact that the Bulldogs were on a losing streak on both kinds of courts—legal and basketball (or as one student put it, "We got beat by Georgia Tech and we got beat by the niggers").[33] This view of the riot as a spontaneous outburst sparked by a basketball loss ignores the whole question of the leadership necessary to convert a basketball audience into a racist crowd. In fact, segregationist organizers had made advanced preparation to stir up trouble after the game no matter who won. That these organizers came out on the night of the riot with a hand-painted "Nigger Go Home" banner was only the most visible sign of such advance preparations. Word on campus that day was that students were making dates for the night game and riot to follow. Several of the students questioned by the FBI admitted that they knew in advance about plans for a post–basketball game march on Hunter's dormitory. The FBI investigation revealed that student militants had distributed firecrackers the day preceding the riot to prepare for a rowdy segregationist display. FBI documents also show that the Athens police chief was so certain that a riot would follow the game (no matter who won) that he went to the dean of students requesting that the contest be canceled—a request that was turned down on the grounds that too many tickets had already been sold. This, along with the close contacts segregationist student leaders had developed with state political leaders to prevent the state patrol from coming to the riot scene, and even those fleeting student contacts with the

Klan, leaves no doubt that, at least for these leaders, the riot was a planned and not a spontaneous event.[34]

One ought not underestimate segregationist student organizers and how well they knew their campus. They understood that on this otherwise apolitical campus, with no tradition of mass political mobilization, athletic contests were the one place where huge numbers of students congregated. So if one wanted to attract a large crowd of students to a racist march under the cover of nightfall in January, a basketball game was not merely the best place but really the only place to commence. Actually, from almost the start of the integration crisis, segregationist student organizers made clever use of the largest athletic events of this season (basketball games) as occasions to recruit anti-integration crowds.[35] Given this context, the connection between the athletic event and the racial mobilization emerges more as a consequence of intelligent planning than as a sign of genuine or innocent spontaneity.[36]

Another of the myths that the FBI documents puncture concerns the riot's dimensions. Some white Georgia alumni minimize the significance of the riot by depicting it as a rather mild and not very violent affair, the racial equivalent of a panty-raid, which was blown out of proportion by the national news media. Here the riot itself is often conflated with an event that occurred earlier in the desegregation crisis when a CBS News cameraman, arriving late on the scene of a UGA anti-integration demonstration, got students to reenact their racist chants for the TV news. Thus, this obviously inappropriate media behavior before the riot allowed white Georgians to imagine that the riot itself was largely the figment of the news media's imagination.[37]

Even some of the historical accounts of the riot have tended to play down its violence. Calvin Trillin's account of UGA's desegregation crisis in his book *An Education in Georgia*, for example, stressed the timidity of the mob outside Charlayne Hunter's dormitory: "It had been a nasty riot, but the group courage that sometimes comes to mobs had never infected it. Although the students could have stormed the dormitory several times without meeting any effective resistance, they never did."[38] Similarly, Thomas Dyer's brief account of the riot in his bicentennial history of the university renders the disturbance less ominous by suggesting that its violence was directed at property ("The group threw bricks at Myers Hall") rather than at persons.[39]

The extensive FBI interviews with Athens police who had been on duty during the riot suggest that both alumni memories and historical accounts of the riot have understated the dangers police encountered at the riot scene, where it was not only dorm windows but police officers themselves who became targets of the angry mob. According to the police interviews recorded by the FBI, on at least two separate occasions when police tried to arrest protesters who seemed to be leading the riot, the crowd found some of that "group courage" Trillin failed to see and sought to physically prevent the police from making arrests. In the first instance, the arresting officer was hit on the side of the head with a rock and lost control of the protester he was trying to arrest. And in the second case, the crowd tried to grab an arrested protester away from the police. Almost all the police officers stressed that the rocks were being thrown not only at the dormitory but at them as they sought both to disperse the crowd and prevent it from rushing the dorm. This led to the injuring of several officers and prodded one to report that "it appeared the students were trying to enter the dormitory, and he believes the only thing that saved the police during this demonstration was the tear gas that was used."[40]

Of course, merely because the officers emphasized the hazards of the riot scene in their FBI interviews does not mean that they were telling the truth. Less than a handful of Athens police were seriously injured at the scene. More police injuries could be expected if the crowd had been extremely violent. In interviews with fellow (and especially federal) law enforcement officials, Athens police may have exaggerated the dangers of the riot scene, with an implicit message of their own courage under fire. Yet the facts that the riot raged for almost two hours, Athens police repeatedly requested reinforcements from the Georgia State Patrol, and they needed tear gas and fire hoses to tame the crowd suggest that they felt overwhelmed by the crowd's size and violence. This was certainly what one volunteer who aided the police during the riot conveyed in a confidential letter to the FBI. He recounted that

> I was called by a friend that was on the scene and was concerned that things were about to get out of hand.... Riding directly to City Hall I found Mayor Snow and several city officials rounding up tear gas and police equipment to send to the scene. One of the gentlemen there took my offer of service and ordered me to take as much tear gas as I could handle and deliver it to [Athens Police] Chief Hardy on Ag Hill. I rode directly toward Ag Hill.... Chief Hardy was spotted and I started passing out tear gas at his instruction. When the gas was all unloaded I looked for the first time at the crowd of people, and immediately realized that this was no crowd of students out for "kicks." Shortly a number of large rocks came out of the crowd at the policemen and their equipment. Police cars were pounded, windows broken and bodys [sic] smashed. Police then used the tear gas. The crowd fought back and the rock throwing increased;

numbers of policemen being hit and injured. At least two men were injured seriously in attempting to arrest the most violent of individuals. Since City Police were the only ones engaged I was asked by an officer to go to the State Patrol and get help and more tear gas. What can a small city police force, ill equipped to handle a violent mob that comes from miles around, do except fight back and get carried away on a stretcher?[41]

The police interviews recorded by the FBI reveal as much about the Athens police force as they do about the riot scene itself. The traditional image of the small-town Southern police as poorly run, unprofessional, and infested with white supremacists bears little resemblance to the Athens police force whose officers spoke to the FBI. Their memories of the riot scene, which they shared with the FBI, were fresh, vivid, and very detailed. In fact, the transcripts of these interviews capture the reality of the riot scene in far more depth than most of the press accounts. The Athens police had excellent intelligence on the segregationist militants. From top to bottom the police knew in advance that a racial protest was scheduled to occur after the basketball game and also that this demonstration would likely be violent. Athens mayor Ralph Snow had advised the police department that he had been tipped off to the fact that the KKK was planning to join the rally. And the police acted upon this information, seeking unsuccessfully to get UGA to cancel the basketball game and informing every officer at the beginning of the night shift of their likely riot duty. Even desk officers were told they would be pressed into service, and a paddy wagon was readied for use as Athens's small thirty-nine-man police department did all that it could to prepare for the riot.[42]

At the riot scene itself the police worked hard to restore order. The entire Athens force was mobilized against the mob. When it became clear that the swelling crowd of 1,500 to 2,000 had gotten out of control, tear gas was deployed to disperse the crowd, along with fire hoses and a police car driven through the mob. This must certainly go down as a rarity in civil rights era history. Our images of the South in that era are of fire hoses and a white police force used against integrationists and African Americans. But here was a white Southern police department suppressing a segregationist mob of whites. All that stood between this mob and Charlayne Hunter's dormitory (in which it must be recalled she was huddling, very much in harm's way, during this frightening assault) was the Athens Police Department (and a handful of university and town officials and firefighters), which at length prevailed.[43]

The contrast between the response of the Athens police and the state patrol to the riot could not have been starker. While the police made advanced preparations for the riot and battled a violent mob, state patrol officers lounged around in their nearby office, drinking coffee and smoking cigarettes. Despite the fact that Athens's mayor and police chief personally appeared at the state patrol office requesting that state troopers reinforce the Athens police, they did not show up in force until the riot had ended. The FBI documents confirm press accounts of the patrol refusing to intervene until verbally authorized to do so by governor Ernest Vandiver—authorization that came much too late.[44]

It is far more difficult to explain than to describe these contrasting police responses to the riot. The FBI documents are not of much use here. It seems likely, however, that politics account for the fact that the Athens police force did their duty that night while the state patrol did not. The state patrol was controlled by politicians associated with Governor Vandiver, who had come into office making the truculent segregationist pledge that "no, not one" Black student would be integrated with whites in Georgia's schools during his tenure.[45] Although of course segregationist in their sympathies, Athens politicians in 1961 had not boxed themselves into a corner with so simple-minded a pledge and were free to let their moderate inclinations prevail. Mayor Ralph Snow, police chief E. E. Hardy, and UGA officials, led by the formidable dean William Tate, also had a local allegiance to the university and an aversion to allowing anyone—even segregationist militants—to damage it.[46]

The FBI's student interviews were in some ways informative and illuminating. As we have seen, the agents got students to admit to colluding with state politicians, engaging in limited contacts with the Klan, and having advanced knowledge of the evening demonstration. These were not insignificant achievements given how guarded and scared the students were during the questioning. However, one comes away from the student interviews as impressed by the FBI's lapses and failures as by its successes. Although the FBI chose well in interviewing some of the riot leaders, especially those who had been arrested, it could obviously have learned more about the genesis of this violent episode had its agents interviewed more students—both leaders and rank-and-file participants in the riot. Only nine UGA students were interviewed. These interviews raised questions about both the organization and ideology of the segregationist resistance on campus, but a second and third round of student interviews were needed to obtain answers to these questions. The FBI failed to do this follow-up work.

Follow-up work was needed, for example, to explore the role that the Demosthenian Society played in planning the riot. One of the riot leaders questioned by the FBI claimed that it was at a meeting of this debating society (which was dominated by militant segregationists from the UGA law school) that initial plans for resisting desegregation were made. This student admitted attending a meeting of more than a hundred students at the society's hall in which this resistance was discussed with all of the leaders of the university's fraternities. It had already been rumored and reported in the press that this meeting was the one where plans were hatched for the riot. The student questioned by the FBI who discussed this meeting claimed that it had confined itself to pondering lawful and nonviolent segregationist protests. It would have been a relatively simple matter to have tested the veracity of these claims about nonviolence by questioning all the fraternity leaders who attended this crucial meeting. But the FBI failed to call these students in for questioning.[47]

The FBI also did not prove itself adept at probing the ideas, motivations, and inspiration for a possible criminal student conspiracy to drive UGA's Black students from campus. The most striking example of this occurred in the FBI questioning of student riot leader Tom Cochran. At the time of the interview with Cochran, the FBI had in its possession a remarkably frank and revealing interview that he had given to a Macon newspaper. Cochran had told the *Macon Telegraph* that he and other segregationist students were aiming at the sort of situation that prevailed in Alabama.

> 'They're integrated at the University of Alabama, legally. . . . But there are no niggers going to school there.' Cochran said he was referring to the Autherine Lucy case in which the female student was finally suspended from Alabama and was unsuccessful in attempts to reenter. Cochran said he was 'in the front lines' at the riotous Wednesday night demonstration outside a women's dormitory where the Negro student, Charlayne Hunter, was staying. He said press accounts attributing the violent demonstration to outsiders and to a small hard core of students were wrong. 'The students started the demonstrations,' Cochran said. 'Everybody knew we had to do it.' He said he had talked earlier to 'several top state officials—I won't name them' and asked the officials what they would do if they were in school at Georgia. 'They said, 'Son, I'd be right in there with you.' . . . 'The suspension of the two niggers here was caused by the demonstration. . . . If we caused them to leave one time, we can do it again.'[48]

To its credit, the FBI did, as we saw earlier, get a reluctant Cochran to admit that he had been in almost constant contact with segregationist politicians during UGA's integration crisis. But the FBI missed the significance of Cochran's words with respect to the University of Alabama. Perhaps the agents did not know enough history to understand that the Alabama model, which Cochran had spoken openly about emulating at Georgia, was a violent one. At Tuscaloosa in 1956, violent racist mobs had hounded Autherine Lucy, posing an immediate physical threat to this African American student, literally forcing her to flee the campus and culminating in her suspension and ultimate withdrawal from the university.[49] If one understands this historical model, it becomes a rather urgent matter to determine how many other segregationist student leaders were guided by it. Was Cochran alone? Or were most of the other UGA militants also inspired by the resistance to Lucy and planning to import to Georgia the kind of racial mobbing that had kept Alabama segregated in 1956? Neither Cochran nor the other students interviewed by the FBI were asked these crucial questions.

In the final analysis, the FBI's record in the Athens case was uneven. The investigation was sufficiently serious to intimidate segregationist students. And in this sense it leads one to question the conclusions of revisionist historians, such as Kenneth O'Reilly, who see a single anti–civil rights movement pattern to all the FBI investigations into racial violence in the South during the 1960s.[50] But, as John Doar suggests with regard to many of the voting rights and voter intimidation cases, the FBI agents did not push hard enough on some of the critical questions needed to solve the Athens case—leaving some ambiguity about the nature, dimensions, and composition of what was almost certainly a criminal conspiracy to assault Charlayne Hunter's dormitory. Nor did the FBI director give his agents the kind of supervision needed to recognize their oversights and follow up on key leads. These flaws not only stood in the way of prosecution but also make it almost impossible for historians to write a definitive history of this riot. We still do not know the identities of most of the students nor the number and names of the student organizations responsible for planning this violence. Since these were lawless acts, no participant in their planning has published a word about them. And none have been willing to speak to historians about these events. Lacking the power and legal authority to compel testimony about the riot from its leaders, historians, unfortunately, may never be able to fill in the blanks left by the FBI's riot probe.

Postscript to Chapter Three

The "G-Men in Georgia" article had its roots in the University of Georgia desegregation crisis research I had done on the *Red and Black*, the university's student newspaper. The *Red and Black* ran a cartoon (reprinted in the photo gallery of this book) evoking student awareness of, and anxiety about, the FBI investigation of the segregationist riot of January 11.[1] The cartoon reflected UGA students' concern that the FBI was watching them. It surprised me that no historian who had read this, or other press references to the FBI role at UGA in 1961, had consulted the records of the FBI investigation of the UGA riot. Since I had, back in graduate school, learned from Athan Theoharis, the great historian of the FBI, how to use the Freedom of Information Act to obtain FBI files, and suspected that they would add to our understanding of the riot, I requested and obtained the FBI files on UGA's segregationist riot, which served as the central source for my "G-Men in Georgia" article.

To say that my research on the FBI investigation of the riot at UGA surprised me is an understatement. Historians of the civil rights movement had emphasized that the FBI and its powerful director J. Edgar Hoover were hostile to the movement owing to their antiradicalism, racism, and deep connections to white supremacist Southern police forces. And movement veterans were bitterly critical of the passive role the FBI had played in the freedom rides and Deep South Black voter registration efforts, doing little or nothing to protect civil rights workers from Klan violence—failing, for instance, to warn freedom riders in Alabama of the advance notice the bureau had of Klan plans for a violent assault upon them—and conducting inept investigations or none at all of many incidents of white supremacist terror. On top of this were Hoover's efforts, first covertly and then publicly, to undermine and discredit Martin Luther King Jr. So I had low expectations of the FBI investigation of the segregationist riot at UGA. But the research led me to see, as my article indicated, that the FBI role at UGA had a surprisingly antiracist impact. This was, as we have seen, because of its timing. UGA's desegregation crisis occurred before the freedom rides, before most of the KKK violence against the historic Southern Black voter registration campaigns of the 1960s, and before Hoover's feud with King had begun. So UGA's segregationist student militants had no idea of the racial politics of Hoover and the FBI or that the FBI investigation of the riot would be half-hearted and fail to result in any federal prosecutions. All they knew was that the vaunted G-men were on their trail, and this instilled a fear in them that any further violence, or even plans for such violence, would place them in legal jeopardy. Thus the appearance of the FBI at Athens in the days following the riot had an antiracist impact in that it had a chilling effect on segregationist student organizing in the riot's wake.

The FBI's files, which were the central source for my account of the bureau's involvement in UGA's desegregation crisis, were so focused on the riot that they did not mention any FBI role in that crisis prior to the riot and its investigation of it—or after that investigation. But the oral history interview with Athens city attorney Judge Barrow, which only became available decades after I published my G-men article, revealed something new: that the FBI had played a role in warning Athens city officials in advance of the riot that racist violence was imminent. Having informants in the Ku Klux Klan, the FBI warned Athens Mayor Snow "that the Ku Klux Klan was taking an interest" in the UGA resistance to integration and "there would be difficulty that night [of the campus riot]."[2] This FBI role in seeking to prepare local officials for the worst led Barrow to praise the bureau and Athens resident FBI agent Bob Cain for their role in the crisis, a highly unusual role for an organization that often was so lethargic about combatting racist violence in the Deep South. And after the investigation, once Holmes had been reinstated and was back on campus, the FBI apparently played a positive role in securing his safety, as Holmes recalled: "When I came back I was protected by the FBI. I was escorted by the FBI for my first 4 or 5 weeks on campus. They picked me up in the morning; they drove me to class; they picked me up after class and took me back."[3]

Since my G-men article was focused on the FBI investigation of the riot, there was no space in it to explore the equal, or perhaps even more surprising, active role of UGA's administration in bringing militant segregationist organizing to a halt on campus. Since this was a belated effort, which began only after the disgraceful riot of January 11 had damaged UGA's reputation, one would be quite justified in characterizing this as too little, too late. Still, it is a part of the desegregation crisis that has not been recognized, and perhaps its crowning irony that a university administration whose unethical segregationist actions paved the way for racist campus organizing and a segregationist riot would, in a way that paralleled the impact of the FBI investigation, belatedly but effectively deploy its disciplinary power to prevent further segregationist student organizing and violence. It is to this UGA administration role, as well as the distorted and self-serving historical memory of the desegregation crisis that the Aderhold administration promoted, that we now turn.

The UGA administration's handling of the desegregation crisis, which impacted the student response to the crisis, was uneven at best. And though there is some useful information in the FBI files on the UGA administration's actions in January 1961, since the main focus of the bureau's investigation was on the rioters, it did not offer anything resembling a coherent narrative or analysis of how the campus administration handled segregationist student unrest and violence. Initially critics in the news media and, later in the crisis, critics on the right in the Georgia legislature, saw the UGA administration's crisis management efforts as little short of disastrous. The UGA administration's response to desegregation can be best understood if it is divided into three phases: 1) massive resistance (which was by far its longest phase); 2) ambivalent compliance; and 3) decisive (but belated) action to prevent further segregationist campus violence.

As was discussed in chapter 1, the massive resistance phase found the UGA administration, in alliance with Georgia's segregationist state government, actively opposing the attempts of Black applicants to integrate the university. This phase began in 1950 when Horace Ward applied to UGA's law school. Over the course of the next six and a half years, UGA's administration used all kinds of administrative delays, doctored admissions standards, a dishonest interview process, and ultimately went to court in its successful effort to deny Ward's admission.[4] UGA's administration used similar tactics in seeking to prevent Hamilton Holmes and Charlayne Hunter from being admitted as UGA's first African American undergraduates from 1959 to 1961, adding the novel and specious claim that the university was so overcrowded that "its limited facilities" and lack of dorm space necessitated turning down these Black students. This time, however, UGA's segregationist administration lost in court, in January 1961. But the university did not relent and even convinced Judge Bootle to stay his integration order on January 9, 1961. And when US circuit court judge E. P. Tuttle promptly overruled Bootle, ordering the immediate integration of the university, UGA again appealed, this time to US Supreme Court justice Hugo Black. But UGA quickly lost this bid as the high court refused to overturn Tuttle's order.[5]

The second phase of the UGA administration's response to desegregation began just as its massive resistance phase was in its final days in early January 1961. This new phase was provoked by the threat of segregationist violence on campus. Bootle's initial desegregation order on January 6—as we saw in chapter 2—sparked an angry segregationist demonstration on campus and in downtown Athens. This was an ominous sign. Indeed, UGA's student foes of integration had gotten off to a faster start than had their predecessors at the University of Alabama in 1956. While Alabama's segregationist student mobs would ultimately drive off Autherine Lucy, that campus's first Black student, these white Alabama students had not demonstrated against Lucy until she registered for her first class. But UGA's segregationist students had managed to hold anti-integration protests before Holmes and Hunter even arrived at the campus in Athens to begin the registration process.[6]

The initial segregationist demonstrations indicated that there was enough racial hatred swirling around on campus to yield violence. The UGA administration seemed to recognize this volatility and took some action to head off trouble. Dean of students Joseph Williams convened an emergency meeting of about a hundred student leaders, urging them to see to it that their classmates behaved "in a manner which befits ladies and gentlemen." He warned against outside agitators and others "who will try to cause trouble."[7] This suggests that the traditionally segregationist UGA administration was coming to the realization that—due to the federal court order—the desegregation of the university was probably inevitable and that the students should be prodded to see that violent resistance to integration was futile and would damage UGA's reputation. But the UGA administration was sending contradictory signals on desegregation, litigating against it until the bitter end while starting in a limited way to prepare students for compliance. On the compliance side, Williams soon displayed weakness and ineptitude (if not outright collusion with those planning the riot) by refusing to cancel a basketball game set for the evening of Hunter and Holmes's first day of classes, despite the fact that local police, students, and others had warned him that segregationist militants were planning to use the game (with its big crowd) as a staging area for a racist riot.[8] Nor did Williams act to criticize, let alone ban, ugly segregationist student demonstrations of the sort that had already erupted when Bootle's integration order was announced.

The dean's ambivalence was further displayed on the night of the riot outside Charlayne Hunter's dormitory when, instead of disciplining the segregationist rioters, he suspended Hunter and Holmes, supposedly for their own safety—though by the time the suspension was announced the riot had ended and neither of them was in any imminent danger.[9] This is why the mayor and city attorney of Athens both publicly objected to the suspensions, as Barrow, Athens's city attorney, later explained: "We protested vigorously. We had fought, we'd had people hurt, we'd had several hundred dollars worth of damage done, and we'd won, and now they were going to undo the whole business and have it to do over again. And we felt so strongly that it was a mistake to yield to a mob that had already been dispersed that we felt like it was our responsibility to make it known that we didn't agree with it, that our responsibility was to the police department, to the city."[10]

There are no smoking gun memos on this, so we do not know Williams's intentions with respect to his most dubious actions before and the night of the riot. But troubling questions remain. Since he was warned that the basketball game ought to be canceled to help prevent a racist riot, why—if he wanted to prevent violence—did he not cancel the game? His rationale was that since tickets to the game had already been sold, the game had to be played.[11] But, of course, the game could have been rescheduled or the ticket holders simply refunded their money. Even worse was his suspension the night of the riot not of the rioters but their intended victims Hunter and Holmes. This was more than unfair; it was reminiscent of what the University of Alabama had done in 1956, suspending not the racist white rioters but the Black student, Autherine Lucy, who was their intended victim. And when suspended, Lucy criticized the Alabama administration for being in cahoots with the mob, the administration expelled her for insubordination. Might Georgia governor Ernest Vandiver (who authorized the removal of Hunter and Holmes from the campus), the UGA administration, and Williams in particular, have hoped suspension would lead to the same fate for Hunter and Holmes at UGA in 1961 as it had for Lucy five years earlier?[12] Since we know that student riot leaders were seeking to duplicate the Alabama precedent, it does not seem far-fetched to suspect that Georgia officials were following the Alabama playbook as well. Plus there was the fact that UGA's administration leaders, including Williams, did not come out with a statement criticizing the rioters on the night of the riot.

But Hunter and Holmes's legal team knew of the Lucy case as well and so advised them not to say anything critical about UGA's administration to avoid providing any pretext for their expulsion.[13] And UGA's faculty finally weighed in, organizing a meeting in the chapel to demand the reinstatement of Hunter and Holmes. Then, two days after the riot and their suspension, Bootle made their reinstatement mandatory via his court order. So whatever the intentions of the mob and Williams, the Alabama precedent would not prevail.

It was not until more than a decade after the publication of my "G-Men in Georgia" article that an oral history interview with Dean Williams done back in 1975 became available. The interview provided new information, but some of it just made Williams's handling of the mob violence all the more baffling. Williams revealed that he had had an informant—"a plant" among the riot's planners—and knew from "about eleven o'clock that morning . . . that there would be a riot" on that evening outside Hunter's dormitory.[14] Why then did he not cancel the basketball game, whose crowd was to be the key organizing tool of the rioters? Williams never addressed that question. Dean Tate would later claim that the decision to allow the game to be played was not Williams's but President Aderhold's, as part of a strategy (and a foolish one) of seeking to calm the campus by not disrupting its normal functioning, including its scheduled athletic events.[15]

Even had Williams and the UGA administration worked more energetically and consistently to head off racist violence prior to January 11, it may be that they initially lacked the moral authority and credibility to prevent the eruption of such violence on campus. This was because the administration in early January 1961 was in the anomalous position of advocating peaceful compliance with an integration order that it was still in the process of opposing in court after having spent years resisting UGA's desegregation. It is understandable, then, that UGA's most militant segregationist students had a difficult time taking seriously UGA's position that, in the wake of the federal court order, the university must peacefully accept its first Black students. Indeed, when the UGA administration at last did clamp down on segregationist militancy and violence in the days and weeks after UGA's January 11 segregationist riot, both those militants and their parents were surprised, and some even felt betrayed. For example, the father of one of the four students suspended for leading the riot complained to Georgia senator Herman Talmadge that this disciplinary action "is most unjust as [UGA dean of men] William Tate told the Freshman men at their first indoctrination that as long as he was Dean, the school would run on a segregated basis. Now the kids thought they were endorsing these words with actions [in rioting against integration] and that his public utterances [on behalf of peaceful compliance with the federal integration order] were either misquoted or made for the benefit of the press."[16]

This irate parent was reacting to the UGA administration's third and last position in the desegregation crisis as it finally took a tough stance—in the wake of the January 11 riot—against both segregationist violence and the political organizing on campus that had yielded such violence at UGA. This hard line was motivated by the damage the riot had done to UGA's reputation as the university was skewered by the national news media as a site of lawlessness and racist violence. The UGA administration's sensitivity to the wave of criticism directed at it in the wake of the riot was evident in the meeting "called by university of Georgia officials ... with thirty members of the press corps" covering integration of the University of Georgia on January 15, "the eve of the" court-ordered "return of Hamilton Holmes and Charlayne Hunter" to the university. At this meeting "the press was severely criticized for overplaying the story," as if the negative publicity generated by the crisis was the media's fault. The journalists "strenuously" objected to this "criticism, denying that they were doing anything more than their job as reporters."[17]

But this meeting seemed aimed at more than UGA public relations. The implication was that the press coverage of the desegregation crisis, in shining a spotlight on segregationist resistance, was actually helping to provoke such resistance by maximizing attention on racial conflict, fueling tension and giving publicity to troublemakers. Whether or not one agrees with this assessment, the fact that UGA administrators had convened this meeting with the news media was a sign that they were finally taking seriously their obligation to promote peaceful student compliance with the court's integration order and saw more restrained media coverage as an important step in calming the waters (although this approach to doing so still reeked of a Jim Crow mentality in which it was assumed, as indicated in the quote below, that the best way to heal race relations was to minimize white-Black interaction). Remarkably, despite the journalists' rejection of the criticism of their coverage of the crisis, they adopted voluntarily these self-disciplined rules for the return of Holmes and Hunter to UGA:

1. They will not question the two Negroes at random on the campus but will confine their questions to a morning and afternoon news conference.
2. Photographers will wait outside the buildings where the Negroes have classes while reporters will meet students in a ground floor classroom. Radio and television sound crews will also be included in the news conference.
3. Sound interviews with the students by television crews will not be made at undesignated times.
4. All members of the press will attempt not to congregate in groups on the campus.
5. The University will issue press cards to working press and will discourage student reporters and others from being with the Negroes.[18]

Beyond this attempt to manage media coverage in the riot's aftermath, the UGA administration in mid- and late January 1961 acted decisively to curb segregationist militancy on campus, essentially decapitating UGA's segregationist student movement. Key leaders of the riot were disciplined, with four suspended, three investigated, and eighteen placed on probation.[19] This not only deprived the segregationist movement of its key organizers, but it also sent a clear message to any would-be successors to them. Unlike the rioters of January 11, who had been told that influential state officials and others would protect them, students in the riot's aftermath knew better: they would be punished and risked losing their student status and UGA degrees if they engaged in violent segregationist protest. This, together with the FBI investigation of the riot, had a chilling effect on such protest activity.[20]

To shut down UGA's segregationist movement, the campus administration warned against not merely violent but nonviolent segregationist activism in the aftermath of the January 11 riot. Within forty-eight hours of the riot the administration had adopted a new policy dictating that "no student demonstration," peaceful or otherwise, for the purpose of expressing dissent against UGA's integration would be permitted. Nor would any group be allowed to assemble except recognized associations such as fraternities and sororities, clubs, and so forth, under penalty of suspension or expulsion. In a memorandum widely circulated on campus three days after the riot, Dean Williams, in effect, temporarily suspended freedom of speech and assembly at UGA, declaring that "students attending or taking part in riots and demonstrations will be suspended or expelled. Members of fraternities and sororities will jeopardize their charters by attending or taking part in such demonstrations and riots."[21] This last provision was a particularly effective deterrent to political organizing since these were among the most influential and reactionary student organizations at UGA.

Segregationist state politicians in Atlanta complained bitterly about these acts as grave violations of free speech, ironic in light of their own history of supporting the suppression of integrationist speech.[22] These free speech complaints were valid nonetheless. But UGA's administration was likely correct in assuming that such suppression was the surest way to prevent further segregationist violence given the anger and strength of the campus's most militant segregationists. It is one of the most striking but little noticed ironies of the desegregation crisis that it took such illiberal actions by UGA's administration at this crucial moment to ensure peaceful progress toward a more liberal and inclusive university.

While angering Georgia's most extreme segregationist legislators who admired UGA's racist student rioters—praised by Peter Zack Geer, Governor Vandiver's executive secretary, as being "possessed with the character and courage not to submit to dictatorship and tyranny"—much of the public both in and out of Georgia credited UGA's administration for acting to ensure there would be no more mob violence on campus.[23] Like the more moderate students in Math 254, many of the letters President Aderhold received from

UGA alumni, even while professing loyalty and affection for segregation, expressed disdain for the lawlessness of the January 11 rioters and held that there was no place for such behavior at the university. For example, three days after the riot, Homer C. Eberhardt, president of Georgia's Bar Association and a UGA alumnus (class of 1921), wrote a supportive letter to Aderhold that "without exception... the alumni of the University are and have been opposed to the desegregation of our beloved university. We feel that we have, over the South, had rather shabby consideration by the federal authorities, and particularly the Supreme Court but we are not among those who would defy legal processes.... In such an hour as this Georgia needs men, not mobs! Men of vision, wisdom, and judgement."[24]

Eberhardt felt that Aderhold was such a man, who would see to it that "our boys" would be taught that they were obligated to be "acting as gentlemen, even in the face of adversity and of" integration, "which is incompatible with" proper "social thinking and practice." Eberhardt expressed "every confidence" that Aderhold would follow the example set by UGA's chancellor from his freshman year back in 1918, "Uncle Dave" Barrows, who chastised male students for responding inappropriately to the first female students admitted to UGA. Eberhardt recalled that "Some of the boys in one of the dormitories began to drop paper bags filled with water from the windows as the girls walked by on the sidewalk below. Uncle Dave Barrows heard about it and called us into the chapel.... 'It is your job to act the part of gentlemen at all times,' he said. 'If we teach you nothing else... but succeed in that you will have learned something that will be worth more to you than all else.' ... That was about all he... needed to say.... The coeds were not further troubled."[25]

This perspective from such UGA alumni, just like that of many of the Math 254 essayists, combined opposition to violence with support of segregation and a sense of white Southern victimhood. In this self-centered view, it was not the Black students targeted by mob violence on January 11 but UGA itself and the white South whose mistreatment most concerned him, meaning being forced to integrate by federal courts that disregarded and disrespected the traditions of the segregated South. There was no thought given to the idea that having barred Black Georgians from their state's leading public university for more than a century was unjust and antidemocratic.

In this reading of history, UGA under Aderhold's able leadership dodged two bullets: the threat from the state government to close the university rather than let it be integrated, and the threat of renewed ungentlemanly behavior (i.e., more mob violence). And in fact, all this was woven into a sentimental reading of how Georgia navigated its way out of the desegregation crisis thanks to its love of the university—that Georgians loved the university too much to see it closed over the integration issue. This enabled the UGA administration to turn back the massive resistance movement and get the governor and the legislature to end the segregationist school closing mandate. As UGA dean of men William Tate explained in 1963,

> when integration came the university was the one institution that could weather it.... The people of the state wanted the university not to close. A lot of people in the state love the university, and the university has always been tied up to the state. We usually have people here from every county.... We have five hundred agricultural extension workers and home-demonstration workers spread out all over the state. Our agricultural people have borne the brunt of shifting from a cotton economy to diversified farming. Ernest Vandiver, the last governor, was a graduate of the university. Carl Sanders, the current governor is a graduate of the university. Both United States senators Talmadge and Russell are graduates of the university. Herman Talmadge's son is here and he is the fourth generation of Talmadges to attend the university. Richard Russell went here; his father was a trustee; his uncle was here. Why he was the fourth Richard B. Russell here.... When this thing [the desegregation crisis] happened I bet a lot of folks said ... "It's a pretty good old university. It's helped us. They've done the best they can. They got their feet on the ground. And my granddaddy went there. I'll help them out."[26]

Tate was right about white Georgia's affection for UGA making it impossible for the state government to shut down the university rather than integrate it.[27] But most of the Georgia politicians he named were, as we saw in chapter 1, architects of the very segregationist regime that had brought UGA to the brink of closing down when it collided with federal courts that had finally deemed its systemic racial discrimination unconstitutional. And judging Aderhold only by how UGA and the state government at the eleventh hour acted to keep the university open and how UGA finally clamped down on its racist student militants, and viewing this as a crisis resolved by love of the university, obscures the roles that racial hatred, discrimination, violence, and the university's disingenuous defense of its Jim Crowism in court played in seeding the desegregation crisis in the first place.

Of all the UGA administrators involved in the desegregation crisis, it is Dean Tate who comes off best in the historical narratives. This is because, as Trillin showed and Hunter-Gault confirmed, Tate was the one most concerned about the safety of the university's first Black students and was on the front lines in opposing segregationist student violence. Thus as Hunter-Gault recalled, when she came to the UGA campus in Tate's car to register for her first classes and a racist student crowd surrounded and began rocking the car, "a very tense moment," Tate sprang into action. The big, burly dean "hurled himself out of the driver's seat and started grabbing at the students closest to him. He was known for snatching up [student] ID cards, and this whirling-dervish act did the trick. While not dispersing, the crowd pulled back far enough for the car to pass and, except for a few 'nigger thises and nigger thats' we proceeded without any more interference."[28] During the riot itself, Tate not only confronted the mob in front of Hunter's dormitory but was injured doing so; he got a black eye battling a student rioter who had struck a police officer, his ankle was hurt by a rioter's rock, and he was hit in the shoulder by a tear gas cannister the rioters had thrown back at the police.[29] This admirable protective role infuriated segregationist militants, including a Klansman at the riot scene who said of Tate, "Someone ought to knock that son of a bitch in the head."[30] And, as historian Robert A. Pratt documents, racists flooded Tate with hate mail, denouncing him as "Judas" and an "NAACP agent."[31]

Yet not even Tate dared to push for any kind of public reckoning with the university's sordid racist past. Indeed, as was typical with white Georgia and UGA's leadership, Tate rationalized and excused the university administration's protracted resistance to desegregation, later telling Hunter-Gault "that he and President Aderhold 'felt that integration was inevitable; it would come. But we felt ... that the longer we delayed it, the less possibility there was of violence.'"[32] This was an absurd argument since, as we have seen, the UGA administration's court battles were designed not to delay but to stop integration, and those battles actually served to foment violence among segregationist students who believed their riot aligned them with UGA's segregationist administration.

In the wake of UGA's desegregation crisis, Tate privately acknowledged the need for Southern campus leaders to recognize that the courts made integration mandatory, writing to a colleague in April 1961 that "things have changed rapidly in the last fifty and ten years; and just as our grandparents had to rearrange their thinking on slavery, so we must rearrange some of our thinking about Civil Rights and Negroes, even under instructions from the courts. I am hoping that the incident in Athens will make the path easier for other institutions."[33] But neither Tate nor any other UGA official went public with any kind of acknowledgment that UGA had spent decades supporting the state's antidemocratic Jim Crow regime, that its academic ethos had been corrupted by racism, and that this shift toward integration forced by the courts represented a step upward for UGA toward meritocracy, inclusiveness, democracy, and academic excellence.[34] Thus Tate and his colleagues left UGA's students and the state with a politically impoverished understanding—really a misunderstanding—of the meaning and significance of the university's court-ordered integration and its legacy.

MISSING FROM THE FBI INVESTIGATION (and thus from my article on that investigation) was any bureau analysis of the role of gender in the segregationist riot at UGA. White female students were almost invisible in the FBI files on the riot, and this was also true of press coverage of both the riot and the desegregation crisis as a whole. In fact, it is virtually impossible from either the FBI report or the reportage of the riot scene to determine how many female students participated in the riot or had been there even as spectators. And the same is true of the nonviolent segregationist protests the week before the riot. Since all but one of the reporters covering the riot and the FBI agents investigating it were men, there was an obvious male bias involved.[35] But it was also true that the target of everyone's attention was on the riot's organizers, and since all of those organizers and leaders of the segregationist militants were male UGA students, the gender imbalance, this focus on the men, made sense. Every prominent leader of the campus's segregationist militants mentioned in the press coverage and in the FBI files was male, as were all twenty-five white UGA students who were the subject of disciplinary action by UGA for their roles in the riot.

Calvin Trillin, who covered the desegregation crisis and the riot for *Time* magazine, was one of the few reporters who wrote anything about women being present at the riot scene. He noted that in preparation for the mob scene, set to occur once the basketball game ended, "some students got dates for the basketball game and the riot afterward."[36]

The one woman the FBI interviewed about the riot "related that she has not received any information to suggest that any female student was connected with the demonstration [i.e., the riot] or that any female student at the University of Georgia had engaged in any overt act to oppose the acceptance of the Negro students.... While ... some of the girls are opposed to integration none of them have actively participated in any of the efforts which have taken place at the school since the Negro students were admitted."[37] Actually, there is photographic evidence refuting this claim and documenting at least one female student's involvement in the initially nonviolent but quite racist demonstration on January 9 when Hunter came to campus to register for classes. An Associated Press photo from that scene has a chilling image of a female student with her mouth wide open jeering right behind Hunter while a male student next to the jeering girl smiles broadly in response to her racist behavior.[38] Moreover, the interviewee who inaccurately claimed no female students demonstrated against integration (her name was deleted by FBI censors) was, by her own admission, "not present on the University of Georgia campus" when the riot erupted. And (perhaps defensively) she understated segregationist sentiment among female students, which included far more than "some of the girls." Recall that the administration's interviews with almost all (153 of the 163) students in Center-Myers Hall, the women's dorm where Hunter was placed, found that the "predominant sentiment" was "for segregation."[39] Unfortunately, the FBI never questioned anyone present at the riot scene about the female presence there, though, again, it is evident that the leaders of the disturbance were all male. But dean of students Joseph Williams, who was present at the riot scene, recalled that while not leading the violence, there was a strong female presence at the riot scene, noting that "there were about as many girls in the crowd up at the front as there were boys" and that both "girls and boys were shooting firecrackers" there.[40]

The best contemporary information we have on female students at the riot scene came not from the FBI but from the *Atlanta Constitution* in its one female-centered article. The report came from inside Center-Myers rather than outside where the rioters were besieging the dormitory; so, revealing as it was about the dorm residents inside, it does not provide information on how many female students were among the rioters or what role they played in that violent scene. The white residents of the dorm knew in advance about the riot, though none told Charlayne Hunter about it. "We knew it would happen," admitted an eighteen-year-old UGA student who resided in the dorm. "There'd been so much talk about it."[41] As to the reaction of these white female students to the violence, this same undergraduate told the *Constitution* reporter that "at first we were all more excited than frightened," but when one of the white girls on the fourth floor was grazed in the head by a rock hurled through her dorm room window, "some of the girls got really frightened."[42] Reflecting a class-based preference for student over blue collar segregationist rioters, two other Center-Myers residents told the reporter "the worst part of their anxiety was the rumor that 'the Klan was coming.'" "That's why we were really frightened," explained one of these students. "We weren't afraid of our classmates. It was the other elements from outside, the *riffraff*."[43] The striking thing in all this, exactly as we saw with the Math 254 essays, was that these white students were so self-centered that they saw themselves as the victims rather than Charlayne Hunter, who was the actual target of the mob's rage.

The reporter failed, however, to get Charlayne Hunter's account of the ways her dorm mates acted when the riot erupted. Not until Charlayne Hunter-Gault's memoir was published decades later did we learn the full extent of her dorm mates' complicity with the mob and their disgraceful behavior as the riot raged. (Of course, Hunter could not offer any insight into the role of women outside among the rioters since concern for her own safety kept her from even looking outside through her windows at the riot scene.) She recalled that the women in her dorm had colluded with the riot's leaders: "All the students" in her dorm except her "had been told by the riot planners to turn off the lights in their rooms when it got dark. With the rest of the building in darkness, the three brightly lit windows of my apartment must have made an inviting target for the mob out on the lawn."[44] And when the rioters' bricks began to break windows in the dorm, injuring one dorm resident, rather than blame the racist mob outside, the women on her floor blamed Hunter. They grew hostile and began hurling insults at her and at the one dorm resident who had had the decency to befriend her. "It was," recalled Hunter-Gault, "hard to sit there and listen to some of the things that were said about me.... I was told I was about to become 'a Black martyr, getting fifty dollars a day from the NAACP.'"[45] And after the police had deployed tear gas to disperse the crowd, some of the gas seeped into the dorm, and the students were told to change the sheets on their beds, some of the white female students in Center-Myers nastily treated Hunter as if she was their maid, making "deliberately loud offers of a dime or quarter to Charlayne for changing" their sheets.[46] Similarly, Tom Johnson, in looking back on the night of the riot, recalled how as a student journalist, he got some of the Center-Myers residents to confide in him and learned that one of the racist female students there had snidely called out to Hunter, "Honey we are so glad you're here. We needed a maid to clean up this place, these halls."[47] Appalled by those remarks, which were among his strongest and most unpleasant memories of that night, Johnson remembered thinking "what a hurtful, hurtful thing to say."[48] The nastiness persisted even as Hunter, after being suspended, was leaving the dorm that night in tears: several of these hostile female students in her dorm "began to hiss."[49]

Given such attitudes and behavior, we are left with the question of why female students did not play a leadership role in UGA's segregationist riot. This was 1961, well before the surge of second-wave feminism, so perhaps Southern women back then were so bound by traditional gender roles that political leadership remained the purview of men. But on the other hand, FBI files reveal that the day after the riot at UGA, "a Special Agent of the FBI . . . observed approximately seventeen women [nonstudents] picketing at the State Capitol Building in Atlanta, carrying signs protesting any State activities which would bring on integration. Four women were observed passing out Ku Klux Klan propaganda, urging continuance of segregation."[50]

It seems likely that a combination of class and gender factors were responsible for the male monopoly on segregationist and riot leadership at UGA. Unlike with the KKK with its blue collar constituency, female students at UGA tended to be more middle and upper middle class, and some were even wealthy, and for them leadership in segregationist resistance, especially if it involved violence, was too radical a departure from their domestic role and likely seemed too masculine. And even had female students been inclined to such leadership, it is likely that they would have been preempted by the male students in UGA's law school, fraternities, and debating societies, some of whom came to the university already aspiring to become leaders in the state's segregationist political establishment, a male preserve—for which UGA served as a kind of leadership academy. What better way for these aspiring junior politicians to launch political careers than to make names for themselves as leaders of UGA's segregationist resistance, and to do so while colluding with some of the state's highest-ranking political figures? Admittedly, though, this is a speculative conclusion, and we need more evidence than has been provided by the FBI and the media if we are to fully understand the role of white female students in UGA's desegregation crisis.

ALL HISTORICAL WRITING INVOLVES compression and selectivity, and this is particularly true when historians convey their findings through historical articles in journals that are limited by space constraints. Reflecting on my "G-Men in Georgia" article after rereading the FBI files on the UGA riot led me to see that while the article does capture all the key insights (as well as the flaws) provided by the FBI investigation, some of the details uncovered by the FBI files that could not be fit into the article are also telling; the closer you probe the riot scene and the FBI records of its interviews with those at the riot scene, the worse it looks.

For example, the issue of whether the students or the KKK planned and led the riot is important, and the files, as indicated in my article (and chapter), show that students and not the Klan planned and led the riot. But when you reflect upon the FBI interviews with UGA students, there is a related point that is equally disturbing: that whether leaders, rank-and-file rioters, or even those privy to the riot planning who claimed not to have been involved in the riot itself, none of these UGA students objected to the Klan's presence in their segregationist protest. Not one of the students interviewed displayed any sense of shame about the fact that this student demonstration was aligned with a white supremacist terrorist organization, not a word of concern or regret. That strikes me as being as shameful as the riot itself.[51] It attests to the utter failure of UGA as an educational institution to intervene in such a way—in coursework or extracurricular life—as to purge or challenge the student body's racism, even in its crudest form.

Such crudeness was also prominently displayed by the rioters in their discourse. So much of my focus in "G-Men in Georgia" and the FBI investigation was focused on the violence—since, of course, the FBI was investigating a violent crime—that the racist language employed by the rioters did not get the attention it deserved. The interviews the FBI conducted with those present at the riot were replete with evidence that the riot had been accompanied and inspired by the crudest racist expression. Chants of "Nigger Go Home" were heard at the riot scene, not surprising, of course, since the rioters initially marched to Charlayne Hunter's dormitory behind a banner with those very words. But this was not all. There were chants of "Nigger lover," though one has to guess whom that chant was directed toward, since it could have been the Athens police, the news reporters and photographers, or university officials present at the riot scene.[52] The rioters also chanted "2-4-6-8, We Don't Want to Integrate," and "8-6-4-2, We Don't Want No Jigg-a-boo."[53] And lest one think such crudity was unique to the emotionally charged riot scene, most of these vile chants (and others equally ugly) were heard at prior segregationist protests at UGA a week earlier. Plus there were the words of student riot leader Thomas Cochran, whose statements to the press suggested that he was addicted to using the N-word even when he was apparently attempting to sound reasonable, as when he told the *Macon Telegraph*, "We don't want to kill the niggers. We're not that inhuman. But we want the press and the world to know that the students at Georgia are not just sitting up here liking it."[54] You can search high and low without finding a word of public criticism from UGA or state government officials of this racist student expression. This may help explain why, according to Cochran, on the day after the riot "you see students walking around with smiles on their faces."[55]

As I reflect back on the FBI files and my "G-Men" study, there is a self-criticism that seems obvious to me all these years later. And that is at the time I published the article, I failed to see that when writing a history of a crime—and both the riot and the alleged conspiracy to riot among students, state officials, and the Klan were criminal activities—and the investigation of it by a police agency, there is the danger that one can start thinking more like a conscientious law enforcement official than a historian, especially when focusing so much on the question of *"who done it?"* This was, or should have been, a key question for FBI agents in 1961 since they were charged with the task of establishing possible guilt for the crimes being probed, so it is understandable that I was drawn into seeking to use the FBI files to solve some of the biggest unsolved mysteries of the riot: specifically, who exactly from the state government encouraged the students to protest, who among these state officials may have been so enthused in urging segregationist resistance and pledging to use their power to see that rioters would go unpunished that they helped incite the riot, and who was responsible for the state patrol's failure to show up to assist the Athens police? These are indeed important matters of historical interest. Still, it is also true that a historian too narrowly focused on such questions can become a bit myopic, leading to a kind of forest for the trees problem.

By that I mean exactly which state officials egged the segregationist students on is important, but equally, and perhaps more important, is the fact that, long before the riot, the state and local officials had established strong records of segregationist loyalty/militancy and resistance to all attempts to topple Jim Crow. So that on the UGA campus in 1961, even the vaguest of rumors of sympathy and collusion by state government officials with the rioters was believable. Thus the FBI files, though only offering one specific state official named by a rioter as being guilty of such collusion, also contained unconfirmed claims by others the bureau interviewed from the campus that state officials as prominent as lieutenant governor Garland T. Byrd, the governor's secretary Peter Zack Geer, and UGA regent and political powerhouse Roy Harris, along with other Georgia politicians who had been cheerleading for the segregationist rioters, had pledged to protect them from being held accountable for their segregationist violence.[56] In other words, whether or not the specifics of each claim of collusion were true, it was Jim Crow Georgia's white segregationist consensus—stretching from the lowly undergraduate up to the governor's office—that in the days and hours leading up to the riot helped paved the way for the violence since it left UGA students feeling empowered and supported by the state's political establishment to express their racism violently. In that sense the criminality can be seen not as the work of a single or handful of individuals but as rather the bitter fruit of the Jim Crow political system itself.

On the legal front, two additional conclusions emerge from the FBI files. The first is the evidence of law students in the riot and what that signified.

One sees in the files, for example, a law student being questioned by the FBI about his attendance at the pivotal student planning meeting for the riot. The law student leaves the room of his FBI interrogation momentarily, consults a more legally experienced classmate who is already a member of the bar, and then tells the FBI agents he wants an attorney present and breaks off the interview.[57] In my "G-Men" study I attributed the participation of such law students in a lawless segregationist riot to some being aspiring junior politicians in Jim Crow Georgia, whose reputations would be enhanced by joining with high ranking state officials to resist desegregation. However, this missed the fact that state law itself in Jim Crow Georgia at the time of the riot was a tool not of equality before the law but of racial discrimination, so on this level there is nothing really surprising about students schooled in segregationist law in UGA's all-white law school becoming so militant in their segregationism as to condone or engage in violence.

As noted in "G-Men in Georgia," the state patrol never showed up to help quell the riot between the time it erupted at 9:45 or 10:00 P.M. and ended at 11:45 or so, not arriving in force until the riot had ended. But there is one detail captured in the FBI files that did not find its way into my article that makes this dereliction of duty seem even worse. When the riot was at its peak at about 11:00, a state patrol officer dropped off some tear gas missiles at the riot scene for the Athens police. That officer could see that the small Athens police force was overwhelmed by the very large and angry mob of rioters, which was why police and Athens officials had urgently requested tear gas and state patrol troopers to serve as reinforcements in the first place. But this state patrol officer, even after observing this tumultuous scene, made no attempt to call in his fellow state troopers. Instead, after dropping off the tear gas, he simply got back in his patrol car and drove off.[58] And the recently available oral history interview with Dean Williams further details the state patrol's negligence. Williams attested that since he knew a riot was coming that night, he convened a planning meeting with law enforcement in the afternoon in which the local director of the state patrol was present and pledged to have troopers on campus before the basketball game was over. But they did not show up then. And the "numerous" times Williams called the patrol during the riot he was told the troopers would "be there shortly," but they did not show up for hours, leaving Williams convinced "that they had orders from higher up the line . . . not to show."[59]

Though my "G-Men in Georgia" study rightly contrasted the dereliction of duty on the part of the state patrol with the dutiful service the Athens police force displayed in quelling the riot, the FBI files confirm that several UGA officials, most notably Dean Tate, put themselves in harm's way battling the rioters. The FBI files also attest that a large part of the press, whether working for an Athens newspaper, for the major dailies in Atlanta and Macon, or for national news media, played an honorable role in the entire desegregation crisis—which is likely the reason reporters and news photographers became targets of the rioters, so that several journalists were injured by rioters' rocks and firecrackers. Their reportage of the riot scene itself and the events leading to it was often quite informative, so much so that the FBI drew upon it considerably in their own investigation. Though not reflected in the FBI files, the TV news coverage—explored and justly praised in a journalists' panel in 2001 at the fortieth anniversary commemoration of UGA's desegregation—was strong as well.[60] Given this record of excellent news coverage, it is no surprise that a journalist, Calvin Trillin, who had covered the desegregation of UGA, would go on to write the first and most enduring book on the university's integration.

Since no one was killed in the UGA riot, there is sometimes a tendency to miss how dangerous the riot scene was. After all, this was uncontrolled violence that went on for more than an hour. This point was driven home to me by the faculty oral history interviews John C. Belcher did, which revealed that a professor claimed to having witnessed a police officer firing his revolver twice at a student after the policeman had been hit by a stone by this student during the riot. This was not mentioned in the FBI reports on the riot, and if indeed this claim was accurate, the shots fired may have gone largely unnoticed because the police officer missed, the student escaped by fleeing into a dark alley, and the noise from all the firecrackers being set off by the rioters drowned out the gunshots.[61]

It is not just such eyewitness accounts and the FBI reports that remind us to take seriously the danger of segregationist violence. There is also the faculty's organizing of a faculty patrol to assist in ensuring no further violence occurred after the riot—a patrol that many felt was needed in the absence of a sizable city police force and virtually no UGA campus police department. That faculty patrol helped prevent further violence, as when it found near Charlayne Hunter's dormitory an armed, unstable man, whom the police came to remove. In light of all this, it is understandable that faculty member and American Association of University Professors leader Thomas Brahana told me decades ago that it was just luck that nobody was killed in the UGA's integration crisis.[62]

Of course, not everyone on campus shared this concern about violence. While UGA's administration was so concerned in the wake of the riot, many fraternity members were not. Pete McCommons recalled being impressed "with the seriousness with which the administration viewed the situation" after learning that in an initiative to avoid violence, UGA assigned its fraternity advisors the task of collecting all the guns and rifles in the fraternity houses, including in his Phi Delta Theta house. A lot of his frat brothers "hunted a lot." So when the advisor came to pick up any guns, he "left the Phi Delt house that night with a trunk full of shotguns and rifles." The Phi Delts, as McCommons explained, "all thought it was amusing. Phi Delts didn't care one way or the other. They didn't want niggers in the university but they weren't going to do anything to stop it. They thought it was rather funny that the Administration was that much concerned."[63]

Part I
The Jim Crow Era UGA

UGA 1932 yearbook illustration mocking Blacks' first attempt to desegregate UGA, after the Civil War. This attempt, foiled by anti-Black violence, is represented via demeaning caricatures of African Americans, and a caption making light of the terrorizing of Blacks—chased off campus by armed white students—as an enjoyable "day of real sport." "Encores" section, University of Georgia *Pandora*, 1932, courtesy Hargrett Rare Book and Manuscript Library, University of Georgia Libraries.

Caricatures of African Americans in UGA yearbook. "Jokes" section, 1914, University of Georgia *Pandora*. Courtesy of Hargrett Rare Book and Manuscript Library, University of Georgia Libraries.

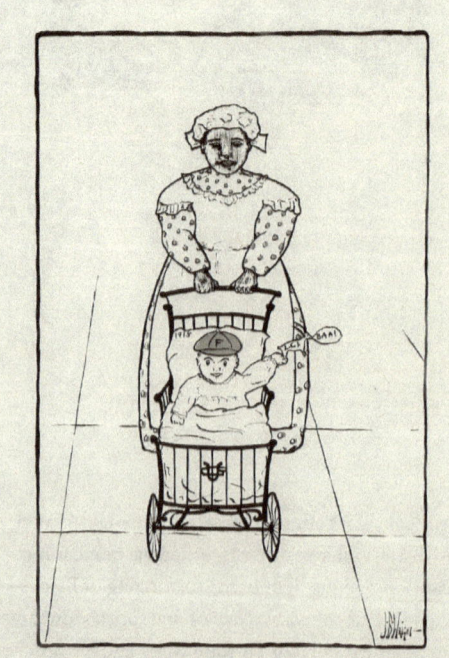

Caricature of African American woman pushing UGA freshman in a baby carriage. University of Georgia *Pandora*, 1912, courtesy Hargrett Rare Book and Manuscript Library, University of Georgia Libraries.

Caricature of African American woman and child. "Slams," University of Georgia *Pandora*, 1912, courtesy of Hargrett Rare Book and Manuscript Library, University of Georgia Libraries.

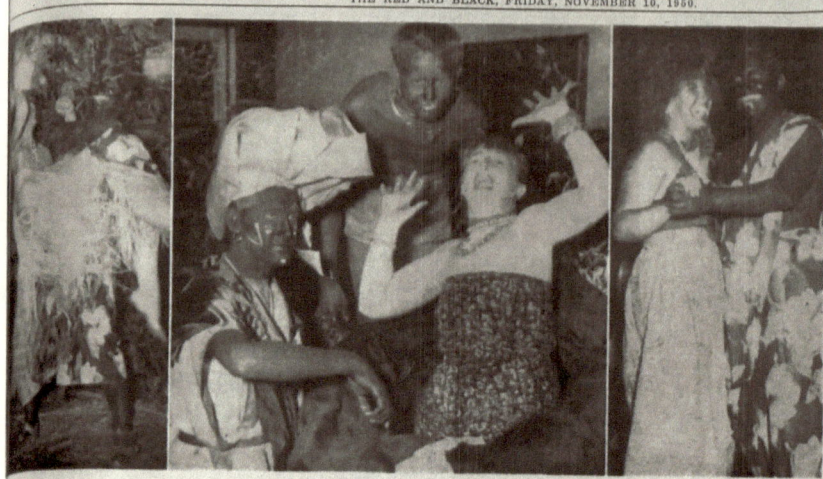

Art students at their "Primitive Africa" party, University of Georgia the *Red and Black*, November 10, 1950, Courtesy Hargrett Rare Book and Manuscript Library, University of Georgia Libraries.

Cartoon refers to jazz artist Duke Ellington as a "damn good nigger" after he became one of the first Black musicians permitted to perform on the UGA campus during the Jim Crow era, the *Red and Black* UGA student newspaper, May 19, 1955. Courtesy of Hargrett Rare Book and Manuscript Library, University of Georgia Libraries.

Part II
UGA's Integration Crisis

Segregationist students hoisting racist banner as they marched to the dormitory of Charlayne Hunter on the night of January 11, 1961, where they rioted, seeking to force UGA's first Black students—Hunter and Hamilton Holmes—out of the university. Bettman via Getty Images.

UGA fraternity member smiling as he dangles a lynched Black puppet in front of news cameras during the university's integration crisis in January 1961. Photo ran in *Life* magazine, January 20, 1961, captioned "Dangling a Doll, a University of Georgia student grinningly shows off home-made Negro puppet hanging on a string. A dean chased him, made him drop the doll and berated him for his crude prank." Courtesy of Joe Scherschel/The LIFE Picture Collection/Shutterstock.com.

"You have to be carefully taught to hate." Political cartoon by Richard Q. Yardley of the *Baltimore Sun*, January 13, 1961, was part of a national wave of media condemnation of UGA's segregationist riot. Permission from Baltimore Sun Media Group. All Rights Reserved.

Atlanta Constitution political cartoon depicts UGA's riot as monstrous while offering no allusion to race, reflecting white Georgians' willingness to criticize mob violence but not the racism that motivated it. "Big Man on Campus," *Atlanta Constitution*, January 13, 1961, Clifford H. "Baldy" Baldowski editorial cartoons. Courtesy of the Richard B. Russell Library for Political Research and Studies, University of Georgia Libraries.

Political cartoon showing the dorm that housed Charlayne Hunter, with its windows shattered by rioters. "Jeepers, I don't know if he's the same as he use[d] to be or not!" *Atlanta Constitution*, January 18, 1961, Clifford H. "Baldy" Baldowski editorial cartoons. Courtesy of the Richard B. Russell Library for Political Research and Studies, University of Georgia Libraries.

UGA students were fearful of being watched by the FBI as the bureau began its investigation of the segregationist riot. "But John how do you know the FBI is here?" University of Georgia *Red and Black* newspaper, January 19, 1961. Courtesy of Hargrett Rare Book and Manuscript Library, University of Georgia Libraries.

AT 72-39

observed a Georgia Bureau of Investigation (GBI) lieutenant and a Georgia State Patrol trooper drive up and the lieutenant left a sack full of tear gas missiles with the Athens Police Department. The state officers then immediately departed, although ▓▓▓▓ said it was obvious that the police department needed help.

▓▓▓▓▓▓▓▓▓▓▓▓▓▓▓▓▓▓▓▓▓▓▓▓▓▓▓▓▓▓▓▓▓▓ said he counted 12 marked Georgia State Patrol cars parked at the station ▓▓▓▓▓▓▓▓▓▓▓▓▓▓▓▓▓▓▓ counted ten uniform members of the patrol sitting around smoking and drinking coffee.

▓▓▓▓▓▓▓▓▓▓▓▓▓▓▓▓▓▓▓▓▓▓▓▓▓▓▓▓▓▓▓▓▓▓ the Athens Police Department needed the assistance of the Georgia State Patrol.

▓▓▓▓▓▓▓▓▓▓▓▓▓▓▓▓▓▓▓▓▓▓▓▓▓▓▓▓▓▓▓▓▓▓ they would be out at the University in about fifteen minutes to take the Negro students to Atlanta ▓▓▓▓▓▓▓▓▓▓ gave no indication they intended to render assistance to the police department,

A page from the FBI's investigation of UGA's segregationist riot showing the excisions made by FBI censors that limit our understanding of the riot. Federal Bureau of Investigation.

Cartoon depicting Hamilton Holmes's election to the Phi Beta Kappa academic honor society. "No Tellin' what'll happen if you give 'em half a chance!" *Atlanta Constitution*, April 26, 1963, Clifford H. "Baldy" Baldowski editorial cartoons. Courtesy of the Richard B. Russell Library for Political Research and Studies, University of Georgia Libraries.

Toilet paper dispenser embossed with the *New Yorker* logo aimed at journalist Calvin Trillin's series of lengthy *New Yorker* articles on UGA's integration crisis and its aftermath. Trillin offered a candid, unflattering account of the white student body's racist behavior. "A New Dispenser Has Appeared on Campus," University of Georgia *Red and Black* newspaper, September 20, 1963. Courtesy of Hargrett Rare Book and Manuscript Library, University of Georgia Libraries.

Part III
Old South, New Day
Rebel Flag, Black Power, and the Struggle over History and Memory

Kappa Alpha social gathering in front of their fraternity house adorned with a Confederate flag. *Pandora*, 1969. Courtesy of Hargrett Rare Book and Manuscript Library, University of Georgia Libraries.

Georgia's state flag, still embossed with the Confederate battle flag, as it had been since the Jim Crow era, at 1996 Olympics in Atlanta, likened to Nazi Germany's flag, at the 1936 Berlin Olympics. Cartoon by Mike Luckovich, *Atlanta Journal-Constitution*. Courtesy of Mike Luckovich.

Cartoon illustrating the political and cultural divide among white and Black students at UGA. "What We Have Here is a Failure to Communicate," University of Georgia *Red and Black*, May 8, 1969. Courtesy of Hargrett Rare Book and Manuscript Library, University of Georgia Libraries.

Black Student Union
(News Release)

History has shown and experience has taught black people that Georgia is deeply entrenched in the southern pig sty of racism and intends to remain so unless it is shaken at its bigoted foundation. This fact is exemplified in the response of the vested university authority to the demands of black students. The gist of the reply was that "hell no black folk have no right to determine their own educational destiny." Once again black students see that white racism is the order of the day and humanitarian efforts take a back seat at the University of Georgia.

Black students are making demands because they can no longer tolerate the concerted efforts on the part of the University to make "honkies" out of black folk. As in the days of the Old South, the Neo-slavemasters have declared that it is illegal, unnecessary and educationally unsound for black people to obtain a meaningful education. Davison declared in essence that it was illegal for niggers to learn about their past, their heritage, and their contemporary racist society from a black perspective. (A good slavemaster realizes that a slave with a book in his hands is a dangerous foe). Hence the efforts of the University to perpetuate the slave mentality among blacks will continue unless blacks cleanse their minds of 400 years of cracker sopping and whitewashing.

Davison's response and the academic community's responses are proof of the blatant racism that permeates the University environment today. Cries of separatism in reverse, black racists, and foes of integration have become substitutes for "niggers and spooks stay in your place." The demands of black students are too urgent to be dismissed as temper tantrums of a hand full of black fanatics.

White racism, covert and overt, prevents whites from understanding that what this society calls an education is nothing more than a course in "HOW TO MAKE IT IN HONKEYDOM." The fork-tongued and power mad administrators speak with tongue-in-cheek when they praise integration. They have taken what was once a great stepping stone in civil rights and have made it a hitching-post of oppression. We realize that the destiny of this state is inextricably intertwined with the destiny of black people, therefore we will not permit the University to castrate black skull.

Black Student Union statement in the university yearbook, 1970, criticizing racism at UGA. The statement expresses strong dissatisfaction with UGA president Frederick Davison's response to Black student demands to improve the educational environment for the university's African American student population. University of Georgia *Pandora*, 1970. Courtesy of Hargrett Rare Book and Manuscript Library, University of Georgia Libraries.

THE BLACK STUDENT UNION
OF
THE UNIVERSITY OF GEORGIA

P. O. Box 2303
University Station
Athens, Georgia 30601

FROM THE OFFICE
OF
THE CENTRAL COMMITTEE

February 21, 1971

Dr. Fred C. Davidson
President - University of Georgia
Old College
Athens, Georgia

President Davidson:

It is with great displeasure that I write this letter. For more than two years the students, faculty, and Administration of this university have known the Black Student Union's opposition to the playing of the racist song "Dixie" both at official University functions and at other times as well. We are insulted by the unpleasant memory of the "Old South" which is created by this song. After all, you wouldn't wear a swastika through a Jewish neighborhood!

Therefore I demand that you act officially, immediately, and concernedly toward the elimination of this biased practice. Moreover, I strongly suggest that you do not employ your previous tactic whereby this practice was stopped only temporarily, because this will definitely meet with a determined, physical backlash. If "Dixie" is the only means by which this university can arouse its students, then it has failed miserably in its task of widening the scope of the student populace.

DIXIE IS DEAD AND YOU CAN'T REVIVE IT.

Power to My Black People,

A. Levert Hood
Chief of Staff, BSU

cc: Dean Suthern Sims
Mr. Roger Dancz
Mr. Joel Eaves

Black Student Union chief of staff A. Levert Hood's letter to UGA president Fred Davison demanding an end to playing the Old South anthem "Dixie" at UGA events, 1971. Courtesy of Alvin Levert Hood and Hargrett Rare Book and Manuscript Library, University of Georgia Libraries.

On Black student alienation over UGA's remaining an overwhelmingly white institution with a small African American student population, few Black faculty, and even fewer Black administrators. "I Need This Place?" University of Georgia *Red and Black*, May 13, 1971. Courtesy of Hargrett Rare Book and Manuscript Library, University of Georgia Libraries.

Attesting to the continuing racial division at UGA, the student government (SA) opposed the Black student drive for an African American Cultural Center on campus. Mike Moreu, *Red and Black*, June 9, 1989. Printed with permission from *Red and Black*, an independent student media organization based in Athens, Georgia.

Poster for the fortieth anniversary of UGA's desegregation; its historic photo generated criticism because it was doctored to obscure the crowd that expressed hostility toward Charlayne Hunter and Hamilton Holmes during UGA's integration crisis. Fortieth Anniversary of UGA's Desegregation, January 9, 2001. Courtesy of Hargrett Rare Book and Manuscript Library, University of Georgia Libraries.

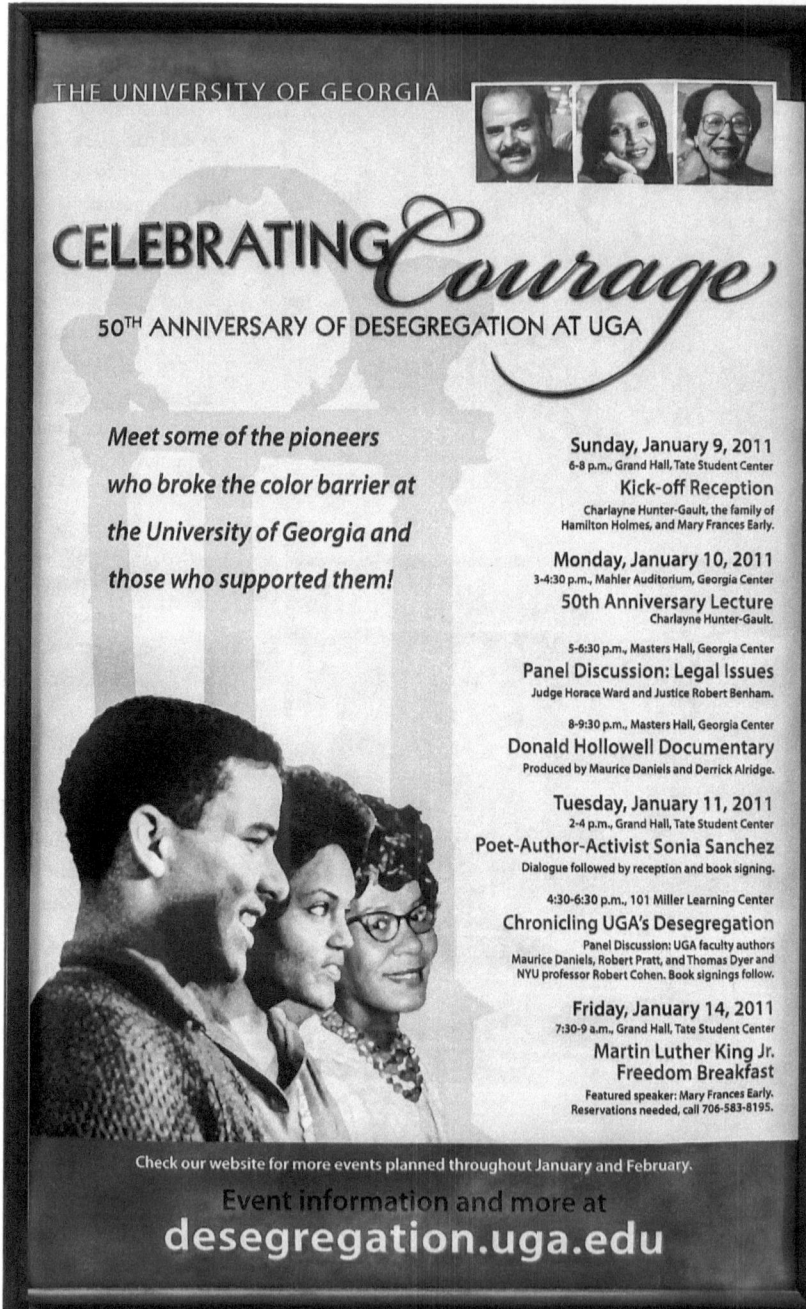

Poster for events marking the fiftieth anniversary of UGA's desegregation, featuring photos of Hamilton Holmes, Charlayne Hunter-Gault, the university's first African American undergraduates, and Mary Frances Early, UGA's first Black graduate student. Celebrating Courage: 50th Anniversary of UGA Desegregation, 2011. Courtesy of Hargrett Rare Book and Manuscript Library, University of Georgia Libraries.

CHAPTER FOUR

Black Memory and University of Georgia's Desegregation Struggle

On one level, whiteness is the starting point for the University of Georgia's desegregation since the university in Jim Crow Georgia existed as an institution run by and for whites. But, of course, UGA's desegregation could never have occurred unless African Americans organized to challenge Jim Crow higher education in the courts and on campus. Since the struggle that smashed UGA's color line was among the major historic events in 1960s America and would ultimately prove transformative for the university, one might expect that UGA would take some interest in documenting the Black history that made this transformative event possible. After all, UGA was a research university, a knowledge-generating institution, and it would seem elemental to think it would research its own history.

But such an expectation runs aground as it clashes head-on with the racial dynamics of UGA, which through the 1960s and 1970s remained an institution whose virtually all-white administration displayed precious little interest in Black history, even the Black history made on its own campus. Thus, we might think of the absence in these decades of UGA commemorative events or published scholarship on its Black history and its desegregation struggle as one manifestation of the afterlife of Jim Crow at the university. What this meant was that UGA not only failed to generate any books, scholarly articles, or conferences on the university's desegregation struggle, but it allocated no funding whatever to conducting oral histories with the key Black organizers, lawyers, and students who were at the heart of that struggle—nor with their families and friends. Nor did UGA in the 1960s or 1970s create a historical archive dedicated to documenting its desegregation or any aspect of its racist past, suggesting that this was a history it would rather forget.[1]

Fortunately for the historical record, among the reporters who covered UGA's desegregation crisis was Calvin Trillin, who in 1963 would do more to probe the origins, meaning, and history of that desegregation struggle than would the entire university faculty and administration back then. Trillin, who in 1960–61 covered the desegregation struggle for *Time* magazine, was dissatisfied by the way his reportage was cut and edited into short squibs by that news magazine. So he returned just before Holmes and Hunter were due to graduate from UGA in 1963, researching and writing a series of insightful, in-depth, and lengthy articles for *New Yorker* magazine that would become the core of his pathbreaking book, *An Education in Georgia: Charlayne Hunter, Hamilton Holmes, and the Integration of the University of Georgia* (1964). As the subtitle makes evident, Trillin realized and wrote of the story of UGA's desegregation as centering on, and originating with, the university's first Black students, their families, and the civil rights organizers of Black Atlanta. Trillin did interviews and wrote biographical portraits of Hunter, Holmes, and their support network. This enabled him to bring them and their desegregation struggle to life on his pages. Such work on Black history and reportage on the Black community was so rarely seen in the national news media in the early 1960s that Trillin received mail from readers who assumed—incorrectly—that he is Black.[2]

And it's a good thing Trillin did all those interviews because by the time UGA faculty got around to probing this history in book-length studies decades later, some of the key African Americans involved in the desegregation struggle had passed away. This was the case most notably with Hamilton Holmes, who died in 1995 and has never been the subject of a book-length biography even though he was involved not only in desegregating UGA but went on to become the first Black student to attend and graduate from Emory University's medical school. It was not until almost a decade after Robert A. Pratt became the first African American history professor at UGA in 1987, and Black social work professor Maurice Daniels emerged as a civil rights biographer and documentary filmmaker, that the university began to add to what Trillin had published about the Black community roots of UGA's desegregation struggle. Pratt's and Daniels's illuminating books on the university's desegregation did not appear until the twenty-first century, and given UGA's long neglect of this history, both had to connect with a civil rights community that had for decades been distant from the university.[3]

With regard to key Black figures in the UGA desegregation struggle, most were too busy getting on with their careers and lives to take the time to write about their part in that struggle. This was true of key members of the legal team that won the desegregation case, such as Donald Hollowell and Horace Ward, and businessman Jesse Hill, who led Black Atlanta's civil rights initiative to end the color line in Georgia's higher education system; and it was also true of Hamilton Holmes, who, after his UGA years, was at work night and day on his medical training and practice. This helps to explain why the only memoir of the UGA desegregation struggle to appear in the twentieth century was Charlayne Hunter-Gault's *In My Place* (1992), a publication made possible because Hunter-Gault alone, of all these movement veterans, was a professional writer. By the time Hunter-Gault wrote her memoir, she had been a nationally prominent reporter for the *New York Times* and was a star news broadcaster for PBS TV, as national correspondent for the *MacNeil/Lehrer News Hour*. Her memoir offers the deepest and most extensive account of UGA's desegregation from a Black perspective.

Even before Hunter-Gault published her memoir she made it clear that, though she viewed Georgia's Jim Crow educational system as racially discriminatory, her educational history was not some simple story of deprivation; the Black community was resourceful and had inspired high educational achievement even in the face of the poor funding and second-hand curriculum materials provided by Georgia's white-dominated school system. As Hunter-Gault explained to an *Atlanta Journal-Constitution* reporter in 1978, Black Atlanta

> was a really terrific place to grow up . . . in many ways—and let me say I wouldn't want to go back to that kind of [unequal, segregated school] system—but growing up like we did gave you a special kind of confidence. At Turner [Atlanta's most highly regarded Black high school, which she attended], we had spirit and unity and celebrations of black history. I think some blacks must feel disoriented today. Oh sure, we had second-hand equipment and books the white schools discarded, but the most important things were the people and the teachers. My English and homeroom teacher, Victoria Sutton, helped teach me that there were no boundaries if you worked hard enough.[4]

Hunter-Gault made a similar point through both the structure and the content of her memoir *In My Place*. Though she would become famous—together with her friend and classmate Hamilton Holmes—for shattering UGA's color line, her life's story and educational history were much too rich and complex to be reduced or subordinated to the role she played in challenging Georgia's Jim Crow educational system. Hunter-Gault was not going to present (i.e., misrepresent) her life's story as a mere pean to racial integration since she had grown up in a world that largely lacked it. It is not that she wanted to deny or take anything away from the historic nature of the Georgia desegregation struggle, whose importance she acknowledged and whose victory—however incomplete—she took pride in, but rather to show that the Black community in Jim Crow Georgia had an internal life that was spiritually, intellectually, and politically independent from white Georgia; that her life, like the Black history of which she was a part, was not dependent upon whites and should not be seen as a mere extension of the white world; and that though race relations were problematic, her precollege years were shaped not primarily by them but rather by her family and the institutions of the Black communities in which she was raised.[5] This helps explain why in her memoir Hunter-Gault did not rush into her moving account of the UGA desegregation struggle, but rather—after a prologue that devoted just two paragraphs to that struggle—she spent more than one hundred pages (almost half the book) on her family background and precollege years, lived mostly in Black communities of the Deep South.

It was that Black family and community environment that helped to give her the determination to pursue her desire to become a journalist, which she described as "a passion bordering on obsession" and a "dream" she held—inspired by her comic book heroine, the intrepid reporter Brenda Starr—even though that career aspiration would have been "if not unthinkable, at least undoable in the [Jim Crow] South" of her "early years." Strengthened and sustained by her supportive family, as Hunter-Gault put it, "No one ever told me not to dream, and when the time came to act on that dream, [which came to involve applying to UGA's Grady School of Journalism], I would not let anything stand in the way of fulfilling it."[6] Her family story was, then, not a tale of deprivation but of intellectual and spiritual growth grounded in a solidly middle class life, provided for by her father, an Army chaplain who served in Korea, and her mother, a well-read high school graduate who had worked as a teacher and office manager of a Black real estate company.

Both Hunter-Gault's family history and some of the relocating that her family did, owing to her father's numerous Army postings, provided her with a racial education. There were the family stories of a beloved minister who had stood up courageously for voting rights despite attempts by the Ku Klux Klan to physically intimidate him, and her father's encounters with racism in the Army. Even more personally, there was her direct experience with racial discrimination at the almost all-white military base in Alaska, where her family resided for a short time. Here Hunter-Gault had been excluded from a social club for teens on account of her race and then witnessed her father insisting that they return to the club, where his protests forced the manager to back down. Afterward her father told her, "You can't let them deny you, and I won't let them deny you or me. Not as long as I have breath in my body. Oh no. I have given too much to this man's army to have someone like that deny me and mine."[7] It is little wonder then that when Hunter-Gault returned to Atlanta, where she would finish high school near the top of her class at Turner High, she would share the racial egalitarianism that drew many Black students into the sit-in movement, "imbued," as she wrote in her memoir, "with an unshakable determination to take control of our destiny and force the South to abandon the wretched Jim Crow laws it had perpetuated for generations to keep us in our place."[8]

Religion was another important legacy of her family background that helped set the stage for her role in the UGA desegregation struggle. It wasn't just that Hunter-Gault was, as she put it, a "P. K." (preacher's kid) and the granddaughter of a pastor, but that her own religious convictions ran deep. This was evident by her conversion to Catholicism as well as the way she internalized the Biblical teachings imparted to her by her grandmother ("Momma") Hunter, whom she regarded as a saint, and who started each day by reading the Bible. Recalling her grandmother's profound impact upon her, Hunter-Gault wrote that "the Psalms were her favorite, and she taught me the Twenty-Third Psalm. So devoted was she to the word of the Lord that as I recited the Psalm I could actually envision myself walking through the valley of the shadow of death.... But when Momma Hunter said, 'I shall fear no evil,' I took heart, learned the lines, and got on out of that valley.... "Thy rod and Thy staff they comfort me ... all the days of my life."[9] It was that psalm and her faith that left Hunter-Gault unafraid of the segregationist hostility and even violence she would encounter during the UGA desegregation crisis, and why to this day she does not consider herself to have been courageous in confronting those dangers. Her faith left her confident that she would not be hurt, that she would endure, so to her this was not a case of courageously confronting danger but not being especially concerned about it since she felt certain that God would protect her.

Turner High School had seemed, as Hunter-Gault put it, "an idyllic island in a sea of segregation," where she could experience a joyful social life, with many friends, and be elected the school's homecoming queen, while excelling academically and working with teachers to sharpen her writing skills for her chosen career in journalism.[10] And yet throughout her high school years in the late 1950s, she remained aware of Jim Crow's injustices and crimes. Most notably for her—and many black youths of her generation—was the memory of the gruesome murder, a modern-day lynching, of the young Emmet Till by Mississippi racists, as he was about her age. This, together with the more hopeful *Brown* decision, made it impossible to ever totally put the Black freedom struggle out of her mind. And when civil rights activists came to Turner looking for outstanding graduating students to help break the color line by applying to a historically white university in Georgia, she was willing to step forward.[11] Both Hunter-Gault and her fellow Turner graduate Hamilton

Holmes were a part of Black Atlanta's professional class (including civil rights attorneys, business leaders, and journalists) that mounted the legal challenge that in January 1961 won the court battle ending more than a century and a half of segregation at the University of Georgia. Some of her friends and classmates had by that time, as Hunter-Gault recalled with pride, already become leading activists in the sit-in movement against Jim Crow in downtown Atlanta—as she herself would have been had she not needed to avoid arrest to serve as a test case for integrating UGA. In fact, Hunter-Gault noted in her memoir that she felt "frustrated" that she "couldn't go to jail" with her friends in their nonviolent lunch counter sit-ins against Jim Crow.[12]

Though it is not possible in Hunter-Gault's memoir to always tell how much of her account of the UGA desegregation crisis reflected her thinking as a young college student and how much it reflected her middle-aged perspective as an accomplished journalist, she offers in *In My Place* a distinctly Black perspective on the crisis. Her narrative is both celebratory regarding Black aspirations and scathing in its criticism of white resistance. Hunter-Gault was aware from the outset that the UGA desegregation case (that made headlines and converted her and Holmes to heroic celebrities in the Black community) was no narrow legal dispute, that for Black Georgians of all classes it symbolized freedom and avenues of opportunity being opened after long years of denial and discrimination. Thus in recalling when word finally came that UGA, on January 6, 1961, had lost its court case, and her return to Georgia from Michigan (where she had been temporarily matriculating at Wayne State University) to enroll finally at UGA, Hunter-Gault noted that at the Atlanta airport she "could see in the eyes and on the faces of Black skycaps and porters, maids and janitors, not the shiftless diffident '*niggah, naggah, naggah, naggah,*' but the same prideful brightness that I saw emanating from my own family as one after another recognized me as I walked through the airport. *Our time has come.*"[13]

As the scene shifts to Athens and Hunter-Gault's first attempt to register for classes on January 9, her memoir conveys the tensions of that time. Three days earlier, angry segregationist students had responded to the integration court order by burning crosses and an effigy of Hamilton Holmes, accompanied by ugly racist chants. And, of course, the resistance to integration had not merely come from white supremacist campus militants but also included threats by Georgia's governor and legislature to close the university rather than integrate it, consistent with the state government's massive resistance policy ever since the *Brown* decision seven years earlier. The UGA administration itself, clinging to its segregated past, was still appealing US district court judge W. A. Bottle's integration order on the very day Hunter-Gault came to campus to register. And since the university's desegregation came (eight months) before the state's major court battle over public school integration in the Atlanta school system led to the start of integration there, this made the integration struggle at UGA especially emotional and symbolic, with the fate of Georgia's white supremacist social order hanging in the balance. As Hunter-Gault so memorably put it, "the entire state was caught up in the fast-moving developments" of the UGA desegregation struggle "that had now placed Georgia in a historic spotlight, white sons and daughters facing their most apocalyptic moment since Sherman marched to the sea. Black sons and daughters their most liberating moment since the Emancipation Proclamation."[14]

Thinking back to her first day on the UGA campus, Hunter-Gault evokes her determination to enroll in the face of white hostility. Aware of the dangers of the moment, she writes of coming to campus early with her lawyers and mother because though "we weren't afraid, we weren't crazy." Yet by the time she arrived there was already a rowdy crowd on campus awaiting her, with the most racist students calling out, "Nigger go home." UGA initially had made no provision at all for her safety. Hunter-Gault and her legal team walked swiftly across campus, and while she was enrolling she heard a cheer from the crowd when word came down that UGA's lawyers had obtained a stay on the integration order. This was, as Hunter-Gault recalled, a "devastating blow. We had come so far, and now this."[15] The stay would soon be lifted by US appeals court judge Elbert P. Tuttle, but it was a reminder of the ongoing resistance of UGA to her presence and Hamilton's at the university. What carried her through that first day at UGA was both her sense of self-respect and her conviction that the Jim Crow Georgia 's subordination of its Black citizens had to end, and was about to end. As she journeyed from Black Atlanta to the white Athens campus on that day, she was empowered by "a heady sense of history. . . . This was the morning when I thought about how I was going to take my first steps on to the campus as if I knew my place, only this time, for the first time, it would be I who would be defining my place on *my* terms, on territory that was their pride but was now mine, too. . . . I would walk onto the campus at Georgia, loving myself and demanding respect."[16]

Among the most insightful passages of the UGA chapters in Hunter-Gault's memoir are those where she stepped back and analyzed *why* there was so much white resistance to UGA's desegregation on the part of the university's students and alumni. Here she demonstrated a keen awareness of UGA's role as one of Jim Crow Georgia's "critical institutions" in which "white privilege and power were nurtured and preserved."[17] Much of the power elite of the Georgia political and educational establishments resisting integration had, as we have seen, UGA roots. As Hunter-Gault noted, "The governor of Georgia was an alumnus, and so was Georgia Senator Richard B. Russell, along with members of the Board of Regents and the state legislature."[18] UGA, in her view, helped groom not only the state's parochial white supremacist elite but an equally small-minded mass of alumni, reinforcing rather than challenging their Jim Crow traditions; it "was the place where the sons of Georgia's majority—small-town farmers and businessmen—passed on their traditions and sense of place, not only in Georgia but in the universe, which also tended to be Georgia." On top of all this, she recognized that UGA existed as a kind of whites only social club where Black classmates would be viewed as totally out of place since UGA was "where the good ol' boys cemented their relations with other good ol' boys, and where they found wives among the good ol' girls, most of whom had come there for that purpose."[19]

The registration process had been an emotional roller coaster for Hunter-Gault as she went from that heady feeling of making history by enrolling, to disappointment when the district court issued its stay halting her enrollment, but then was hopeful again when the appeals court quickly lifted the stay. And this emotional tumult continued after Hunter-Gault (on January 11) attended her first classes, which had seemed a positive sign, but one that was followed by a nighttime riot as a mob of racist students besieged her dormitory, where they broke dozens of windows, hoisted a "Nigger Go Home" banner," and were only dispersed after the Athens police deployed tear gas against them. For Hunter-Gault the worst part of the evening was not the ugly riot but rather the UGA administration's response to it, which was to suspend her and Hamilton, supposedly for their own safety (even though the riot had ended before these suspensions were issued). For Hunter-Gault the disappointment over this suspension ran deep, as it led her to feel that her efforts to pursue her dream of attending UGA's journalism school and dissolving the university's color line had been futile. "All I could think was: I've failed, I've failed. I began to cry, and as hard as I tried, I couldn't stop."[20] So when she left with the police to head back to Atlanta, the news photos showed her walking from her dormitory in tears, clutching a statue of the Madonna. Though those photographs led readers to believe she had been driven to tears by fear, that conclusion was, Hunter-Gault insisted, mistaken, and it bothered her as she had not been afraid: those were tears of frustration.[21]

Press accounts and Trillin's book documented the ugly riot scene outside her dormitory, the women's residence hall Center-Myers, but what they missed, and what Hunter-Gault revealed in her memoir, was that the white student residents of her dormitory had, as we have seen, colluded with the mob. She learned that "all the students had been told by the riot planners to turn off the lights in their rooms when it got dark. With the rest of the building in darkness, the three brightly lit windows of my apartment must have been an inviting target for the mob out on the lawn."[22] Hunter-Gault's memoir was also the first published account to record the hostility of her fellow dorm residents that night, whose upset about the broken windows and tear gas led some to lash out at her, denouncing her as a paid pawn and martyr for the National Association for the Advancement of Colored People (NAACP). They yelled insults not only at Hunter-Gault but at a classmate who had befriended her and, as we have seen, spoke down to Hunter-Gault as if she was their maid.[23]

Two days later, Judge Bootle ruled that UGA had to readmit Hunter-Gault and Holmes. But along with this good news, she and Holmes knew they were returning to a university whose students had rioted against their presence, in alliance with Ku Klux Klan members, and done so with the Georgia political establishment's support. Well-connected Atlanta reporters, whom Hunter-Gault got to know and respect during the desegregation crisis, revealed that leading state officials had signaled to segregationist militants on campus that they could riot without consequence, and as we have seen, the state patrol had not shown up at UGA for hours after the riot started. She noted too that none of these political leaders had condemned the racist violence at UGA and that Peter Zack Geer, the Georgia governor's executive secretary, had praised the rioters for their "character and courage" in refusing to "submit to dictatorship and tyranny."[24] Nonetheless, she remained, as she later put it, "upbeat" in the wake of the court order, telling the press "that the ugliness was far outweighed in my mind by 'the friends I made who impressed me as being really sincere.'" Holmes, however, was, as Hunter-Gault indicated in her memoir, "less sanguine," indicating that while he would return to UGA "with an open mind," he did not "think anything could make up for what happened Wednesday night."[25]

Hunter-Gault then devoted most of her memoir's closing chapters to what she termed the "almost quiet time," the years she spent matriculating at UGA once the violence and desegregation crisis itself had come to an end.[26] True to her word, she sought to remain upbeat, reconnecting with a small circle of new friends at UGA, which would come to include Walter Stovall, who (as will be discussed in chapter 5) would become her first husband. And there were a few supportive faculty she looked back on with fondness, along with a handful of Black students who were admitted to UGA before she graduated in 1963.

But her memoir also conveyed the enduring unfriendliness of most UGA students, who proved unwilling and unable to adjust to the idea of a multiracial university. On those pages, she revealed the hostility that some of the students in her dorm exhibited upon her return to the university, where "for roughly a week, girls on the second floor above my room would take turns pounding the floor for hours at a time." This harassment, on top of "all the other tensions of either real or anticipated problem[s]," left her sleep-deprived and drowsy in her early morning class sessions.[27] Plus there was the reactionary Kappa Alpha fraternity, which lowered its Confederate flag again (as it had back on her first day of classes) in protest against her and Holmes's court-ordered readmission to UGA. Hunter-Gault was candid about her annoyance at the ways in which the UGA administration dragged its feet in putting its Jim Crow past behind it: keeping her out of the cafeteria her first semester, refusing to allow her to move from her isolated dorm room to a floor where she would be integrated with other UGA students, and barring her Black friends outside UGA from joining her for campus events.

The contrast between this mistreatment on campus and the warm reception she received as an invited speaker at civil rights movement events both in Georgia and the North was especially striking to Hunter-Gault. Those outside trips were like "a lifeline to a different world.... The incredible affirmation" they provided helped her "through the cold spells" of the unfriendly campus, which "despite the thaw, blew through from time to time."[28] In spite of her considerable social skills (she had been homecoming queen of her high school and had many friends there and at Wayne State), sometimes being the lone Black student in her dorm and her classes at UGA amid a still segregated college town yielded extreme isolation. Memorably evoking this experience, Hunter-Gault recalled that "one day, as I sat in front of my mirror in my bedroom at school, I looked up and realized as I saw myself that I had not uttered a human sound in several days. I had gotten up, gone to class, sat down, taken notes, gotten up again, gone back to my room and studied, and gone to sleep. When I calculated how long it had been, I remember being mildly surprised and smiling to myself. I really was the right one to desegregate the University of Georgia because I had no problem being alone. In fact, I had always relished my solitude. Except that up to now it had always been by choice."[29]

Though the term had not yet been invented when she was attending UGA, Hunter-Gault would from a twenty-first century perspective come to see that she had been impacted by the "microaggressions" directed at her in her UGA years. While, of course, the first semester with the riot had been far worse, after that in both her classes and attempts at an extracurricular life, she experienced more subtle slights—such as when she signed up to work on UGA's student newspaper, the *Red and Black*, "but never got an assignment." Or "when professors went a whole term without addressing" her in class.[30] All this did take a personal, physical toll, leading her to spend considerable time those first semesters in the university infirmary beset by stomach pains.

Resourceful as she was, however, Hunter-Gault managed to make the best of this difficult situation. Thus, when the *Red and Black* refused to give her news to cover as an aspiring journalist, she used her Atlanta connections and was able to get more exciting and important journalistic experience working for the *Atlanta Inquirer*, a new African American newspaper founded by her friend and mentor Carl Holman. Hunter-Gault would, through her reportage, contribute to the *Inquirer's* cutting-edge coverage of the Student Nonviolent Coordinating Committee and the Black Freedom movement in this hub of activism, linking her to this world of Black protest in Atlanta that she had admired and would likely have been a part of had she not gone to UGA.[31]

What emerged from Hunter-Gault's UGA years, evoked so powerfully in her memoir, was a contradictory amalgam of pride in her role in expanding Black educational opportunity, in defying the odds in gaining admission to and graduating from UGA, and gratitude to the Black community, her family, and friends who had made this all possible, together with a critical perspective on the university's continuing recalcitrance about shedding the remnants of its Jim Crow past. A similar duality endured, appearing in her memoir's closing pages and in her 1988 UGA commencement address (which we will discuss in chapter 7), where we find her, as the university's first Black graduation speaker, glorying in the demise of Jim Crow yet concerned about the continuing underrepresentation of Blacks at UGA.[32]

SINCE HAMILTON "HAMP" HOLMES never published a memoir or did a comprehensive oral history, the record of his experience during the desegregation crisis and his subsequent reflections on it—as well as his longer-term view of UGA—is not nearly as rich as that of Charlayne Hunter-Gault. But Calvin Trillin's *An Education in Georgia*, grounded in interviews with Hamilton and his family, as well as in accounts of some of his speeches in 1963, offers valuable insights into Hamp's desegregation experience, as do Hunter-Gault's brief reflections on her friendship and interaction with Hamilton, and quotes from Hamilton in the Atlanta press from the early 1960s and beyond. What

Trillin makes clear is how deeply connected Hamilton's politics and career aspirations were to his distinguished family background in Black Atlanta's professional class and in his family's tradition of civil rights activism. As Trillin put it in 1963, Hamilton "is not only a third generation college graduate; he is also a third generation integrationist."[33] Hamilton's grandfather, Hamilton Mayo Holmes, the patriarch of the Holmes family, was a prominent physician. Hamilton's father, Alfred "Tup" Holmes, was a businessman, and his mother, Isabella Holmes, a teacher. In the mid-1950s Hamilton's father, grandfather, and uncle had filed suit in a court case that ended in the desegregation of the Atlanta public golf course. With such a family background it would have been surprising had Hamilton *not* volunteered to challenge Georgia's Jim Crow line in higher education. In fact, Hamilton credited his activist father with his own decision to challenge the color line, recalling that toward the spring of his senior year in high school "my old man ... said 'I've been a paying a lot of taxes for years'" for state universities that did not accept Blacks. "'Why don't you go to Georgia Tech?'" so his tax dollars would finally be used for nondiscriminatory education. And Hamilton responded, "Daddy, no, I'm going into medicine," which meant UGA, so "we decided to write a letter" to UGA's admissions office.[34]

Intellectual integrity and dedication to academic excellence ran strong in Hamilton, as you might expect in one who had been the valedictorian of his high school and aspired to attend medical school, following in his grandfather's footsteps. That academic intensity played a key role in carrying the desegregation struggle to UGA. Initially the civil rights organizers who initiated that struggle had thought the Jim Crow line could most safely be challenged at Georgia State in Atlanta, but when they brought Hamilton and Charlayne to that campus, Hamilton found its courses offerings, as described in its catalogue, too limited and indicated he wanted to head north to UGA, and Charlayne agreed—even though Athens was remote from Atlanta and its Black community. This mindset also contributed to his willingness to abandon his happy campus life at Morehouse—Atlanta's leading historically Black men's college, which he attended for a year and a half while his Georgia application and desegregation suit dragged on—for UGA. He realized that Georgia had better science facilities, which would be most useful in preparing him for medical school.[35]

Holmes's academic accomplishments and intensity also shaped his response to the shenanigans UGA officials pulled when they argued in court that he had been rejected for admission not because he was Black but because his interview at the university proved that he was unqualified. This slanderous claim was especially offensive to Holmes since he took great pride in the high quality of his academic record, which would subsequently be affirmed in his UGA years when his sterling academic record as a premed student led to his election to the Phi Beta Kappa academic honor society. His no-nonsense approach to college work not only led to such academic success but served as a kind of refuge from the social isolation he experienced at UGA. Even though he could not find friends among white UGA students, he could view his college years as successful in the sense that he had refuted their white supremacist assumptions through his superior academic performance—as Holmes's father put it, "making those crackers sit up and take notice."[36]

All of this contributed to what we might term Holmes's model minority approach to the struggle against racism and discrimination in academia and the workplace. Holmes essentially equated his brand of academic intensity and diligence with the struggle for equality, viewing such dedication to excellence as the best weapon against discrimination. Since Holmes had proven the racists wrong via his academic excellence, he reasoned so should other Blacks as a route to respect, meritocracy, and career opportunity.[37] It was, in Holmes's view, not enough for Blacks to equal whites' academic performance; they had to prove themselves superior academically to their white classmates to earn their respect and make it impossible for whites to make a case for white superiority or supremacy. And in fact, Holmes offered this as a key part of his message when he spoke in Black communities and at events organized by civil rights and human relations organizations during his UGA years.

In what Trillin in 1963 termed Holmes's favorite speech topic, "Higher Education and the New Negro," Holmes argued that to take advantage of the new opportunities opened up by the civil rights movement, Blacks, in a world of scientific and technological advances, needed to attend and excel in universities in order to compete for good jobs. This was especially true, Holmes insisted, since "ours is a competitive society.... This is even more so for the Negro ... [who] must have more training than his white counterpart and be more qualified if he is to beat him out of a job." The lesson, Holmes concluded, was that "we must strive to be superior in order to be given an equal chance." And this was his guiding principle in his work at UGA, where, as Holmes explained, "I cannot feel satisfied with just equaling the average grade there. I am striving to be superior. If the average is B, then I want an A. The importance of superior training cannot be overemphasized. This is a peculiar situation, I know, but it is reality, and reality is something we Negroes must learn to live with."[38]

This also connected with Holmes and Hunter-Gault's disappointment with the slow pace of desegregation at UGA. In a speech Holmes gave to a

Black Atlanta audience in 1963, he vented his anger that in the two and a half years since they entered UGA, there had been no Black student applicants one year and only half a dozen the next. Holmes believed "there should be ten, or fifteen, or even twenty times more Negro students at Georgia." Both had expected far more than this handful of Black students. Through a twenty-first century lens, UGA itself seems clearly at fault for this situation since it made no effort at all to recruit Black students. But back in 1963, with Jim Crow still casting its long shadow over UGA—and its administration only two years away from its court battle to keep the university white—neither Holmes nor Hunter-Gault expected any pro-integration initiatives from the UGA administration. Instead, they looked to the Black community of Atlanta, whose civil rights leaders had recruited them, and they bemoaned the community's failure to recruit more Black students and create scholarships to help them afford a UGA education. To Holmes, this signaled the need for a better understanding on the part of the Black community of the importance of advanced education in the competition for employment, as outlined in his "Higher Education and the New Negro" speech.[39]

Both Holmes and Hunter-Gault realized that desegregation was not a one-day event but an ongoing process. And though they took pride that their admission had ended UGA's Jim Crow regime, they understood that process was moving at an unsatisfactory, glacial pace. Holmes spoke publicly in 1963 about the role that white student hostility played in keeping the campus mostly white. He characterized "the atmosphere" at UGA as being "just about the same as it had been in January 1961. The only difference is that there is no overt resistance. The atmosphere is definitely an atmosphere of uncordiality."[40] Such an atmosphere was hardly conducive to attracting more Black students to UGA. The implication of this, though Holmes did not say so explicitly, was that though UGA's segregationist rioters had failed to stop the first Black students from attending UGA, like-minded segregationist students had succeeded in forging the kind of cold and unwelcoming atmosphere toward Black students that helped keep the campus almost all white, and not just for the moment but for the foreseeable future. Holmes deemed this "a big problem. It has bothered me. And I don't know how it can be overcome."[41]

Holmes learned that such candor about the campus's chilly social atmosphere evoked resentment from white students. He was infuriated by a hostile column that the editor of UGA's student newspaper ran in its pages during Holmes's last year at the university, attacking him for his speeches criticizing UGA. The column sought to place the blame for all his problems at UGA on

Holmes himself, implying that he lacked school spirit and so had not engaged in the extracurricular activities that could have prevented him from going friendless at UGA, depicting him as a self-isolating grind who did nothing but study and give speeches. Yet the column itself attested to the kind of attitudes that had created that cold atmosphere in the first place, suggesting that Holmes did not belong at UGA and that he had been brought to the university as a result of coercion by the courts: "Holmes," the column asserted, "entered the university forcibly as an alien. He attended as an alien. And when he graduates this June (with honors, I understand) he will still be an alien. The treatment he has received, the friendless atmosphere he has encountered: he could have expected no more and he has received no less."[42]

This column actually revealed more about UGA's white student body than it did about Holmes, notably its scoffing at him as if it were OK to view and treat him as a pariah. But on top of this was the way it embodied the utter cluelessness of the majority culture, its inability even to consider the kind of discrimination and belligerence Holmes had encountered at UGA, and the refusal to speak to Holmes before publishing such a harsh column. Had this editor done so, he might have seen how unfair and inaccurate the column was, for example on extracurricular life, in suggesting Holmes's indifference. Actually, Holmes had been a star football player in high school and might well have played for UGA's football team had it not barred Blacks from doing so during his years at UGA. Nonetheless, Holmes had taken an interest and attended some UGA games in his senior year (he had not done so earlier out of concern for his own safety).[43]

And though Holmes did devote a great deal of time to his studies, this did not mean that, as the *Red and Black* editor suggested, he was a hermit who did nothing but prepare for his classes. In fact, the reason Holmes made the long trip back to Atlanta almost every Friday after his last class was so that he could be among his friends (and family) over the weekends and do the kind of socializing that seemed impossible on the unfriendly Athens campus. Holmes found the contrast between Black Atlanta and white UGA so stark that he could feel it just from taking a walk: "At home, when I walk down the street, I speak to almost everyone who passes. It's been that way all my life. All week [at UGA] I look up at people, wanting to speak, and people turn their heads. I guess that bothers me more than anything else."[44] The weekly trips to Black Atlanta were essential to Holmes's ability to endure the chilly campus atmosphere, as he later explained: "My going home was an outlet for me that allowed me to be cool. If I had stayed [in Athens] the whole time, I would have been very, very hostile."[45]

The reality was that in light of some of the worst experiences Holmes went through at UGA, it was an understatement to term the campus unfriendly. Aside from the riot itself, Holmes had experienced episodes of harassment. One day he found that all the tires of his car had been flattened. Racists from UGA's most hostile fraternity, at another point, blocked his car and were crowding around him menacingly, which ended without violence only because Holmes, with a flashlight in his pocket, managed to convince the frat boys that he had a gun. It is little wonder, then, that Holmes chose to live off campus with a Black family all through his UGA years and that, as Trillin noted, near the end of his final academic year at UGA, "Hamilton . . . had never eaten in a university dining hall, studied in the library, used the gymnasium, or entered the snack bar. He had no white friends outside the classroom. No white student had ever visited him, and he had never visited one of them."[46]

While researching his biographical segment on Holmes for his *New Yorker* articles on UGA's desegregation, Trillin, after driving back with Holmes in the Georgia student's car to the home of the Black family that hosted him, was struck by what he saw as he looked back at Holmes's car. "On the front bumper was a red and black sign reading 'Georgia Bulldogs,'" a booster bumper sticker for the UGA football team (the Georgia "Dawgs"). Trillin had seen "similar decals or bumper stickers on the cars driven by Charlayne and Mary Frances Early [UGA's first African American graduate student]." So he asked Holmes "why all the Negro students went in for such things." Holmes replied, "Well, we do go to school here. . . . It's school—spirit? No, not spirit. I'm trying to think of another word. I'll let you know."[47]

This bumper sticker discussion raises an important point about the Black desegregation experience and the way the first African American students at UGA processed it. It was complex, conflicted, and its emotional impact was, to say the least, not easy to convey—as we saw with Holmes as he struggled unsuccessfully for the words to explain why he displayed that Bulldog sign. On the one hand, the insulting admissions process and UGA's lies and slander in *Holmes v. Danner* had been horrible, as were the riot, the harassment, coldness, and microaggressions. But the formal education had been useful and mostly positive. And it was also the case that one of the main goals of the desegregation struggle was to open UGA's gates to Black students, to make it their place too. After all, UGA had been the college of their choice; its name would be on their diplomas. So taking some pride in at least the positive side of UGA was in a way a testament to the fact that those years of struggle had accomplished something worthwhile for themselves and something historic for the university, Georgia, and its Black community.

These contradictions were equally visible four years later when Holmes was interviewed by an *Atlanta Journal* newspaper reporter in May 1967, on the occasion of Holmes's approaching graduation from Emory University's medical school. Now that he was about to complete his education as Emory's first Black medical student, Holmes, in looking back on his UGA years, praised Georgia as "a pretty good school" that provided him with "a good background in the basic sciences" that prepared him for his medical schoolwork. And he had positive things to say about his professors at UGA, whom he termed "helpful and cordial." But Holmes also stressed that while he was a student at UGA, "I never enjoyed it." While "it was a good education and it helped me to mature an awful lot, the big drawback was the social life. It was nonexistent.... The students were cold and unfriendly. I was never quite accepted." And he contrasted UGA with Emory, where he had made friends among his fellow medical students and found his medical school experience "pleasant and enjoyable." The reporter concluded that despite such criticisms, "Holmes, who will be 26 in July, speaks of his life on the [UGA] campus without bitterness."[48]

Had UGA's leaders been interested in recruiting African American students or cared about Holmes in 1967 and read this *Atlanta Journal* article about his dissolving the color line at Emory, as he had at Georgia, they would have seen the opportunity here. Holmes, the first African American male to attend and graduate from UGA, was—despite his criticisms of his unfriendly classmates—crediting the university for helping to pave the way for his success in medical school and his emergence as a highly qualified physician. He could obviously serve as a role model and recruiting magnet for other aspiring African American students who might follow in his footsteps at UGA. But UGA in 1967—as we shall see in more detail later in this study—had yet to develop a strong interest in such recruitment, and its leaders seemed reluctant to move UGA with any dispatch beyond its Jim Crow past. Thus, they did nothing in 1967, nor much in the following decade to reconnect with Hamilton Holmes, who would have no official ties in these years with the university he had sacrificed so much to desegregate. But Holmes did return to UGA in 1977 to speak to a predominantly Black audience at the Martin Luther King Jr. memorial event, and true to form, he argued that "education is the key to the future of the black man.... The end result of the sit-ins, boycotts, and demonstrations is that we have opened many doors. We must be prepared to take advantage of our opportunities."[49] It would not be until the 1980s, however, as generational change began to take hold within the UGA administration, that its leadership would finally reconnect officially with Holmes, leading to an invitation in 1983 to become the first Black trustee of the Georgia Foundation. Despite his initial hesitancy, Holmes, out of concern about continuing the struggle to diversify the student body (and also bring in more Black faculty), and in accord with the same kind of school loyalty that had led him to post a Bulldogs bumper sticker on his car back in 1963, said yes to that invitation.[50]

One ought not, however, underestimate the magnanimity Holmes displayed in being willing to officially reconnect with UGA. Given all that he had been through, with the administration slandering him in the court case, as well as the riot and student hostility, he would have to have been almost superhuman to have not carried some bitter feelings from his UGA years. And in fact, contrary to that *Atlanta Constitution* reporter's upbeat conclusion in 1967 (mentioned above), Holmes, in a 1977 radio interview, admitted that when he "left Georgia I was a little bitter.... And while I will not go so far as to say that all whites were bad people, I in general did not trust the white race and I felt that anything we got had to be taken, essentially, but I have mellowed a lot over the years."[51] Holmes linked that mellowing to the fact that much of UGA's faculty treated him fairly, and that both at Emory and in his medical practice he had experienced many whites who focused on the high quality of his professional work, not his race.[52]

ALTHOUGH IT WAS A LONG TIME COMING, Vernon Jordan's memoir, *Vernon Can Read!* (2001), published forty years after UGA's desegregation, was well worth the wait. Jordan's role in the UGA desegregation case is less well known today than his work as advisor and transition team head for president Bill Clinton, and as executive director of the Urban League and the United Negro College Fund. But his role on the legal team that won *Holmes v. Danner* and UGA's court-ordered integration was not unimportant, and his memoir's discussion and historical contextualization of both this court case and the lawyering that made this victory possible is brimming with insights. Jordan's account is brief but offers a distinctly Black perspective on UGA's desegregation.[53]

That perspective was expressed even in the title Jordan chose for the chapter where he dealt with UGA; it was not the university but the Atlanta-based civil rights attorney Donald Hollowell who got top billing in that title: "Mr. Hollowell."[54] Hollowell—together with the NAACP's eminent lawyer Constance Baker Motley—led the all-Black legal team that argued the Georgia case. Jordan, only twenty-six years old at the time, was the youngest attorney on this team. Fresh out of Howard University School of Law, he served as Hollowell's first intern (he called himself Hollowell's "first law clerk") and was, Jordan writes, "in awe of him."[55] And such admiration was well deserved. Though Hollowell is most well known nationally for his work as an attorney for Martin Luther King Jr., in Georgia he was already famed in the African American community as the state's most accomplished legal advocate for Black rights. So much so that among Atlanta civil rights workers, whom he represented in court, one of the popular chants went, "King is my leader, Hollowell is my lawyer, we shall not be moved." Hollowell was revered in Black Atlanta as "Georgia's Mr. Civil Rights."[56]

For Jordan, the UGA case, though quite important, was a subset of Hollowell's larger struggle against Jim Crow Georgia's use of the courts to oppress and discriminate against its Black citizens. In fact, the first cases discussed in Jordan's chapter that covered UGA find Hollowell battling even more serious, literally life-and-death matters, where the state courts, which were still excluding Black jurors, rushed to judgment against Black defendants in capital cases. Hollowell found it difficult to prevail in some of these cases given the racism of the Georgia jurists and other state officials who could have prevented such unjust executions.[57]

Such cases are a reminder that the Jim Crow system, upheld by many of the state's UGA-trained prosecutors and judges, did far more deadly things than maintain segregated schools—enabling us to see the place of UGA's racial history and desegregation struggle in relation to this larger pattern of injustice and Hollowell's struggle against it. Indeed, when you check the biographical record of the jurist and politicians whom Jordan mentioned as refusing to take seriously Hollowell's attempt to secure a stay of execution for Nathaniel Johnson, a young African American whose rights had been trampled, you find a trail of Jim Crow UGA graduates (judge Francis Scarlet, UGA law school, class of 1913; Henry Neal, counsel to Georgia governor Vandiver, UGA, BA, class of 1943, UGA law school; and Vandiver himself, who, as we have seen, had taken his undergraduate and law degrees at UGA).[58] But, as Jordan shows, when Hollowell had the opportunity, he used the federal courts skillfully, as in the Preston Cobb case, stopping the execution of this fifteen-year-old after an all-white jury sentenced this Black teen to death.[59]

Jordan's memoir demonstrated that for Georgia's Black communities, having strong legal advocacy asserting Black rights was a relatively new and much appreciated development, that when Hollowell had begun such work in Georgia in 1952 there were less than fifteen practicing African American attorneys in the whole state.[60] Thus when Hollowell and Jordan came to Reidsville, Georgia, to defend James Fair, an eighteen-year-old African American who, as Jordan put it, "had been arrested, tried, convicted [and] ... sentenced to death ... within 48 hours," the Black community showed its appreciation in a highly personal way. The Black lawyers could find no place to eat as the restaurants near the court were for whites only, so they ate bologna sandwiches in Hollowell's car. On the third day of the trial, a local Black woman told Jordan, "We've been watching you lawyers eat bologna for two days now.... Don't eat [that] today.... Come to my home for lunch." When Jordan and Hollowell followed her advice and the directions to her home, they confronted, as Jordan recounted, a dazzling scene: "We saw a beautiful ... table set for royalty. Her best silver, china, and crystal, a lace tablecloth, beautifully folded white napkins, and the most exquisite Southern cuisine I've ever eaten. Some ten black women and their husbands joined hands with us for grace. Our hostess's husband said the blessing. I shall never forget one sentence in that prayer: 'Lord, we can't join the NAACP down here, but thanks to your bountiful blessings, we can feed the NAACP lawyers.'"[61]

In discussing the UGA desegregation case, Jordan found similar Black solidarity and also similar obstacles for the legal team. The Black attorneys daily commuted the 150-mile round trip from Atlanta since no Athens hotels were open to African Americans. Jordan found that supporters of integration came to court daily. "This was," he wrote, "never just Hamilton's and Charlayne's case.... Everyone knew that if we won, all other black children in Georgia—in the country for that matter—would have a significant victory. So black people came to court."[62] Jordan noted that the courtroom itself offered a refuge from segregation, and one that much of the local Black community had never experienced before in Jim Crow Georgia. Blacks who came out to watch the trial, "accustomed to Georgia's segregated state courts," were "a little confused at first.... They hung back, not sure where they were supposed to sit. We were, of course, in a US federal court, which was not segregated. It took a short while before they figured this out, and then sat where they wanted."[63]

Jordan's account spotlights the brilliance of the legal team's leadership, both Hollowell and Constance Baker Motley, whose excellent strategy for the case proved essential to victory.[64] He compared Baker Motley's cross-examinations to "a barber sharpening his razor.... No one was better prepared for courtroom battle than she was. She planned every detail of her direct examination, anticipated every possible issue that could be raised on cross-examination, and prepared a response to hypotheticals."[65] And, young as he was, Jordan himself contributed to the court victory when during discovery, in poring through mountains of admissions files, he found evidence that a white female student with an almost identical academic profile to Hunter's had been admitted at a time when UGA had claimed a lack of space and had closed off all admissions (which had been UGA's excuse for rejecting Hunter). This was a "smoking gun" that helped pave the way for the integration order.[66]

Beyond such legal skill, Jordan's memoir evoked the humanity, solidarity, and compassion that the lawyers for Holmes and Hunter directed toward these young plaintiffs. Jordan was especially impressed with Horace Ward (who we shall discuss in more detail shortly), who after being rejected for admission to the UGA law school because of Jim Crow had earned his law degree in the North and joined the legal team to, as Jordan wrote, "make sure that other black students had the opportunity to do what he could not do: attend the University of Georgia." This, Jordan concluded, "has been so much the story of black advancement: one person being rebuffed, and then supporting those who rise up to make other attempts when the right moment appears."[67] Ward, as historian Robert Pratt documented, not only confirmed all this, but made it clear that he drew upon his own experience with UGA's hostile and dishonest interview process to reassure Holmes when "evidence" from his almost identical interview was used by UGA in *Holmes v. Danner* to justify rejecting Holmes's application. Ward, recalling his effort to help Holmes keep his morale up when he had felt so wounded by UGA's insulting conduct, explained, "I knew what he was feeling, and I could understand why there were times when he didn't want to go on. The way they interviewed him, asking him about red-light districts and such, and bringing up other indiscreet personal matters, was rough on him. But we had to explain to him that these kinds of things were to be expected, because the bottom line was always that they were not seeking to qualify you, but to *disqualify* you, and at that time it really didn't matter to them how they did it."[68] Similarly, Baker Motley comforted Hunter when she was glum about having to be in court in Athens rather than with her friends around the Christmas holiday, which startled Hunter, since she had assumed the lawyer was so focused on the case that she barely knew Hunter existed.[69]

Jordan recalled that while still aglow from their court victory, other hurdles remained, including the backlash by state officials who had threatened to close down the university rather than abide the court-ordered integration. And then there was the threat of violence on the campus itself from militant segregationist students and the Klan. Jordan was keenly aware of the dangers since he and the other civil rights lawyers had faced similar dangers in other cases. In fact, he had felt the tension when he delivered subpoenas to high-ranking

Georgia officials early in the case—not something that would be well received from a Black lawyer by these segregationists. And since Jordan would decades later be seriously wounded by a white supremacist wielding a rifle, his UGA narrative is especially attuned to the physical dangers the students and their legal team faced on the campus. He recalled getting out of his car that first day on campus and escorting Charlayne "through a howling mob, who saw this bright young woman (and me) as their mortal enemies—no southern hospitality, no Christian spirit of brotherhood—just unbounded hatred and fear on open display."[70]

Reflecting on why he and Hunter were able to come out of that first day unscathed, Jordan credited the news media. The presence of reporters and news cameras made it risky for UGA's militant racists to riot in broad daylight. Jordan was right about this since the segregationist rioting, cross burnings, and effigy hangings were all done in cowardly fashion at night under cover of darkness. And as Jordan noted, the media helped the cause of equality and justice in another important way: its cameras captured the ugliness of the daytime student crowds with their racist chants and the young white faces contorted with hatred. And the news media simultaneously conveyed the stark contrast between the civility of those representing the civil rights movement and their foes. In Jordan's words,

> as in other instances where blacks have sought to exercise some of the basic rights of citizenship—going unmolested to a lunch counter, enrolling in a state university for which they were paying taxes, sitting where they wanted to on a bus—there was always great dignity that stood in marked contrast to the baseness of those who came out to jeer. Look at the old film footage and newspaper pictures from those days: schoolchildren versus the mob, young adults trying to get an education versus the mob, peaceful diners versus the mob. It comes through so clearly. There's just no question who was out of moral line.[71]

Despite all the ugliness and resistance, Jordan came away from the UGA struggle feeling optimistic. The hard work on this just cause had yielded both an important victory and an encouraging lesson: "*Holmes v. Danner* taught me that sustained social agitation, moral suasion, and political action can create an environment in which people in power feel compelled to do the right thing."[72]

But Jordan had seen too much injustice in the state courts to conclude that this important victory via the federal courts would quickly end Jim Crow Georgia's misuse of its own judicial system, that white Georgia jurists and prosecutors in those courts would continue trampling Black rights, rushing to jail, and even executing African America defendants. There were, as Jordan aptly put it, "limits of law in a society unwilling to do justice."[73]

THE MOST RECENT MEMOIR by one of the pioneers of racial integration at UGA was that of Mary Frances Early, a music educator, who in summer 1961 became the first African American graduate student at Georgia, and in 1962 the first to be awarded a UGA degree. Because Early entered the university six months after the court-ordered admission of Holmes and Hunter and after the initial UGA desegregation crisis and riot, her entry into the university in June 1961 came at a time when UGA's integration was no longer generating headlines and television coverage. Owing to this timing and the fact that she had not been a party to the litigation that had resulted in UGA's desegregation, Early never obtained the celebrity status that Holmes and Hunter did. Nonetheless, her experience at UGA was a significant part of the history of the university's desegregation, and her memoir *The Quiet Trailblazer: My Journey as the First Black Graduate of the University of Georgia* (2021), is an important document on Black memory and UGA's desegregation struggle.

Like Hunter-Gault and Holmes, Early was a product of Black Atlanta's middle class. Her father was a restaurant and grocery store owner and her mother a teacher. Early had attended the same Black high school as Hunter-Gault and Holmes. And like Holmes she was its valedictorian there and won the same honors at Clark College, the historically Black college she graduated from in Atlanta in 1957. In her youth she had experienced and witnessed painful episodes of racial discrimination on buses, at gas stations, and movie theaters. As a music major and teacher, she was especially aware of and indignant about such discrimination in musical venues. In her work as a music teacher, she would not stand for racial insensitivity toward the students in the Black school in which she worked. Thus when, at a young people's concert, in an audience participation part of the performance, the Atlanta Symphony Orchestra began playing the Old South anthem, "Dixie," Early instructed her students (fifth, sixth, and seventh graders) not to sing and to be seated, and they heeded her words.[74]

Early had begun her graduate education at the University of Michigan, one of the top music education programs. She transferred out of Michigan and applied to the University of Georgia as an act of solidarity with Charlayne and Hamilton after reading with horror of the segregationist riot at UGA on January 11. While Early's mother was politically sympathetic, she initially opposed the idea of Mary Frances attending Georgia out of concerns for her safety. To reinforce her point about the dangers of confronting violent racists, she told Mary Frances for the first time about the racist murders of four African Americans in her hometown, Monroe, Georgia, in 1946, which were terrifying. But Mary Frances was determined and convinced her mother that going there was the right thing to do, standing with Charlayne and Hamilton in their struggle to banish Jim Crow from UGA.[75]

The application process, as discussed in the introduction to this book, involved a nightmarish interview in which UGA admissions officers asked her the same kinds of insulting questions they had used in their interview with Hamilton Holmes (and Horace Ward before him), designed to help keep Black students out of the university. They would never ask a white applicant, "Had she ever visited a house of prostitution?" Early understood that this question was designed to undermine her "self-esteem and dignity," but she kept her composure, not wanting, through an angry response, to give the admissions officer an excuse for rejecting her. So she simply told them the truth, which was that she was "a teacher, a professional, and had no reason or desire to visit a house of prostitution."[76] The registrar also sought to discourage her by telling her UGA might not accept the graduate credits she had already earned at the University of Michigan. Early thought that was absurd since Michigan's music graduate program had such an outstanding reputation, but she again avoided becoming argumentative and did not object to his ridiculous assertion.[77]

If all this was not enough, Early later learned that the Georgia Bureau of Investigation had conducted an FBI-style background probe of her, seeking some pretext that could be used to reject her application to the university. This resulted in an eleven-page investigative report on whether she had broken any laws or had any character flaws—checking on whether she had an illegitimate child, venereal disease, used drugs, shop lifted, and so forth.[78] Unable to find any reason to reject her, the university admitted Early and she began classes in the summer of 1961. Her admission did make one of the Atlanta papers, though since Holmes and Hunter had already completed their first semester at UGA in the aftermath of the desegregation crisis back in January, Early's coming to the university did not generate much media coverage.

Since UGA's first two Black undergraduates would be away for summer vacation, when Early began her graduate program that summer, she was the only African American student on campus. She took heart from the welcome she received from speech professor James Popovich, who sent her a friendly letter even before she arrived at UGA, and from the warm reception accorded her by Corky King, the Presbyterian campus minister (the one person at UGA who was so openly supportive of integration that he would soon be fired) and several students. Her hope was that since, unlike Hunter and Holmes, she was enrolling in a graduate program, the white students would be more mature than the undergraduates who had been so hostile to UGA's first two Black students. The supportive nature of most of her professors in her music education program also left her hopeful.[79]

These hopes were quickly dashed, however. Even before Early began her coursework, she encountered hostility from UGA graduate students. Told that she needed to take the GRE to complete her admissions, she showed up at the Ag auditorium to take the test, but when she took a seat all the students already there abandoned the row of seats near her. This was, Early recalled, "not a very good start to taking an important exam. I was both insulted and crestfallen. As it turned out I did pass the GRE with flying colors but I really had to focus on the questions because the incident greatly affected my inner psyche."[80] She got a similar response from the students in several of her classes and when dining on campus. In her first meal at the cafeteria, white students greeted her with catcalls and threw slices of lemon at her from their iced tea glasses, several of which struck her. It only ended when the manager came out and got the students to stop. Early remembered being "so angry and insulted over the incident that I found it difficult to eat my lunch."[81]

Early found that the worst part was never knowing what to expect, that ordinary campus experiences, such as a research trip to the university library, though usually uneventful, could in a moment turn into an ugly racist incident. One such incident, recounted by Early in her memoir, is especially striking since it occurred on the front steps of the university library, an institution one associates with higher learning but instead became a place where she faced, as she put it, "ignorance and stupidity." About to start researching a paper on Latin music, Early approached the library's entrance, where she encountered a group of male students who had "spread themselves across the front steps as if to block my entrance. One of them said 'I smell a dog.' Another said 'That's not a dog, that's a [N-word].' I was hurt and humiliated but continued to walk towards the steps. I decided I would be the bulldog I was supposed to be—and barge through their barrier if necessary. Just as I neared the top step, they broke ranks and laughed loudly."[82] Once in the library, Early did start her research but was too upset that night to get much done. She was surprised by how much such harassment impacted her. "I had thought," Early reflected, "that I could handle any situation at UGA. I was, after all, twenty-five years of age and self-selected. No one had asked me to attend UGA. Transferring there was *my* choice, but I was human, and the slights and troubling incidents really got under my skin at times."[83]

As with Hunter and Holmes, Early was also impacted by the remnants of Jim Crow maintained by the UGA administration. After being invited by her professor to join the university's summer chorus, she was informed that the administration barred African American guests since the desegregation of the university only applied to students.[84] And while she was happy to be housed with Hunter as her dorm suite-mate, she was irritated, as Hunter was, that UGA would not allow either of them to move to another dorm floor since the administration preferred that the Black students room in isolation from their white dorm-mates.

Despite all these indignities, Early, as a talented, diligent graduate student and a veteran music teacher, excelled in her master's program. Since it was a one-year MA, Early, though having come to UGA after Holmes and Hunter, would graduate a year before the two undergraduates did, making her the first African American student to get a UGA degree.

Early did not ask permission from UGA officials but simply went ahead and invited her friends and family to the summer commencement ceremony, making this the first racially integrated graduation audience in UGA's history. Though the news media did not spotlight this event, Early was well aware of the significance of what was happening on that hot August day in 1962: "I was overcome with emotion. It felt surreal. This was truly a watershed moment. After more than 175 years of an all-white University of Georgia, the university was about to confer a degree on an African American.... It felt so rewarding to realize that I had done my part in bringing about equality and social justice in the state of Georgia. I also realized that I had helped pave the way for others to make that journey."[85]

As with Holmes and Hunter, UGA's administration for decades did nothing to keep in touch with Early after her graduation or to seek her help in recruiting Black students. She was contacted once in 1968 by the music department about her election to a national music honor society on account of her outstanding grades as an MA student. But that was it. This seemed to Early one last insult from the university. As she wrote in her memoir, "I heard nothing from UGA. It was though I had never attended.... I was summarily forgotten as the first person of my race to receive a degree. And so I placed UGA at the back of my mind and went on with my career. I was initially angry over the slight, but my inner strength helped me overcome that hurt and anger, and my career, which was very demanding, was deeply satisfying."[86]

Much like Holmes and Hunter-Gault, Early went on to a very successful career. She emerged as a leader in her field of music education, first as a teacher, then as director of music for the Atlanta public schools. She also had an impact on higher education, serving on the faculties of Spelman and Morehouse Colleges, and chairing the music department of Clark Atlanta University.

It was not until the twenty-first century that UGA finally began to officially honor Early for her important role in the university's desegregation. That recognition grew out of the oral histories that UGA professor Maurice Daniels conducted in the late 1990s for his foot soldiers documentary film project on UGA's desegregation. Daniels's interviews with key architects of the UGA desegregation struggle Vernon Jordan, Jesse Hill, and Donald Hollowell alerted him to Early's importance. After Daniels interviewed Early, he featured her in the documentary and hosted her at the premier of the film at the UGA campus in 2000.[87] This in turn called the UGA administration's attention to the university's shameful neglect of its first Black graduate. In other words, it had taken a connection to Black memory of the UGA desegregation struggle to cure white UGA of its long-term case of amnesia regarding Early. UGA's belated but substantial moves to make amends and recognize its first Black graduate culminated with the naming of Georgia's college of education in her honor in 2019. The story of this long overdue recognition is narrated in one of her memoir's closing chapters, "My Reconciliation with UGA," and it is a heartwarming story.[88] The contrast between this recognition and all those years of neglect was for Early so stark as to be almost unbelievable. "If you ever want to feel like the world had stopped turning," wrote Early, "try getting a phone call from a university president telling you that the University of Georgia has decided to name its outstanding college of education in your honor. I was speechless when that call came through, and I still have to pinch myself to believe this really happened."[89]

HOLMES, HUNTER-GAULT, AND EARLY all had in common their Atlanta roots and background in that city's African American middle class. This was not surprising since the relative affluence of that community and the organizational sophistication of its civil rights activists made it a natural center for the challenge to Jim Crow in Georgia educational institutions. But all this attention to these Atlanta-rooted avatars of integration contributed to the neglect of an important question: What about Athens? After all, this was the north Georgia college town where UGA was located, and in 1963 it had a Black population of some 10,000.[90] The role that the Athens Black community played in UGA's desegregation struggle, the degree to which it benefitted from it, and the memory of Black Athens regarding that struggle and the larger story of its community's relationship with UGA are all stories badly in need of attention. The memoirs and histories of UGA's desegregation say little about Black Athens other than mentioning one Black Athenian, Rev. Archibald Killian, the intrepid community leader who housed Hamilton Holmes in his UGA years.[91]

The last account to appear in print on these questions about Black Athens dates back to 1964 when Calvin Trillin devoted just four pages to this subject in his book *An Education in Georgia*.[92] Trillin offered perceptive class-based arguments: that the Black community of Athens, lacking Atlanta's large Black middle class and extensive civil rights organizational network, was in no position to challenge Jim Crow at UGA; and that one consequence of school segregation and the relative poverty of Black Athens was that its public schools were poor—burdened with "half educated teachers" capable of preparing very few of even its top students for college work.[93] Trillin's point about class and race here is important and impossible to dispute: that although the state's well-endowed and leading public university was located in Athens, it had done just about nothing to improve the Black schools in its college town and had resisted making the university accessible to even the local Black community's best students. It is also notable that unlike Hunter, Holmes, and Early, the one Black Athens student at UGA when Trillin wrote *An Education in Georgia*, Mary Blackwell, was working-class. Her father was a taxi driver supporting his ten children.[94]

But Trillin did get one thing wrong in this account. He made the mistake of assuming that there was some connection between academic merit and UGA's admissions record from 1961 to 1963 regarding Black applicants from Athens. He wrote of the three Black Athens classmates of Blackwell who UGA had rejected, that "nobody in Athens complained about prejudice in the rejection of three Athens Negroes who had applied for admission to the same class, because nobody in Athens pretends that the town's Negro high school could conceivably produce more than one or two students able to meet the relatively undemanding minimum requirements for admission to the University of Georgia."[95] Putting names to these numbers, Mary Blackwell (now Mary Blackwell Diallo) in 2022 attested that her three Black high school classmates who had been rejected by UGA—Ola Lumpkin, Eleanor Shaw, and Joan Liston—were all well qualified for UGA. They went on to attend historically Black colleges, and two of them later returned to Athens to earn graduate degrees at UGA. Blackwell Diallo took this as evidence that the basis for their rejection by the UGA admissions office "was racism, pure and simple."[96]

Blackwell Diallo also challenged Trillin's view that poorly qualified Black teachers were responsible for the lack of qualified Black applicants to UGA from Athens. She argued that the fear the Jim Crow system had generated in students, and the fear of Black teachers in Athens's Black high school that they would lose their jobs if they encouraged their students to apply to UGA, had more to do with the limited Black applicant pool. The fear ran so deep, according to Blackwell Diallo, that her admission to UGA "was like an open secret [at her high school] that no one dared to acknowledge in any public forum, even though I was the first African American from Athens to be admitted there. Our school newspaper did not report it, nor was it mentioned during my high school graduation ceremony."[97] This is why when Blackwell Diallo returned to UGA in 2022 to be honored for her role in the university's desegregation, she brought with her as her invited guest Dr. Walter Allen, her high school band leader, who had had the courage to transcend that fear and encourage her and three of her classmates to apply to UGA. Allen had even arranged for her and her three classmates to meet with Charlayne Hunter. Allen convinced them, as Blackwell Diallo put it, that "we had every right to attend the University of Georgia because we were well qualified."[98]

Even though she provided a valuable corrective to Trillin on the teacher quality issue, Blackwell Diallo was essentially attesting that there were four rather than one Athens students who applied and ought to have been admitted to UGA—which is still a very small group. So her rebuttal to Trillin does not negate his larger point (and evidence) of the way educational inequality in Jim Crow Georgia added to the distance between UGA and students in Athens's Black high school. Trillin also found that in the Black high school algebra had only recently been added, while there were twenty-six courses offered at Athens's white high school that were not available at its Black counterpart.[99] So there was a disconnect between the school curriculum and college preparation. The fear Blackwell Diallo documented would only have compounded such problems.

The UGA–Black Athens chasm challenges us to add another dimension to our thinking about what we mean by desegregation. Ordinarily viewed narrowly as ending Jim Crow on campus, there is the added desegregation question concerning the relationship (in 1960s UGA's case one even might question the existence of any meaningful or positive relationship) between the historically white university and the nearby Black community. So one metric of desegregation might be the degree to which the university conceives of its service function as multiracial, seeking to benefit the local Black community along with its traditional white constituency. In the educational realm this might involve intervention to ensure that the Athens public schools were maximizing their college preparation—something that was obviously not happening in 1963 when only one Black Athens student was enrolled at UGA. And one could argue it is still not happening much in our own century when the public schools of Athens/Clarke County are 80 percent Black, the poverty rate 29.9 percent, the testing performance is in the bottom 50 percent of Georgia's more than 200 school districts, and the Athens/Clarke County public schools manage to send in total only a few dozen students a year to UGA.[100] It is little wonder then, that as recently as 2018, UGA's dean of social work sounded a Dickensian note as she contrasted the predominantly affluent UGA community with its struggling neighbors in high-poverty Black Athens: "There's been almost two Athens."[101]

Black Athens's memory of UGA in the 1960s is not confined, however, to the university's admissions policies. Indeed, when a memoir of Black Athens emerges, it may focus as much on what UGA took away from the Black community via land grabbing as what it did or did not add to the community through the desegregation of its admissions. The university's use and abuse of eminent domain in the 1960s to evict some fifty African American families from the nearby Linnentown neighborhood in order to build UGA dorms and parking lots has become an ongoing sore point, as those displaced have recently returned to demand just compensation.[102] From a Black Athens perspective, then, the desegregating 1960s may seem less triumphal than UGA presents it in its commemorations since in that decade UGA may have *evicted* more local Blacks from their homes than it admitted to the university.

NO ACCOUNT OF BLACK MEMORY and UGA's desegregation can be complete without a discussion of Horace T. Ward. One could argue in fact that Ward did more than anyone to pave the way for UGA's desegregation. We might well think of Ward as the founding father of the UGA desegregation struggle. Ward was not only the first African American applicant to UGA; he also battled the Jim Crow university longer than any other applicant, first applying for admission to UGA's law school in 1950, persisting through unconscionable delays by the UGA administration, until he was drafted into the Army in 1953, and then once discharged in 1955, renewing his attempt to have a federal court order UGA to admit him. Ward abandoned this integrationist marathon only when the court threw out his case in 1957. And even this setback could not deter him in his dedication to overturning UGA's racist admissions policies. Having earned his law degree at Northwestern University, Ward, as we have seen, returned to Atlanta and worked on the legal team in *Holmes v. Danner* and, in what must surely be seen as a kind of poetic justice, helped to win the case that resulted in gaining for Holmes and Hunter what had so unjustly been denied to him: admission to UGA.[103]

And his UGA desegregation crusade was only one chapter in a remarkable life. As a Morehouse man, Ward shared the connection of Holmes, Hunter, and Early with Black Atlanta. But he differed from them all in that his roots were not in Atlanta's middle class but in working-class LaGrange, Georgia. His mother was a domestic. He never knew his father, but Ward's stepfather was a laundry worker. Ward was, then, more of a self-made person than any of the UGA's other Atlanta-based integration pioneers. He came the furthest, from working-class youth to bachelor's and master's degrees, to lawyer, state senator, and finally to federal district court judge (appointed by president Jimmy Carter).[104]

It seems evident too that Ward's protracted battle for admission to UGA's law school did more to expose the unethical nature of UGA's white supremacist leadership than any other Georgia legal case would, and in more sickening detail. His application to UGA and his court case led the university's leadership to use a range of dishonest tactics, from endless delays (in the hope that his need for a legal education would push him to give up on UGA and go to another law school), to revamping its admission process just to keep him out (this included suddenly requiring letters of endorsement from a judge and an alumnus of the law school), to convening a kind of kangaroo court "interview committee" staffed by white supremacist professors to "interview" Ward when its real purpose was to slander him so it could offer a pretext for rejecting his law school application. The timing of his draft notice has led historians to suspect it was engineered to disrupt his battle for admission to UGA. And parts of this experience would help win the *Holmes v. Danner* case (most notably, as we have seen, the use of the phony "interview" with Ward, which the judge recognized was deployed against Hamilton Holmes precisely as it had been used against Ward).[105]

Ward's case is also important for the very reason it has been largely forgotten: he lost. This makes it more typical of the Jim Crow era than the UGA case (*Holmes v. Danner*) that finally banished segregation. It reminds us that for decades the battle to end racial discrimination in the Jim Crow South was a David versus Goliath struggle, with rich white institutions and their lying admissions officers, high priced lawyers, and all the time in the world to delay, arrayed against Black applicants eager to get on with their education and careers. Figures like Ward, and generations of Black applicants turned away from historically white universities and colleges, reveal what Jim Crow higher education really meant, and so—though biographers and historians might in a few cases bring them to life on their pages—they will rarely be celebrated by Southern universities seeking to embrace a triumphant desegregation story. Nor will Southern universities recognize the stories of those who thought it futile to apply, leaving instead, as if pariahs, their home states and forced to seek higher education, as Ward did, in a northern state or simply abandon their dreams of educational opportunity.

Historian Robert A. Pratt and biographer Maurice Daniels have done much to illuminate Ward's life and work.[106] Still, I wish we knew more about Ward's reaction to each of those lies and evasions UGA directed at him in the 1950s. Ward's all too brief foreword to the biography of him by Daniels offers a memorable observation on both the sacrifices he and other Georgia desegregation pioneers made and the formidable skill and support needed to challenge Jim Crow higher education: "Among the factors not commonly known are the tremendous amount of resources, time, energy, and money expended. Also the emotional strain on the plaintiffs and their parents were staggering. These cases required ... courageous plaintiffs, and skillful lawyers, together with dedicated parents and diligent supporters in the community."[107]

Sounding very much like the judge that he was, Ward concluded that in his application effort both he and UGA "were laboring under major misconceptions." Ward thought that as a young law school applicant he had erred initially in thinking that, in light of his qualifications and the prior judicial precedent (*Sweatt v. Painter*, 1950, in which the Supreme Court had ordered the admission of a Black applicant to the University of Texas's law school), he would be admitted without having to file or win a court case against UGA. He realized he had underestimated UGA's determination to keep out any and all Black applicants. And according to Ward, UGA erred in believing he was an NAACP tool and "not a bona fide candidate for admission to the law school."[108] Ward was equally critical of the judge who threw his case out on a technicality without considering the merits of the case, and why UGA officials refused to admit him to their law school. This was, Ward believed, an erroneous decision.[109]

It is unfortunate that his busy career left Ward with no time to write a memoir, as he surely would have added significantly to our understanding of Black memory and the struggle to desegregate UGA. I know this because I was among the group of historians at UGA who in 1996 invited him to speak at our civil rights conference on the campus, which he had not set foot on (or been asked to) since 1961. His speech at that conference (and my conversations and correspondence with Ward) left no doubt that having waged the longest desegregation struggle in Georgia history, he had deep insights into this painful history. He spoke eloquently and in a generous spirit about the freedom struggle: listening to him—especially on the UGA campus—was a moving experience, which left many of us regretting how much the university lost by rejecting Ward and then for decades ignoring him.

Ward's speech was all the more memorable because, from his perspective as a federal judge, he could look back and even find some humor in his long, losing battle to get into UGA's law school, telling us, "I should be the best trained lawyer in the state. I spent seven years trying to get into one law school and three years trying to get out of another."[110] Having recently read with horror the transcript of the UGA faculty committee that had used insulting and deceptive questions to trip up Ward, and its report offering slanderous accusations against Ward (so they could justify rejecting his law school application), I was amazed that Ward could find humor as he looked back on this grim history.[111] He jokingly remarked, "The screening committee said that my statements during the interview were evasive and inconclusive. Now some would say those are good qualifications for being a lawyer."[112]

Such lightheartedness offers a hint of something impressive about Ward, and something he shared with Holmes, Hunter-Gault, and Early: a refusal to get torn up by bitterness. To varying degrees all these pioneers of desegregation had at some point experienced feelings of bitterness, and how could they not given the abuse that they endured? But in the end, all of them let go of that bitterness so that they could continue their lives and their work for a more just society. As Ward explained in a 1994 interview with Maurice Daniels,

> it's best to deal in a live-and-let-live philosophy, and to stand on whatever foundation you have built rather than go back and live in the past. I don't harbor any ill will against anyone because of their efforts to keep me out of the University of Georgia. I think they were wrong, especially on a constitutional basis; as a matter of fact, I know they were, but I don't live in the past. I know some of these people now, they're getting old like I am, some of them are my friends now, but I don't have any bitterness toward them; it would be counterproductive.[113]

Ward's case attests, as do the reflections of Hunter-Gault, Holmes, Early, and Blackwell Diallo (along with those of Black Athens), that UGA's desegregation, while representing genuine progress, had too much pain associated with it to be converted into a simple, triumphalist story—as it often comes off in twenty-first-century UGA PR. Yes, these pioneers of integration, as Ward indicates, chose not to dwell on the unpleasant memories of that time. But the racism and cruelty they encountered at UGA was such that it took years to overcome the bitterness it left behind. Black memory of the desegregation struggle in the 1950s and 1960s reminds us that it was an important step, but only a step, toward equality. And we cannot do justice to this history if we whitewash it to the point that we obscure the decades and decades of racial discrimination practiced by Jim Crow Georgia, and its leading public university, that made this struggle necessary.

CHAPTER FIVE

Freedom Dreams and Segregationist Nightmares

Charlayne Hunter, Walter Stovall, and University of Georgia's First Interracial Marriage, 1963

Though January 1961 is the time most associated with the University of Georgia's desegregation—because that was the month when a federal court order forced UGA to admit its first African American students—the desegregation of UGA's student dining halls did not occur until two months later. This occasion was covered by a late March Associated Press story headlined "Negro Student Eats Meal at University Cafeteria," which reported that "Negro coed Charlayne Hunter ate supper in a student cafeteria at the University of Georgia Monday night, the first member of her race to do so in the 175-year history of the state-supported institution."[1] The delay in the desegregation of the cafeteria was caused by the segregationist mindset of UGA's top administrators. They thought that the best way to avoid racial conflict was to keep the university's two Black students separated from UGA's 7,100 white students wherever possible, especially when it came to social life. This is why Charlayne Hunter had been given a suite of her own and was sole resident of the first floor of her dormitory, and would never be assigned a white roommate. It is also why her dorm room included a kitchenette, and the university got her and Holmes to agree to refrain from using the university's dining halls during their first quarter at UGA. So during her first two months at UGA, Hunter either cooked her own meals or dined off campus with Holmes and the Black family with whom he lived.[2]

Before long, however, Hunter got fed up with this forced isolation, and she came to suspect that it was contributing to her stomach problems, which her physician thought "might be related" to her "less than assiduous eating schedule." Besides, Hunter, as she put it in her memoir, "believed I had a right to eat there [at the UGA cafeteria]." Initially, her attorney, Donald Hollowell, burdened with other civil rights cases, including work for Martin Luther King Jr., was in Hunter's view pursuing this "secondary push for desegregation with less vigor" than she would have liked.[3] But in early March, Hollowell took this matter up with Judge Bootle, who ruled that Hunter and Holmes must have access to the cafeteria and all university facilities.[4] When, on March 20, 1961, Hunter did finally take her first meal at the Snelling Hall cafeteria, there was no major disruption. A few of the hundred or so white students there stopped eating when she entered the cafeteria and "glanced at her," but "then they continued their meals."[5] It is also true, however, that this first interracial dining experience was marred by racism. When Hunter ate this meal with her friend Marcia Powell, who, as Hunter recalled, "was more an object of scorn than me, as the white-girl traitor," white students called her "openly and loudly 'nigger-lover.'"[6]

What the dining issue revealed was that while the UGA administration would comply with court-ordered desegregation, the Jim Crow inclinations and attitudes of its leaders with regard to race were essentially unchanged, especially when it came to social life on campus. If this was true with respect to interracial dining in 1961, it was all the more true with regard to interracial dating. Campus administrators who had been raised in Georgia during the Jim Crow era simply could not comprehend, let alone approve of, the racial egalitarianism of Charlayne Hunter and Walter Stovall, who would date as UGA students and marry after graduation in 1963. So the subtitle of this chapter would have mortified UGA's leaders, who viewed the marriage as a terrible break with how they saw their university. Socially UGA for them was more akin to a whites-only country club than an educational institution that could lead students to depart from traditional racial norms. So to call the Hunter-Stovall union the University of Georgia's first interracial marriage was for the university's leaders a point of shame rather than pride.

The Hunter-Stovall marriage was also a "first" quite unlike the firsts that Hunter and Holmes had become when they won their struggle to attend the University of Georgia as its first Black students in 1961. The difference was that educational integration opened the doors of UGA to other Black students, whereas interracial marriage was such a powerful taboo that neither Black nor white students for years would prove willing to duplicate the precedent set by the Hunter-Stovall marriage. And in fact UGA's first interracial couple had to leave the state to marry, and they left the South to live as husband and wife. One should keep in mind too that years (and as we will see, even decades) after the first Black students entered UGA, the social life among its undergraduates remained largely segregated. So the prospect of Black and white students dating each other was slim, and marrying remote, in such a bifurcated social atmosphere.

All this underscores how remarkably independent and nonconformist Hunter and Stovall were in 1963, and how at UGA for most students the color line was not something they could even conceive of challenging when it came to marriage. To reflect critically on this, we might consider James Baldwin's observation that "the sexual question and the racial question have always been entwined.... If Americans can mature on the level of racism, then they have to mature on the level of sexuality."[7] This proved, as we will see in this chapter, an impossible task for most white Georgians at UGA and across the state in 1963.

JUST AFTER LABOR DAY, 1963, Charlayne Hunter confirmed rumors that had been swirling around Atlanta since early summer. Hunter announced that she and Walter Stovall III, a white University of Georgia journalism student with whom she had been seen socializing on campus, had been secretly married in the spring. The couple had left the South, moved to New York City's Greenwich Village neighborhood, and expected a child in December.[8] News of this interracial marriage was the most controversial concerning Charlayne Hunter since January 1961, when she and Hamilton Holmes became the first African American students to attend the University of Georgia.

This news came only three months after Hunter and Holmes graduated from UGA, and the response to it was a reminder that the kind of bigotry that had kept Black students out of the university for almost two centuries remained alive and well in 1963. Neither the fact that Holmes and Hunter had attended and graduated from the university nor the presence of a handful of new Black students at UGA, who by matriculating followed in the footsteps of Holmes and Hunter, had done much to liberalize racial attitudes either on or off the campus. And interracial marriage was still a crime in Georgia, punishable by eighteen months in prison or a $1,000 fine.[9] So the response to the interracial marriage, among most white Georgians who expressed an opinion, was predictably racist, angry, and ugly.

The files of University of Georgia president O. C. Aderhold attest to this bigotry. Even without reading the angry letters themselves, one can see and feel the racism by glancing at the visuals that irate UGA alumni and others sent to UGA's president. For example, a real estate executive sent Aderhold a racist cartoon that had been given to him by "one of our loyal alumni," which, this businessman explained, indicated "how strongly a lot of folk feel about it."[10] The cartoon depicted a grotesque image of a very pregnant Black woman, with stereotyped features (thick lips extending from ear to ear), sitting atop a convertible headed north, saying, "I's got a belly full of this university."[11] Actually Charlayne Hunter was a talented journalism student who would go on to become a prominent reporter for the *New York Times*, PBS, and National

Public Radio. She spoke standard English at least as well as any white student. But the conventions of race-baiting cartoonists dictated that African Americans be depicted as simpletons who spoke in Black dialect. The cartoonist's racist imagination resulted in an image that bore no physical resemblance to Hunter, an attractive young woman who had been the homecoming queen of her high school. Since the cartoon was designed to mock interracial sex as if it was something new, Hunter had to be depicted as purely Black when in fact she was a light-skinned African American. From Florida came a photo clipped out of a newspaper depicting University of Georgia football players sitting on a bench reading brochures and so not paying attention to an attractive, scantily clad white female cheerleader who was doing her cheerleading routine. Under the photo the outraged letter writer fumed, "Those white boys love that nigger stuff so good they will not even look at a white girl. It is pitiful. That's what it is just pitiful."[12]

Less crude but no less irate came a letter from Atlanta attorney Young H. Fraser, an alumnus of the University of Georgia's class of 1911. Fraser wrote Aderhold, charging him with being naive in allowing the university to become racially integrated and failing to realize that Black aspirations ended not with white classrooms but with white bedrooms. "When the University permitted integration it invited social equality and promoted intermarriage between the races.... The only way to prevent such happenings is to insist upon total segregation in our schools and colleges." In this way the university had contributed to "mongrelization," posing a threat to a key mission of society, "that the white race should be preserved for posterity."[13]

In responding to this letter, Aderhold revealed that as president of the university he was no more willing in 1963 to defend racial equality than he had been two years earlier when in the Hunter-Holmes desegregation suit, as we saw in chapter 1, he virtually perjured himself attempting to keep UGA all white, testifying under oath and in defiance of common sense that the university did not discriminate racially.[14] In the same tradition Aderhold did not challenge any of Fraser's racist assumptions. Instead, UGA's president simply blamed Washington for the whole Hunter-Stovall affair. He told Fraser, "There is one comment I would like to make. When you say the University permitted integration you may recall that integration at the University was a result of a federal court order specifically putting colored students in the University." In other words, it was federal judges, not university administrators, who had opened the door to intermarriage by forcing the university to admit "colored students."[15]

President Aderhold's public posture on the Hunter-Stovall marriage was consistent with this private correspondence. Upon learning of the interracial marriage, Aderhold released a press statement jointly with UGA's dean of students and the dean of the school of journalism (in which Hunter and Stovall had been students) declaring that the marriage "greatly surprised and shocked" them. The primary issue was, of course, that "interracial marriage is prohibited by Georgia law." The second issue was that the couple had apparently kept their marriage secret while they were students—violating UGA's prohibition on secret marriages. Had word of this secret marriage come out prior to Hunter's graduation, "dismissal rules would have applied." The statement concluded by relegating Hunter and Stovall to pariah status at UGA. Neither of them, the deans and university president affirmed, "will be permitted to return to the University of Georgia."[16]

The secrecy issue, which became conflated with the racial issue, was actually blown out of proportion by Aderhold and the deans, who invoked it in a disingenuous and discriminatory manner. They made secret marriages by students sound as if they were a dire offense that led to dismissal of the offending students. Actually, a private memorandum drawn up by Aderhold's staff indicated that the most serious punishment that UGA imposed upon students for secret marriages was not expulsion but merely suspension—which rarely extended beyond a single academic quarter. In fact, of the five secret marriage cases reviewed in this memorandum, dating back to 1958, the case closest to Hunter's was one in which a student disclosed her marriage after graduating in 1959. And what did the university do in that case? "Violation of regulation noted, but *no other action taken*."[17]

The UGA administration's hostile response to the Hunter-Stovall marriage was in sync with that of the state's political leadership. Georgia governor Carl B. Sanders denounced the marriage as "a disgrace and a shame."[18] Taking a cue from Aderhold, the governor rebuked the couple for breaking Georgia law and violating UGA rules on secret marriages. Sanders found it "tragic that they should falsify their status at the University."[19] In this same spirit Roy Harris, the most vehement segregationist on Georgia's Board of Regents, called for an investigation to determine whether this violation of university regulations and state law ought to lead to the revocation of Hunter's diploma. State attorney general Eugene Cook conducted just such an investigation. But since the marriage had occurred in early June, shortly after her graduation, the secrecy rule was not applicable to Hunter. So Cook could find no university rule violation that would enable him to revoke her UGA degree.[20]

As one would expect, the white Georgia media was filled with denunciations of the interracial marriage. The diatribes by the state's most militant segregationists, however, combined their normal racist vitriol with an almost gleeful quality. Much as these Jim Crow partisans hated the very thought of Blacks and whites marrying, this particular marriage in a bizarre way warmed their hearts because they thought it validated the warnings they had been issuing for years that interracial schools would lead to interracial sex. This is why one clever Georgia editor headlined his column on the Hunter-Stovall marriage "Segregationists Happy Over Mixed Nuptials," noting that it was proof "positive that token integration brings intermarriage."[21]

The opinion pieces by such prominent Georgia segregationists as former governor Marvin Griffin and regent Roy Harris adopted this "I told you so" posture. Griffin gloated over how such prominent "members of the liberal element" in Georgia, including "Ralph McGill, publisher of the *Atlanta Constitution* have had a button lip, and have had nothing to write or say about the Walter Stovall–Charlayne Hunter mixed-marriage." Such liberals might claim that the goal of school integration was legal equality, but its ultimate consequence was, in Griffin's words, to "bring half-breed children into the world," a consequence they did not want to own up to but that segregationists had loudly and accurately predicted. Griffin went on to accuse liberals nationally of covering up their own complicity in ushering in a horrid new age of interracial social equality that had been created by their integrationist social engineering. "And they are engineers. They are attempting to ditch, drain, and damn this country ... for political gain and expediency.... Why have not Bobby Kennedy, Jake Javits, Hubert Humphrey et al come out of hiding and told the American people in a loud voice that this [miscegenation] is what they have been working to accomplish?"[22]

All this disapproval of interracial marriage seems true to form, pretty much what one would expect from white Georgians at a time when they were still having a difficult time coping with the shock of desegregating schools, universities, and lunch counters. But at the heart of this chapter in Georgia history is a story that breaks with this mold and undermines any stereotyping of white Georgians as segregationist automatons. And that is the story of Walter Stovall himself. Stovall's story has been largely neglected even by historians of UGA's desegregation, in part because the focus is on Holmes and Hunter and the breaking of the color line in higher education by these two intrepid African Americans.[23] But Stovall too crossed the color line and he too paid a price for that action, becoming a pariah in his home state.

Nothing in Stovall's family background even hinted that he would emerge in 1963 as the white student who most brazenly defied Jim Crow at the University of Georgia. His parents lived "conventionally" in the small, segregated south Georgia town of Douglas. In Stovall's words, on race his parents followed the "local mores ... played by the local rules." There was no occasion in which Stovall ever heard segregation questioned in his home. His father, a chicken feed manufacturer, said little to young Stovall on questions of race, but his mother, according to Walter, "was a racist."[24]

It was not until high school that Stovall first encountered any opposition to the Jim Crow system in which he had been raised. In the aftermath of *Brown v. Board of Education*, discussion of racial justice "was just beginning to percolate a little" in the whites-only public high school from which Stovall would graduate in 1956.[25] During one such discussion, Mary Dean George, a younger classmate of Stovall's, questioned segregation. Appealing to her classmates' sense of fairness and decency, she asked them to consider whether they would sit next to a Black student if their school integrated. Even a half century later, Stovall recalled vividly both the words of this dissident student and her confident manner—"how very sure she was of what she was saying"— since even this limited kind of questioning seemed so "very bold" in that south Georgia context in the 1950s.[26]

Neither Stovall nor his classmates were ready to take up the challenge posed by Mary Dean's question. As Stovall put it, if you said "yes" to integration and joined her in expressing a willingness to sit next to a Black student, "well you were a Nigger Lover. OK. But that was all right because you weren't going to sit next to one any way" since the *Brown* decision was a long way from being enforced in south Georgia, where the schools remained strictly segregated in the 1950s.[27] With his own "agenda" centered on an athletic career, Stovall as a high school student never even considered endorsing or joining the struggle for racial equality: "I was a football player. Desegregating the school was not part of something I was doing."[28]

Stovall's initial encounters with Southern higher education took him no closer to challenging Jim Crow. Entering Vanderbilt University, whose undergraduate population was all-white in fall 1956, he proved an indifferent student. He disliked the campus's social elitism, viewing the school as "a rich kid's place."[29] Stovall flunked out of Vanderbilt, and after briefly doing better as a transfer student at Valdosta State in Georgia, soon grew weary of his studies there too and flunked out again. Eager to "get away from this academic stuff," Stovall enlisted in the Army, which would on race (and on life in general) offer him "a better education than any" he "had anywhere along the line."[30]

Stovall's service in the Army quickly and profoundly transformed his views on race. "The idea of racial equality really came alive in me when I got into the Army," recalled Stovall.[31] The Army was the first racially integrated institution into which Stovall had become a part, and it caused him, as he recalled, "to adapt to a different reality. Like my drill sergeant was black in basic training. I mean the whole thing was just integrated, period."[32] Stovall trained and roomed with African American soldiers, even taking hits off the same cigarettes they smoked. He came away from the Army experience comfortable with integration. "The Army was," as Stovall put it, "where my eyes and head got opened up."[33]

The Army experience was also significant for Stovall in that by exposing him to Europe—he was based in Paris, where, as a medic, he worked as an X-ray technician—he came to know and value a cosmopolitan way of life that was much more diverse and tolerant than the small-town world he had been born into in Georgia. "I really lucked out ... getting stationed in Paris.... You got to see the world, see people that ... you normally would not have met [in Georgia] because most people who were from the South stay there and just get recycled in the place."[34] Stovall set about learning French at the Alliance Francaise. He found himself envisioning a life outside of Georgia, aspiring to return to Paris after his Army days, where he hoped to work as a foreign correspondent.

Just how far his Army experience had removed him from the mindset of Jim Crow Georgia was evident even before he returned to the South in 1962. While still in the Army and Paris, Stovall had read press accounts of the desegregation of the University of Georgia by Charlayne Hunter and Hamilton Holmes, and he looked upon it as an exciting and positive step toward moving Georgia, as he had been moved by the Army, away from its racist past. He thought that what Hunter had done in Georgia was "very courageous," and so as he was about to get discharged from the Army and enroll in UGA, he thought "the first thing I'm going to do" at the university was "meet this Charlayne Hunter. ... I mean I know the rest of it [what white Georgia was all about]. This [challenge to Jim Crow] was what I don't know down there, [and wanted] to find out how that works."[35]

Befriending Hunter or Holmes proved difficult even for those few white UGA students inclined to reach out to the school's first African American students. With the student body still overwhelmingly segregationist and resentful of the court-ordered presence of Hunter and Holmes, students who welcomed them, as we have seen, risked social ostracism. Indeed, for merely walking Hunter across campus one female student was shunned by her sorority.[36]

Stovall, however, proved immune to such peer pressure. Having entered UGA as an older student and an Army veteran, he was not interested in being a part of the undergraduate social scene and had no connections to the campus's Greek houses. He had not come to UGA to party but was there, after his educational misadventures at Vanderbilt and Valdosta State, to finally excel in school (which he did by making the dean's list), get his credential as an aspiring journalist in UGA's journalism school, and leave the South for reporting work that he hoped would lead him back to Paris. He had few friends on campus, and these were mostly limited to fellow veterans who shared his skepticism about segregation.[37]

Rather than feeling pressured to conform to UGA's segregationist norms, Stovall came to Georgia with a critical outlook on the whole campus culture and that of the society that bred it, viewing both as hopelessly parochial. "I never liked the University of Georgia, period. I didn't like their football team. I just never liked the idea of the place. It was like some kind of social club."[38] Nor did he think much of the quality of education at its journalism school, which he saw as "a joke" and a place where "I didn't think you could learn anything," but he knew he needed the degree to get access to jobs in journalism.[39] Stovall felt that, thanks to the Army, he "had grown" up and grown away from the provincial social world of white Georgia and its racist traditions.[40] He had evolved into precisely the kind of independent-minded person who was comfortable defying segregationist norms—all of which set the stage for his friendship and then his romance and marriage to Charlayne Hunter.

So by the time Stovall first met Hunter in 1962 at Athens's only racially integrated restaurant, the coffee shop of UGA's Georgia Center for Continuing Education, he had evolved into that rare white Georgian who was both cosmopolitan and critical of the South. This cosmopolitanism, along with the personal warmth he directed toward Hunter—at a time when most white students shunned her—was among the first things that attracted her to him. After a number of brief, friendly encounters, and learning of his time in Europe, Hunter asked Stovall, who had a heavy Southern accent, to speak in French, partly for her amusement. But when he did, what came "out of his mouth" was, as Hunter-Gault recalled, "a language so beautifully accented that it contained not a trace of roots in the 'whites only' South that went back three hundred years. It seemed to transform him too, causing me to let down just a little of the guard I always maintained in that environment. Hmm, I thought, here's somebody different."[41]

Hunter was right about Stovall being different from most UGA students back then, who, as Stovall put it, "hadn't been anywhere else" but the Jim Crow South "and didn't want to go anywhere else.... I was something she didn't believe existed ... a cool cracker. I mean I was a cracker [by birth] but on the other hand I was not one [socially or politically]."[42] In his own way Stovall was as critical of white Georgia as she was. This is why in her memoir Hunter-Gault credited Stovall with sharing her critical sensibility and educating her to what the small-town world of white Georgia looked like from the inside. "Through Walter," Hunter-Gault wrote,

> I began to get a glimpse of the white world of the South that I had never seen, one that had its share of deprivation, too.... The environment he described [in Douglas] was a stultifying society that in its own way kept most whites in their place—self-centered, socially homogenous puritans, whose worldview was restricted to the Protestant church on Sunday ... a limited range of weekday activities ... and Friday-night football. Everybody wrapped himself in the Confederate flag but the Black Citizens, who washed and ironed it.... Walter also provided a window into small-town white public education: it was designed to teach you to read, write, and do your sums, and prepare you to go to a non-threatening, non-challenging place like the University of Georgia, where you would be educated to take your place in that little world, thrive in it, and see to it that it continued in perpetuity just as it was.[43]

Although aware that Stovall's time in the Army and Paris enabled him to break with and defy Jim Crow, she also thought that his character played a major role here. Hunter-Gault referred to this as Stovall's "sense of honor that was as deep and old fashioned as his manners. To him being unfair was dishonorable and he saw clearly that segregation was unfair."[44] Of course it took the years out of Georgia to enable him to apply his ethics to race, yet it does seem that his ideals about honor evolved out of his Southern roots and at the same time left him profoundly alienated from the South. As Hunter-Gault explained, "his nature ... his sense of honor has probably been his greatest quality," enabling him to defy the white South and to insist "on having a decent white South."[45]

Among the most striking aspects of Stovall's turn against Jim Crow was that it was so experiential in its roots and so disconnected from the writings of Southern white liberals. The editorials of such progressive Southerners as Ralph McGill did not influence Stovall at all. He viewed such writers as all talk and no action. Even in retrospect Stovall remained critical of them for looking on "the racial dilemma as an abstraction.... It was all very nice to write editorials about it but they wouldn't have a drink" with an African American. Stovall noted that when he worked as an intern on the *Atlanta Journal* in 1963, even the best white reporters there who wrote informative civil rights stories nonetheless "spent all their social time with a bunch of white people." And even had dissident Southern white writers been more consistent on race, it still would not have been formative for Stovall since, as he put it, "when I was a kid I didn't read anything. I was a jock."[46] For Stovall, then, his support for racial integration and equality was rooted in his lived experience in the racially egalitarian Army rather than books or the press.

With regard to the question of racial intermarriage, Stovall was ahead not only of white Georgia but of most whites in both the North and the South. A Gallup Poll from the time that Hunter and Holmes first applied to the University of Georgia revealed that 92 percent of whites in the North and the West disapproved of interracial marriage, as did 99 percent of white Southerners. Nationally as late as 1968 the overwhelming majority of whites in the United States, 76 percent, opposed intermarriage. It is little wonder, then, that this same year even liberal Hollywood was reluctant to spotlight interracial marriage. Columbia Pictures almost shut down production of *Guess Who's Coming to Dinner?* because its executives feared that America was not ready for a feature film on interracial marriage.[47]

Given this larger racial context, it seems logical to view the Hunter-Stovall marriage as a political event and a daringly radical one—which is how it was widely perceived back in 1963. One can read portions of Hunter-Gault's memoir *In My Place* (1992) in this way. Near the end of that memoir, she described her relationship with Stovall as "an act of love and defiance."[48] The defiance was, of course, most notably directed toward the Jim Crow South. Crossing racial lines to marry meant defying law and custom in Georgia; it meant refusing to be cowed when the deans called her in to warn against dating across the color line. It meant being determined, as Hunter-Gault put it in her memoir, to "show ... all the hypocrites in the world how we lived our beliefs and didn't just pay them lip service."[49]

There is no question that it took courage for Stovall to join Hunter in defying the greatest taboo of the Jim Crow South, and this was why a quarter century later, when Hunter-Gault, by then remarried and a famous journalist, in delivering the UGA commencement speech—the first by an African American—praised him for his "courage.... I would wish for you all such courage, conviction, and commitment to ideals and principles."[50] When William Tate, UGA's dean of men, sought to intimidate Stovall out of continuing to date Hunter, it soon became clear that Stovall, as an older student and Army veteran, would not be intimidated, as some young freshmen might. "I'd been intimidated by much better than him" is how Stovall thought about it. When Tate, seeing that intimidation wasn't working, started "to talk about southern life" and conforming to its racial norms, Stovall just nodded, unmoved, since, in his words, "I'd moved on from that."[51] And when dean of women Edith Stallings advised him not to "rock the boat," Stovall's mindset was that "well the boat has already been rocked. In fact, the boat was rocked before I got here," when Hunter and Holmes had desegregated UGA.[52]

Despite these memorable stories about their defiance of Jim Crow sexual rules that appear in Stovall's oral history interview and Hunter-Gault's memoir, neither of them saw their marriage as purely or even primarily political. And this was true both in 1963 and retrospectively. At several points in Hunter-Gault's memoir, and when she first announced her marriage in September 1963, she stressed that she saw their marriage in personal rather than political terms. She never said in 1963 that she was marrying Stovall to make a statement about the South's hypocrisy on race or to further the cause of civil rights but instead asserted that she was marrying him simply because they had fallen in love. "This is a personal thing," Hunter told TV reporters the day after she announced her marriage. "My personal life should not have anything to do with that which affects masses of people. And so I can't be too terribly concerned about that because I have my own life to live."[53]

Having spent more than two years in the civil rights movement spotlight as a symbol for the cause of racial equality when she desegregated UGA, Hunter had grown fatigued with that role and felt she was entitled to run her own personal life. She found it irritating that within the Black community a debate raged about the political wisdom of her marriage (because some thought it fanned white sexual fears of school integration and thus set back the movement's crusade for educational equity). She found this debate dehumanizing since it implied that her personal life ought to be sacrificed for the sake of political expediency. Hunter thought she had already made enough such sacrifices to last a lifetime, being the lone Black female undergraduate in an often-hostile white student body in a segregated town. Thus, in her conversations with journalist Calvin Trillin back in 1963, "Charlayne ... was interested to note how few of the people she had told of the marriage during the summer had bothered to wish her happiness before beginning an analysis of how the [civil rights] Cause would be affected."[54]

This distancing of herself and her marriage from the civil rights movement seems linked to the larger Black community's reservations, ambivalence, and even opposition to interracial marriage. Hunter-Gault noted in her memoir that even before their marriage some of her friends "were wildly disapproving" of her relationship with Stovall. She "found the things they said to be racially insensitive and totally at odds with the Movement position articulated by Dr. King: that people should be judged not by the color of their skin but by the content of their character."[55] Actually, even King had, earlier in his career as a civil rights leader, been something of a trimmer on the issue of intermarriage. Seeing white fears of miscegenation as a distortion of the movement's goal of nondiscrimination, he had quipped that Blacks wanted to "be the white man's brother not his brother-in law."[56]

A similar message came from National Association for the Advancement of Colored People (NAACP) executive secretary Roy Wilkins, who responded to the Hunter-Stovall marriage not by saluting it as a step toward complete racial equality but by dismissing it as a rare exception to the rule that Blacks on campuses with whites were pursuing educational opportunity, not sexual proximity: "Of all the tens of thousands of Negroes that have gone to colleges in the north, east, and west over all these years, the percentage of intermarriages has been infinitesimal."[57] This evading of the intermarriage issue was, as historian Peggy Pascoe has documented, part of a larger NAACP strategy dating back to the 1940s of ducking this sexually explosive issue so as not to jeopardize its desegregation efforts.[58] Reflecting these same priorities, the *Atlanta World*, a conservative Black newspaper, headlined its lead editorial on the Hunter-Stovall marriage "The Goal is a Good Education Not Intermarriage."[59]

Since the mainstream civil rights organizations in 1963 were a long way from placing the right to marry across racial lines anywhere near the top of their list of priorities, Hunter did not really have the option back then of seeing it in the same or even similar political terms as such movement priorities as school desegregation. Indeed, with the prevailing view within the movement being that intermarriage was at best a political distraction and at worst a tactical mistake that promised to spark a racist backlash, Hunter was almost forced to see her marriage in 1963 more in personal than political terms. The political language needed to discuss intermarriage as a human right had not yet entered the mainstream of the civil rights community.

Up to the present, Hunter-Gault insists that her "marriage was a personal matter not an intellectual or political decision at all." She links this to her sense of independence, which had been what had brought her to UGA in the first place. As important as she had been to the movement as a trailblazer for university desegregation, she never saw herself as some functionary of the civil rights establishment. She had come to UGA both to end its segregation and to pursue her individual career and educational goals, and the latter was for her at least as important as the former: "Hamilton [Holmes] and I didn't say we wanted to go to the University of Georgia so we could become historical symbols of civil rights. In a real sense that happened. We were in a real sense a part of the movement. Still the notion that we wanted to do this for ourselves, to secure schooling, to meet our career ambitions, was pure. That it had a positive impact on the struggle on civil rights made me happy, but it was really secondary to our educational goal."[60]

With this individualistic mindset so central to who she was, it would never have occurred to Hunter to make judgments about her personal life on the basis of whether her actions would enhance the progress of the civil rights movement. So when it came to her marriage Hunter insists that she "didn't care what the people in the movement thought about any of that. I had been here [in Athens] by myself. I was here because of my independent spirit. Nobody was here for me. I didn't feel anyone else had a claim on my ashes or could tell me what to do."[61]

This may sound like a surprisingly individualistic outlook for someone who had become an icon of the civil rights movement, with its communalist ethos—idealizing "the beloved community." Here it must be recalled, however, that though Hunter and Holmes are associated with the period of mass civil rights protest in the 1960s (because they entered UGA in January 1961), they had actually become civil rights pioneers earlier, applying in 1959 to this all-white university, setting the stage for their historic and ultimately triumphant legal challenge to educational Jim Crow two years later.[62] This was a time when the civil rights movement was in a lull, before the first great mass movement of the students who sat in at the lunch counters beginning in Greensboro, North Carolina, in February 1960, before the freedom rides, the Student Nonviolent Coordinating Committee's mass voter registration campaigns, and the massive March on Washington, before Students for a Democratic Society had become a mass organization. So while supported by the NAACP and the civil rights leadership of Atlanta, Hunter and Holmes had sought to enroll at UGA as individuals, not as part of a booming mass movement. In this sense the individualistic and independent streak that guided Hunter in her choice of a marriage partner was quite consistent with her decision to risk so much to attend UGA in the first place. As Hunter-Gault put it, "I knew it [her marriage to Stovall] wouldn't be well received here [at UGA].

But did we care? No. My coming here wasn't well received here either [and, as we have seen, sparked segregationist rioting in her first week of classes]. I felt I had the right to lead my life my way."[63]

Such independent mindedness also shaped the way Hunter handled the marriage decision with respect to her parents. She consulted with neither her mother nor father about her decision. Charlayne's father, Col. C. S. H. Hunter, a former Army chaplain, divorced and serving as a minister in Tampa, told the press "the fact that she withheld" news of the marriage "from us is good evidence of what she thought our reaction would be." But he also noted that given her determination to marry Stovall, "I couldn't have stopped her." Hunter publicly expressed reservations about the marriage, recounting that he was "shocked and disappointed when I heard about it. I never dreamed she would take that turn. I would have preferred her to have married a Negro.... Any well thinking Negro wants the best for his child, and under our present society's customs, a Negro husband would have been best for my daughter.... I don't think they've committed a crime or anything like that, but I'd have preferred it the other way [marrying a Black man]."[64]

Despite these reservations and his view that they "erred in judgment," he defended his daughter's and Stovall's rights to "freedom of choice. It just shows we can't control the direction of human emotion by legislation, mores, or customs. I'm going to stand by her right down the line."[65] Charlayne's mother, Althea Hunter, told the press that, since Charlayne was twenty-one, the decision of whom to marry was hers. Though stopping short of endorsing the marriage, she did say that Stovall "seems like a gentleman." While not complaining about the marriage, she noted that since the news of it had become public, the phone in her Atlanta home "jangles mercilessly. On the other end are whites with crude threats, vile insults." But her friends in the Black community were supportive.[66]

Though Hunter-Gault's claims about the autonomy and personal integrity of her private life are convincing, they cannot fully eclipse the political dimension of her marriage. Certainly it is true that the marriage decision was not political in the sense that she was marrying to make a political statement or to promote the civil rights movement. There was, as we have seen, no tactical gain and arguably far too much tactical risk in such a marriage to make it something worth even thinking about in terms of political calculation. Nor is there evidence Hunter or Stovall sought each other out for the thrill of flouting social and political conventions by crossing the sexual color line. But the fact that both of them were radically egalitarian enough on race not to allow race or the tactical concerns of the mainstream civil rights groups to stand in their way as a couple was in its own way not merely political, but radical. In this sense the personal, in the phrase popularized by second-wave feminists, is political when you live your egalitarian values in your private life—and not letting race pollute one's choice of a life partner is certainly that.

What was involved here was not a political cause but a political sensibility. It implied that allowing racism to inhibit one's choice of a marriage partner was not merely wrong but crazy. Indeed, Stovall, when reflecting back on the white Georgia outrage over the marriage and the whole segregationist mindset that bred it, spoke of the partisans of the Jim Crow tradition as "a screwball lot.... They were just nuts"—using words and phrases about insanity persistently and in a more than metaphorical way.[67] "People who went ballistic when you start tearing down these [Jim Crow] traditions. I mean you can call the Inquisition an institution.... That's really what it was like. You just couldn't believe the idiocy of the whole thing."[68]

Part of what made the whole scene seem so crazy was that even the most mundane things that a couple would ordinarily do together were made impossible by Georgia's Jim Crow system. In most Athens restaurants, for example, Hunter and Stovall could not dine together. Reflecting on this decades later, Hunter-Gault wrote that Stovall gave up going to the Varsity, a popular fast food place near the UGA campus, "because he knew they would not serve me—although at the time he said it was because the chili dogs tasted funny."[69] Nor could they go to the movies and be seated together because the theaters were segregated. And even going to the Black theater in Athens proved problematic because the police tailed them all the way home—an experience Mary Frances Early, the second Black female student at UGA and Hunter's roommate, found so frightening that she told Hunter her first would also be her last time going to the movies with the interracial couple.[70]

So it was initially only through "long drives in the afternoon" and private time in Stovall's apartment that the couple could spend time together. As Stovall put it, the racially repressive environment in their college town meant "you couldn't go out" together downtown or on campus. "And through our sneaking around we'd spend whole weekends in this apartment of mine." This was, of course, restrictive but, ridiculous as it was, it did not seem all that oppressive since it forced the young lovers to spend lots of time with each other in private as a couple, which they enjoyed immensely since, as Stovall reminds us, "we were hot young things."[71]

Hunter and Stovall's daring form of racial egalitarianism was rare anywhere in the America of 1963, and rarer still in Georgia and the rest of the Deep South. About the only place you find it is in the radical wing of the Black freedom struggle, among Student Nonviolent Coordinating Committee organizers, and others closest to the front lines of the direct-action battle against Jim Crow. These activists tended to be unwilling to back away from the issue of interracial sex.

In Georgia the media voice of these activists was the *Atlanta Inquirer*, a Black newspaper edited by Carl Holman and which Hunter wrote for as a student journalist, where she befriended Holman. This was the one paper in the state that responded to the Hunter-Stovall marriage by both mocking the white Georgia establishment's outraged denunciation of the marriage and daring to point out the hypocrisy of such white attacks on miscegenation—since white men in the South had been illicitly pursuing interracial sex for centuries, using their superior political, economic, and legal power to impose themselves sexually on African American women. The *Inquirer*'s initial editorial on the Hunter-Stovall marriage pointed out that "for many years in the South, white men, prominent white men, public officials, financiers, if you please, have engaged in sadistic kitchen maid–room and non-descript 'marriages.' Today in Atlanta white and black brothers and sisters live two separate lives. The negro children live across the tracks from their father's mansion. White Southerners for over 100 years have been sadist fathers by taking advantage of Negro women."[72]

To the *Inquirer* the contrast between this grim history of sexual abuse across racial lines and the news of the Hunter-Stovall marriage grounded in free choice, love, and equality was dramatic and in its own way inspiring. Thus the *Inquirer* editor concluded that "I can only suppose that this is the marriage of two persons whose love for each other is strong enough to sustain them in spite of the obstacles which they face, a love of such depth is not found every day and for that reason should be cherished and nurtured, for great love can bring only good to all who are touched by it."[73]

Hunter-Gault's memoir echoes this radical egalitarianism on race and also the historically informed sarcasm about white Southern sexual hypocrisy. Thus, in discussing their decision to marry, she contrasts her and Walter's free choice to live as husband and wife (which was, as she put it, "every segregationist's nightmare") with the South's hidden history of sexual abuse in which the interracial sex was a coercive relationship between "concubine and master."[74]

Hunter-Gault's sexual border crossing seems to have been made possible more by a radical sensibility than by radical politics in the formal sense of being connected to a political cause or movement. And it is not only her rejection of a political reading of her marriage that leads to this conclusion but also her nonchalant attitude toward the growing movement to abolish antimiscegenation laws, and in particular to the epochal legal breakthrough in this movement: the US Supreme Court's 1967 ruling in *Loving v. Virginia*, which found antimiscegenation laws unconstitutional. For those who embraced interracial marriage as a political cause and an essential step toward social equality, *Loving* was a major event, a historic victory to be cherished. But this was not the way Hunter-Gault remembered it. Though, of course, glad that the court upheld the principle of racial equality in the realm of marriage, she did not "recall having a big reaction" to the ruling. In fact, she had no specific memories about the decision or her response to it back in 1967 and speculated that "I probably looked on it as any reporter would, as an important story." But she did not see it as validating her own marriage. "I wasn't going to live my life as a symbol and so did not see my marriage that way." And Stovall's reaction to *Loving* was almost identical to hers.[75] Both in 1963 and in retrospect, Stovall discussed their marriage in the same terms that Hunter-Gault did, stressing that it was wholly personal, an act of love rather than a statement about civil rights. "We were a couple of people" who were in love with each other. Though the mere fact of their interracial marriage did challenge Jim Crow, "we didn't talk about it that way," according to Stovall. "The politics of it was dealt with by [the segregationist] papers.... We didn't."[76]

There were, however, a number of ways in which politics connected to the romance. Part of the reason Stovall wanted to meet Hunter was because he had read of her in the press, owing to her courageous desegregation struggle. In other words, she was a political celebrity who, as Stovall put it, "was in the papers all over the world." But that just facilitated their meeting; it did not mean they would end up romantically involved or married. The fact of her political celebrity was, in Stovall's words, "the superficial part. We just clicked." The other way that the political context entered into their romance was that it tested their love and commitment. All relationships involve tests of a partner's love and willingness to make a lasting commitment. But this was all the more true when, in order to marry, one had to defy the racist norms of a whole society. As Stovall explained, "It's like Charlayne was sizing me up. 'Is this guy for real? Is he really going to go through with this whole thing?' And I did."[77]

As to the political firestorm that was sure to ensue when the marriage was announced, Stovall and Hunter expected it. As Stovall put it, he and Hunter "knew it [their marriage] was not going to be on the society page. No, we didn't talk about it all that much because we knew" how racists would respond—there were "no guesses about it." Focusing on their relationship, the move to New York, and the need to find jobs and housing, the political implications of their marriage were something that the young couple was too busy and too radically egalitarian to fret over.[78]

This was a very different way of expressing racial egalitarianism than would be seen less than a year later among the civil rights workers in Mississippi during Freedom Summer, 1964—whose rejection of the taboo on interracial sex has attracted extensive attention from historians. These Black and white volunteers in Mississippi's freedom movement embraced interracial sex as the ultimate political statement, a way of proving that one's commitment to racial equality went beyond mere words.[79] Hunter and Stovall shared the Mississippi volunteers' egalitarianism but expressed it differently in part because the context was so different. During Freedom Summer the volunteers were part of an activist movement culture forged amid hundreds of fellow civil rights workers, a culture that could champion new sexual norms in explicitly political terms. But at the University of Georgia in 1963 there was no such movement culture and nobody to try to impress with one's politics. Hunter and Stovall were quite isolated in their egalitarianism and so had no incentive at all to make explicit the political implications of their marriage, a job that was done all too well by their racist detractors.[80]

Whether or not one sees the marriage as a political event, there is no question that the response to it was political and that the newlyweds were forced to deal with that response in ways that were both political and personal. The fact that Hunter felt compelled to announce the story of their marriage to the press, and that she and Stovall did a nationally televised interview with CBS News about their decision to marry, attests that this was widely viewed as a politically charged event (though both insisted in that interview that love, not politics, led to their marriage).[81] This publicity was linked to Hunter's celebrity as one of the first two African American students to attend the historically white University of Georgia. Indeed, Hunter was so well known in Georgia that the state's newspaper editors could refer to "Charlayne" in their headlines with confidence that their readers knew that they were referring to Georgia's most famous female student.[82] Accustomed to such publicity, Hunter weathered this political storm well. Stovall did too, though, new as he was to such media attention, he found his instant celebrity status and the media's meddling into his personal life "unsettling."[83]

The personal and political came together in a most unpleasant way as the media frenzy sensationalized the marriage in soap opera style. The *Atlanta Journal* quoted Walter Stovall as saying that his father had used apocalyptic terms when he learned of the marriage, pronouncing it "the end of the world."⁸⁴ This quote was repeated in the Georgia and national newspaper coverage as well as by CBS News. Walter, however, told CBS News back in 1963 that that as far as he knew, that quote did not represent his father's reaction to the marriage. He did tell CBS that there had been some "bitterness and some resignation" toward the marriage on the part of his family, but this almost certainly referred to his mother—who, though a racist initially unhappy with the marriage, said little about it so as to avoid dividing her family—and not to his father.⁸⁵ Walter Stovall later characterized "the end of the world" quote as an "incredible fabrication" authored by a racist reporter who ought to have been "put in a mental ward."⁸⁶ The reality was that when they were first married, Stovall kept his distance from his family in the hopes of shielding them from attacks by their south Georgia neighbors. So he never had extended conversations with his parents in the days immediately after the marriage went public.⁸⁷ But such facts eluded the press, which circulated the melodramatic "end of the world" quote far and wide. Had Hunter believed its accuracy and taken it to heart, it would have made any kind of family amity almost impossible.

Hunter-Gault and Stovall's avoidance of civil rights discourse in discussing their marriage, and their casual reaction to the *Loving* case, suggests that for both of them the marriage was far more about love than *Loving*, and that their radical sensibility almost at a subconscious level paved the way for them to make what for an egalitarian person was the straightforward human decision to marry the one that person loved irrespective of race. When CBS News asked Stovall how "did this [marriage] come about?" he replied, "Well it's very simple. We met. We fell in love"—to which the reporter responded, "Under the circumstances in Georgia, this is a little difficult isn't it?" Stovall replied, "It is."⁸⁸

The CBS News interview captures perfectly the tug-of-war going on between this interracial couple pursuing marriage as a personal matter and the media's public politicization of the marriage. Here we see Walter Cronkite pronouncing the Hunter-Stovall marriage "an event in the integration revolution that could have profound effects," and his reporter predicting that the wedding might be taken as proof that integration yields the very intermarriage that segregationists predicted.⁸⁹ Unrattled, the newlyweds insisted that their marriage should be a private matter and an event centered on love and family.

Although it may sound sentimental, love did prove to have more influence on the newlyweds and their parents than did the kind of political concerns that CBS and the Southern press had raised. Charlayne's parents were obviously concerned about the white racist reaction to the wedding and troubled by her decision to flout racial norms. But despite these reservations, even her reluctant father quickly came around to supporting her. And Walter's parents at least attempted to end up in the same place. They traveled to Greenwich Village to meet their new daughter-in-law. At that meeting Walter's father told Charlyane that "he never said what the press claimed he did in response to our marriage," never termed it the "end of the world." Charlayne's response to this assertion was "I believed him."[90] Who would have predicted that Walter's father, a conventional white businessman from segregated south Georgia, would choose to reconcile with his antiracist son and African American daughter-in-law? The fact that he tried to embrace his interracial family (with Walter's racist mother going along with this) and that Charlayne chose to reciprocate, is a hopeful part of this story and suggests that Georgia had the potential to turn the page on its Jim Crow past.

The dynamics of the Stovall family response to the marriage are actually more complex, however, than the reunion above might seem to imply, and they reveal how difficult it was for a conventional white Southern family to defy its community's racial norms. This family response had been a private matter until decades later when the Stovall family correspondence finally (in 2011) opened to the public. These letters—which for almost a half century were hidden away by Walter's mother in a briefcase under a bed in the Stovall house in Douglas—show us a small-town Southern family that was initially unprepared to process or accept the fact that one of its members would defy the white South's deepest racial taboo. The response evolved through several stages, starting with disbelief, resistance, and anguish, followed by varying levels of acceptance that took years to deepen and was never quite complete among Walter's parents.

Walter's parents learned that he and Charlayne were dating during the spring semester of 1963 when they visited him in Athens. Although, according to Walter, there had been "no hostility" in his parents' response, they did make quite clear their opposition to the relationship. His father, who was mayor pro tempore of Douglas and had been planning to seek the mayoralty of their hometown, told Walter that because of his "relationship with Charlayne" he "had decided not to run for Mayor." And his mother indicated her disapproval by implying that "she preferred that he not come to Douglas between the time that school was out and the time he reported to work [for his summer internship at the *Atlanta Journal*]." The interracial relationship was initially so disturbing to his father that he could not bear to write about it— even privately. Walter complained about this form of denial, noting that in their correspondence that spring, his father "had not mentioned anything about Charlayne and him and acted as if nothing had ever happened."[91]

His parents' disapproving response to his relationship with Charlayne left Walter disinclined to discuss with them his plans to move from dating to marriage. So the first of his relatives he revealed those plans to was not his parents but his aunt Martha. The most well traveled and liberal member of the Stovall family's older generation, Martha was a librarian who had moved to Massachusetts, and she, like Walter, had lived for a time in Europe. Of all his relatives, Martha was the most sympathetic to Walter and the most admiring of Charlayne. And when told in early May 1963 of his marriage plans, Martha wrote him that she "admired Charlayne for her bravery and courage in making herself the test case of the university" and praised her as "sensitive, perceptive, as well as intelligent." But like the rest of the Stovall family, Martha initially opposed the marriage. She tried, as diplomatically as she could, to explain to Walter why she "was opposed to biracial marriages" as well as to marrying before one had graduated college and secured a job. Among the arguments she used against the marriage was the tactical liberal claim "that their marriage right now would harm integration." Walter gave Martha permission to let his parents know of his marriage plans, which she did, while also urging them to discuss the marriage with Walter rather than continuing to avoid the issue. Martha thought—and confided to Walter's parents—that there was still hope that he might change his mind about his marriage plans.[92]

Next to Martha, the Stovall family member whom Walter spoke to most intensely about his marriage plans was his younger sister Lynn, a Mercer College student at the time. Lynn became involved in these conversations later in the summer of 1963. She first learned of the relationship in July when William Tate, UGA's dean of men, began phoning her at the family home in Douglas to let her know that Walter and Charlayne had been seen together around Athens and were dating. Tate was apparently seeking to get Lynn to alert the family to the relationship, hoping they could talk him into ending it. Lynn's initial response was disbelief, and she assumed that talk of this relationship was idle gossip. But when she discussed this matter with Walter, he confided to her that the rumors were true and that he was planning to marry Charlayne. Lynn, like Martha, but more heatedly, at first sought to talk Walter out of his marriage plans.[93]

Lynn's dialogue and arguments with Walter did not change his mind, but they did lead him to write her a letter in late July, a remarkable document that both critiqued her position and that of the Jim Crow South and explained his own thinking about race with great eloquence. The letter came after a long phone conversation with Lynn that Walter felt "for the first time in a long time perhaps generated more light than heat and I was glad about that."[94]

Walter argued that Lynn's (and the rest of their family's) opposition to his marriage was rooted not only in prejudice but selfishness—that rather than welcoming a marriage rooted in love, or thinking about his happiness, the family was concerned mostly that an interracial marriage would undermine its own status in small-town Georgia. "As I see it," Walter wrote, "your quarrel with me is that I have made life untenable for you in Douglas and have left you holding the bag." Walter agreed that her old friends in Georgia disapproved of intermarriage but, referring to his own experience abroad, he advised her that such friends and their prejudices ought to be left behind. "Having seen a major portion of the globe and having known people all over it who had the widest diversity of viewpoints" had led him to "re-evaluate . . . the ideas that I held when I was a boy who had never been cut off from" the Jim Crow South. "To have done less" would have left him intellectually and morally impoverished "because an inquisitive mind must be receptive to new ideas if it is to endure."[95]

Part of the problem, and one of the cornerstones of the family's deference to Jim Crow, Walter explained to Lynn, was that it had bought into the provincialism of Douglas the narrow-mindedness of a Southern small town. And it was a provincialism that repressed freedom not only in racial matters but in almost every aspect of life. "Most of my upbringing," wrote Walter, "was based on one big Don't," which fostered an inability to think independently about "what my purpose is, sex, religion, race, gambling, fashions, the works." Nobody in Douglas, Walter charged, was supposed to question its religious institutions, though its leading congregation had built a huge, luxurious church while a third of the town lived at the poverty level. "Neither my mother or father ever told me the facts of life, consequently the only thing I know about sex is that it is a sin. The only thing I know about money is that you aren't supposed to spend it." And one is not supposed to question Jim Crow, the town's biggest racist, who rails against "niggers" as "worthless bastards" flunked out of school "and can't hold a job . . . etcetera, ad nauseam." He confessed to Lynn that questioning and rejecting the fallacies of one's youth was not an easy process—that he had initially become "the most confused country boy that had ever dared to think an original thought"—but that it was crucial to his becoming a whole person and one who was true to the universalistic Christian ideal.[96]

It was on this last point that Walter was most critical of Lynn and his whole family. He wrote her that she and the rest of the family "aren't living up to the

Christian ethic" since they were "denying me my desire to act like a member of the human race.... People are people. Color is of no importance in my way of thinking.... Color in relation to intelligence or ability is an anthropological absurdity. Therefore I take people for wha[t] they are ... with no consideration for their hue." Lynn had told Walter that she was "unprepared" for such an egalitarian view and that his acting on it would lead him to become a pariah in his own hometown because he was "ten years ahead of the South." But Walter chided her for invoking the South in this way since she was, inadvertently, saying that she—like their parents and emblematic of the white South—was unprepared to act as a genuine "human being" who treated all as equals. "If being a human being is as you say ten years ahead of the South, then it is my decision to discard the South and remain a human being.... Perhaps my family actually does know these basic human values. If they do, they have never revealed it to me."[97]

With these differences unresolved even with those he was closest to in his birth family, it is little wonder that when Walter and Charlayne made the final decision to marry, he did not share the news personally with any of them. He did not even phone his parents to tell them of the marriage before this news became public. Walter also thought it would be easier for his parents if he announced the marriage after he and Charlayne had left the South for New York so that the town and state's anger over the wedding would be directed at him, the self-exiled son, rather than his parents. Thus the Stovall family learned of the marriage not from Walter but from a phone call from an Associated Press reporter after Charlayne and Walter publicly announced it shortly after Labor Day.[98]

Despite the prior discussions with Walter about dating Charlayne, this news came as a shock to the family. As Lynn put it, when she got the news from the Associated Press reporter, "I couldn't believe it; I was sort of prepared but that was the finality right there." Their anguish and sense of loss was intensified by the way the family's friends in Douglas responded. As Lynn recalls, "All of a sudden word got out over Douglas ... and people started pouring into our house. It was like a funeral. People stayed all night with us. Food was brought in."[99] The family correspondence added to this mood, as relatives, friends, and neighbors literally sent sympathy cards as if someone had died—many of them were religiously tinged, advising the family to look to Jesus, that their faith would get them through this terrible ordeal. The dominant assumption here was that the marriage, which was for Walter and Charlayne a happy event, was an occasion for mourning since the nightmare of every respectable white family in the Jim Crow South had come true.[100]

The morning after they got the news, Lynn "heard daddy weeping in the other room." And her mother told Lynn, "this is going to be the end of your daddy." Later that day, when Lynn, her mother, and aunt went out for lunch at the Dairy Queen, "we were all wearing sunglasses. We didn't want anybody to see us," especially the pack of reporters in front of their house.[101] The event was so traumatic that initially Lynn favored dropping out of Mercer for the semester. But when her friends urged her to reconsider, she agreed to return to school. Back at Mercer, the controversy followed Lynn when an anonymous caller telephoned her and in a phony Black accent asked her out on a date.

Given this racist milieu, it is striking that Walter's parents not only refused to disinherit him but traveled to New York to see the newlyweds. Perhaps the urging of Martha played a role here, since she kept in close touch with Walter and Charlayne and urged his parents to do the same. Not all of Walter's relatives, however, shared Martha's liberalism. In fact one of his uncles was so angry over the marriage that he and Walter never spoke again.[102] And when Walter's uncle Edwin learned that Walter's parents had not only visited the newlyweds in New York but brought gifts—including a dress for Charlayne—he was outraged and fearful for his brother's future. His letter to Walter's parents conceded that Blacks "need help" but denounced the "national *mania*" for integration and expressed "contempt for "that race of people's characteristics, morals, habits, potentials, etc." Edwin warned that "if you tell people that you took the negro girl out to eat or brought her a dress, you are going to jeopardize further your social acceptance and your business.... We pray for all of the family that their pain may be eased somehow." And to dramatize the need to keep secret their trip to New York and kindness toward Charlayne, Edwin closed his letter with "Now Burn This!"[103]

In the long term the family member for whom the marriage proved most transformative was Lynn. This was a gradual process. After her initial shock and opposition faded, she spent her next few years trying to avoid the issue and hoping that in her job as an Atlanta school teacher no one would recognize her connection to Walter. But over the years, her emotional ties with Charlayne and with Walter and Charlayne's daughter Susan helped her to see that the kind of attitudes that would have banned such a marriage were wrong. She became a strong liberal, socializing with the progressive Emory University graduate school classmates of her liberal husband, who at one point said to her that, had it not been for Walter's marriage to Charlayne and the way it changed her, they would likely never have connected and married themselves.[104]

As for Walter's parents, though their reconciliation with Walter seems impressive in the context of their times and location in south Georgia, it was far from perfect. While his parents embraced Charlayne and Susan, even decades after Walter and Charlayne's marriage had ended, they were still in the 1990s unable to shed the last remnants of their segregationist background, arranging to meet their granddaughter in Macon (where Lynn lived) rather than in their hometown of Douglas. This arrangement upset Walter, who repeatedly pressed Lynn as to "why won't mother and daddy invite Susan to Douglas." Walter, as Lynn put it, "did not like that. He wanted Susan in Douglas," to which Lynn replied, "Speak to them about it. Don't speak to me. I . . . can't make them do anything."[105] And Lynn really could not change the situation since whenever Susan came south they would say, "Well, let's just meet in Macon." This was in the 1990s, at a time when, now remarried, Charlayne Hunter-Gault was a famous television news broadcaster. Lynn, in response to her parents' request, would drive to Atlanta (where Susan was staying with Charlayne), pick Susan up, and drive her to her home in Macon to meet the grandparents. This arrangement contributed to Walter's growing estrangement from his father.[106]

Within the Stovall family the degree of the break with that Jim Crow past at first glance seemed to vary along generational lines. The earliest and most dramatic break had come, after all, from the younger generation, Walter himself, of course, but Lynn later made a complete break as well. A generational explanation breaks down, however, when Walter's aunt Martha is factored in since—after her initial and restrained opposition—she quickly emerged as the Stovall family member who was closest to and most supportive of Walter and Charlayne. Martha was at the other end of the political spectrum from Walter's racist uncles. It was political geography, in the final analysis, more than generation that had the most effect on these family dynamics. What Walter, Martha, and later Lynn all shared was their flight from Douglas; they all landed in more cosmopolitan settings, which for Walter and Martha included Europe and the North and for Lynn, Atlanta and its sizable liberal subculture. Walter's parents, by contrast, remained in Douglas. Hard as they tried, and much as they succeeded in being loving parents, in-laws, and grandparents in their private lives, they could never quite manage to stand up publicly to Douglas and its small-town mindset on race. And so they chose to slip off to Macon to avoid causing any stir in Douglas over their multiracial family. Love had inclined them to stay the course with that family but whatever its power, that love was not strong enough to render them indifferent to the prejudices of their small town. That distance from Macon to Douglas, and those car rides from Atlanta to Macon, attest that though the elder Stovalls had traveled quite a distance from the Jim Crow past, there were some miles of the journey away from the era of segregation that they would never traverse, and an illiberal legacy that they could never fully overcome.

As to UGA, its integration had made it possible for Hunter and Stovall to meet. But, of course, that integration had been involuntary since it occurred under federal court order and was resisted in court by UGA's administration, in the streets by its white students, and resented by both. Lynn Stovall may even have understated things when she told her brother that his racial egalitarianism had rendered him ten years ahead of the South. And the credit for Walter's democratic ethos belongs to himself, the integrated US Army, and Charlayne, not to UGA, whose deans—who were not ten years ahead of anything—tried to stop the interracial romance that would lead to the marriage, and whose top officials denounced the marriage. The negative response of these UGA leaders to Hunter and Stovall's relationship and marriage is one of many indications that, for years after the university's admissions color line had fallen, Jim Crow had a considerable afterlife at the University of Georgia.

JUDGING BY THE HEADLINE in a front page *Red and Black* story in 1972, one might conclude that UGA had progressed little regarding its acceptance of interracial dating since Hunter and Stovall dared to date and then marry back in 1963. That headline read "Peers Hassle Interracial Couples."[107] The article revealed that interracial dating remained so frowned upon at UGA that all but one of the few students who had dated across racial lines, willing to speak to the *Red and Black* reporter, asked to remain anonymous. Transfer students from northern universities agreed that "interracial dating is prevalent in the North but has been slow to come to this campus." On the other hand, the article noted that though "the idea of interracial dating has not been totally accepted here ... the trend toward black and white interracial dating is increasing." Unlike the Hunter-Stovall experience in 1963, the main opposition to such dating came not from the UGA administration or leading Georgia politicians but—as indicated by the article's headline—from fellow students. Indeed, it was "peer group" pressure from students opposed to interracial dating that led most of the few who engaged in such dating to believe those relationships must be "kept secret."[108]

Though the article was vague about white student opposition to interracial dating, it implied that the old white Southern taboo against it remained strong, citing traditional parental opposition as a major obstacle. What was new—and likely overstated—was the article's claim that opposition to interracial dating was stronger in the Black than in the white student peer culture of UGA. Though the article did not document this comparison, it did offer compelling Black testimony that the key reason Black student culture at UGA looked down upon interracial dating was that there were so few Black students, and their numbers were so skewed in terms of gender balance. As one African American female student explained, with Black female students outnumbering their male counterparts by a six-to-one ratio, "each black male has approximately six black females to choose from to date. If he decides to date a white girl, we get uptight and resentful of the white girl." Another Black female student explained, "At this campus it's ... a small black community within a large white city. The trend is more toward a unity between black men and women." In this sense she saw it as "a matter of black pride to stay within the race." All this led Black male students, as one put it, to "feel bad about dating white girls because I feel like I'm cheating."[109] Still, "the majority of black students interviewed said that if they were aware of interracial dating among their friends, they might resent it but would not try to break it up." As one Black student explained, "the real friends of the interracial couple would leave them alone and let them work out the problems without intervention. There will be enough problems without outside hassles."[110]

The consensus among the students interviewed for the article was that in 1972 interracial dating remained difficult at UGA. The *Red and Black* reporter revealed that most of those he interviewed attested that "serious interracial dating does not last long here because outside pressure tears it up." A typical remark he noted was that dating across racial lines was "just not worth it. The couple could eventually be made so unhappy that nothing is left of the relationship." One of those who had been involved in an interracial relationship advised that "you've got to be brave and strong before you try it." A white student formerly involved in such a relationship concluded that "the bad outweighed the good." Nonetheless his "advice is to go ahead and try it but prepare to be hassled."[111]

The difficulties involved in interracial dating at UGA in 1972 attest that Lynn Stovall was prescient in arguing that her brother was way ahead of his time (as was Charlayne Hunter) in dating across racial lines a decade earlier. And given the secrecy involved, to this day we do not know whether any of those relationships proved lasting and resulted in UGA's second or even third and fourth marriages across racial lines. But on the other hand, the fact that nobody was openly denouncing such relationships in racist terms, that there was no public discourse about them leading to "mongrelization," is a sign of progress away from UGA and Georgia's white supremacist past. And so was the fact that the campus student newspaper would run such a fair-minded article in 1972 on interracial dating, which not only ended on a positive note but offered something one would never have encountered a decade earlier: nonracist humor, and antiracist analysis whose source was a Black UGA basketball star, the one student included in the article who did *not* insist on anonymity and spoke openly of his perspective. The article concluded that

> perhaps basketball player Tim Bassett gave the most reasonable view of interracial dating when he said: "I don't like to call it interracial dating but rather just meeting new people. With all the talk about brotherhood going around, I wonder how you can you can learn to associate with people in another race if you aren't friends with them." Bassett sees nothing wrong with interracial dating and said that perhaps he hasn't been hassled for dating white girls because of his size. "Not many people would hassle a guy 6'8" who weighs 225 pounds," he said with a laugh. However, Bassett thinks that the acceptance of interracial dating will be slow to come here but will eventually be accepted. "The main thing is communication," he said. "That's all it is."[112]

Illuminating as the *Red and Black* article was on the state of interracial dating, it said nothing at all about what interracial dating can and, in the case of Hunter and Stovall, did lead to: marriage. This is likely because the article was written and published in 1972, a time when, despite the *Loving* decision of the US Supreme Court (1967), interracial marriage was still banned by Georgia state law. Georgia was one of the last states to comply formally with the *Loving* decision; it did not repeal its antimiscegenation law until 1979.[113] If one uses that repeal date as a yardstick, one could say then that with regard to interracial marriage, Walter Stovall and Charlayne Hunter were, to extend Lynn Stovall's phrase, not ten years but sixteen years ahead of their time in comparison with the part of the South in which they were raised.

Neither Stovall nor Hunter ever expressed the slightest regret about marrying for love in defiance of Jim Crow Georgia's color line. To the contrary, even though their marriage later ended in divorce (which had nothing to do with race), and both happily remarried, they looked back with pride on their relationship, at how much they had learned from each other, and the stance they had taken to follow their hearts and not defer to the norms of a racist society. And they felt pride and joy in their daughter Suesan, who is an accomplished artist.[114]

It is also true, however, that Walter Stovall's story in relation to UGA does not have that redemptive chapter that Hunter-Gault's, Holmes's, and Early's stories do. Not only did Stovall leave UGA and the South before he graduated, but he and the university never reconciled. Eager to turn the page on its Jim Crow past, UGA has since the 1980s honored Hunter-Gault, inviting her back to speak, naming an annual civil rights lecture after her and Holmes, re-naming the academic building for her and Holmes, endowing an English professorship in her name, and naming the education school for Early.[115] But the university has done nothing to acknowledge Stovall for defying Jim Crow as no other white UGA student did during the desegregation era.

Walter Stovall's willingness to defy the racism of his native state exacted a toll even as it enabled him to cross racial lines—as few did in 1963—to marry the woman he loved. With Stovall already alienated from the South, white Georgia's hostile response to his marriage "reinforced that alienation." In Hunter-Gault's words, he "turned his back on the South" and as both a journalist and novelist never wrote about his native region. Hunter-Gault thinks that this sense of alienation, though a plus in enabling him to marry her, was "also a negative. It haunted him. It was like a demon. . . . It broke my heart. It was as if he was running away from those demons." She thought that if he could have written about the South, "he could have been another Faulkner. But for some reason he couldn't confront it in his writing. . . . Maybe it was too painful." It was "unfortunate," she thought, that the world he knew personally, knew best, and was capable of probing the most deeply, he could not bear to write about—which was why, she thinks, he was less successful an author than he might have been.[116]

CHAPTER SIX

Decades of Desegregation
The Slow Death and Afterlife of Jim Crow at University of Georgia, 1963–1989

Historians of race and the University of Georgia owe a large debt to Calvin Trillin, one of the great journalists who reported on the Black Freedom movement and its segregationist foes in the 1960s. After covering the legal battle over the UGA color line in *Holmes v. Danner* and the university's desegregation crisis, Trillin returned to UGA in 1963, on the eve of Hunter's and Holmes's graduation, to write a series of long *New Yorker* articles on the genesis and evolution of the struggle to integrate the university. This culminated, as we have seen, with the publication of his book *An Education in Georgia*, the first and still among the most perceptive accounts of a Deep South campus desegregation struggle. Among Trillin's insights, the most important was his recognition that integration was not a brief and triumphant event—as it is still often presented in history textbooks—but a long, protracted, and often painful process.[1]

Trillin understood that while a historic milestone was reached the day that Holmes and Hunter first attended classes at UGA, ending almost two centuries of segregation there, equally important was the experience they had in their years as students in this previously white university located in a Jim Crow college town. Through in-depth interviews with Hunter, Holmes, white UGA students, administration, and faculty, Trillin documented that campus housing, social events, and extracurricular activities (as well as downtown Athens restaurants and stores) remained segregated during their years at UGA. Trillin also offered portraits of the very small group of African Americans who followed in Hunter's and Holmes's footsteps, enrolling at UGA up through 1963, documenting both their aspirations and the discrimination they faced at the university and off campus. Trillin showed that though Holmes and Hunter took pride in their role in opening up UGA to African American students, they were disappointed that so few Blacks enrolled, and they were unhappy that the coldness of many of UGA's white students toward them proved so enduring.

Trillin's example of exploring the desegregation process over time needs to be extended. That process did not, of course, end in 1963 when Trillin published his *New Yorker* articles or *An Education in Georgia*. It continued as the faculty, the curriculum, UGA facilities, athletics, and extracurricular life more generally, as well as downtown Athens, gradually desegregated over the course of the 1960s, 1970s, and beyond.[2] Take, for example, the important student activity of bringing in guest speakers. Though the color line in UGA student admissions fell in January 1961, it was not until 1964 that an African American was invited by students to address an audience at the university. This was state senator Leroy B. Johnson, the first Black elected to the Georgia legislature since Reconstruction. The lag time between the admission of the first Black students and this invitation to the first Black speaker was a product—and reminder—of the fact that UGA's integration initially was at a token level, that the mere handful of African American students at UGA did not constitute enough of a critical mass in 1961, 1962, or 1963 to be hosting guest speakers.[3] This, plus the provincial state of mind, the myopic white-student focus on white speakers, and events by and for white students, meant that the idea of inviting Black speakers was as alien to the UGA student body in 1961 as it had been in 1951, 1941, 1931, and in the rest of the Jim Crow era. And unlike with the admission of Hunter and Holmes, no court was going to order UGA to host a Black speaker. This had to be done voluntarily by UGA, and so it took three long years for anyone in the white UGA student body to volunteer.

Even where there was some interest in breaking with the Jim Crow past, as there was with regard to hosting "mixed race" musical events—so that great Black jazz and R & B musicians could be brought to campus in place of the often-mediocre white bands that bored students—the white student body, as late as 1962, continued to be too timid to defy UGA's conservative administration. When students raised the idea of ending this racist prohibition, dean of students Joseph Williams "argued that the campus 'is not quite ready' for mixed race entertainment."[4] Some UGA students dissented from this decision, including student government leaders and the editor of the campus newspaper, but they did not defy the dean, as one might think a real option in the 1960s, a decade we associate with student rebellion. Instead, they deferred to a dean who was still very much a captive of the Jim Crow past.[5]

Such timidity was consistent with the old Jim Crow tradition of students usually deferring to rules barring multiracial music groups from campus which, as we saw earlier, was why the UGA Jazz Club had canceled its invitation to Dave Brubeck's jazz quartet in 1959 when its leader learned that the bass player was African American. "Mixed race" was a term used at UGA to bar not only integrated musical groups but events involving all-Black bands.

The bans' impact was especially evident in UGA's campus-wide events, such as homecoming and the "Little Commencement" dances, which in the 1940s through the early 1960s almost always featured (mostly second-tier) white musical bands.[6]

Toward the end of the Jim Crow era, however, there were several notable exceptions to the "whites only" musical event restrictions on the UGA campus. These involved jazz greats Louis Armstrong and Duke Ellington. Armstrong played at a UGA women's fraternity dance in winter 1955, followed by Ellington playing at the Little Commencement dance that spring quarter.[7] Having a famed Black musician featured at a campus-wide dance was such an unusual occurrence at UGA that the student newspaper responded to Ellington with a bizarre political cartoon depicting him playing at the university and terming him a "damn good nigger."[8] Two years later, Armstrong returned to play at a dance on the UGA campus, as part of his 1957 southern tour that had been violently disrupted by white supremacists who thew a stick of dynamite at his concert in Knoxville, Tennessee.[9] He would draw a packed house at UGA's Stegeman Hall, but his appearance almost did not come off because its student sponsor, the Interfraternity Council, displaying characteristic political timidity, was on the verge of cancelling Armstrong if the Georgia legislature acted on a bill it was considering banning such "mixed social events."[10] Fortunately, the bill was defeated through a technicality. But for the rest of the decade, into the early 1960s, white bands remained the norm at UGA dances.[11]

It may seem odd that a fraternity organization was involved in hosting Armstrong, since Fraternity Row was staunchly segregationist. Here it must be kept in mind that generally not even politically conservative UGA students tended to think that events with Black musicians posed any threat to the segregationist social order, especially when those musicians were entertaining white fraternity members and their white dates at a Greek House dance.[12] So the fraternities seemed disinclined to have this part of their social lives rigidly policed for such matters of racial purity. Actually, in the musical realm the fraternities in the 1950s were considerably more progressive than the UGA administration when it came to scheduling entertainment. This also had to do with musical preferences. Having Black and interracial bands largely banned from campus meant that the dances there featured big band-style music, which seemed out of date. So the fraternities used their semi-independent status to host in their off campus houses Black R&B groups, and in 1950 even featured an interracial group Al Jackson's Dukes of Rhythm.[13] This helps explain why the Interfraternity Council would become involved in the failed effort in 1962 to get UGA to lift the ban on mixed-race musical events.

Though there was no announcement of the breakthrough at UGA, by spring 1963, this remnant of the Jim Crow era seemed on its way out, as Black R&B singer Clyde McPhatter played at the campus-wide Greek Week dance.[14] And when Jackie Wilson in May 1963 played a concert sponsored by the Chi Phi fraternity that same semester, he drew a crowd of some 3,500, which Dean Tate termed "the largest crowd he'd ever seen at a function of this type."[15] By the mid-1960s major Black musical recording artists, such as James Brown, Stevie Wonder, the Temptations, Clyde McPhatter, and the Platters were regularly appearing at UGA.[16] Note, however, that the bands of these Black musical stars do not seem to have been interracial when they played at UGA, and it is not clear when the first racially integrated band appeared on campus.

In contrast to the racial progress in UGA's music scene during the 1960s, the afterlife of Jim Crow at UGA was strikingly displayed in and beyond this decade in the racially discriminatory admissions practices of the university's white fraternities and sororities. In June 1965 US commissioner of education Francis Keppel declared that discriminatory fraternities were in violation of the Civil Rights Act of 1964, and that universities tolerating such discrimination would lose their federal funding. UGA dean of men William Tate and dean of students Joseph Williams indicated that they were taking no action toward compliance and had heard no word directly from Washington on this matter. Dean of women Louise McBee was even more evasive, telling the *Red and Black* she "didn't see how such an act could be enforced" and acting as if there was nothing wrong with Greek houses practicing racial and religious discrimination. She argued that "if someone should ask me if fraternities and sororities discriminate I would have to say yes.... Discrimination of a kind is practiced by all organizations that cannot accept all who apply for membership."[17] This ignored both the illegality of racial discrimination and the authority of the UGA administration to drive Jim Crow off frat row by withdrawing university recognition from Greek houses that excluded Blacks and other minorities—an authority it would never invoke.

By 1970, the university required signed statements from fraternities and sororities that "they did not practice racial discrimination," but, as Tate attested, those statements were meaningless since "every Negro that went through fraternity rush, and every [Black] girl that went to a sorority house dropped out, and none of 'em got picked."[18]

Resistance to letting go of the Jim Crow past was a multigenerational affair. Parents of UGA students at times proved more recalcitrant than their sons and daughters. Tate recalled, for example, that shortly after Charlayne Hunter was assigned to a room in Center-Myers, he had a difficult encounter with the father of a resident of that dorm. This parent didn't want his daughter living in the same dorm as a Black student—and was apparently also concerned about the potential for further violence in the aftermath of the riot outside the dorm. So he came to Tate for help, after he had told his daughter to pack her bags, as he was withdrawing her from UGA. His daughter had responded defiantly. As Tate recalled it, she had told her father, "'Daddy, I want to be a Journalism student at University. I made an A average last year. I'm gonna have to live with nigras this way the rest of my life, and I'm going to classes, and I'm not goin' home.' And she walked out of Myers Hall with her books and walked over to the School of Journalism, with her father telling her to pack up and go home."[19] The father asked Tate, "Don't I have the right to tell my daughter to go home?" Tate replied, "You have a right from a legal point of view, I guess, because she is under 21, but I'd think a long time if I had a daughter at the University who wanted to continue before I let her go home." The father started crying, and after sitting in Tate's office for a few minutes, gave in to his daughter and went home.[20]

By the late 1960s, when UGA finally began assigning roommates in the dorms across racial lines, Tate encountered similar problems. After a white south Georgia student was assigned a Black roommate, his father, as Tate put it, "hit my office like a ton of bricks," threatening all kinds of trouble "if you don't move my son out of that room."[21] When Tate told him that, according to a court decision on this issue at the University of Kentucky, he could not arbitrarily reassign roommates on account of race, the father blew up, saying, "Well, I'm goin' to be talking to the governor in an hour.... My boy's going to have another roommate." But he had not talked to his son, and when he did the son told him, "Father, I want to come to the University of Georgia. This boy's got better SAT scores than I've got. He's assigned to me by what the University has to do, and I'm not going to raise a ruckus about it, and I don't want you to."[22] So the father relented.

Some of those in the older generation having a hard time adapting to integrated dorms were university officials themselves. Aware of how sensitive this living arrangement could be among those raised in the Jim Crow South, UGA's housing staff initially would ask if the white student knew that the roommate the student was about to be assigned was Black, to ascertain if this was acceptable to the white student. But this quickly led to an investigation by federal officials, concerned that, as Tate put it, "we have a segregation policy in the dormitory. They sent a fella down here to interview me—fact is three of em' came down, gave me a hard time."[23] And UGA in the mid and late '60s would often assign single rooms to Black students at the end of their hallways so that there would be as little racial interaction as possible.[24]

Employment was another area in which UGA was slow to change. From clericals to professors the academic workforce was white from the time Holmes and Hunter entered the university in 1961 to and beyond their graduation in 1963. As one faculty member recalled, back then "the role of Negro employees on campus was almost exclusively at the unskilled level. All the janitors and maids were black, as were practically all unskilled laborers in construction and on the crew of the Physical Plant and Landscaping." Sociology professor John Belcher noted that "probably the first white-collar position held by a Black on the University of Georgia took place about 1965." Belcher had received a call from the student placement office indicating that a Black student was eligible for a federally funded work-study job and was asked "if he would be willing to accept a 'colored girl' in this position." Belcher said yes, and the reaction to her presence speaks volumes about how novel the idea of racially integrated white collar work was to the campus community back then. As Belcher explained, "She started doing clerical work at a desk in the office of the Sociology Department. People walking by the office would glance through the window in the door and see her hard at work at a desk. The general response was to glance through the door in passing, walk one or two paces on past the door, stop suddenly, return to look through the glass again, and then walk on, shaking the head in disbelief."[25]

And so historians need to explore this longer narrative arc of desegregation, probing the Black experience at UGA for the generations of students who came after Hunter and Holmes—and later Black faculty and administrators—as well as the university's white student majority, which struggled with, and at times resisted, the process of shedding the remnants of its Jim Crow past. This involves doing a more complete Black history of UGA into and beyond the 1960s; it also means recognizing that while some UGA administrators and faculty did try to build a new and more democratic university, there was also lots of lethargy and some pushback. In the absence of any meaningful accountability or critical reflection on its racist past by Georgia politicians or UGA's top administrators, much of white Georgia continued to assume that UGA belonged to it, proving largely indifferent to the Black experience at the university, and unsupportive or hostile when Black student activists organized to demand democratic change.

It would require an entire book to do justice to this larger story of Black UGA and the death and afterlife of Jim Crow on and off campus, but I would like to offer some glimpses of what this history encompasses, and some thoughts about what it seems to reveal. There is no question as to where and with whom this discussion should begin. By far the best source for probing race and memory at UGA post-1963 is Charlayne Hunter. As a *New York Times* reporter, Hunter returned to UGA late in 1969 to report on race and the university, and how it compared to her own experience and Holmes's as UGA's first Black students. This was her first visit to UGA since her graduation in 1963. Hunter's article reflected not only her formidable talent as a reporter but her unrivalled insider's knowledge of what it meant to be a Black student at UGA, which enabled her to raise the most searching questions with both whites and African Americans about race, equity, change, and continuity at the university. The article she published in the *New York Times Magazine* in January 1970, after this trip back to UGA, is brimming with insights about both the progress and obstacles that limited the progress in race relations at the university.[26]

Hunter opened her article by recalling her tumultuous first days at UGA, when with Hamilton Holmes, she broke the color line at the university: the riot outside her dormitory, when "a brick and bottle had shattered the window in my room, sending chunks of broken class within a foot of where I was standing," followed by her and Holmes's suspension "for our own safety," and court-ordered readmission to the university. The white student hostility in her dormitory "continued for a long time" that first semester as "the girls above me—I was the sole resident of the first floor —would pound the floor, night after night, late into the night."[27] This would leave her suffering "with physical and mental exhaustion" that first semester, which was why during the sessions of her mid-morning world history class, she often found herself "fighting desperately," but not always successfully, "to stay awake and avoid confirming the stereotype that all blacks are lazy." This contrasted dramatically with the first UGA class Hunter observed almost nine years later when she "entered that same classroom—this time wide awake, and found not a course in world history, but one in African history, part of a new black-studies program; and not one exhausted black girl, but five outspoken black men and women among the students, and a young black man with a heavy Afro haircut teaching the course. By the end of the hour, as the white students sat quietly taking notes, the black instructor was acting as a referee for two of the black students who were engaged in a vehement clash of opinion on the subject of pan-Africanism."[28]

Another encouraging sign of progressive movement Hunter observed in 1969 was a generational changing of the guard, as some of the old UGA administrators aligned with Georgia's Jim Crow regime either had retired or were about to, and their replacements were younger educational leaders with no ties to that regime. She found O. Suthern Sims, UGA's young acting dean of student affairs, "a welcome change from the tight-jawed, close-minded segregationist who preceded him." Sims "greeted" Hunter "warmly" and said he hoped she "found the university to be a lot different from what it had been when" she entered UGA. Sims told her that UGA would no longer list apartments unless they were rented on a nondiscriminatory basis, and that the administration no longer confined its Black students to segregated "black rooms" as has been done to her; it stopped such segregation in 1967. Hunter soon learned that it took pushing from Black students during those four years after her graduation to get UGA to end the dorm discrimination she had complained about as an undergraduate. Sims said UGA had eliminated all "forms of racial segregation that you can take any legal action against."[29]

While impressed that Sims and his colleagues opposed de jure racial discrimination, Hunter implied that they seemed passive when it came to de facto, informal modes of discrimination. Sims contended that the university could address legal or official forms of segregation but had no power when confronted with segregationism "attitudinally." When you're talking about attitude, that "is a tough one." And this passivity had led to tension between the administration and the campus's Black students. As Sims explained, "Our blacks come in and they're experiencing disgust and hostility, and it becomes a real paradox—'You do something about it now,' they say. But we can't just unilaterally rule against attitude. That's a fascist state." This stance reminded Hunter of what she had heard from her segregationist classmates in 1961, "the white students who vowed not to accept desegregation despite the fact that it was being shoved down our throats. You can't legislate morality, they were fond of saying."[30]

Sims's upbeat view of progress toward racial equity was also contradicted by the enrollment statistics. Though noting that no one knew the exact number of Black students at UGA, the best estimate in 1969 was "approximately 125" out of a total student enrollment of 18,000.[31] And the university's limited interest in increasing Black student enrollment was indicated by the fact that it had only recently hired its first African American admissions counselor to recruit Black students, and he was a graduate student doing this work only on a part-time basis. Moreover, when another dean boasted to Hunter that UGA had received funds to "increase the faculty by more than 500—which he termed 'a breakthrough for educational excellence,'" she asked him how many of these new faculty hires were Black. The answer was *one*: Richard Graham, a music therapist.³² Though Hunter did not comment on this, such numbers spoke for themselves, attesting that as of fall 1969 there had been even less progress in desegregating the faculty than the student body.

Hunter's interviews with Black UGA students were quite revealing about both the problems they encountered at the university and their efforts to get the administration to address those problems. One positive note was that Hunter conducted these interviews over lunch at a steakhouse in Athens that in her own student days refused to serve African Americans. The most depressing part of the interviews was the degree of frustration, a sense that university authorities would not intervene decisively to end racial discrimination. For example, James Hurley, a freshman from Atlanta who had made the freshman football team and hoped to play on the varsity of UGA's historically white football team, was told by "a sympathetic coach . . . that Georgia would probably dress him, but that if he was really serious about playing football he'd better look elsewhere."³³ And he did, transferring to Vanderbilt when it offered him a football scholarship.

One sign of progress was that, small as it was, the 125-student population was sufficient to generate a critical mass to form an activist organization, the Black Student Union (BSU), which since 1967 had championed the rights of UGA's African American students. Though it only had thirty members, the BSU managed to pressure the administration to end its discriminatory dorm assignments and helped win the establishment of a Black studies program—though the BSU felt it was much too modestly funded and structured, as they had wanted a major, autonomous department rather than a small program.³⁴ The students believed that they just got the runaround from UGA on their demands for an end to racial discrimination on its athletic teams.³⁵ And they were angered by the administration's refusal to take action against UGA's racist fraternities. Of special concern was the same fraternity that had harassed Holmes and Hunter in 1961, the Kappa Alphas, who were still at it in 1969. "There are still incidents in front of that house," the Black students told Hunter. "Black women are constantly subject to verbal abuse and getting things thrown at them."³⁶ The BSU asked for a ban on this racist fraternity, but UGA president Fred Davison refused to act. He also turned down the BSU demands for new policies to bring back to UGA Black students who had dropped out.

The relationship between BSU leaders and Davison was tense, which is reflected in the heated rhetoric found in some of the organization's correspondence with him. For example, more than a year after the interviews Hunter did with Black students for her 1970 *New York Times* article, the BSU sent an irate letter to Davison protesting the playing of the song "Dixie" at campus events. This letter's angry tone was apparently motivated by the Black students' perception that only militancy could get any meaningful response from the administration of a white institution whose leadership was insensitive to Black students' views and needs. BSU chief of staff A. Levert Hood wrote to president Davison (on stationery adorned with a clenched black fist):

> It is with great displeasure that I write this letter. For more than two years the students, faculty, and Administration of this university have known the Black Student Union's opposition to the playing of the racist song "Dixie" both at official University functions and at other times as well. We are insulted by the unpleasant memory of the "Old South" which is created by this song. After all, you wouldn't wear a swastika through a Jewish neighborhood!
>
> Therefore I demand that you act officially, immediately, and concernedly toward the elimination of this biased practice.... I strongly suggest that you do not employ your previous tactic whereby this practice was stopped only temporarily, because this will definitely meet with a determined, physical backlash. If "Dixie" is the only means by which this university can arouse its students, then it has failed miserably in its task of widening the scope of the student populace.
> DIXIE IS DEAD AND YOU CAN'T REVIVE IT.[37]

If the BSU came across to its detractors as abrasively militant, Davison came off all too often as arrogantly dismissive of Black student concerns. In the late 1960s, Davison seemed almost to glory in saying "no" to the BSU. At a time when Georgia had elected the segregationist Lester Maddox as governor, perhaps Davison did not want to be seen as knuckling under to Black militants. Or perhaps it was that he saw the goal of racial equity on campus as at best secondary to his larger goal of converting UGA from a relatively provincial institution to a leading research university—and never caught on to how those two goals could connect. Having been born and raised on the white side of the color line, Davison, who took his UGA degree in veterinary science in the Jim Crow era (1952), seemed ill-equipped to relate to Black students. A Black student complained that when she met with Davison, he referred to African Americans as "nigra[s]" and "colored people," and that when asked to "show respect by using the proper phraseology," Davison replied "that he would not change his speech pattern because of some personal idiosyncrasy of hers."[38] Some BSU activists—among themselves—in turn mocked his unpresidential behavior by terming him "the horse doctor."[39] Davison conveyed apathy about the need to improve the racial climate on campus, telling an interviewer in 1969 that "I don't create the living environment.... I can't guarantee relationships between students or even between students and faculty."[40]

Whatever Davison's motivations, his response to the BSU's twenty-two demands in March 1969 (and similar demands in the next few years) was to turn most of them down as wrong-headed, impractical, or illegal, without stopping to consider that the students had brought up serious racial problems that merited action, and that if he did not agree with the BSU solutions to those problems he should offer some solutions of his own.[41] For example, the BSU, reflecting a common Black student concern about racist and racially insensitive faculty (documented in Hunter's *New York Times Magazine* article), demanded the establishment of ad hoc committees to investigate "redneck" professors. Davison rejected this idea as a violation of academic freedom. But he offered no alternative solution that could have addressed this problem—for example, establishing teacher training workshops and instructional guides for faculty on teaching a racially diverse student body—with no threat to academic freedom.

Similarly, Davison refused to act on the BSU demand to halt the playing of the Jim Crow "Dixie" anthem at campus events, which so offended Black students, a refusal he justified by claiming this would amount to censorship. But he could easily have asked the UGA marching band's director to consider Black student views in deciding what songs to play (and three years later the band director would, with no censorship involved, decide to stop playing "Dixie" and also changed the band's name from the Dixie Redcoat Band to the Redcoat Band).[42] And while rejecting the BSU's proposal for the use of pass/fail grades and readmission of failing Black students to address the Black dropout problem, he offered no proposal to address this problem with Black student attrition. His defensive responses about the BSU demands for more serious efforts to recruit Black faculty, students, and student athletes were equally weak. Davison may have been correct in claiming that he lacked the power to simply dissolve the racist Kappa Alpha fraternity since it was a recognized student group, but he certainly did have the authority to require that the fraternity desegregate, something he was too timid even to mention. And perhaps most cowardly of all was Davison's evasive response on the BSU demand for the removal of Roy Harris from the University System of Georgia Board of Regents. Obviously fearful of the political clout of Harris, arguably the state's most powerful and unrepentant segregationist, Davison said nothing about the merits of removing this white supremacist from the university's highest governing board but simply pointed out that only the governor determined the board's membership.[43]

The recent oral history interviews of Black UGA alumni attest that the grievances the BSU aired were genuine. This was evident, for example, in the recollections of Nawanna Lewis Miller, who vividly recalled being made to feel like an "intruder" almost from the moment she set foot on the almost all-white UGA campus in 1969, when the band played the Old South anthem "Dixie" at her freshman orientation.[44] And she recalled going to see a professor in his office because he gave have her a C grade on a paper with no explanation, and him telling her that she received this low grade because he "just could not give an A to a Nigra."[45] For Miller the tears over such injustice were real, as was her desire to do something about it, which led her to become active in the BSU. The comradery, the Black cultural activities, and the protests of the BSU seemed to her "an oasis" and about the only good memories of her UGA years—during which, like Hamilton Holmes years earlier, she sought refuge every Friday by traveling home to Black Atlanta.[46]

The late 1960s was the era of Black Power, when nonviolence was often seen as passé by young militants who sought to battle racial discrimination "by any means necessary." In this mindset, the BSU in January 1968 held a "stand-in" aimed at ending racial segregation in the bathroom facilities that Black cafeteria employees still had to contend with in the UGA student center's Bulldog Room.[47] The protesters demanded the removal of the "white" and "colored" bathroom signs; they "walked to the head of the food line" in the student center cafeteria and simply refused to move until the signs came down. When white students objected to this stand-in disrupting their lunch, and some sought to use physical violence to end the protest—which the Black activists viewed as a racist assault—a scuffle ensued,[48] and as one female BSU activist told Hunter, "I climbed up on top of a table and started throwing forks and knives and trays.... Anything I could get my hands on. That's one of the reasons they leave us alone. They think we're crazy. Imagine, thirty black kids got 18,000 honkies scared to death."[49] The uproar led the UGA to remove the signs, an offensive remnant of the Jim Crow era.

Hunter's interviews touched on this daring tactical approach taken by BSU activists in the late 1960s and early 1970s. The BSU engaged in confrontational protests that were simply not possible for Hunter when she was one of only two Black students at UGA. In fact, Hunter told a reporter in 1970 that "the critical difference" between her UGA years and those of her successors in 1969 was that these African American students "aren't taking this stuff....

If Hamilton [Holmes] and I wanted to complain about something [in 1961] all we could do was complain to each other. Now there are enough blacks to work on all fronts where they feel inequities exist.... When I was here I had to get my car door repainted because someone scratched 'nigger' on it. These kids faced the same thing but they started fighting back; and they say that when they did, everything stopped."[50] Hunter learned that Black students—even those not connected to the BSU—found the image of Black militancy useful since it led to white fears of retaliation, yielding an almost complete stop to white harassment of Black students.

The glacial pace of UGA's desegregation of its intercollegiate athletic teams was another concern, and one that was especially galling to the BSU and the Black student community. At a time when African Americans had long since emerged as star players in professional and intercollegiate football and basketball, UGA's persistent whiteness seemed almost incomprehensible. It had gotten to the point that, as BSU chairman Levert Hood explained in 1971, UGA Jim Crowism in athletics had even left UGA behind other formerly all-white Deep South teams, including UGA's archrival in athletics, Georgia Tech. This, according to Hood, led him "and other black students [who] attend a Georgia-Georgia Tech" basketball game to cheer for Tech "because they've got a black on their team and our own team doesn't."[51] As to football, Hunter told an interviewer in 1970 that back in 1961, Hamilton Holmes, who had been a high school football star before coming to UGA, "wanted to play football, but they told him it was too soon, he'd have to wait. Who would have thought that it would have taken more than nine years?"[52] This long delay in desegregating UGA football—which historians have noted but not done much to explain—likely contributed to the university's poor record in attracting Black students in the 1960s and early 1970s, as Hunter observed in 1970: "If there were four or five black boys on the football team, you'd have black boys all over the state identifying with them and wanting to come."[53]

Nor was it only Black students and alums who noticed UGA dragging its feet on the desegregation of its sports teams. So did the federal government. The US Office of Education in April 1967 sent a compliance team to Athens to speak to UGA administrators about desegregating its athletic teams.[54] These federal officials were coming to see to it that UGA was getting into compliance with the desegregation requirements of Title VI of the 1964 Civil Rights Act. Universities receiving federal aid were required to comply with the act's antidiscrimination provisions. The Southeastern Conference was a special focus for the Office of Education because as of April 1967 only two Southeastern Conference universities, Kentucky and Vanderbilt, had begun to offer athletic scholarships to African American students.[55] It would not be until fall 1971 that UGA awarded its first football scholarships to Black students, freshmen who would finally integrate UGA's varsity football team in 1972.[56]

In its initial stage, moreover, it was not only the glacial pace of the football team's desegregation that was so striking. It was also the repetition of the pattern of continuing racial discrimination even as the desegregation process finally began. Recall that well after Hunter's admission to UGA in 1961, she was barred during her first quarter from dining in the cafeteria where the white students ate and kept from living on the same floor of her dormitory as white students. Similarly, almost a decade later, when the first African American was able to join the football team, he was treated poorly, as he explained to his outraged religious history professor Robert Ayers: He "had not been awarded financial assistance, nor had he been given a room in the athletic dorm, or even permitted to eat at the training table with the other athletes. Having meager funds, he ate many meals in his own dorm room, using many dietary supplements."[57]

Beyond athletic fields, the BSU was also not alone in its concern about the underrepresentation of Blacks in the UGA student body. The National Association for the Advancement of Colored People's Legal Defense and Education Fund, the Southern Education Foundation (an Atlanta-based philanthropy that focused on Black educational opportunity in the South), and the US Department of Health, Education, and Welfare (HEW) in the 1970s confronted the university on its lack of racial equity as part of broader reports and actions on the poor statewide performance on such equity in all of Georgia's public colleges and universities. In 1973 HEW rejected as inadequate the state of Georgia's eleventh-hour plan to desegregate its thirty public colleges and universities. HEW threatened to cut off the federal funding of these state colleges unless the plan was revised satisfactorily.[58] When the Southern Education Foundation released its report on desegregation in 1975, UGA had one of the worst records in the state's higher education system. In the state's four universities, twelve senior colleges, and fourteen junior colleges, Blacks constituted 11.7 percent of the student population. But at UGA, its 634 Black students in 1975 accounted for only 3.3 percent of the total student enrollment.[59] All this occurred in a state in which more than 25 percent of the population was African American.

It is this poor desegregation record that gave UGA Black student protests of the 1960s, '70s, and '80s a similar focus. Always, as the editors of UGA's student newspaper noted in May 1979, on the twenty-fifth anniversary of the *Brown* decision, at or near the top of the list of Black student demands was "more black professors, more active recruitment of black students to increase enrollment, more financial aid to blacks."[60] And yet by 1982 Blacks represented only 5.2 percent of the UGA student body and 1.2 percent of the UGA faculty. All of this was well below the standards the University System of Georgia Board of Regents had adopted in 1978 in response to the federal government's calls for meeting meaningful desegregation goals. According to those standards, UGA was supposed to enroll 2,646 Black students by 1983, but UGA missed that mark by a whopping 53 percent, with a Black enrollment of 1,235 (which equaled only 5.6 percent of the total student population).[61] The *Red and Black* editor put it well when he concluded that "the enrollment of Hunter and Holmes [in 1961] was not the first trickle before a flood of black students at the University. Rather it was the first drop before the trickle."[62]

UGA's top administrators claimed that the numbers were limited because of a lack of qualified Black students and intense national competition for top Black faculty. But Eddie Daniels, the university advisor to Black student organizations, noted in 1983 that UGA "has a reputation for making excuses for the shortage of black faculty, staff, as well as students."[63] Lack of leadership in this desegregation work was linked to the fact that the UGA administration itself had not even by the late 1980s desegregated its own ranks. According to Maurice Daniels, then a social work professor and member of the Minority Advisory Committee to UGA president Charles Knapp, as of fall 1988, Blacks were not represented in any "key UGA administration positions.... Of the six University vice presidents and 13 school deans, none are black. There are some very dynamic scholarly blacks who need to be in some of these positions."[64]

The most candid UGA administrator when it came to discussing race relations and the poor performance of the university administration in this area was Ben Colbert, who in 1969 became the first African American hired in an administrative capacity in the history of the University of Georgia. Though Colbert worked hard in his position as a minority recruiter and helped increase Black enrollments from abysmal to low (83 Black freshmen and a total of about 300 Black students in a student body of over 18,000 as of fall 1971), he realized that UGA's top administrators had little interest in accelerating the desegregation process. As Colbert explained to a local reporter, "the main problem" was that "the University does not really care if he has any success in recruiting blacks and offers no hint of caring what happens to the black students once they are actually on campus."[65]

Colbert found that UGA lacked a serious desegregation strategy, and that having one Black recruiter in the admissions office did not constitute such a strategy. It was faculty and student affairs staff and university leaders who were needed for "this business of relating to the black community," which is why he was in 1971 "pained by the fact that there are virtually no black administrators or faculty members at the University of Georgia. You need to have more black people" in those positions. Colbert was aware that in response to recent BSU demands for recruiting more Black students, President Davison pointed to Colbert's work, which confirmed the Black recruitment officer's sense that "their reason for hiring me was a surface thing . . . [in this] showcase position. . . . They really wanted me to sit and look good for people. . . . Everyone knows they are racist and so they try to disprove that by having my position."[66]

Colbert believed that his position was created not of the UGA administration's own initiative but because of outside pressure. When Colbert was approached for the position in the fall of 1969, the Black student population had been very small, which, as Colbert put it, "was of course embarrassing not from the university's point of view but from the point of view of agencies concerned with civil rights, particularly the HEW. They are the ones who said: 'Perhaps you ought to get into minority recruitment.'"[67] Colbert attested that UGA was having a hard time making the transition from a Jim Crow institution that from 1950 to 1961 had waged an energetic campaign to keep Black students out, to a multiracial university that devoted similar energy to recruiting and retaining Black students and to hiring Black faculty and administrators. Coming as they did from Colbert, who worked for UGA and whose job it was to help with this transition, his words carry considerable weight.

As to UGA's white students and their attitude toward Black UGA students, Hunter's 1970 article offered critical insights. Hunter noted that in her years as a student, after the initial desegregation crisis and its racist violence ended, most white students "were too preoccupied with fraternity and sorority parties to really concern themselves about us." And from what she was "able to glean from various sources," this "was still pretty much the case" in 1969.[68] One white freshman from a small town in Georgia told her, "I just sort of don't feel anything toward" Black students. "But I don't feel anything against them." This student said there was "discrimination emanating . . . from the way people talk about them and stuff." Hunter found that these interviews confirmed what BSU activists told her about the cold atmosphere on campus toward Black students. Especially memorable was the candid remark of one white student that he "wouldn't be comfortable if I were black on this campus. There's an awful lot of discrimination. It's just the way people have been raised to feel about blacks."[69]

The social and political chasm between Black students and the white campus majority was most visible when African American students became vocally critical of UGA. This was evident, for example, in a rally the BSU held on campus in April 1969 on behalf of its twenty-two demands for a more hospitable campus for Black students. The rally drew "some 500 white students" who "showed up as uninvited guests, and the rally became a tense exchange between black and white students."[70] Here you had a conservative crowd of white Southern students exposed—many for the first time—to a radically critical Black perspective on the university and American society, expressed in the language of Black Power and Black militancy, which did nothing but anger the most vocal of these whites. One Black organizer of the rally vowed that the BSU would win concessions from the administration, "or we will march from one end of this campus to the other, like Sherman." The rally began with one Black protester clad in dungarees reading what he termed a "black interpretation of the Gettysburg Address.... Four score and seven years ago white racists brought forth on this continent a new nation dedicated to the proposition that only white men were created equal" and that Black people were "highly resolved that racism of the honkies, by the honkies, for the honkies shall perish from the earth."[71] Another BSU speaker argued that it was a shame that so many white students "refuse to acknowledge the sins of your fathers" in propagating racism in the Jim Crow era.[72]

Prominent among the grievances cited at this rally was the Eurocentrism of the UGA curriculum. As one speaker complained, "There's not one course in this campus required in black history and culture. Are you trying to tell me our culture and history is not worth anything? In our fine arts department here not one black painter or sculptor is mentioned. The university has two courses in western civilization so you can learn about Greece and Europe. But how many of you have ever heard of Ghana or Nigeria?" In a voice "charged with emotion" the speaker asked, "Are you trying to tell us the only way for blacks to make it is by white standards? If you are, to hell with you."[73] This indictment of the curriculum provoked a white heckler, who shouted, "Go somewhere else, if you don't like it here." William Kennedy, an African American freshman and Vietnam veteran, responded, "Go somewhere else? I've been somewhere else. I fought your war in Vietnam and came back to the home of the free and the brave. I see the brave, but I'll be damned if I see the free." He continued, "All I want is a good education." And in a swipe at the history of segregation on UGA's football team, the Georgia Bulldogs, Kennedy remarked that "some day I'd like to sit down to a Georgia football game and see some black Bulldogs running up and down that field." Another speaker took aim at UGA's most racist fraternity and its Confederate flag, and in articulating the BSU's demand that Kappa Alpha's charter be revoked, stated that Kappa Alpha "represents the kind of society we're trying to destroy. That flag is coming down!"[74]

The BSU speakers sought to defuse the tension at the rally by taking questions from the crowd. One of those questions was about the BSU demand for a separate Black dormitory. Expressing Black alienation from the white student majority, a BSU speaker replied with a note of irony that "we know you don't want us in your dorms, so we want to set this thing up so you won't feel discriminated against."[75] Asked about whether the BSU was willing to negotiate its demands for a Black studies department and a Black grading system (designed to cut down on Blacks dropping out of UGA), BSU activist Leonard Lester asserted, "Our demands are not negotiable. We feel what we're asking for is necessary for a black education."[76]

This meeting made quite an impression on the *Red and Black* news editor. He was struck by the white hostility to the Black students and their demands and noted that "many of the questions were prompted by animosity" toward the African Americans "and what they were doing.... There were catcalls and jeering.... A type of tension and animosity hung over more than 1,000 students who milled around the area."[77] He thought it was fortunate that the racial tension had not led to violence. "Tempers are still hot, and feelings high on the ever present problem [of race] at the University.... There is still a great deal of misunderstanding." But he also reported that when in the question-and-answer segment white students finally were exposed to the logic behind the BSU demands, some of the them "started questioning among themselves if perhaps there was some justification for what the black students were calling for."[78] In the aftermath of this stormy rally and heated letters to the editor about it, the *Red and Black* ran a political cartoon that was less optimistic, featuring a bearded Black student, sporting an Afro haircut, trying to speak across a brick wall—labeled THE WALL 1969—to a group of clean-shaven white students on the other side of that wall, and with the cartoon captioned "WHAT WE HAVE HERE IS A FAILURE TO COMMUNICATE."[79]

The racial divide was also displayed vividly in the controversy over the appearance at UGA in 1974 by William Shockley. Attempting to revive racist eugenics' pseudoscientific theories of Black inferiority, Shockley engaged in public debates about his racist "theories." UGA's right wing Demosthenian Society sponsored such a debate. BSU activists disrupted this event when

"50 Blacks charged into the already crowded auditorium, shouting 'To hell with Shockley.' The predominantly white audience attempted to drown out the Black students shouting by applauding vigorously when Shockley was introduced. At one point fist fights almost broke out between white and black students, and on two occasions blacks charged on to the stage."[80] This BSU disruption of the Shockley event was widely pilloried by white students, UGA's student government, and the student newspaper as a horrendous free speech violation, and President Davison apologized to Shockley. While it is true that the BSU had committed a free speech violation here, the editorials and letters that appeared in the student newspaper and the statements of student government officials and Davison display an almost astonishing degree of ignorance and racial insensitivity regarding why representatives of UGA's small Black student population would find it so offensive to have Black intelligence and alleged inferiority subjected to this kind of public debate.

This white discourse depicted the Shockley incident simply as a free speech issue without any consideration of how UGA's history of racism and ongoing racial tensions shaped the BSU's perspective on the Shockley event and paved the way for its disruption.[81] In fact, reporters at the Shockley protest noted that that this dispute was "part of a much larger problem at the University of Georgia." The "group of blacks who charged on to the stage ... later told newsmen that there is considerable discrimination and racial unrest on the Athens campus." Among the grievances the BSU activists mentioned was "few black graduate students, no black coaches, discriminatory practices in recruiting methods, degradation of black students in the classroom, and lack of black representation in administrative positions in housing."[82] In this context, a Black protest leader explained, bringing Shockley to campus was both "an insult" to UGA's Black students and indicative of bad faith in the process of improving race relations at the university: "We've been trying to sit down at a table and talk things over with the whites, but bringing Shockley on to campus shows us whites are not sincere, and only want to add fuel to the fire."[83]

For all its radicalism, the BSU was at least hopeful enough to organize to change UGA. But race relations were so bad at UGA in 1969 that most Black students Hunter spoke to had given up on UGA as an institution that could be reformed, or one whose activities beyond the classroom attracted them— which was why most Black students did not even join the BSU. And their criticism had a bitter edge, as with one student who explained to Hunter that "a lot of things have happened that made me develop negative attitudes about whites that will be with me the rest of my life."[84] But Hunter felt that their experience of dissatisfaction with their treatment "as blacks in" UGA's "microcosmic white society" was one of the most useful educational lessons of their college years; it would prepare them for their roles in the larger society. So she thought in this sense "the university will have succeeded far better than" UGA's disillusioned Black students "may be able to realize now."[85] And the prominent roles that BSU veterans would later play in society—including the first Black chief justice of Georgia's Supreme Court—suggests that she may have been right in reaching that conclusion.[86]

One should not overlook, moreover, that there was a positive and rewarding side to Black student life at UGA. There was community-building within the Black student community, which included the founding of Black student fraternities and sororities; and socializing at hangouts with fellow Black students, such as in the Bulldog Room and off-campus houses—one of which was called The Black House—where African American students resided. Lifelong friendships were forged by students in such settings. And there was a sense, by the early 1970s, that the Black student body, small as it was, had begun to have an impact on campus. For example, it pushed the UGA student government to take steps toward cultural diversity, particularly in the area of entertainment, by hosting such prominent African American musicians as B. B. King; Earth, Wind, and Fire; and the Commodores, and the politically engaged Black speaker Dick Gregory. And, of course, there were also academic classes, the best of which were intellectually stimulating, fostering academic achievement, and for those who graduated, helping lead to successful careers.[87]

HUNTER'S ARTICLE, though focused primarily on students, did deal briefly with the UGA faculty and the examples Black students gave of the racial bias and insensitivity they encountered from some professors.[88] What she missed, however, was that by the late 1960s a generational and political split had developed between some conservative older faculty (allied with like-minded UGA administrators) and more progressive younger faculty. This resembled the contrast Hunter's article had made between the retired and retiring administrators who had been holdovers from the Jim Crow era and the younger and more progressive administrators who succeeded them. The difference was that in the case of the faculty, some of the old guard was not bowing out gracefully but instead actively resisted the rise of a more liberal and inclusive university.[89] Of course we need to be careful to avoid generational stereotyping since some of the older faculty had been sympathetic to desegregation in the early 1960s and remained progressive as the decade wore on.⁹⁰ But it is also true that some of the old guard sought to stand in the way of change, a tendency that was particularly pronounced in UGA's history department, as was embodied in its "compatibility" controversy rooted in the repressive acts of the department head in 1969, and which erupted into a full-scale scandal in 1970 that rocked the department, made headlines nationally, and led some of the department's most productive and progressive younger faculty to leave UGA.⁹¹

One of these departing UGA faculty members, Robert Griffith, a leading historian of McCarthyism, published in 1971 a revealing account of the "compatibility" controversy, that illuminates not only the history department scandal but the larger political atmosphere in Georgia and at UGA, which slowed the university's transformation to a major research institution at which faculty desegregation could emerge as a high priority. At the dawn of the 1960s, UGA was, in Griffith's view, "a conservative, provincial state institution, one which integrated its student body in 1961 only after great difficulty, much notoriety, and considerable ill grace."⁹² A decade later UGA retained "much of the staunchly conservative character," which Griffith held was in part a reflection of Georgia's reactionary state politics, in which Lester Maddox was governor from 1967 to 1971 and Roy Harris, "onetime president of the White Citizens Council of America, served as a member of the state board of regents." But UGA was also a difficult institution to liberalize and democratize because, as Griffith put it, the university was weighed down by the "cautious parochialism" of its top administrators, "most of whom are native-born alumni ... selected most often for their 'loyalty' to the institution rather than for their teaching, scholarship, or command of the dynamics of higher education." Making matters worse was the "rigid chain of command system" in which UGA was governed, giving this conservative administration apparatus disproportionate power—with departments governed not by chairpersons elected by the faculty but rather by department "heads" selected by the deans, and these unelected department leaders exercised "almost baronial authority over the faculty."⁹³

By the mid-1960s these political tendencies and governance weaknesses were causing great tensions at UGA because this was one of those rare times of prosperity in which the Georgia state legislature was willing to fund an impressive expansion of the university's faculty. As Griffith explained, "in 1967 alone, 351" new faculty "were hired" by UGA, many of them from outside the Southeast.⁹⁴ Most valued professional achievement over "institutional loyalty" and were liberal in their politics. A few, through their involvement in the civil rights and antiwar movements, threatened to disrupt the school's traditional conservatism. Almost all "posed a challenge to the provincial and authoritarian character of the University. The University was not prepared for such an influx of outsiders."[95]

In UGA's history department this time of expansion had resulted in an unprecedented seventeen new faculty hires in a single year—1967. Among these new history faculty were a "handful who were politically active" and "sometimes contemptuous of... the social conservatism" of some of the senior faculty. The department head appointed by the dean in 1969, Robert G. McPherson, represented the most conservative wing of the senior faculty.[96] In fact, he was the son of the UGA history department's former head, and the son was appointed by the dean who was himself the son of a former UGA professor.[97] This connection to the department and UGA's reactionary past, which had also included the long reign of the white supremacist E. Merton Coulter as history department head, led young faculty critics to liken the department's governance to that of a plantation, according to Will Holmes, who was a young assistant professor back then.[98] Before long, McPherson began lashing out at these new UGA faculty. McPherson's first move came in 1969 when he fired a teaching assistant—highly regarded by the young faculty—because this graduate student, a Vietnam veteran, had spoken out against the Vietnam War. For historian Charles Crowe, his "personal baptism in the new regime came when" McPherson, in "objecting to his efforts to create two Black history classes," issued "a tirade of orders, threats, and insults which reminded me of the Infantry basic training I took more than 20 years ago.... I will not be allowed to accommodate in 1970–71 the several hundred interested students despite my willingness to teach ... Black History as an extra course and without pay."[99]

The generational conflict within the history department escalated as McPherson in 1970 began to use his power to freeze salaries and limit raises for dissenting younger faculty, torpedoing the promotion applications of some of the most talented and productive newer faculty. "The final blow," as Griffith put it, came in late February when McPherson, after consulting with the provost and dean, "issued a memorandum on the evaluation and retention of assistant professors. 'The criteria for retention,' he wrote, 'will be the individual's total contribution to the department and the University, based upon *compatibility* (his emphasis) as well as teaching and research.' At the same time McPherson told a number of associate and full professors that economic coercion would be used to end disagreement among those tenured faculty not covered by the memorandum." This memorandum ignited an explosion of criticism from the newer faculty, who interpreted "compatibility as a code word for stifling dissent" and denounced McPherson's edict as "a threat to academic freedom, political non-conformity, and the primacy of professional values."[100]

Such criticism was soon aired in the local press and the Atlanta papers as well as national magazines, damaging the department's reputation. Within two years of the issuing of the compatibility memo, eight history department faculty members left UGA, largely due to the negative political climate it generated, including some of the most well-published and progressive younger historians.[101] So this conservative backlash was delaying the transformation necessary to give UGA a top-tier history department. Charles Crowe, in an irate letter to George L. Simpson Jr., the University of Georgia system chancellor, protested McPherson's pattern of acting "on whim and political prejudice rather than on professional standards" and explained why such a transformation was both desperately needed and so difficult to achieve:

> You must know, Mr. Chancellor, that the University is far from a great institution. In recruiting faculty . . . we are hampered by the national image of football, fraternities, and rednecks. Professors . . . must live in a very provincial town and send their children to an inferior school system. The University does little to improve the educational, political, or cultural life of the town. About one third of all Georgians are Black, and the University does almost nothing for Black people. With a few notable exceptions, the most senior faculty have little professional standing (it was extremely difficult to recruit able faculty in the forties and fifties and few Georgia administrators wanted to). . . . The faculty and the students have no adequate institutional means to seek redress, and a petty authoritarianism often prevails in administrative offices. . . . Many of the older professors are watchful, suspicious, and withdrawn. (Men have been made to pay for free expression of professional and political opinions). How can free and zestful intellectual inquiry in the classroom flourish under these conditions? . . . Possibly you do *not* believe that all is well in Athens, that storks really bring babies, that an administrator who persists in addressing young Black militants as "Nigrahs" despite polite correction (see U. of Ga. *The Impression*, May 1969, p. 30) can cope with student protests at a time when campus protest is exploding all over the nation.[102]

Gradually, UGA's history department would recover from this scandal and the loss of a generation of promising young scholars that it caused.[103] But there is no question that the "compatibility" controversy delayed the department's upgrading, and this connects with its faculty's belated desegregation, which did not occur until 1987. While of course we need to be cautious about generalizing from this one department to all of UGA, it does not seem unreasonable to suggest that institutional conservatism, perpetuated by some of the older faculty and allied deans, along with an overcentralized and often mediocre university administration, bore some responsibility both for making more difficult UGA's transformation into a major research university and for the glacial pace of Black faculty hiring from the 1960s to at least the early 1980s.

Additional evidence of generational tensions within the UGA faculty on the issue of race surfaced when younger faculty dissented against that hard-line stance President Davison took in response to the BSU grievances in the late 1960s and early 1970s. In March 1969, for example, a group letter was initiated by Harrell Rodgers, a northern-born assistant professor in UGA's political science department, expressing to Davison "extreme disappointment with your ... totally non-conciliatory approach ... to the black student demands." Most of the dozen UGA college of arts and science faculty signatories to this letter were assistant professors.[104] Similarly, Brett W. Hawkins, a young associate professor in political science—also from the North—wrote scathingly about Davison on race and complained that unproductive senior faculty, who could not "get a comparable job elsewhere," set the tone for much of the UGA professoriate, and they seemed to think all UGA had to do was "comply with the law" and not take Black student concerns seriously. "Is it," asked Hawkins,

> courage to publish statements about administrative forms and legalities? Is it courage to say "we admit nothing." "We have no room to improve because we do not discriminate now?" ... That is the president's posture. ...
> The president should have said that we are trying to do better and are painfully aware of vestiges of the past. By failing to find any merit publicly with the black student demands ... President Davison has encouraged division, conflict and violence with his rigidity. By taking the familiar course of pandering to the environment, concealing conflict, and asking for faculty support without genuine consultation he has worsened the conflict. Once again the President, his administration, and faculty supporters have indicated their insufficient vision, experience, and capacity to make Georgia great. The University of Georgia has too many "responsible" people who are irresponsible to the University's potential greatness. They can't even see it.[105]

Since the faculty in UGA's political science and history departments—including the liberal dissidents among them—as in most of UGA were white in the 1960s and 1970s, this and almost any discussion of the UGA faculty back then focuses upon white academics. But by the 1980s, the ranks of Black faculty across the university, though still very small in numbers in relation to the white faculty, did reach enough of a critical mass at UGA to establish (in 1980) the Black Faculty and Staff Organization on behalf of a more diverse professoriate, staff, and student body, becoming in its own right a significant force for change and against racial discrimination.[106] In this sense one could say that since faculty desegregation trailed behind that of the student body, the Black faculty was organizing in the 1980s in a manner that paralleled what we have seen with the BSU and its student organizing in the late 1960s and 1970s, giving voice to a small but demanding Black community on campus. So when the story of this later chapter of UGA's desegregation gets written, its focus will shift somewhat, focusing more on Black faculty organizing—in contrast to the 1960s and 1970s, in which, of necessity students were more central since they were the spark plug of that earlier era's Black struggle at UGA.

ALTHOUGH THE UNDERREPRESENTATION of Blacks at UGA throughout the late twentieth century was continuous and so gives 1961–2000 a kind of coherence as an era, the 1960s and 1970s come across as distinctly more tense and race relations rawer than in the 1980s and 1990s. This seems linked to the fact that in these earlier decades there were more whites in the student body, and in the faculty and administration, who had been raised in the Jim Crow era and were infected by its racism. Here it must be kept in mind that though the segregationist militants who had rioted on campus against UGA's integration in 1961 had long since left the university, the type of segregationist hotheads who had organized that riot had certainly not gone extinct in the student body by the late 1960s.

There was in the late 1960s and 1970s UGA student body still a small but vocal racist right wing on campus that could be counted on to express their hostility toward Black students and the civil rights movement in crude and tasteless ways. Much as militant racist students had distributed firecrackers in preparation for their riot outside Charlayne Hunter's dormitory in 1961 and hurled them during the riot, so their successors used such fireworks in 1968, but this time in an even sicker display, as part of their celebration of Martin Luther King Jr.'s assassination. The night of the assassination, joyous white students in the Tucker Hall dormitory shouted, "They did it! They shot the nigger." Such cries were heard through the night. "The campus was alive that night with boys throwing firecrackers and yelling to show their exuberance."[107] These were the same types of students who would hurl racial epithets at

Black students and harass them whenever the opportunity presented itself, behavior President Davison's administration did next to nothing to stop. The racist right even had its own white supremacist organization on campus in the late 1960s and early 1970s, the Campus Conservative Club, which, as historian Christopher Huff has shown, was so right wing and nostalgic for the Jim Crow era that it burned its Young Americans For Freedom charter and in 1972 hung in effigy UGA's bandleader for daring to order an end to the playing of "Dixie" at Bulldog football games.[108]

Making matters worse, the Long 1960s and the 1970s, it must be recalled, came before, both on campus and off, the valorization of the civil rights movement gained steam nationally, with the establishment of the Martin Luther King Jr. national holiday in 1986. So the early MLK birthday commemorations at UGA were small and mostly Black affairs with no administration support. And in fact the BSU felt compelled to write UGA administrators in 1970 to explain why Black students would not be in classes on January 15 and to articulate their support of the Southern Christian Leadership Conference's "drive to make Dr. King's birthday a national holiday."[109]

The commemoration of King's birthday in 1970 indicated just how isolated Black students were. It featured a march by nineteen Black sorority students on campus singing freedom songs. The *Red and Black* reported that "there was scattered jeering by white students and some mocking of the singing," but "in a departure from past years where black demonstrations or speeches have generated heated reactions from University white students . . . there were no counterdemonstrations. NO ONE drove by in cars and shouted obscenities."[110]

In this cold atmosphere, the MLK day events back in the 1970s were occasions not for expressions of interracial solidarity but rather Black students airing their grievances as a small campus minority that felt besieged as well as terribly underrepresented. Thus in the 1971 King event one speaker explained what it was like to be a Black male student at UGA, where he "must assume . . . that every southern belle will look at you like a mad rapist, the university policeman will bust you for breaking in line at registration, and if you talk about Angela Davis or the Black Panthers you will be arrested for conspiracy to blow up dorms."[111] A reporter on the scene noted that these remarks "got rousing applause," and the Black students "readily tell you that the bleak picture he painted of life at UGA is an accurate one."[112]

Race relations among UGA undergraduates seemed at a low point in February 1974 after a fight broke out between members of a Black fraternity and a white fraternity. The conflict took on crisis dimensions when some 200 Black students marched on Davison's office to demand improvements in the campus racial climate.[113] Perhaps chastened by the outbreak of violence across the color line in the Greek letter organizations, Davison was uncharacteristically responsive to the Black protesters in that he met with them at length while BSU leaders aired their grievances about the lack of Black representation on campus and advocated the formation of a Black cultural center on campus. And while most of the students' demands would not be granted, at least this time, unlike back in the 1960s, Davison was not dismissive of their concerns.[114] Davison did, however, offend some of the protesters by characterizing those who had picketed outside during his meeting with the BSU, chanting and singing freedom songs, as having "serenaded" him. This led one Black student protester to reply,

> for the record, Mr. Davison, we were not out there in freezing weather with numb faces, hands, and feet to serenade you or anyone else. Every one of our songs were songs protesting the black man's experience, particularly those here at the University of Georgia. The obvious lack of accurate perception of our motives by the president demonstrates another gap in the black-white communication line here at the University of Georgia. Mr. Davison has provided black students here yet another legitimate reason to keep on crying at the top our lungs: 'Up Dat House.' We fail to understand why even he can deny the necessity of a black cultural center.[115]

The following year, Black student activist Gail Hall used MLK's birthday to speak out against UGA's violation of King's spirit and that of the Civil Rights Act he championed. She termed UGA's having "only 5 black professors" on its huge faculty "a disgrace," along with its only "couple hundred Black students," underpaying of Black maintenance workers, and refusal of "top administrators" to "redress . . . black grievances," which "in the past have only been likened to serenades."[116]

By the late 1970s, such complaints on King's birthday had spread beyond undergraduates. The 1979 Black King day event featured UGA law students organizing a freedom rally and a one-day boycott of classes protesting the lack of Black law school faculty.[117] Speakers from both the Black student body and the off-campus Black community in Athens noted that while twelve states had recognized King's birthday as a holiday, Georgia, his birthplace, had not. Nor had UGA recognized the slain civil rights leader's birthday as a university holiday, leading protesters at the 1980 King day event to change the words to the freedom song "Ain't Gonna' Let Anyone Turn Me Around" to "Ain't Gonna Let [UGA president] Fred Davison Turn Me Around."[118]

Such rhetoric suggested Black disappointment with UGA's campus climate endured long beyond the supposedly heady days of integration in the 1960s. As to the off-campus world in Black Athens, there were just a few signs of hope, some connections between activists on campus and the Black community. Though the New Left was never strong at UGA—owing to the conservatism of its student body—the antiwar movement of the Long 1960s, second-wave feminism, and gay liberation had generated a core of a few hundred activists. Some of these activists in 1970 did something quite unusual for the UGA campus: reach out, together with some Black students, to the Black community of Athens in its protests against what they saw as the way their schools were subordinated to their white counterparts in the plans for public school integration. These interracial protests, which also involved a few UGA faculty, generated mass arrests and charges of police brutality in Athens during the spring semester of 1970.[119] But neither these protests nor the racial issues that sparked them drew any comment or concern on the part of the UGA administration—which never seemed to give a passing thought to using its resources or expertise to assist Athens's Black community. In its relationship, or really its lack of a relationship with its Black neighbors, UGA ended the 1960s much as it began that decade, a white institution off on its own, with most of its students living within their monoracial bubble.

DESPITE ITS ROUGH BEGINNINGS with those anti-UGA administration chants during the Black rally on Martin Luther King's birthday in 1980, in terms of symbolism the 1980s would become the most important decade of change on race at UGA since the 1960s. The first major symbol of change was African American football star Herschel Walker, who led UGA to its first consensus national football championship in 1980. Charlayne Hunter-Gault remarked on "the interesting parallel in his experience and mine. Here they were yelling for Herschel in a completely different way that they used to yell at me."[120] The striking contrast was, of course, that where once UGA students jeered her with racist epithets, now a new generation of UGA students cheered for Walker and urged him to carry the Georgia team to victory. Indeed, as historian Charles H. Martin noted, "After star halfback Herschel Walker helped Georgia win the national championship, one die-hard Bulldog fan even exclaimed, in words that would have been blasphemous a decade earlier, 'Thank God for Earl Warren!'"[121]

Walker represented the first of several important symbols of change at UGA with respect to race in the 1980s. The national football championship offered a powerful testament to the fact that when the university acted in a meritocratic fashion, as it finally had become accustomed to doing in athletics by 1980, less than a decade after its football team's belated desegregation, UGA could soar above every university in the nation.

The 1980s brought a rapprochement between the UGA administration and the pioneering Black heroes of the university's integration, its first two African American students. UGA finally got around to honoring Hunter-Gault, appointing her to the journalism school's advisory board in 1981. At about this same time UGA reconnected with Hamilton Holmes, whom historian Thomas Dyer, chair of UGA's bicentennial, invited to serve on the alumni committee that planned the bicentennial of the university. Holmes agreed and was an active member of the committee.[122] In 1983 Holmes became a trustee of the UGA Foundation, the university's key organization for raising private funds and using them to upgrade the quality of education at UGA. In 1985, with permission and assistance from Holmes and Hunter, UGA established and funded the Holmes-Hunter Signature Lecture, an annual event focused on race relations, civil rights, and Black history.[123]

The decision to honor Holmes and Hunter was obviously of great symbolic importance for a university that had in 1960–61 opposed in court their admission to UGA and then had ignored its two most famous Black graduates for decades.[124] But even the *Atlanta Journal* article on the creation of the lectureship implied a relationship between this decision to honor Hunter and Holmes and the fact that "UGA President Fred Davison has been the subject of recent criticism over the low percentage of black faculty and about morale problems among black students at UGA."[125] This was a reference to the upsurge of UGA Black student protest in the early 1980s, led by the BSU, objecting to the continuing paucity of Black students and faculty at UGA under the Davison administration.[126] This leads to the question of whether the Holmes-Hunter lectureship was created, at least in part, as a public relations move designed to distract attention, via new integrationist symbolism, from the long-term failures of UGA on the substance of desegregation at the university.

Given Davison's failures on campus racial issues, it is a fair question. However, it should be noted that the idea for the Holmes-Hunter lecture series came not from Davison but from Thomas Dyer, an exceptional figure in the UGA administration. Dyer had been a doctoral student of Charles Crowe, the leading faculty critic of the history department's "compatibility" policy, and the first UGA historian to teach a course on Black history. Crowe had participated in the Selma to Montgomery march, been an antiwar activist, and written major articles on the racism of the Southern populist movement. Dyer, in this same tradition, wrote an important and critical book on Theodore

Roosevelt's racism and, as a UGA academic vice president, had taken great interest in expanding Black faculty hiring. In presiding over UGA's bicentennial events and involving Hamilton Holmes in this effort, Dyer had developed both a friendship and admiration for Holmes. Dyer wanted the bicentennial to "build some much needed bridges" between Blacks and whites—and saw the lecture series as helping to do just that. In addition to the lecture series, Dyer had Davison, at the inaugural lecture, present to Holmes and Hunter UGA bicentennial medallions reserved for eminent scholars and alumni.[127]

For Dyer and many present at the UGA chapel for the first annual Holmes-Hunter lecture in November 1985, it was not the keynote speech by civil rights leader Vernon Jordan—illuminating as it was in its indictment of President Reagan's civil rights record—but rather Hamilton Holmes's remarks that were the most memorable. Those remarks came after Holmes and Hunter had been awarded their bicentennial medallions at this lecture that had been named in their honor. Jim Minter of the *Atlanta Constitution*, who had witnessed the segregationist riot at UGA in 1961, was present in the chapel when Holmes spoke twenty-four years later. Minter noted Holmes's words and captured the emotions of the moment in a powerful column that he titled "Tears in the Chapel": "Dr. Holmes rose from his seat . . . and touched the silver medallion. . . . 'I will never forget this,' he said. 'I will cherish it forever.' . . . He began to cry. 'I have come to love this place,' he said. . . . 'People look at me and say, you're crazy man. How can you love that place? But I do . . . love this university.' . . . For a moment, he could not speak. . . . Quietly, his tears spread throughout the Chapel, helping to wash away a past which today seems not only cruel but ridiculous."[128] Of course, UGA's troubled racial past cannot really be washed away with tears, but the Holmes-Hunter lecture series suggests that the past can be better understood by a university that explores racial problems and dares to honor those who challenged racism within its gates.

In announcing the Holmes-Hunter lectureship's creation in 1985, Davison paid tribute to UGA's first two Black undergraduates for having "made contributions of enduring and lasting significance to the University of Georgia."[129] This praise for Holmes and Hunter was well deserved, not only because of their important role in pushing a very resistant UGA out of its Jim Crow past, but their generosity in agreeing to loan their names, their ideas, and their energy to the lecture series. It would have been quite understandable if either or both of them refused so public a connection with a university whose discriminatory traditions had taken much of the joy out of their college years. Instead, both welcomed the opportunity to help establish a lecture series that would analyze racial problems and, as Hunter-Gault put it, "always be a window of truth on the world."[130]

Yet UGA remained so overwhelmingly white—with only about 5 percent of UGA's student population Black as of 1985—that, as Grace Elizabeth Hale noted in her book *Cool Town: How Athens, Georgia Launched Alternative Music and Changed American Culture* (2020), even the most culturally rebellious white UGA students of that decade, those who founded and participated in the indie rock scene that made Athens a countercultural center, birthing the famed rock groups R.E.M. and the B-52s among others, barely noticed that their bohemian clubs, style, and music, like UGA itself, was mostly white and distant from Black students, Black Athens, and its very different music scene. These cultural rebels, Hale noted, thought of themselves as progressive on race, yet they were oblivious to the fact that in Athens they were pioneering an indie cultural world (that would soon go national) whose ostensibly liberal "color blind" approach to race "allowed white participants to be proud of their racial liberalism without having to think very much about why so few people of color were drawn to their 'alternative' culture."[131] Decades after desegregation, then, UGA was still intellectually, culturally, and socially a largely segregated world, where students from the fraternity houses on Milledge Avenue to indie rock's Forty Watt Club downtown still thought of white as normative.

Those who were in the best position to know, most notably Jeff Cooper, UGA's veteran minority recruitment officer, thought UGA in the 1980s could be doing much better in both the recruitment and retention of African American undergraduates; Cooper believed the university needed to fund more extensive recruitment trips (UGA's were shorter and less effective than those of other universities), and that Georgia's less generous scholarships tended to limit its appeal to Black students. This resource problem, Cooper noted in 1988, carried over into the area of retention. Black student retention was more than 7 percent lower than its white counterpart, and the major reason for this was economic: financial problems were the top reason Black undergraduates did not complete their UGA degree programs, which could have been addressed by UGA via greater financial aid. Cooper viewed this retention problem as even more serious than the recruitment problem.[132] Similar concerns were raised into the 1990s (and beyond) by UGA officials who spoke of a "Black brain drain" as top African American students across Georgia were lured to colleges outside the state by more generous scholarship offers.[133]

Throughout the 1980s and beyond, the whiteness of UGA had a way of being self-reinforcing. Black students, who often attended high schools that were predominantly Black, found the overwhelmingly white environment of UGA alien and difficult to cope with, and not one they could easily promote in the Black community. "It's a big culture shock," noted a Black UGA student interviewed by a local reporter in 1983. "I remember lying on my bed my freshman year, and asking myself why am I here?" "'Culture shock'" is, the reporter noted, "a term many black students used to describe how they felt during their first months at UGA. And many black students feel the university could ease some of the shock by developing more black programs."[134] Even Hamilton Holmes Jr., a fourth-generation integrationist who followed in his famed father's footsteps by doing his undergraduate work at UGA, admitted in 1990 to feeling "'a little uncomfortable' when he looks around and doesn't see any other black faces in his classes. . . . 'I'm the only black student in two of my classes.'"[135]

Black and white students, even when living in the same residence halls, tended to remain socially segregated in the 1980s, rarely hanging out or partying together, and interacting at the most minimal level. This in why in reporting on the racial situation in UGA's dorms in October 1988, the *Red and Black* concluded that "university housing [was] not harmonious."[136] This atmosphere bred tension, especially when white students acted in racially insensitive ways, as when two white male students appeared at a party dressed in blackface, sporting the colors and Greek letters of a Black sorority, which sparked outrage among African American students.[137]

As to the Greek houses, they remained UGA's most segregated student institutions.[138] The only change that UGA had successfully promoted was with regard to their governing bodies. The white and Black fraternities and sororities had since the 1970s been governed by entirely separate councils that did not communicate with each other. But in 1985, at the university's prodding, the white Interfraternity Council and Pan Hellenic made the Black Greek Council a subcommittee of their councils. The idea was to increase communication between the white and Black organizations in the interest of establishing an amicable relationship. The reality, however, was that those on the different sides of the Greek organization color line had little contact, and the white Greeks, with their large houses, and the small Black fraternities and sororities, all of which lacked such houses, operated in entirely separate worlds.[139] The UGA administration would never find the courage to order the all-white fraternities and sororities to desegregate, a remarkable evasion on the part of UGA (as well as federal government officials) since such racially discriminatory housing affiliated with a public university was, and remains, unlawful.

The white fraternities and sororities had such a reputation for racial insensitivity that there is little record of Black students even trying to join these organizations at UGA. But in a revealing case, one African American transfer student came close to seeking such fraternity membership in fall 1988. The student, Joseph Alexander, had been a member of the Tau Kappa Epsilon (TKE) at Seton Hall University in New Jersey, where 20 to 25 percent of the members were Black, 35 to 40 percent were white, and the remainder were from other minority groups. So when he arrived at UGA he planned to affiliate with the TKE fraternity, unaware that it lacked a single Black member. And when he went to the TKE house, the remarks he heard there indicated, as Alexander put it, "that they're not too open-minded when it comes to race," which made him feel uncomfortable and unwelcome. "I think I would have affiliated if I had felt more comfortable with it." Alexander was also struck by how his Black friends reacted upon learning that he had even considered joining a white fraternity: "It just blew me away that they would be so taken aback" by his interest in TKE. "I do think there is such a thing as a Southern mentality," Alexander concluded. "Both races have been brought up not to deal with each other."[140]

That the racial parochialism of the traditional white fraternities was going strong more than a quarter century after UGA's integration can be most readily seen with regard to the Kappa Alpha fraternity. Not only did this fraternity continue to fly its enormous—sixteen-by-twenty-foot—Confederate flag from its frat house, but as late as June 1988 it was publicly defending this practice and denying its racial implications. Kappa Alpha members explained that "racism is not an issue here at all."[141] The flag was flown, they claimed, "not to alienate anyone, but to evoke the South's heritage.... The flag was symbolic of the Old South and the ideals it represented—reverence toward God and chivalry toward women."[142] Of course outside of the white student bubble on frat row, better educated UGA students were well aware that the Confederacy and its flag actually symbolized racial slavery and a regime bent on preserving it—and that if there was "chivalry" toward women under that regime, it was certainly not directed toward enslaved Black women, whom slaveowners bought, sold, and sexually abused. As one UGA student told a *Red and Black* reporter, "The Confederate flag is offensive to him as a black and as a human being. It's a symbol of people who built their wealth on the oppression of others."[143]

The white sororities displayed similar insensitivity. A June 1989 sorority reggae theme party featured a Black caricature with huge lips and eyes. "It was offending," said the president of UGA's Black Affairs Council. "You think they would have known better than to draw a slave." This incident led that council to propose the creation of an African American cultural center "to promote racial sensitivity and give blacks a place to nurture their identity." The idea for such a center drew the opposition from the UGA student government and newspaper on the grounds that it represented "favoritism" toward Blacks and would "foster self-segregation"—curious arguments on a campus that housed white fraternities and sororities, whose "self-segregation" had drawn no such objections from these white student leaders. Perhaps the most revealing comments made in this whole dispute was the *Red and Black* editor's argument that an African American cultural center would not foster interracial dialogue because "if you go by past events [designed to draw Blacks and whites together] you're probably not going to see a lot of white students up there"—attesting to how little Black-white dialogue and socializing there was.[144]

In contrast to the huge rebel flag and the other remnants of Jim Crow on frat row, UGA in the 1980s seemed to be at last breaking with that past when it came to graduate students and faculty, becoming more serious about its minority recruitment efforts. The graduate school, which had only begun to fund minority recruitment trips in 1974, was by 1984 finally breaking the $100,000 level in funding such recruitment.[145] This was still a fairly modest sum, but in light of UGA's history, it did represent a significant advance. UGA's recently appointed president, Charles Knapp, an unusual figure for a Georgia president in that he was not a Southerner, displayed in the late 1980s considerable dynamism regarding the promotion of an African American presence at UGA. He broke the color line in the upper echelon of UGA's administration in late 1988 by appointing the university's first Black vice president, Bryndis Roberts Jenkins, who headed the office of legal affairs and served as a key advisor to Knapp on minority affairs. Knapp would act on the BSU's longstanding demands for a support structure, establishing the Office of Minority Services and Programs (1989) and the African American Cultural Center (1994).

Also notable was the Black faculty cluster hire in 1988, which in a single year nearly doubled the number of African American tenure line faculty at UGA from twenty-nine to forty-nine.[146] But considering that the first fulltime UGA Black faculty member, music professor Richard Graham, had been hired in 1968, this impressive Black hiring initiative under Knapp could hardly make up for the university's pathetic rate of African American faculty hiring, which had amounted to a little more than one per year in the two decades since the color line in faculty hiring had ended. Thus, even with the Knapp initiative, UGA's faculty was still less than 3 percent Black.[147] And it would not be until 1991 that UGA hired its first African American department head, John Morrow, of the history department—190 years after UGA held its first classes, in 1801.[148]

For those who had sacrificed so much for the ideal of a desegregated university—the vision of UGA as a university whose student body, faculty, and administration reflected the sizable Black presence in the state of Georgia—it was impossible, decades after the start of integration, to be satisfied with the incremental changes represented by the still small numbers of Black faculty, students, and administrators. This is why Hamilton Holmes, on the thirtieth anniversary of the *Brown* decision, while noting the "obvious" increase in the number of Black students at UGA since he and Hunter had entered the university, stressed that "the University hasn't made much progress in hiring black faculty and administration. The system hasn't made as much progress as it could have" in the decades since *Brown*.[149] Similarly, Hunter-Gault was not willing to be a symbolic ornament of racial reconciliation. Ever since attaining her position as an honored UGA alum in the early 1980s, she used it to press the university's leadership to do more to further and expedite the process of student and faculty desegregation. As will be discussed in more depth in chapter 7, Hunter-Gault would offer pointed criticism of UGA in her historic 1988 commencement address (the first such address ever given at UGA by an African American), noting UGA's failure to change the status quo in which Black students and faculty remained a small minority at the university. And she carried this message further by publishing this speech in her memoir *In My Place* (1992) and by making the same point on the fortieth anniversary of UGA's desegregation in 2001, when UGA again honored her and Holmes, this time by naming its academic building for the two of them. Making it clear that—honored as she was to have a campus building bear her name and Holmes's—such integrationist symbolism could not make up for UGA's inability to better serve the Black community, Hunter-Gault remarked that "if anyone had given Hamp [Hamilton Holmes] and me a crystal ball into which we could have looked to the future forty years hence and seen only six percent students of color . . . I think we might have sat down under the Arch [at UGA's campus entrance] and cried."[150] As Hunter-Gault explained to historian Robert A. Pratt in 2000, "I don't think I will ever make my peace with" UGA "until black students and black professors there are as comfortable as whites and until I'm convinced that they [university officials] have made every effort to ensure that. But from what I can tell that's not yet happened."[151]

Hunter-Gault's candid and critical perspective on the racial realities of UGA, past and present, contrasts dramatically with the flowery discourse that has emanated from UGA's presidents. Listen, for example, to what President Davison went on to say about UGA and race when he announced the founding of the Holmes-Hunter lecture series in 1985. Davison claimed that the Holmes-Hunter lectures "will be a permanent and continuing reminder to future generations of students and faculty that this university gives primacy to the principle of equality among all people—in education and all human endeavors."[152] This was a noble sentiment but also an utterly ahistorical statement since the key reason Holmes and Hunter were such important historical figures and were being honored by the university was that UGA had for more than a century and a half rejected "the principle of equality among all people," erecting a color line that Holmes and Hunter became in 1961 the first Black students to overcome; that took years beyond 1961 to remove from UGA's athletic fields, faculty, and administration hiring; and that persists in UGA's fraternity and sorority houses.

Davison's celebratory rhetoric has been typical of UGA presidents even into our own century. While, of course, it is admirable that these UGA leaders affirm the value and importance of equal opportunity, it is important to reflect on how for much of the university's history its leaders and graduates impeded such opportunity for Georgia's Black population. You will not hear UGA's presidents discuss the fact that for generations the university was a party to cheating Jim Crow Georgia's African American citizens, who were taxed to help subsidize a university they were barred from attending; that UGA-trained prosecutors and judges in Jim Crow Georgia staffed a racist judicial system that made a mockery of the ideal of equal justice under law; that UGA-trained politicians who served in Georgia's legislature and executive branch, and both houses of Congress ranked among the white South's leading proponents and defenders of legally ordained racial segregation; that even after being forced by a federal court order to dissolve its color line, UGA moved with all deliberate slowness to open its doors to Black students and faculty; and that though UGA students rioted in partnership with the Ku Klux Klan against the campus's desegregation, this sparked no conversation at all by UGA's or the state's leaders about the educational failure of a university that could produce such racist and lawless students, and how that failure might be addressed through more critical teaching about white supremacy.

Since this depressing and central racist characteristic of UGA's past and its lessons about white supremacy have not been part of the university's presidential oratory, the idea of taking some dramatic—as opposed to merely symbolic or incremental—action to right these old wrongs almost never comes up. In fact, the task of honestly confronting UGA's long history of racial discrimination has been left to its critics, to historians, and to UGA's Black students, faculty, staff, and alumni—most notably, Hunter-Gault herself—all of whom lack the influence that UGA's presidents have with Georgia's political elite. This presidential aversion to discussing UGA's history of racism connects with a similar aversion of some of its most politically powerful alumni in the Georgia governor's chair and Georgia legislature; these UGA-educated politicians have recently, as mentioned earlier, banned by law as "divisive" any candid discussion in its public schools of the state's racist past and its legacy.[153] A decent respect for history and the search for historical truth and justice demands that we challenge such historical amnesia. Reflecting on race, education, and equity at UGA requires that we remember the university's longtime support of slavery, Jim Crowism, and racism, as well as their legacies and opponents.

CHAPTER SEVEN

New Day or Old South?
Late 1990s University of Georgia Student Reflections on Campus Race Relations in Their Time vs. 1961

More than any other work of history I have published over the past three decades, my article "'Two, Four, Six, Eight, We Don't Want to Integrate': White Student Attitudes Toward the University of Georgia's Desegregation" has followed me into the classroom. This is because of the way it resonates with undergraduates who had never before candidly explored the history of collegiate racial attitudes and racism. This holds true for the students I teach today at New York University and those I have taught at UC Berkeley and the University of Georgia (UGA). Generally when students are taught about the history of race, their focus in high school and college is on the heroic Black Freedom struggle rather than on the foes of racial justice: segregationists who opposed the civil rights movement, and whom the movement struggled to defeat. So they find it new and thought-provoking to probe the mindset of segregationists—all the more so when those segregationists were, like themselves, college students. Indeed, since my article focused upon, and quoted extensively from, the essays UGA students wrote (in their Math 254 class) amid the desegregation crisis of 1961, just a week after UGA's segregationist riot, one gets to hear in their own words Southern white students' views on race, segregationist militancy, and violence. This gives today's students a window into an era where racial inequality was ascendant but also being challenged by intrepid African American students and their legal team, who would overcome the color line of this historically white university. And since the issue of racial justice remains a live one on campus, confronting this history of collegiate racism has had continuing relevance to students decades after the death of Jim Crow in American higher education.

Of the many students for whom I have assigned the "Two, Four, Six, Eight" article, those who became the most deeply engaged with this history were my UGA students when I taught there in the 1990s. This was because the article was about their predecessors, UGA students in 1961. This included UGA's first two Black students and how they and the racial integrationist ideal and movement they represented were viewed by the university's white student majority when UGA desegregated in 1961. Some of my students had personal connections to this history through the stories they had been told by uncles, aunts, and parents who were UGA students back during the desegregation crisis. The UGA classroom experience was also unique in that my students, recognizing that the article was about their campus, were provoked by it to reflect comparatively on its history and their place in it, offering insight into the ways their university had and had not changed on matters of race since desegregation began in 1961.

In my final years on the UGA faculty, I asked my students, after reading the "Two, Four, Six, Eight" article, to write an essay comparing the racial dynamics at UGA as they had experienced it in the 1990s to those reflected in my article and the Math 254 essays from 1961. Were they more impressed with the changes or continuities? And along with their views on this question, I asked that they discuss this question with a fellow student from a different racial background to get both white and Black perspectives on it. Since UGA's student body and my classes in the 1990s were overwhelmingly white—but with a small Black minority that tended to display a distinctive historical sensibility—such dialogue was necessary if the students were to avoid parochialism.

In both the years, 1997 and 1998, when I posed these questions to my large (hundred-plus) classes of educational history students at UGA, some definite, consistent patterns emerged. All agreed that the days of racial violence and majority support for Jim Crow at the university had long since ended. The crude racist stereotypes found in those Math 254 essays struck many of my students as "one-sided, absurd, and cruel." "I was embarrassed for the writers," explained one of my students. However, this same student noted that "I have come into contact with white students, most of whom were born and raised in the South, that share some of the opinions of these early [1960s] writers."[1] This student also observed that though racist views were commonly expressed at UGA in the 1990s, this was not done in public, as was the case in 1961, but rather privately within the white student community.[2]

In fact, white students in my class agreed that "racist and prejudice[d]" ideas could be easily encountered in private conversations with white classmates, along with the "N" word. As one student reported, "A friend of mine says that 'Niggers are lazy.' After stating his opinion, I thought about the generalization that an educated person had just pronounced. Laziness isn't limited to the black population and in my eyes, it hasn't bypassed my friend."[3] Another student noted the attitude of a friend "who seemed to be shaped by his Southern upbringing. He is a true 'Dixie' boy and does not care to associate with ... African American[s]. ... He goes to classes with them, but does not sit by or speak to them. He shares the view of his family of avoiding blacks."⁴

In explaining this shift at UGA from public (1961) to private (late 1990s) racist expression, one of my students argued that this shift was due to "Political Correctness." In other words, the antiracist ethos promoted by the faculty, the university itself, and the academic community nationally—often mocked on the right as a form of "political correctness"—ensured that overt racist expression would be scorned, with the result being that "racist and prejudice[d] ideas tend to be kept more in the closet," conveyed by whites to whites only in all-white private settings.⁵ While obviously it is a form of progress that racist discourse had become too unpopular at UGA to find a public forum in the 1990s, with such expression going covert, this racism often escaped the notice of UGA faculty and administration, undermining the university's ability to recognize that racism was a persistent student problem that needed to be addressed. This seems to be what Hamilton Holmes had in mind when he told a Black UGA student audience at a Martin Luther King Jr. birthday march in 1990 that "racism is still here—it has become more subtle in some ways, but when racism becomes subtle, it becomes harder to fight."⁶

Since Black students constituted only about 6 percent of the student body (in 1997, there were 1,840 African American UGA students out of a total student population of 29,693, and in 1998, 1,823 Black students out of a student body of 30,009), and whites were so predominant at UGA in the 1990s, many of the white students in my class subconsciously took whiteness as normative and had not given much thought to the nature of race relations at the university until I asked them to analyze it.⁷ Some had not even noticed that all their friends were white, and thus they were surprised that when they turned to the part of the assignment that asked them to get the views of someone from a different racial background and realized for the first time that they had no Black friends (and thus no one to consult on the assigned questions). As one student explained, "I am embarrassed to report that I do not have a single black friend to discuss" the status of UGA race relations with. "Whites and blacks do not fall into the same social groups. This is evidence that we are not as far [from the segregated UGA of 1961] as I would like to believe."⁸ Though this kind of apologetic response was the most common, one student was defensive about his lack of Black friends, attributing it to "demographics.... The black population is only a tenth of the white population. Does this mean that every white guy or girl should make friends with the first dark skinned person he or she sees? Of course not.... My point here is I didn't ask a black person this [assigned] question [on race relations at UGA]... and I don't think it says anything except that for every nine or ten white persons their [sic] most likely will be one black person, plain and simple."[9]

Some saw their isolation from Blacks at UGA as an extension of their earlier educational experience in high schools that had been de facto segregated. One such student, a twenty-one-year-old female junior from Atlanta, saw bigotry as quite evident among her many UGA Kappa Alpha fraternity friends in the 1990s, who "are still very racist and still fly the GA state flag [emblazoned with the Confederate battle flag] with meaning."[10] She traced her own racial isolation to the fact that she had attended "a private school" while living "in the upper class area of Atlanta." And UGA represented more of the same:

> In my three years attending UGA I can only account for one conversation that I ever had with a black person. I think that is extremely sad and extremely embarrassing, I am not a prejudice[d] person, but the opportunity had never been there. In my experience blacks and whites lead separate lives on campus. Different fraternities, different sororities, different places of residence, different places we eat, different ways of talking, etc. To me black people are foreign. I have never had an African American as a friend. No, I had nobody to ask (no black person) [the assigned questions about race at UGA]. The point right there tells you how separate we are.[11]

This kind of social segregation at UGA in the 1990s was so striking that it led some of my students to argue that the continuities in race relations were at least as noticeable as the changes since 1961. One such student, who was white, argued that

> the attitude toward black students (minorities) has remained the same. Students say they have changed and made progress, but actions speak louder than words.... Although there are a few black students in our classrooms, very few enter "our" social life. Rarely do you see a black student downtown in the bars and social clubs. If you do, many times it is one of the athletes. People stare and pretend not to notice. Finally someone notices it is so and so on the football team. Then it is ok for them to be there. Last year... I was out with several of what I consider to be good friends when a black student called to me. I left the group I was with to go talk to him. I greeted him with a hug... talked for a few minutes—while being stared at the entire time. When I went back to my "group" several guys remarked about "Who was that?" "Where did I know him from?"

But when I told them my black friend's name [a prominent UGA athlete] they wanted to meet him. It was a disgusting eye opener.[12]

Several of my students—both Black and white—made similar observations about the white student social scene in downtown Athens being unfriendly to Black students. One white male student recalled an incident when that cold atmosphere ruined his evening when he went downtown with a friend, who was a female African American student. She had suggested to him that they drink "at least one hurricane" to celebrate Mardi Gras.

Not needing much arm twisting, I agreed and we set out for Harry Bissett's [a New Orleans–themed bar in downtown Athens]. As we walked into the bar (the crowd was all white and many Greek and Confederate shirts were donned for the occasion) I felt as if people were looking at my friend (who was preceding me) and thinking "What's this field hand doing in the House?" When I mentioned this to her, she agreed with my assessment of the situation. Needless to say, after consuming our hurricanes we left. This event proves the point that on the surface we may feel we have an Integrated society, but we do not. Even though an African American was allowed into Harry Bissett's and served, she was definitely not well received.[13]

As with the Math 254 essays, there were students in my UGA classes in the 1990s who wrote of being exposed to racist attitudes in their Georgia hometowns and in their families. One student who grew up in a small north Georgia town wrote that while most UGA students were far more progressive on race than their predecessors from 1961, she knew from her precollege home life that "there are lingering remnants of those days of hatred." So for her, as a child and teen, "racism was a part of every day life. My father did not allow my brother and sister and I to watch a television program with an African American in it. But thanks to my mother, who held some racial stereotypes but nothing like the ignorant hatred of my father, I learned that it was wrong to treat other people differently based on the color of their skin."[14] Even so, she came to college with "many misconceptions about African Americans." But in this case, UGA's racially integrated dorms made all the difference. Her freshman roommate was an African American student who helped her transcend the racial miseducation she had experienced at home: "She helped me understand so much, and I will be forever grateful to her as a future parent and teacher, but most importantly as a human being."[15]

Looking at both UGA's segregationist past and her family's own racist history, a white student in my class stressed that the university "had come a long way" as a place "where blacks and minorities are allowed equal opportunities." She told of her grandfather, a blue collar worker with a grade school education, who lived in a small community in Barrow County, and who "like most [white] southern men in the 50s and 60s . . . didn't like colored folk. . . . My grandaddy used to drink a lot and go out looking for trouble with his buddies. They'd say in their drunken state 'I'm gonna go kill me a n———,' grab their guns and nobody would hear from them again for a few days. My mom never really found his white robe but she suspected he was a member of the KKK or a similar organization."[16] In her youth she "heard the 'N' word a lot" but came to disdain the bigotry it represented. She wrote that she did have Black friends but none of them close and admitted that being around large groups of African Americans made her "feel uncomfortable and out of place." She also expressed strong opposition to the idea that Georgia "was not finished paying . . . [its] debt to the black community because of slavery. Things like that burn me up. Give me a break—the people in question were not even alive back then. They had no control of their ancestor's deeds, just like I had no control over my grandfather's." She also aired resentment of the existence of "separate Miss Black UGA," even noting that "I've often thought of auditioning for it." And she felt the same about the United Negro College Fund which was, in her view, unfair since it was "based on the fact that you're black. . . . If there were a college fund for whites, there would be a total uprising."[17] So the essay seemed to argue both for equality and resentment of Black assertiveness on behalf of it, a position common among conservative whites on UGA's campus.

One of the students in my class, who began his schooling in the Atlanta area but later moved to a rural Georgia county (Habersham), based his analysis of race relations at UGA in the 1990s on an urban-rural contrast. In his urban community there was a cosmopolitan atmosphere that pervaded his junior high school, where "we had people from over thirty different nations. People of all races got along, [and] the only division was between classes, and that was not pronounced."[18] This was "dramatically" different from the rural school he later attended. It was a complete shock . . . that the blacks, the whites, and the Asians kept to themselves. The lines were drawn, and when they were crossed fights would erupt. Most of the fights . . . were over some of the most idiotic things."[19] He saw this same division on campus and thought that the most forward-looking students were from cosmopolitan urban areas and the most narrow minded and bigoted were from provincial rural counties. "You can," he explained,

> walk across campus, and see races intermingled, but at the same time you can see people in their own little group often based on race. Most often the integrated groups are from areas in the state that have integrated classrooms, and the racially . . . [exclusive] groups are from rural areas where a voluntary separation is the unspoken rule. From my observations, and discussions with other white and black students, this is also their view point. It is a sad truth that not all people have woke to the new day! Some are still asleep in the past! Those from the rural areas still hold some of the same views as [the segregationist protesters in 19]61. Thankfully . . . the number of people that would side with Charlayne [Hunter] have greatly increased from the few who became her friends at UGA in the 60s. The sad thing is that not all have changed their views from that of the [segregationist] majority in [19]61. Time and education will hopefully heal the wounds, and all of the people of the world will unite as one.[20]

Unlike those students in the Math 254 class in 1961, some of the white UGA students in the 1990s had attended racially integrated high schools en route to college. But contrary to the prior student's assumption, those experiences were not always helpful in breaking down racial barriers and isolation at UGA. One such student recounted that she had grown up in a small town in Georgia beset by racial tensions that went unaddressed by the inadequate teachers and administrators who set the tone of her racially integrated high school. She recalled that "I heard the word 'nigger' used by almost everyone I associated with. I went to school with about 50 percent black student ratio but would never call any of them my close friends. My high school crowned (and still does) a black and white Homecoming Queen and our school never had a prom because the community preferred that blacks and whites have separate proms, and of course, the school wouldn't permit this, so we have separate proms outside of school."[21] In assessing the impact of all this upon her racial attitudes, she noted that "growing up in this warped little town, I think I did develop some racist views, although I would never have admitted it at the time." And high school just compounded the problem: "At my school race was absolutely never discussed in class—it was simply ignored. Racial comments were common, as were racial fights, and this caused me to be really uncomfortable." At UGA, however, in my class she finally had the opportunity to study the history of racism in Georgia and to rethink her prior assumptions: "This class is actually the first class I have ever taken that had discussions about race. At first I felt uncomfortable, but now it is much easier for me. I've really learned a lot about racism in [Georgia's] past—things I had never heard before . . . and honestly I actually cried when I read Charlayne Hunter-Gault's book. I am now more aware than ever of the need for multicultural education in the schools. I am the perfect example."[22]

Another student from a small town in Georgia—this one near the Georgia-Alabama line—recalled horrendous racial conflict in this "white town mainly consisting of old Southerners who believe in segregation because that's how they were raised to think."[23] She initially went to a K-8 school "with its enrollment of about two hundred students (all white)." When a Black family moved to town and enrolled two children in the school, "many [white] parents looked down on the school for allowing the blacks to enroll, but what could the school do, forbid them to enroll and contend with federal law? I think not." Before long, however, the Black family was "chased away." "Shots" were "fired" into this Black family's home "from a vehicle that was passing by and soon after that the black family left the community. I guess living down the street from an ex-Grand Dragon of the Ku Klux Klan did not do anything to ease their minds either. So the people of the community made it known they were not welcome here. Anyway, I ended up switching schools when I was in eighth grade."[24] In this new school, for the first time she "attended classes with black people." But here too she encountered racism from white classmates "who were appalled that I was talking to black people." She credited the values of her home for her willingness to defy such racism: "I have always been taught to be kind to everyone. My family is not in the same mindset as everybody else in our community. Maybe it is because my family moved to Georgia from California when I was five, or maybe it is because my family does not succumb to the rule of thumb of society and tends to go against the norm."[25]

For this student, UGA seemed an oasis of toleration in comparison to the racist small-town world of her youth. "College differs from high school in that students do not seem as quick to judge people by skin color. . . . Today while attending college, I notice that people are not as close-minded as they once were."[26] Of course there were exceptions: She did encounter some white students who held the same racist beliefs of her small town, refusing to associate with Black students. But this mindset she found less widespread than in her prior schools, so that at UGA interracial friendships were not scorned. She found divergent views and experiences among her Black friends at UGA. Some say "they believe that blacks are treated as equals on campus by faculty and other students . . . given the same opportunity as whites both academically and socially." But other Black friends at UGA told her African American students "feel that they are discriminated against because they are black.... That ... if the teachers were white ... blacks had to work twice as hard as a white student in order to receive a grade that a white student would receive for half the amount of work.... That black students were particularly discriminated against when it came to Greek Life at the university.... That they had to form their own fraternity and sorority because they were not allowed to be a member of the [white] fraternities and sororities ... on campus."[27]

White students in the fraternity and sorority system seemed the least willing of my students to confront issues of historical racism and its legacy at UGA. When discussing the all-white character of their Greek letter organizations, most would cite the presence of Black fraternities and sororities and take them as evidence of a mutual desire for racial separation, a false equivalency that ignores the fact that these Black organizations emerged in the Jim Crow era because African Americans were barred from attending white colleges and universities. Nor was there a single white Greek house member who expressed any desire to change this segregated status quo. In fact, one student mentioned in her essay that she "went through [sorority] Rush here at UGA this past fall, and there was not one black girl going through at all." She took this as evidence that Black and white students at UGA had no desire to "hang out" in the same social organizations—as further evidenced by the fact that in their Greek organizations "black students have their own Rush and no white students were invited to participate." So she "mentioned nothing" about integration to those running the all-white rush process.[28] "I am not a racist," wrote another sorority member in my class, "but I cannot honestly say how I would feel about having a black sorority member or if my brother was to date a black woman. These are obviously racist attitudes but I think I still learn more about races every day, and I have much more liberal attitudes than my parents.... I must remember not to pass the racial views that were passed to me on to my children."[29] Another of my students, who thought the progress and changes at UGA on race since 1961 had been "tremendous," also noted that at UGA he sees "racial inequality daily" and offered as exhibit A his fraternity friend's statement that "it is just not seen as cool or normal" for white students "to hang out with blacks. My fraternity would call me a 'nigger lover' and laugh at me."[30]

This is not to say, however, that even within the white fraternity system at UGA, everyone was a racist who went along completely with its whites-only mindset. Thus one of the students in my class claimed that the white Greek houses in the 1990s remained segregated not because of racial hatred but because of "feelings of discomfort" and the awkwardness of rooming with Black students with whom they had so little contact. This student conceded that some in the fraternity system's leadership "do still feel hate towards blacks," but such views were far from universal in that system. In support of this point, she cited her experience at "a fraternity party in about the third week of school. Three black students showed up, and the president of the fraternity was furious. He told the pledges to kick them out, but they refused. The majority of brothers agreed with the pledges' decision, so the black students remained at the party. This probably would never have happened two decades ago. I do not think black students [back then] would even consider going to a fraternity party."[31] Yet while certainly significant, this anecdote does not address the question of why fraternity members failed to offer such dissent regarding their leadership's continuing discriminatory practice of reserving fraternity membership for whites.

UGA's Greek houses in the 1990s resembled their predecessors in the Jim Crow era not only with their discriminatory admissions practices but with their embrace of the Confederate flag. Back then some white Georgia students would defend the flag as symbolizing their Southern heritage rather than slavery, segregation, and racism, but such arguments fooled no one and it was difficult to believe even they took them seriously. And to walk past those houses beneath enormous flags with the stars and bars waving was chilling, a sight that evoked the Old South in a way that made it hard to believe these were the residences of students in a late-twentieth-century university. As one of my students put it,

> if you go down Milledge [Avenue], you see Confederate flags flying from the fraternity houses. To me, these flags represent the old racist South. Maybe it is because I am from the North, but I just don't like to see these flags flying around campus. If UGA students have changed their racial attitudes, why do these flags still wave? ... There are some prejudices against blacks on this campus from students who have been raised by parents with the prejudices that were evident [at UGA] in the 1960s. I do believe they can change their views, but it is hard when you have been taught that blacks are inferior your whole life.[32]

With their limited experience in probing racial problems and bigotry, a good number of the white students in my classes were shocked about what they learned and heard. One of these students spoke to her former roommate, who was African American, and was startled to learn that one of the reasons she transferred out of UGA was because of the cold atmosphere on campus toward Blacks, especially in her dormitory. "When she told me this," the student wrote, "I was a little hurt at first, afraid that I had added to her unhappiness. But she was quick to explain that I was one of the few reasons why she stayed the entire year and did not leave after the fall quarter."[33] The Black student explained that "the racism she encountered was not obvious. It was more subtle and hidden": White girls from her dormitory floor would never speak with her outside the dorm when they encountered her on campus. And when her boyfriend "would come to visit her in the dorm, many of the girls would look uncomfortable when they saw a tall black man coming down the hall. . . . I guess I did notice this then, but did not want to acknowledge it," wrote the white student. "Some of the things she said never occurred to me, but when I began to think about them, I realized how difficult that year must have been for her."[34]

Another student wrote of being amazed and appalled when "a black guy" in her speech class described an incident in which "a Confederate flag was thrown at him out of a car" whose passenger yelled, "Nigger go back to Africa," along with his other encounters with racism in their college town.[35] "Another shock came" to her when she asked a white student about the state of race relations at UGA in the 1990s and he responded, "They are fine. I think they [Black students] are treated equally by UGA. I think they tend to segregate themselves. There are too many minority opportunities. I firmly believe that affirmative action is the work of the devil." She concluded that "this guy would have fit in perfectly with UGA students in 1961."[36]

One of the few students in my classes who had extensive contacts and friends on both sides of UGA's racial divide in the 1990s offered a nuanced, critical, yet optimistic assessment of how race was lived on campus then, and how it compared to the newly desegregated UGA of 1961. Opening with more positives than negatives, she held that "obviously circumstances for blacks are better now than they were in 1961, but they are not ideal. Segregation persists in our Greek system and in [other] social groups. Fortunately, a variety of programs, such as the CLASS program and the BESTeam, have been implemented to help African American students deal with minority status and academic issues. Also cultural advances, such as Afro-American Choral Ensemble and Black History Month observance are available. . . . Students attending in the [19]60s would" not have had access to "such advances." But many Black students feel that "only lip service is paid to the most significant racial issues."[37] The Black students she interviewed have to "deal with racism on a daily basis both at the University and in Athens, which is manifested in many ways: the pressure of being the only black student in a classroom, getting 'attitude' from a white cashier, and combatting various prejudices from whites ... Some things have not changed since '61—there are still those who believe blacks are inferior and that the races should not mix." Nonetheless, she believed that though uneven and marred by problems, racial progress since '61 was real: "At UGA although we are officially integrated many believe this is mere tokenism and that beneath the surface little mixing occurs—an oil-and-water, us vs. them attitude dominates every aspect of University life.... Considering though, that it's only been a generation or at most two since UGA first opened its doors to blacks, the situation is good. The university can boast special programs, integrated dorms and athletic teams, some minority faculty, and an affirmative action program. But though the political dust may have settled, ignorance is constant ... persists and must be patiently dealt with."[38]

Some of the most progressive white students in my classes tended to be more aware than the average student that campus racism reflected in the Math 254 essays had not vanished. As one of them explained, "The old spirit of racism lives on, on the bumper stickers of rebel flags and the t-shirts of the Greek system (i.e. Heritage Day, etc). Most likely ignorance will always be present here in the sewer of society, more commonly known as the South." Another noted, "I have never had a black professor.... In a school of over 30,000 do you find something wrong with that? I do. I don't have any black friends and can name only one black person I have become an acquaintance with in my two years here."[39] Race, another student observed, "is still a very touchy subject." At UGA

> we have people from all walks of life and places. I think racism is found most in the deep rural South. Something I first encountered when I moved from Gwinnett County to Alpharetta where there are a lot of "rednecks" with prejudice. The thing that strikes me as funny is that even as I write this condemnation of racism I am stereotyping a group. When I was first coming to this school I was to live in Creswell Hall, which everyone equates to the "black" dorm. When I told people in high school where I was going to live they said things like "that's where all the black people live." This surprised me as I thought "Who cares?" The reactions of these people shocked me but if that wasn't enough I confronted this in college as well. Freshman year when I told people where I lived they responded with "Cretwell" in what they thought to be a funny black way of speaking and "Cres-hell?" When I asked them why they called it that they said because it was such a trashy, dirty dorm, or that it must be hard to

study with black people playing rap music so loudly all the time, or that black people were just generally loud. It blew my mind, and today when people ask me where I live[d] freshman year I get much the same response, sometimes with comments like "I'm sorry, that must have sucked," but with no reasoning behind it.... The stereotyping and negative attitudes disgusted and amazed me.[40]

Among the most well informed of my students on race was a white student who had family members who were veterans of the civil rights movement in Atlanta. He knew of the 1995 US Supreme Court decision, based on a University of Maryland case, barring (the Benjamin Banneker) scholarships that targeted Black students; he linked this to the larger right wing movement against affirmative action. He saw this whole movement to kill affirmative action as "cheap, covert racism" and feared that with the "death of affirmative action" higher education at places like the "University of Georgia will be heading backward to January 1961," posing additional obstacles in the way of Black enrollments at UGA.[41] He wrote that his Black friends at UGA found the whole topic of affirmative action "complex and unsettling" and were relieved that they were graduating before all educational programs benefitting minorities were eliminated.[42]

The African American students in my classes acknowledged that at UGA there had been positive changes since 1961, including the hiring of Black faculty and the rise of Black enrollments from a handful to close to 2,000. Yet all agreed "that there are some aspects of the UGA's life that have not changed since 1961." Social life, as one Black student noted, was still among "the segregation issues.... All of my close friends are black. I have not been invited to a white party since I entered the University in Fall '94."[43] The Black students felt that, unlike the situation faced by Charlayne Hunter and Hamilton Holmes at UGA, in the 1990s "no group is seeking [to] offend [or] unnerve" them, but on the other hand "the hate has become more masked," which is "dangerous" too.[44] "Sure, I am allowed to live in a dormitory with white students," wrote another Black student in my class, "and I don't receive the threats that Charlayne Hunter did, but I feel the chill of isolation as they [white students] rush by me in groups, not bothering to speak to, or even acknowledge me. I also feel the chill of isolation as I watch them scurrying around downtown drinking and partying, making no comfortable room for me." And when she asked fellow Black students—one a freshman and the other a senior—she found that they too felt "detached from the spirit of UGA." The senior observed that "our social activities, such as parties, remain the same, about 95% divided. Racism has changed on the surface but not inside the hearts of some white students."[45]

Another African American student bemoaned the way white students romanticized their racist ancestors and clung to a white supremacist view of Southern history: "I don't like the way many white Georgians are so obsessed with the 'Old South.' Many say 'Why bring up history and slavery?' but at the same time they display Confederate flags, and white fraternities and sororities even have Antebellum events" promoting nostalgia for plantations and the Southern slave regime.[46] One Black student noted the intense parochialism of many white students who "instead of wanting *to learn about* other cultures . . . *protest* multicultural [course] requirements."[47] Another linked this nostalgia for the Southern past with white discomfort with any Black presence at UGA: "Many of UGA's white students would like to return to the 'Old South' before UGA was integrated."[48]

Although there were some interracial friendships and even some dating across racial lines, Black students found the norm among their white counterparts was a lack of sensitivity to the problem of racism on campus and to what it meant to be a Black student in a student body that was overwhelmingly white, Southern, and ignorant about racial realities past and present. One of the Black students in my class noted after speaking with several white students that "basically all the feedback was the same and so was the uncomfortable manner in which they [white students] spoke to me."[49] Most said that they disapproved of the racist views of the kind aired by the Math 254 students in 1961 and stressed that their generation of white students was more enlightened. But there was nonetheless evidence of a white backlash against the Black student presence at UGA, expressed in the language of the then current right wing attack on affirmative action in university admissions. As one white student told this Black student, "I apologize for the attitudes in the past but black people didn't meet some requirements of UGA then and some don't meet them now. The university allows them to come in just to even out the numbers."[50] "I was," wrote the African American student, "disappointed in his opinion which he believed to be true. At the same time, I respected his honesty . . . [since] I felt that some of the other [white] students I questioned felt the same way but would not tell me to my face because I was black."[51]

Similarly, a Nigerian student told another of my students that she "overheard [white] students say they feel that blacks are dumb and are only here because of affirmative action." As my student noted, "This comment echoes that of the students of 1961 when they said blacks were [mentally] slower than whites."[52] Carrying this argument even further, one of the most right wing white students in my class wrote that she "found numerous opinions voiced by the Math 254 class that I agree with." She argued that "what has changed in . . . race since 1961 . . . [is that at UGA] whites are repressed instead of the blacks. Now whites are backed in a corner and have to allow blacks with lower grade points to the school in the name of affirmative action."[53] Such views are not surprising given the strength of Southern conservatism, but on a campus that was overwhelmingly white and where Black students were a very small minority, it is striking that this student, and others in my classes, begrudged the presence of even a limited number of African American students—and viewed that presence as illegitimate.

There was a notable awkwardness as well as tension in a good deal of the Black-white conversations about race that the students wrote about. This reflected the very different takes on racism as Black students felt some of their white classmates were unaware of and insensitive to racial problems, while white students thought Blacks overly sensitive on racial matters, so much so that they thought Blacks saw racial slights where they did not exist. For example, Black students noticed that white students "would rather stand on a crowded [campus] bus than sit next to them."[54] But when this issue of bus etiquette came up in a personal way for one of the white students in my class, she was offended: "I got on a crowded bus and sat next to a black [male student] whose friend was sitting behind him. When the bus cleared at the next stop, I got up and moved one seat forward so that I would be more comfortable and I assumed he would too. When I got up and moved I heard him say to his friend: 'See some people can't even stand it for 10 minutes.' I felt like telling him that was a very selfish and ignorant thing to say. The bus was almost empty, so why should I sit next to him and deny us both a more comfortable place to sit?"[55] Similarly, another student in my class wrote of her "first real experience: with racial tensions," which began with an issue regarding elevator etiquette. This occurred when the resident advisor from her dorm

> took me and three other white girls to an African-American meeting. One black girl said that when she got in the elevator none of the white students looked at her or spoke to her. Since the four of us from my hall were the only white girls there I felt like she was talking directly to us. I remember wanting to defend myself by saying that I do not talk or look at anyone on the elevator. I just stare straight ahead. My RA [resident advisor], who was black, got up and spoke. When she got up she pointed us out as being the girls on her hall, and then continued to say that she was the only minority in our hall . . . and that we did not participate in the activi-

ties she planned because she was black. I wanted to speak up, and deny it, and explain why it was that anyone hardly ever went but I was not allowed the chance to. Until that point my RA and I had a very good friendship, or so I thought. I did not realize I was a racist simply because I was white. It was that same night when I was discussing the incident with one of my best friends, who also happens to be Black, and she said, "To us everything is about race."[56]

Among the most perceptive summaries of the roots of the racial tension at UGA in the 1990s came from one student who linked this tension to the contradictory assumptions about racial realities on campus and the strikingly different historical sensibilities that divided white students from their Black classmates. "Most white students," he explained,

> believe there are few racial problems on campus. Some think that blacks sometimes look for racism where there is none present. Most white students don't have racist views that are as strong as their ancestors and believe that blacks unjustly blame them for the degradation they experienced under slavery, segregation, and discrimination. They feel that there is no need for Affirmative Action here at UGA because all people are viewed as equal, that much discrimination does not exist, and view it as a measure to replace highly qualified white students and employ[ees] with unqualified black students and employ[ees].... I believe that it is important to understand our past to help us come to terms with the present. Blacks and whites have a history together that is mixed with suffering, turmoil, discrimination, slavery, and etc. that we have not been able to come to terms with. Whites prefer to forget the past and can't see why blacks don't. Black students cannot forget the past because many of the problems of today are a direct result of the past and we are living in a society where we fear that social conditions of the past may resurface.[57]

He also noted that these very different and conflicting views on race made it difficult for Black and white students to dare to discuss race. Indeed, since so little was done to foster such discussions at UGA, he experienced my class as the first time he had ever seen students encouraged "to address controversial issues pertaining to race.... It allows black and white students to discus [sic] issues together they would not have gotten a chance to discuss with members of the opposite race."[58]

Perhaps the student most shocked by her exploration of how race was lived at UGA in the 1990s versus 1961 was the white student who had begun with the assumption that race relations were excellent at UGA in the 1990s. But after she reflected on numerous examples of social segregation and then interviewed her disillusioned Black next-door neighbor from her dorm, she came to realize that the state of race relations at UGA was so troubled that her Black neighbor had totally given up on connecting with her white classmates. This Black student said, "she chooses not to hang out with white people because for the most part we were all racists." This shocked the white student, so she asked, "why she thought whites were racists." She responded that white students "are all concerned with appearances and luxuries and for the most part blacks don't have all those luxuries. She made herself out to be oppressed and blamed her families [sic] hardships on the white population.... She seemed to hate white people, and she even told me that she would not like to have any white friends. She likes how the two races stay away from each other, and she liked the fact that we don't mix. She said the day she receives an apology from white people about the way her ancestors were treated was the day she treated a white person with respect."[59]

For all her bitterness, this Black student had hit on an important historical truth. Georgia and UGA had never been held accountable, never promoted public understanding of their long history of racial discrimination and service to the Jim Crow system. It is little wonder, then, that right wing white students, with their arguments about Blacks being unqualified to attend UGA, were clueless about the fact that the UGA administration had spent more than a decade—1950 to 1961—battling to keep out of UGA some of the most highly qualified students ever to apply to the university simply because they were Black. These included Horace Ward, whom the color line kept out of UGA's law school, and who went on to become a distinguished civil rights attorney who would be appointed to a federal judgeship by president Jimmy Carter; Charlayne Hunter-Gault, whom UGA tried but failed to keep out of its journalism school and who would become a world famous journalist for the *New York Times*, PBS, and NPR; and Hamilton Holmes, whom UGA sought but failed to keep out of its premed program and who became the first Black graduate of Emory University's medical school, a surgeon, and medical director at Grady Memorial Hospital in Atlanta.

We cannot know what difference it would have made had UGA educated itself and its students about its shameful racist history, had white Georgia not hidden behind the myth that it was victimized by federal courts ordering integration when in fact those court orders would finally liberate UGA from its decades of provincialism and racial discrimination, making possible the university's emergence as a first-rate institution of higher education. My "Two,

Four, Six, Eight" article and the Math 254 essays, when discussed in my classes, could not, of course, end the racial tensions at UGA, but they did provoke most students to take a good hard look at campus racism past and present.

As the student essays make clear, the racial realities at UGA in the 1990s were so complex that my students differed in both describing and explaining them. While all recognized that the age of Jim Crow and racial violence had long since ended, racial tensions, social isolation, and pockets of segregation persisted at UGA. I take it as a hopeful sign that most of my students regretted that persistence, but on the other hand few of the essays indicated much thought about how to end the racial divide on campus, and there was some skepticism about whether it could in fact be ended.

Cultural, political, and historical differences kept the white and Black student populations divided from one another. Of course, racial divisions are present on many campuses—north and south—and with Jim Crowism dead we should be cautious about assertions of Southern or Georgia exceptionalism. Still, it is hard to avoid concluding that greater student familiarity with UGA's service to Georgia's Jim Crow and slavery regimes and with the Black struggle to democratize UGA and Georgia could be a valuable tool for racial understanding, and perhaps reconciliation and healing. Also valuable would be more decisive action by the UGA administration in areas such as Greek house desegregation. Segregated fraternities and sororities persist into our own time, and in fact, yet another racist scandal involving a white UGA fraternity made headlines in 2020, surfacing bigoted discourse far more hateful and obscene than that found in any of the Math 254 essays in 1961.[60]

As was mentioned earlier, back in the 1990s teaching about UGA's desegregation crisis inevitably led me to interact with students whose relatives had been a part of that crisis. One such student wrote of his uncle (UGA class of '64), who had "witnessed the riot in front of [Charlayne] Hunter's dormitory." This uncle, like many UGA students back then, tried to evade the racist implications of the riot by claiming that it was "provoked by the disappointing [overtime basketball] loss to Georgia Tech."[61] But the more he talked the more he undermined this specious argument, for he also told his nephew he remembered "his friend tying a noose around a black doll and parading it around" during UGA's desegregation crisis. His friend "was on the cover of *Life* magazine."[62] The uncle also recalled "much obscenity that night" and that he would "never have been a part of such violent action and was ashamed that so many of his friends did" engage in such racist violence. In the end he dropped the basketball loss rationale and instead asserted that "hatred feelings from the Civil War were still very real, and that instigated much of the actions."[63] The Math 254 essays offer a window into such hatred and the desire of some UGA students to transcend it and the ugly violence it provoked. And here was my student's uncle, a UGA alum of those turbulent years, taking a step toward such transcendence by at last reckoning with the hatred that had led his classmates to engage in racist violence.

NO UGA ALUM OF THE desegregation crisis has done more to assess its meaning and legacy than Charlayne Hunter-Gault, who in her first days integrating the university was, of course, the target of a violent segregationist mob. Hunter-Gault reflected on that same question my UGA students would probe, which is the title of this chapter, "New Day or Old South?" What had become of the university and Georgia itself on the question of racial equality since she and Hamilton Holmes crossed its color line in 1961? Had UGA been transformed by desegregation? Or was there a substantial amount of continuity and resistance to the egalitarian integrationist ideal? Hunter-Gault reflected on all this in 1988, a decade earlier than my students did. The occasion for her reflections was the twenty-fifth anniversary of her and Hamilton Holmes's graduation as the first African Americans to be awarded bachelor's degrees by UGA. And the event in which Hunter-Gault shared these reflections was itself historic. She had been invited to give the commencement address, making her the first African American graduation speaker at UGA since the university's founding in 1785. One could say, then, that the speech itself represented, at least symbolically, a new day and a dramatic break with the Old South; the university was honoring the most famous representative of the struggle against its Jim Crow past and celebrating its emergence as a multiracial institution of higher education.

Striking an upbeat note, as befitted such a joyous occasion, Hunter-Gault thanked all those who had made it possible for her to gain entry into UGA and to graduate, including her family, her legal team, and the small circle of classmates who had defied the segregationist ethos of the university by befriending her. Reminding students of the political atmosphere in her student days, Hunter-Gault quoted the commencement speaker at her graduation in 1963, Georgia's segregationist senator Richard Russell, who spoke of "the majesty of local law," which she characterized as "a not so veiled reference to" the white South's resentment of the *Brown* decision and its preference for its Jim Crow laws.[64] She also pointed out that what "the majesty of local law" meant in her student days was that she could not take a bowling class because the town of Athens was still segregated, and that if Blacks wanted to attend a

UGA football game they could only do so by sitting "in isolation" in the remote stadium seats known as "the crows' nest."[65] But the implicit contrast her presence offered, that where in 1963 UGA's graduation speaker was a segregationist and now in 1988 the commencement speaker was its most famed integrationist, symbolized the new day that had dawned at UGA.

Hunter-Gault also evoked the spirit of racial healing in her speech by reading a letter sent to her recently by a UGA student of her time who had witnessed the riot outside their Center-Myers dormitory and had learned some enduring lessons, though as Hunter-Gault pointed out, those lessons were "a long time coming and not the usual ones taught in an academic setting."[66] This UGA alum wrote Hunter-Gault that she had grown up in Jim Crow Virginia and "entered the university a very ignorant child," blind to "the suffering of blacks" in the segregated South. But as she "watched from the window that night" in "shock" as the racist mob besieged their dormitory, "for the first time I understood unreasonable cruelty, and I have not been an innocent since that night. I have tried ever since 1961 to treat all people with respect, and I now have a good number of Black friends.... I wonder how many of the 'privileged' white girls in Center Myers have been able to use their potential as you have; when I think of some of the attitudes, there is irony and I have to smile to myself."[67]

But like my students a decade later, Hunter-Gault was well aware that racial tensions and inequities remained. This is why she told the graduates,

> no one here today would pretend that the Old South is dead and buried, that the events of the past twenty-five years, even my presence here today, have transformed our peculiar world into one that is beyond recognition. The Confederate flag still flies in places on this campus ... and it would still be unwise for me to spend too much time in certain municipalities a few hours' drive from here. To be sure, there are more than two Black students in this graduating class—there are 300 in a class of 6,200. Taken together with the number of Black students in the entire student body—1,200 out of 26,000—permit me to say that we have all failed in our responsibility to this institution and this state for lo these many years.[68]

Linking UGA's failings on racial equity with the rightward tilt of American politics, Hunter-Gault noted that the "lessons I learned on the campus that have stayed with me for life have provided me with sharp radar for disharmony and intolerance. And in recent times that radar has been sounding alarms. From the college campus, where dissent is now often mean-spirited, to the [Reagan] White House, where former education secretary Terrell Bell recalled that he was 'shocked to hear...sick humor...racist cliches and other ethnic slurs.'"⁶⁹ So for Hunter-Gault, UGA in 1961 "found itself established as one of the first battlegrounds of a New South" but one that "is still aborning."⁷⁰

Sounding another hopeful note, Hunter Gault praised UGA president Charles Knapp for his "bold stroke" in initiating the hiring of "fifteen new Black faculty members for the upcoming academic year.... When people at the top exercise aggressive leadership ... they set a tone and create an atmosphere that make things happen."⁷¹ Hunter-Gault expressed confidence that "the presence of more black faculty members here will not only attract more black students to this campus, but their presence will move this place—our place—to a new phase in its pioneering history. A place that could be a model for a more perfect union. A place in which people of color are on the ascendancy."⁷²

Some of this optimism about Black faculty hiring echoes that of Thomas G. Dyer, UGA's vice president for academic affairs, who had written Hunter-Gault about this Black faculty hiring initiative just a few weeks before her commencement speech. He expressed confidence that these hires would make UGA a national leader in Black faculty recruitment and then in Black student recruitment.⁷³ Dyer, as we have seen, was a dedicated supporter of integration and had also played a key role in establishing, in 1985, the annual lecture series on civil rights named for Hamilton Holmes and Charlayne Hunter-Gault. Certainly this hiring initiative, and one championed by such high-ranking UGA administrators, did represent a move in the direction on greater equity and diversity.

And yet, as Dyer conceded in his letter to Hunter-Gault, even with these new hires UGA would still only have a little more than 50 African American faculty out of a total UGA faculty in 1988 of 1,900.⁷⁴ Its impact was certainly not enough to touch most of my UGA students a decade later, some of whom mentioned never being in a class with an African American professor in all their years at the university. Nor had the positive symbolic step of naming that lecture series for Hunter and Holmes had much of an impact on my students, though that series brought to campus each year one of the leading figures in the Black Freedom struggle. Not one of my students mentioned that lecture series in their essays on race at UGA in the late 1990s. This calls to mind a lecture on campus by Hamilton Holmes that I attended, sponsored by a Black student organization. This was in the early 1990s, soon after I joined the UGA faculty. His talk was memorable, but so was the fact that the room was half empty, with few, if any, white students present. That racial dynamic was depressing and one more affirmation of the conclusion offered by one of my students later in that decade that "UGA to me is integrated by law, but vastly segregated within."[75]

In light of my students' essays, the Hunter-Gault speech at UGA's graduation in 1988 seems all the more striking as it explored the same problems, failures, and limited progress on desegregation that would be still very much in evidence a decade later, when my students reflected on these issues at UGA in the late 1990s. It is also striking that the mixed reaction to her speech confirmed the complexity of race relations at UGA and how difficult it was even to promote dialogue about them. I had heard from colleagues that Hunter-Gault's speech provoked considerable resentment from white students and alumni who were present for it. The coverage of the speech by the *Red and Black* confirmed this. For example, a graduating advertising major told the *Red and Black* reporter he "felt the speech was inappropriate.... I just don't think it was the time or place" for her to discuss race relations at UGA.[76] Similarly, a journalism major expressed to the *Red and Black* reporter resentment of Hunter-Gault's discussion of UGA's failures regarding Black admissions and Black faculty hiring: "She shouldn't have chastised us—It's the administration that should be chastised."[77] (Actually her speech did not single out UGA's students for blame regarding these failures.)

But the editors of the *Red and Black* found the speech both memorable and accurate. In an editorial titled "Coming Full Circle," they expressed agreement that desegregation had moved far too slowly since Hunter-Gault's UGA graduation in 1963. Indeed, they noted that the racial realities of UGA in 1988 left them with a sense of déjà vu when they reflected on her words about her own graduation a quarter century earlier. Hunter-Gault had said that with just her and Hamilton Holmes the only Black graduating seniors in 1963 amid a graduating class of 1,600, these two Black students felt "lost in a crowd" at the graduation ceremony. And this, the editors noted, would also be true in 1988 when "some 300 black students graduated in a class of more than 6,000." The editors, much like many of my students, saw other parallels between UGA in 1963 and UGA decades later: "The numbers may be different, but as Hunter-Gault suggested, things haven't changed all that much. The University community is still largely segregated. Whites socialize with whites, black with blacks. Today only 1,200 of 26,000 students are black. The figures for black faculty, though improving, are even worse."[78]

Though conceding that some might not like to be confronted with such searching criticism, the *Red and Black* argued that the truth needed to be faced even if it seemed painful: "Hunter-Gault's words were stinging at times, encouraging at others.... It wasn't your traditional graduation speech. But who expected it to be? Hunter-Gault saw the opportunity Saturday to state what she's been feeling for 25 years, to state it at this critical moment in the University's history of race relations, to state it before the largest and most influential audience possible. She succeeded.... Her speech was historic." The editors ended with an important question that evidenced their understanding of the long-term nature of the struggle for desegregation and racial equity at UGA, wondering whether Black graduating seniors a quarter century after 1988 would still be so small a minority as to feel "lost" in an immense white crowd, as had been the case in 1963 and 1988. Will we "have simply come full circle again[?] Or will the University have forged way ahead [in its percentage of graduating seniors who were African American]?"[79]

Twenty-five years later, that question could be answered: as of 2013 the number of UGA graduating seniors who were Black had risen from 300 to 539, but the percentage had only risen from 5 percent in 1988 to 6.69 percent (539 out of 8,050 graduates), which does not seem to meet with the *Red and Black* editor's hope that UGA would have "forged way ahead," and which very much resembles the white majority campus world that my students there wrote about so memorably in the late 1990s.[80]

Coda
Commemorations

In the twenty-first century, the University of Georgia (UGA) has hosted three major commemorations of its desegregation in which veterans of the desegregation struggle, historians, journalists, faculty, and students have reflected on the fall of the university's color line. The first of these occurred in January 2001, on the fortieth anniversary of the entry of Hamilton Holmes and Charlayne Hunter into UGA as its first Black students. Impressive commemorative events at UGA would subsequently occur on the fiftieth and sixtieth anniversaries of desegregation, in 2011 and 2021. All three commemorations were addressed by UGA presidents and Charlayne Hunter-Gault; they drew large crowds and signaled official recognition of desegregation as a key milestone in the university's history, and in that sense these were symbolically significant events.

Of the three commemorations, the fortieth was the most memorable. It involved renaming for Holmes and Hunter UGA's Academic Building, the place where they first registered for classes in 1961. And this commemoration brought back to UGA key participants on both sides of the desegregation struggle. Most notable among them were the lead attorneys for the plaintiffs in *Holmes v. Danner*, Donald Hollowell and Constance Baker Motley, along with Horace Ward, who was both a member of that legal team and—as we have seen—the African American who unsuccessfully sought admission to Jim Crow UGA eleven years before the court-ordered admission of Holmes and Hunter in 1961. Leading political figures from Georgia's white power elite of the early 1960s also spoke at the fortieth anniversary commemoration, among them Ernest Vandiver, who was the state's governor during UGA's desegregation crisis, and Carl Sanders, president pro tempore of the Georgia Senate during the crisis. Sanders had been Governor Vandiver's floor leader in the Senate and later ascended himself to the Georgia governorship.[1] This would be the last appearance of two of these three eminent lawyers and both these former Georgia governors at a UGA desegregation commemoration, all elders who have passed away in the years since.

Vandiver made the most dramatic gesture of the fortieth anniversary commemoration. In a meeting with Charlayne Hunter-Gault, he apologized for the militantly segregationist pledge he had used in his campaign for governor in 1958, that in Georgia "no, not one" African American would attend school with whites if he was governor—which aligned him with the white South's massive resistance movement aimed at blocking implementation of the *Brown* decision's mandate for racially integrated schools. In her speech at the commemoration, Hunter-Gault praised Vandiver for having "the decency, grace, and yes, the morality" to admit that he had been wrong.[2] And Vandiver, in his public remarks at the commemoration, added that his segregationist pledge had been "intemperate," and that he should never have said those words.[3]

Both Vandiver and Carl Sanders sought, in their fortieth anniversary remarks, to take credit for Georgia's abandonment of massive resistance in January 1961. They discussed their role in getting the state government to repeal its segregationist laws, most notably the section of the Appropriations Act of 1956 that mandated the defunding of any school in Georgia that was racially integrated. Vandiver recounted how unpopular this stance was in 1961, that when during UGA's desegregation crisis he convened a meeting to discuss the choice between court-ordered integration and closing the university, and he asked the state's leading politicians there what to do, one after another (dozens) told him to close the school until he got to Sanders, who insisted that education was so important that the state must not close its leading state university.[4] Vandiver presented himself and Sanders as the voices of moderation, who opted to keep the university open, choosing open schools and obedience to federal law and avoiding the bitterness and bloodshed seen in Deep South states whose governors defied the federal courts to maintain Jim Crow.

It is true that Vandiver and Sanders did better than their counterparts in Alabama and Mississippi, who used their states' segregationist crises demagogically for neo-Confederate posturing and defiance of federal authority that fostered white supremacist militance and terrorism. This is why in her remarks at the commemoration, Constance Baker Motley agreed that whoever convinced Vandiver to comply with the integrationist court order at UGA deserved thanks.[5] But on the other hand Vandiver, at the commemoration, glossed over the unflattering details of his shift away from massive resistance, most notably the *grudging way* that it was made—without the slightest hint that segregation itself was wrong, undemocratic, un-Christian, and discriminatory—which added to the racial tension at UGA in 1961 and helped pave the way for the segregationist campus riot there. Vandiver had accused the federal court of improperly imposing its will on the state government that he headed, as if the antisegregation court order was itself undemocratic.[6] In fact, he denounced the court order as "harsh and vicious."[7] This affirmed the same sense of white victimization that we saw in the UGA students who opposed integration, including the rioters. And even as Vandiver finally, on January 10, 1961, acceded to the court-ordered integration of UGA, he championed legislation to preserve a segregationist local option for white Georgians in their own school districts so they could opt out of integrated educational institutions—supposedly ensuring that no student "could be forced to attend school against his will with any member of the opposite race."[8] This was part of his strategy of what he called, back in 1961, "lawful resistance to integration."[9] Nor did Vandiver say a word in his commemoration remarks about his executive secretary, Peter Zack Geer, who had praised UGA's segregationist rioters for supposedly defying judicial tyranny, or explain what role he or anyone in his administration had played in preventing the state patrol from showing up on the UGA campus to help quell the campus's segregationist riot outside Charlayne Hunter's dormitory.

While it is understandable that time constraints, civility, and gratitude for Vandiver's apology to Hunter-Gault seemed to make it impossible to surface these problems at the commemoration, unless we confront them, we will not be in a position to understand what role UGA played in the social order of Jim Crow Georgia. That understanding becomes possible when we raise questions that Vandiver did not address in his commemoration remarks: Why were he and Sanders unwilling to say a positive word about racial integration during the UGA desegregation crisis? What role had their education at UGA played in perpetuating their adherence to segregation? Why, in their UGA education, had they not been impacted by the findings of modern social scientists refuting traditional white supremacist, segregationist assumptions? Why had so many UGA graduates like them perpetuated a racially discriminatory political system, and in their case helped to lead it? How, why, and when did they finally reject white supremacy and segregation? Why had it taken forty years for Vandiver to apologize for his racial demagoguery?

This last question seems especially important when we consider Vandiver's record as governor well after the UGA desegregation crisis. Governor Vandiver opposed the historic Black Freedom movement that championed desegregation and human rights in Albany, Georgia, in 1962. The governor in a press conference during that struggle denounced Martin Luther King Jr. for his role in supporting, and briefly leading, the Albany movement, depicting King as a self-serving outside agitator: "The people of Georgia are sick and tired of Martin Luther King. The nation is tired of Martin Luther King." King, in Vandiver's view, was "attempting to stir up strife" and violence and had "no respect for the law."[10]

Though Sanders was considered a moderate by Georgia standards, the same questions and doubts apply to him. Sanders in his commemoration speech exaggerated his liberalism by depicting himself as a lonely progressive in Georgia politics who had paid a price for his conscientiousness, damaging his own political future by being the only state official in Georgia to support Lyndon Johnson's presidential campaign in 1964. But what Sanders neglected to mention was that back in 1964 he qualified that endorsement by stating that while he supported LBJ he did not support the Civil Rights Act that Johnson had championed and signed. Nor did Sanders mention at the fortieth anniversary that as governor of Georgia he had denounced the interracial marriage of Charlayne Hunter and Walter Stovall as "a disgrace."[11]

It is likely true that for an occasion such as the fortieth anniversary of UGA's desegregation, there was a temptation to put one's best foot forward, especially among such veteran politicians. So it is not surprising that neither Vandiver nor Sanders proved willing to dwell on the negatives concerning their Jim Crow past. But such evasions are emblematic of the way historical memory has worked for decades among white Georgians. Though whites supported, benefitted from, and, some, served in Georgia's antidemocratic political system, an authoritarian enclave grounded in white supremacy and injustice and a system that had to be toppled for democracy to come alive even as a possibility in Georgia, this reality seems too grim even to be acknowledged, let alone explained. Also grim is the fact that those who championed genuine democracy and equality before the law in Jim Crow Georgia almost always came from the other side of the color line.

THOSE WHO CAME FROM THAT black side of the color line and had battled most persistently and effectively to smash it gave the most insightful remarks at the fortieth anniversary commemoration's plenary session. And—unlike their white counterparts—they were candid about the history they had made, and sugarcoated nothing. This is not at all surprising since the speakers included some of the civil rights movement's leading voices for justice. Two of those speakers from the Holmes-Hunter legal team—Baker Motley and Ward—had risen to become federal judges, and the third, Hollowell, had been Georgia's most revered civil rights lawyer.[12] Their egalitarianism and solidarity with each other and Holmes and Hunter and the cause of equality before the law shone through in their remarks.

Hollowell chose not to discuss the UGA desegregation case but instead focused on how and why he became a lawyer in Jim Crow Georgia. Hailing from Kansas, it was not until he served in the Army that he experienced racism at its most severe—which awakened him to issues of rights and the law. When his marriage led him to Atlanta, Hollowell learned there were whole regions of Georgia that had no Black lawyers at all. So there was a desperate need for legal advocates for Black rights, which Hollowell felt drawn to fill. And Hollowell soon attracted dedicated, aspiring civil rights lawyers, including Horace Ward and Vernon Jordan, to work with him. This team of lawyers devoted to challenging injustice in Jim Crow Georgia was ideally suited to working with Constance Baker Motley of the National Association for the Advancement of Colored People's Legal Defense and Educational Fund to overturn Georgia's educational color line. So it is not surprising that at the fortieth, Hunter-Gault, with great personal warmth, paid tribute to all these lawyers, referring to Hollowell as serving as her surrogate father during the desegregation struggle.

Ward expressed quite movingly his feelings of solidarity with Holmes, Hunter, and Early, making the point that he was gratified that they were able to gain the admission to UGA that had been denied to him back in the 1950s. The point was that a movement for justice persists so that when one effort on behalf of equality fails, others continue the struggle, ultimately prevailing. Ward added that he was proud to have been part of the legal team that made this victory possible. Ward conveyed how hurt he had felt when UGA made bogus claims about his unfitness for law school, a reminder that there was an emotional price paid by those who challenged Jim Crow. Ward also told the story of how, after escorting Charlayne to the campus building that now bears her and Holmes's names and getting lost afterward as he left via the back exit, he was spotted by a hostile white student who sneeringly told him never to return to the UGA campus. In fact, he would not return to UGA for thirty-five years (a story that resonated personally for me since I was among the planners of the UGA civil rights conference that extended to Ward an invitation to come back to the campus in 1996, and I wrote the letter to UGA's president asking him to personally welcome Ward to campus upon his return). For Ward the rejection and exile from the university had been a low point, but the fortieth anniversary commemoration symbolized redemption, an important victory for human rights. It left him feeling that he and his comrades in this struggle for justice were, as he put it, "vindicated" in both the victory and this celebration of it.

Constance Baker Motley's memoir was titled *Equal Justice Under Law*, and that ideal was the focus of her remarks. Her struggle against Jim Crow education was the most geographically diverse of all the lawyers who spoke at the fortieth. Indeed, other than Thurgood Marshall himself, who had hired her for the National Association of Colored People's Legal Defense and Educational Fund, Baker Motley was arguably America's most well-traveled courtroom foe of Jim Crow. She spoke of educational desegregation struggles she had helped win at the Universities of Mississippi, Alabama, and Florida as well as UGA. She insisted that the most important factor in these victories, as in less successful cases, was the quality of the judge—and she noted with some disappointment that W. A. Bootle, the courageous and fair-minded judge who had so ably presided over *Holmes v. Danner*, was not in attendance at the fortieth anniversary.

Nothing that was said at the fortieth was more pointed or revealing than Baker Motley's rebuke of Georgia for failing to live up to the letter and spirit of *Brown v. Board of Education. Brown*, she insisted, did not merely obligate universities to accept qualified students of color when they applied for admission; it also mandated that the states dismantle their inequitable and segregated dual public school systems and merge them into one equitable, high-quality public school system. This, she maintained, had never been done in Georgia, the implication being that the state's political and educational leaders had failed to embrace this egalitarian ideal, this vital and necessary task, and that as a result of such ongoing inequity, state universities such as UGA remained largely white and not much of a force for greater educational and racial equity. UGA desegregation scholar Maurice Daniels, who MCed the fortieth, made a similar point in his introductory remarks, noting that forty years after the desegregation crisis only 6 percent of UGA students and 4 percent of the UGA faculty were African American.[13]

The keynote speech at the fortieth, given by Charlayne Hunter-Gault, was much more candid about the ugly realities of the Jim Crow era than either of the Georgia governors would be in their remarks at the commemoration. Hunter-Gault alluded to the violence—the racist terror, the lynchings—that had been used to reduce Blacks to second-class citizens and keep them down. She spoke too of the meanness and pettiness of the system, which she and Holmes had experienced at UGA, he with harassment from white students who flattened the tires of his car, and she as she went for days without anyone speaking to her in a dormitory with over 200 of her fellow female students, and when a rioter's brick smashed the window of her dorm room, spewing glass near her. Though Hunter-Gault never feared for her own safety during that riot, in its aftermath, when she and Holmes had been suspended from UGA and were to head back to Atlanta, she experienced real terror when Holmes insisted he would drive there from Athens in his own car. She feared that he might be attacked in one of those small racist towns along the way.

Acknowledging her teenage flair for the dramatic, Hunter-Gault recalled throwing a tantrum so as to prod Holmes not put his life at risk, which worked, as it apparently proved so embarrassing to Holmes that he agreed to drive to Atlanta with her and the police.[14]

Citing the African poet Mongane Wally Serote and his *Freedom Lament and Song*, Hunter-Gault insisted at the fortieth that her and Black Georgia's story should not be read as a simple tale of oppression—"not just a sad tale, and must not be." That there was love and beauty that would outweigh the ugliness. Though literally second-class citizens, Blacks refused to see themselves that way and would through community and solidarity unite to topple Jim Crow, as she, her family, friends, and legal team did at UGA. Their love and support, and especially her own friendship with Holmes, whose sterling character she compared to Martin Luther King's and Nelson Mandela's, was central to their success in desegregating UGA. And Hunter-Gault paid tribute to the small circle of white students whom she credited with displaying real courage in defying the bigotry of UGA's white undergraduate majority by befriending and standing by her—as did progressive white faculty members who petitioned to demand that she and Holmes be reinstated after the riot and then proved so welcoming to her.

Opening up in a very personal way, Hunter-Gault noted that even forty years later she could recall exactly what she had been wearing that day when she first walked across the Athens campus. The "olive drab green jumper ... and the blouse with the flowers to match ... boots 'hip' as we said in those days, above the ankles, with knee high white sox." Dressing to look her best had been important to her, Hunter-Gault said, because back in 1961 she was a fashion-conscious nineteen-year-old ready to start a new school year. But according to Hunter-Gault, dressing well those first days at UGA had an added significance, serving as her personal "armor" that helped preserve her self-respect and "deflected such things as being called 'nigger'" by the crudest members of UGA's segregationist student body.

Hunter-Gault was affectionate toward UGA, making it clear that this was a university that—despite all the travail—had helped to shape her, that she had no regrets that she and Hamilton had made UGA their place too and in the process brought down the color line that had for too long closed UGA to African Americans. She expressed the hope that UGA would do more to make a reality of the egalitarian vision that had led her and Holmes to the Athens campus in 1961, adding that the racism she and Holmes had faced in 1961 had not gone extinct, and that UGA still had its work cut out for it if it was to become a truly integrated university, as she and Holmes had envisioned. Among the most powerful lines in her speech, quoted earlier in this study, was where she asserted that if back in 1961 "anyone had given Hamp and me a crystal ball in which we could have looked to the future forty years hence, and see only six percent [African American] ... students in a student body of 34,000 I think instead of walking through that [historic] Arch [at UGA's entrance] we might have sat down and cried." As she had done back in 1988 as UGA's first African American commencement speaker, Hunter-Gault had used the university's podium and her celebrity status to go beyond nostalgia and to push the university toward a deeper commitment to racial inclusiveness.

The most fitting tribute to UGA's desegregation, however, may not have been such memorable remarks of these veterans of that tumultuous time, but the protests mounted by a new generation of UGA students eager to implement the egalitarian vision of *Brown*, Hunter-Gault, and Baker Motley. This group of UGA diversity activists had delayed holding a demonstration until after the fortieth so as not to disrupt the events honoring Holmes and Hunter and the ending of UGA's color line in 1961. But less than twenty-four hours after the commemorative events, the protesters held a press conference expressing "their dissatisfaction with the University's current diversity, citing its 6 percent black enrollment." The student protesters dressed in black, "which they said symbolized both respect for the desegregation anniversary and dissatisfaction with the University's current commitment to diversity." Their spokesperson charged that "the administration here does not address our needs and concerns and does not make us feel welcome." The students made six demands, which they had "also circulated at Tuesday's anniversary events," among them the establishment of "an office and staff and infrastructure devoted solely to recruit and retain minority students."[15]

UGA's vice president for student affairs Richard Mullendore criticized the protest and said he was "disappointed" at its timing. It's "really a shame to see anything detract from what's been happening this week," namely the fortieth anniversary commemoration.[16] To the contrary, the students' demonstration detracted from nothing. Their protest shared the same democratic goals and criticisms of UGA that Hunter-Gault, Baker Motley, and Daniels had articulated in the commemoration itself. The protesters were, through their activism, affirming that the desegregation struggle is not a museum piece and is not over. It lives and breathes in all who work still for a more inclusive university.

THE ONE CONTROVERSY CONNECTED to the fortieth anniversary commemoration of UGA's desegregation concerned not what was said or done at that event but the poster used to promote the commemoration. The photo featured in the poster aroused criticism on campus because it seemed an exercise in avoidance; it showed Hunter and Holmes in a car near the campus entrance on their historic first day at UGA but obscured the hostile crowd of white students who chanted ugly racist epithets and made plain their resistance to desegregation. Some charged that the poster's photo had been doctored to sugarcoat this historic moment. It is true that the white crowd gathered near the university's entrance, by UGA's historic arch, appeared way off in the corner of the photo, and its image was so blurred that it seemed intentionally smudged.[17]

It turned out that Rick Fiala, who designed the poster for the university, had indeed intentionally doctored the photo. Denying any political motivation, he said he had decided to use what he termed the "'motion blur' technique to create a dramatic atmosphere."[18] It is unclear, however, how blurring the crowd of white students who opposed desegregation would make the photo of Holmes and Hunter more dramatic, solely spotlighting their image. One could well argue that to the contrary, it was the presence of those white students that made the early moments of integration, captured in the original photo, especially dramatic since their hostility was the key source of tension and even danger for Holmes and Hunter. Whether or not Fiala was aware of it, his blurring of the crowd in obscuring this tension and danger had, as UGA journalism professor Conrad Fink explained to a *Red and Black* reporter in December 2000, perpetrated "a distortion of history.... This photo has been changed so that the meaning is substantially altered."[19]

Fiala denied that he had blurred the crowd to avoid embarrassing the white alums who had been in that assemblage and who might be upset if they could have been identified in that photo as those resisting integration. The UGA administrator who commissioned the photo work for the poster and admired the result of its doctoring, echoed Fiala, arguing that "we didn't alter" the photo "to cover up the issues involved."[20] But, in fact, the blurring of the crowd accomplished just such a cover-up. Indeed, this obscuring of the segregationist crowd, and the endorsement of that blurring by a university official, brings back memories of another case of UGA hiding the identities of its alumni expressing racist ideas. That occasion involved not a photo but the Math 254 essays written by UGA students in mid-January 1961 that I quoted and discussed in my *Georgia Historical Quarterly* article in 1996 (reprinted as chapter 2). After that article was published, I learned from subsequent researchers that the names, and even the initials, of those essays' authors were no longer accessible, that UGA's archives made the essays available only with their authors' names and initials removed.[21] Perhaps, then, a privacy concern or even a subconscious desire not to embarrass alumni with their reactionary past played some role in the removal of both the names from the essays and the identifiable white students' images from the photo. And it could be that for UGA officials blurring the memory of segregationist students, with their mean and hateful acts, seemed a way of turning the page on the racist past, aligning best with their approach to the desegregation commemoration as an upbeat occasion centered on Holmes and Hunter's history-making obliteration of UGA's color line.

Even if we accept Fiala's claim that the crowd image itself was altered not on political but aesthetic grounds to spotlight Holmes and Hunter, the critics still have a point since the selection of this particular photo for use in the poster resulted in hiding UGA student racism. After all, there are many historical photos from that day of UGA's integration in January 1961 (as well as the next week) that clearly show Hunter and Holmes walking near or driving away from hostile white student crowds whose most rowdy members are not on the outer fringe but rather at or near the center of the photographic image. Yet none of those were selected for the poster. Here again there was an unwillingness to focus on the racist past and a choice to accentuate the positive instead, the birth of a new and multiracial university, owing to the heroism of Holmes and Hunter.

To place this photographic choice into context we have only to compare it with the UGA photos Charlayne Hunter-Gault selected and published in her memoir, *In My Place*. All three photos she used documenting her first day at UGA included crowd shots, and two of them featured captions that conveyed the crowd's racial hostility. These included the chilling Associated Press photo of a white female student, mouth wide open, taunting Charlayne as she walked on campus, while a male student, cracking a wide smile, is depicted looking at that white girl, enjoying the way she was tormenting Hunter. Hunter-Gault captioned this photo, "As students called out 'Nigger go home' and a variety of other unoriginal taunts, I found myself more bemused than angry or upset." Another photo included in her memoir depicted Hunter and Holmes in Dean Tate's car, surrounded by a large group of unsmiling UGA students. This photo Hunter-Gault captioned, "As we focused our attention elsewhere during registration, a boisterous crowd advanced on Dean William Tate's car, but the Dean routed them and prevailed."

The photographic documentation Hunter-Gault's memoir provided of UGA student racism and resistance to integration was not confined, however, to that day when she first came to campus. She also included a shot of a nighttime anti-integration demonstration by UGA students wielding a Confederate battle flag in downtown Athens. Even more disturbing was the photo in her memoir of segregationist rioters holding aloft their "Nigger Go Home" banner—with the caption attesting that in Hunter's first two nights at UGA she was "serenaded" by students chanting those same words on that banner, words about which Hunter-Gault recalled, "I had a hard time relating to myself."[22] There was also a photo of the tear gas clouds from the riot outside her dormitory and a shot of her in the patrol car about to leave UGA after she was suspended following the riot. Clearly, then, the very thing that the fortieth anniversary poster photo obscured, Hunter-Gault was emphasizing in her photo selection: the vocal racism of many in the UGA student body in 1961.

In fairness, it needs to be acknowledged that the brief documentary film screened at the fortieth anniversary commemoration did offer a candid account of that racism and the riot as well. But it is also true that the poster, as the public face of the commemoration, reached many more people than attended and saw the film. That less-than-candid poster embodies a continuing feature of white historical memory and amnesia in Georgia (and beyond), a reluctance to discuss and confront the state and its university's grim racist past. This was the same reluctance—as we saw in the introduction to this book—that I encountered from alumni and senior faculty as I researched and presented my findings on that past back in the 1990s. More recently, I again encountered this reluctance to engage with UGA's troubled past when the editor of a major Georgia publisher wrote me that the prospect of publishing the book you now hold in your hands left him with a sense of "trepidation," which is why this book on Georgia's racist history could not be published in Georgia.

This same reluctance was equally evident in 2011, when the fiftieth anniversary commemoration of UGA's desegregation was promoted via a poster that featured six photos, none of which showed racist white students rallying, taunting, or rioting. All six were close-ups, first from their student days, and then from middle age, of Holmes, Hunter, and Early. The title and theme of the commemoration and its poster was "Celebrating Courage: The Fiftieth Anniversary of the Desegregation of the University of Georgia." The poster beckoned, "Meet Some of the Pioneers Who Broke the Color Barrier at the University of Georgia and Those Who Supported Them!" As to why it took courage to desegregate the university, the poster and its photos offer not a clue.[23]

This white Georgian inclination to avoid focusing on the racist past seems even more intractable now that the state's Republican governor and right wing–dominated legislature—with their Orwellian-named Protect Students

First Act— have outlawed teaching about that past in public schools on the grounds that it is divisive.

The Black Freedom movement's anthem and rallying cry, "We Shall Overcome," means more, far more, when we take a good hard look at the racist resistance to democratic change and are actually able to understand what it was that needed to be overcome back in the Jim Crow era and what still needs to be overcome today.

The issue here is much bigger than a poster or an approach to publicity. It is about how we learn about the past and whether we are willing to confront our long history of racism. Maybe it is easier to reflect upon such questions by thinking about them in a non-US context. If one were to design a process to de-Nazi Germany after World War II, that obviously could not be done merely by celebrating the Allied victory and the liberation of the death camps. Those victories and liberation are, of course, worth celebrating, but the deepest and most troubling questions are those associated with probing how a murderous regime fueled by bigotry could come to power in the first place. Similarly, while it is important to recognize and commemorate those who brought down the color line, that cannot by itself bring about our own counterpart to de-Nazification, which requires understanding why white supremacy for so long dominated the history of Georgia and UGA, why white supremacy endures, why Georgia (along with other red states) has been fleeing from probing its racist history, and why the state has recently banned the teaching of that history in its public schools. With white nationalism and white supremacist violence surging in twenty-first-century America, a reckoning with the history and legacy of Jim Crow seems both essential and long overdue. It is my hope that this book will help to foster such a reckoning.

REGARDING THE FUTURE OF EFFORTS to advance UGA's desegregation process and to overcome Georgia's legacy of racial inequality, the most important remarks at the fortieth anniversary commemoration of the university's integration were offered by Charlayne Hunter-Gault. In her keynote speech she alluded briefly to the struggle to preserve affirmative action; this was a matter of real significance since affirmative action had become pivotal to the incremental gains in Black student admissions at UGA. But by 2001 affirmative action had been under assault for years across the nation by wealthy conservative foundations that funded attacks upon it via voter propositions, court cases, and other means. Hunter-Gault sounded optimistic about the resistance to these attacks, noting how impressed she was that, in contrast to the Jim Crow era when top officials in the Georgia state government pledged themselves to massive resistance against the *Brown* decision's school integration mandate, there seemed to be bipartisan support for the defense of affirmative action among Georgia's political leaders.

Though Hunter-Gault did not mention it in her speech, what pushed her to comment on the threat to affirmative action was the recent US district court decision in the case of *Johnson v. Board of Regents of the University System of Georgia* (2000). This case involved three rejected white female applicants who claimed that the university's affirmative action policies, designed to increase Black student enrollments, had discriminated against them. The district court sided with these white plaintiffs, ruling that UGA's use of affirmative action was unconstitutional.[24] Even a glance at the enrollment statistics for UGA the year of this decision attests that whatever its legal rationale, the court had lost touch with political reality in fretting over discrimination against white applicants: 26,354 UGA students identified as white, dwarfing the university's 1,818 Black student population in 2000.[25]

Hunter-Gault's remarks about the defense of affirmative action in Georgia would prove too optimistic. No bipartisan coalition to defend affirmative action would emerge in Georgia politics. It is true, however, that the UGA administration appealed the *Johnson* case to the Eleventh Circuit Court of Appeals. But when that court too ruled in August 2001 against the university, UGA simply gave up its defense of affirmative action. In contrast to 1961 when UGA took its opposition to integration all the way to the Supreme Court, in 2001 UGA failed to take its defense of affirmative action to the high court, offering no appeal of the circuit court ruling. On the other hand, it is worth noting that in contrast to the Jim Crow era, when the district court was way to the left of UGA, ordering the university to integrate in 1961, by 2000 the UGA administration was more progressive on race than was the district court, battling to use racial preferences to enhance Black admissions in a court that rejected them. And when the circuit court tossed out UGA's use of affirmative action, the university's representatives publicly criticizing the court's ruling included an administrator that in the Jim Crow era would not even have been imaginable: Vanessa Smith, an African American, who served as the associate director of UGA's Office of Minority Programs. Smith viewed this verdict as one in which the court was "telling us that diversity is not important." She pointed out that the lawsuit itself had had a chilling effect on Black student recruitment (there had been a 19-percent decline in Black freshmen in the aftermath of the lawsuit).[26] "Frankly," Smith observed,

"I think the lawsuit has hurt us.... I think the students and lawyers of the lawsuit may have failed to see the struggles and strides for minority students to get here in the first place."[27]

The setback the courts visited upon UGA's minority recruitment work more than two decades ago was just one of many precursors to the conservative-dominated Supreme Court's recent decision, *Students for Fair Admissions Inc. v. President and Fellows of Harvard College and the University of North Carolina* (2023), outlawing affirmative action in all US college and university admissions. Since only one of the six justices who voted for this decision was a Southerner, it is evident that this undermining of Black college recruitment is a product of a national and not merely a Southern movement. At its heart this is a movement fueled by white resentment of the very idea of racial preferences designed to benefit African Americans. Whether expressed crudely by the bigoted UGA students interviewed and quoted in my classes in the 1990s or dressed up in fancy legal jargon by Supreme Court justices this year, the impulse is the same. In both cases the white majoritarian logic insists that the rights of non-Black college applicants must not be abridged by admissions programs that seek to compensate African Americans for decades, even centuries, of anti-Black discrimination in higher education. After treating Blacks for so long as a group to be excluded—as a pariah caste—by racially discriminatory universities, these same universities are now barred from treating Blacks as a group for the purpose of compensating for all those years of discrimination. To reinforce this point, the conservative majority, citing the late justice Lewis Powell's words from the first major anti–affirmative action decision by the high court (*Bakke v. Regents of the University of California* (1978), argued that "permitting past societal discrimination to serve as the basis for rigid racial preferences" was unconstitutional since as a result of such preferences, "the dream of a nation of equal citizens would be lost."[28]

Putting aside for the moment the irony (not mentioned by the court) of citing Powell in a case involving racial integration, when prior to his years as a justice he helped lead Richmond, Virginia's, efforts to evade the *Brown* decision's school integration mandate, we must ask, to use the majority's own phrase, what happens to "the dream of a nation of equal citizens" in a nation whose Black population is so grievously underrepresented in its leading universities and colleges? How does the Supreme Court propose to change the kind of situation we still see in Georgia, where only 7.5 percent of UGA's student population is Black in a state where some 30 percent of its residents are African American? The court offers no answer. How could it, after outlawing the most direct means of battling such underrepresentation and constraining redress for the sake of the conservative delusion that the United States has a "color blind Constitution"?

If readers of *Confronting Jim Crow* examine the court documents from the *Students for Fair Admissions* case, they will notice that it is not the ruling of the conservative majority but the dissents of the liberal minority that are the most candid on the history and legacy of racial discrimination at the university, and closely aligned with my own findings about UGA. This is particularly striking in the segment of justice Sonia Sotomayor's dissent that discusses the University of North Carolina (UNC)—which along with Harvard was one of the two universities whose use of affirmative action in their admissions process was being challenged and would be found unconstitutional in this court case—since UNC, like UGA, is a Southern campus still struggling to overcome the legacy of its Jim Crow past. Sotomayor's dissent explains that "to this day UNC's deep seated legacy of racial discrimination continues to manifest itself in student life. Buildings on campus still bear the names of members of the Ku Klux Klan and other white supremacist leaders.... Students of color also continue to experience racial harassment, isolation, and tokenism. Plus the student body remains predominantly white: approximately 72% of the student body identify as white, while only 8% identify as Black. These numbers do not reflect the diversity of the state, particularly Black North Carolinians who make up 22% of the population."[29] For Sotomayor such data constitutes powerful evidence of the persistence of the racial inequity and injustice that affirmative action was designed to help overcome. Rejecting the claim of the conservative majority that color blindness is somehow a path to equality, she concludes that "entrenched racial inequality remains a reality today. That is true for society writ large, and more specifically for Harvard and the University of North Carolina, two institutions with a long history of racial exclusion. Ignoring race will not equalize a society that is racially unequal. What was true in the 1860s and again in 1954 is true today. Equality requires acknowledgment of inequality."[30]

While Sotomayor and the dissenting minority urge us to confront the legacy of Jim Crow, as I have in the pages of this study, the conservative majority of the court chooses to evade such a confrontation with racial reality. Much like red state America, whose political power produced that majority, the Supreme Court retreats from pursuit of justice and equity where the rights of Black Americans are concerned. This impulse to retreat and evade is so strong that in states such as Georgia, bound by its recent legislation barring critical discussion of race from its public schools—and where teachers have been fired for merely using children's books deemed divisive by repressive school authorities—public school teachers will almost certainly be barred even from teaching about Justice Sotomayor's dissent (if they have the courage to do so).[31] A large part of our nation is clearly not in a place where it can grapple with Sotomayor's dissent, the evidence in this book, or the justice's compelling conclusion that racial "equality requires acknowledgment of inequality." All this just makes W. E. B. Du Bois's words about the previous century seem prophetic for our own, that the problem of the twenty-first century "is the problem of the color line."

Acknowledgments

This book would not have been possible without the assistance of the University of Georgia's talented and diligent archivists who gave me access to crucial historical sources. My thanks to Jill Severn and Ashton G. Ellet of the Russell Library and Mary Palmer Liennemann of the Hargrett Rare Book and Manuscript Library. The Hargrett's Black Alumni Oral History Project, overseen by Steven G. Armour, is a great gift to researchers of the African American experience at UGA, and my thanks to all who served as interviewers and interviewees for that project. I am grateful to Black Student Union veteran Alvin Levert Hood for encouraging me in this study and granting permission to reprint his powerful letter demanding that UGA stop having the Old South anthem "Dixie" played at campus events.

My research on UGA's troubled history of race, as discussed in the introduction, began back in the 1990s when I was a UGA faculty member. Sadly, some of those who did the most to inspire the research that led to this book have passed, but their words and spirit are as vivid to me now as when I first encountered them almost thirty years ago. The late William S. McFeely made a huge difference in my work. Bill made generous use of funds from his endowed chair to fund a memorable conference at UGA on the Black Freedom movement's impact on small towns. That conference brought me into contact with a number of veterans of the UGA desegregation struggle, who were an inspiration, including the late Donald Hollowell and the late judge Horace T. Ward. One of my most pleasurable tasks in helping with that conference was to drive Donald Hollowell from his home in Atlanta to Athens. I learned more on that drive about the struggle against Jim Crow than I did in any graduate seminar. Somehow Mr. Hollowell managed to cover a huge amount of history, while also breaking off to tell stories that charmed my four-year-old son when he was getting bored with the long drive.

Similarly, Judge Ward was remarkably insightful about the struggle for racial justice, both in his remarks at the conference and in our conversations and correspondence that followed. Ward displayed such an evidence-based approach to history (including his own—he asked, and I sent him documents I had been reading on the UGA faculty committee that so rudely and unfairly interrogated him to justify UGA's refusal to admit him), and was so deeply analytical about his case that my first thought was that he had the historical sensibility of a top historian, but then it occurred to me that these were the same qualities of a fine judge, which he clearly was. The injustice he had suffered at the hands of the university at which I worked could never seem an abstraction after meeting Judge Ward.

I am grateful too to the late Thomas G. Dyer, the first historian of UGA (and author of its bicentennial history) to include a chapter on its desegregation, and who as a member of the university administration pushed hard to address the shameful underrepresentation of Blacks on UGA's faculty. Tom, as a colleague, friend, and neighbor, encouraged my work on UGA's history and generously shared his correspondence and memories of the struggle for a more inclusive university. The late John C. Belcher's oral histories of UGA's integration crisis were of enormous value to this study, as were the insights of the late Thomas Brahana and Horace Montgomery in my oral history interviews with them.

Other friends and colleagues at UGA who facilitated my work on UGA's history include Robert A. Pratt and Maurice C. Daniels, whose books on the struggle to desegregate the university are of enduring value, as are the documentary films Maurice Daniels produced on this history. I am also grateful to them and Derrick Alridge (now of the University of Virginia) for their fine work in helping to organize the commemorations of UGA's desegregation in our own century.

It was through one of those commemorations—the fiftieth in which I was a panelist—that (thanks in part to a freak snowstorm that stranded us at the Georgia Center) I had the chance to meet and interview Charlayne Hunter-Gault, whose brilliant writings on UGA have meant so much to me. I am grateful to Charlayne for sharing her memories of the history she and the late Walter Stovall made in defying Jim Crow bigotry in their marriage, and for connecting me with Walter, who, in a moving and profound oral history interview schooled me in his very personal and very critical view of both UGA and the parochial world of white Georgia in the Jim Crow era. This book is dedicated to the memory of Walter Stovall and to all those who, like Walter, dare to publicly reject racism. My thanks as well to Lynn Stovall Cass and Mary Frances Early for sharing their memories of Georgia's response to interracial dating and marriage in 1963.

It was through the fiftieth anniversary commemoration that I met Calvin "Bud" Trillin, whose pioneering history of UGA's integration introduced me to this subject and to the university itself. Thanks to Bud and his willingness to speak every year to my NYU classes in our shared Greenwich Village neighborhood, and to do so a number of times with Charlayne, I along with my students have been able to keep learning about UGA's history even while hundreds of miles away from Georgia.

Early in my UGA years I attended a talk given by Hamilton Holmes. His words on behalf of equal opportunity and education were powerful, and, in a manner that is hard to describe, Holmes radiated integrity and intelligence. I came away from the talk deeply impressed but troubled by the fact that I did not see a single white student in the audience. This combination of Holmes's eloquence and the white absence was a striking example of what we lose educationally as a university when students self-segregate, and this experience in its own way helped pave the way for this book.

As explained in the introduction, the work on slavery at UGA by Chana Kai Lee and Scott Nesbit offers a model for the kind of critical history of the university and race that has been of great influence on me. And I am grateful to them for their scholarship and courage, and to Chana for her kindness and encouragement.

Crucial support for my work on Georgia history has come from John Inscoe. John encouraged me and edited my first articles on UGA's desegregation back in the 1990s and has been a critical reader of my work—including the first draft of this study—and a great friend ever since. His work as editor of the *Georgia Historical Quarterly* was an inspiration to me and generations of historians who were taking a good hard look at the way race, class, and gender was actually lived in the "Peach State."

At a time when right wing political leaders have been trying to ban, distort, or sugarcoat the history of racism in the United States, I am grateful to my friends and colleagues who have stood up for free speech, academic freedom, and honest, critical history. These include Eric Foner of Columbia University; Bill Bigelow and Deborah Menkart of the Zinn Education Project; Vann Gosse and his colleagues at Historians for Peace and Democracy; Stacie Brensilver Berman, Diana Turk, Cynthia Copeland, and Michele Mitchell of NYU; Sonia Murrow of Brooklyn College; Janine Drake Giordano of Indiana University; and Jon Zimmerman of the University of Pennsylvania. Their work has helped inspire my own. A special thanks to my students at UGA for your honesty and trust in sharing your perspectives and experience with race in Georgia.

There is, as mentioned in the preface, a Berkeley connection to this study. My teacher, the late Leon Litwack, in his brilliant lectures and books and in our private conversations, sparked my interest in African American and Southern history. And so did the late Mario Savio, both through his activism and our oral history interview and conversations many years ago.

I am deeply grateful to Andrew Winters of the University of North Carolina Press for his faith in this project as well as the wise advice he so generously shared, and to the board of the press for taking on so critical a history of race at a time when such history has become ridiculously controversial. My thanks to Bettina Aptheker of UC Santa Cruz for her critical reading of the introduction and her encouragement and friendship, and to Olga Margolina for her fine work on the book's illustrations. And to Alrick Brown and Emilie Clark for their friendship and helpful advice on the images used in this book.

Special thanks to Joy Ann Williamson-Lott, for her friendship and her path-breaking work on academic freedom, free speech, and student politics in the Jim Crow South, which helped make this book possible.

My wife Rebecca Hyman, my son, Daniel, and my daughter-in-law, Lucia Hsiao, helped make this work possible, and so much more.

Notes

Author's Note on Derogatory Language

1. Sara Pauff, "NAACP: Quote Needs Explanation," *Red and Black*, Feb. 16, 2005.
2. Sara Pauff, "Hunter-Gault: Keep Epithet," *Red and Black*, Feb. 10, 2005.
3. Charlayne Hunter-Gault, "Slur Is an Integral Part of History," *Red and Black*, Feb. 10, 2005.
4. Grayson Irvin, "Hunter-Gault Responds to NAACP," *Red and Black*, Feb. 21, 2005.

Preface

1. I am using the dictionary definition of "antiracist" as one who opposes racism and advocates racial equality.
2. Sidna Brower Mitchell, "A Student Editor Calls for Calm," in *James Meredith Breaking the Barrier: Celebrating the 60th Anniversary of James Meredith's Enrollment at the University of Mississippi*, ed. Kathleen W. Wickham (Oxford: Yoknapatawpha Press, 2022), 77–85.
3. Mitchell, "Student Editor," 85.
4. Mitchell, 82.
5. Mitchell, 83.
6. Mitchell, 85.
7. Edward E. Meek, *Riot: Witness to Anger and Change* (Oxford: Yoknapatawpha Press, 2015), 1, 7.
8. Meek, *Riot*, 7.
9. Meek, 2.
10. Meek, 4.
11. Charles Eagles, *The Price of Defiance: James Meredith and the Integration of Ole Miss* (Chapel Hill: University of North Carolina Press, 2009), 362.
12. Trent Lott, *Herding Cats: A Life in Politics* (New York: Regan Books, 2005), 29.
13. James W. Silver, *Mississippi: The Closed Society* (New York: Houghton Mifflin, 1964; reprint, Jackson: University of Mississippi Press, 2012), vii.
14. Lott, *Herding Cats*, 42.
15. Eagles, *Price of Defiance*, 366.
16. Robert Cohen, "Politicians Dictating What Teachers Can Say about Racism Can Be Dangerous," *Washington Post*, Feb. 3, 2022, www.washingtonpost.com/outlook/2022/02/03/politicians-dictating-what-teachers-can-say-about-racism-can-be-dangerous/.

Introduction

1. Richard Fausset, "What Donald Trump Didn't Count on in Georgia," *New York Times*, May 22, 2022, www.nytimes.com/2022/05/22/us/what-donald-trump-didnt-count-on-in-georgia.html.

2. Tina Burnside and Devan Cole, "Georgia Gov. Kemp Signs Bill into Law That Limits Discussion of Race in the Classroom," CNN, Apr. 28, 2022.

3. Jennifer Brett, "'Solid' Republican Brian Kemp Plays Up Rural Roots and Business Bonafides," *Atlanta Journal Constitution*, Oct. 12, 2018, www.ajc.com/news/solid-republican-brian-kemp-plays-up-rural-roots-business-bonafides/OTAH07LgnwgnnwKQG2CyFI/.

4. "The Baldwin Hall Controversy," UGA & Slavery, eHistory, https://slavery.ehistory.org/baldwin-hall. Accessed May 20, 2023.

5. Calvin Trillin, *An Education in Georgia: Charlayne Hunter, Hamilton Holmes, and the Integration of the University of Georgia* (1964; reprint, Athens: University of Georgia Press, 1992), 40.

6. Trillin, *Education in Georgia*, 40.

7. Holmes v. Danner, 191 F. Supp. 394 (M.D., Ga, 1961).

8. Georgia in 2019 passed a law "prohibiting state and local agencies from renaming any building named for a 'historical entity.'" In 2021 the regents of the University System of Georgia translated this law into official university policy, perpetuating the university's traditional naming pattern in which segregationists and slave owners had buildings that carried their names. See Nick Anderson and Susan Svrluga, "University System of Georgia to Keep Names on Buildings with Ties to Slavery and White Supremacy," *Washington Post*, Nov. 22, 2021, www.washingtonpost.com/education/2021/11/22/university-system-georgia-building-names-white-supremacy/; Jeff Amy, "Georgia Regents to Not Rename Buildings Associated with Slavery, Segregation," Associated Press, Nov. 23, 2021, www.fox5atlanta.com/news/georgia-regents-to-not-rename-buildings-associated-with-slavery-segregation.

9. For a striking example of the rich historical discussion that can be generated by a building name changing initiative, see Patricia Nelson Limerick, *What's in a Name? Nichols Hall: A Report* (Center for the American West, University of Colorado, Boulder, 1987).

10. "Prank, Riot, and Shock on Georgia Campus," *Life*, Jan. 20, 1961, 24. This picture is reprinted in the photo gallery of this book.

11. Robert Dince interview with John C. Belcher, June 6, 1975, Charlayne Hunter-Gault Papers, Richard B. Russell Library, UGA. Dince, a professor of business administration, also recalled in this same interview that having caught sight of this student with his lynched Black puppet from his office window, he rushed outside and "grabbed the student, demanding to know his name, which he refused to give me. Then I pushed the student down to the ground and knocked the doll away, and I said 'Don't be such a goddamned fool.' The student cursed at me, and said 'We're going to get you for that, you fat bastard.'"

12. I did not know that this second photo existed until an editor at *Time* dug it up in the Time-Life photo collection and ran it in 2015 with my article comparing the University of Oklahoma's racist fraternity scandal that year with similar racist behavior at UGA in 1961. See Robert Cohen, "The Historical Roots of Fraternity Racism," *Time*, Mar. 12, 2015, https://time.com/3742109/history-fraternity-racism/.

13. Cohen, "Historical Roots."

14. Cohen, "Historical Roots," History News Network, https://historynewsnetwork.org/article/158761; also see Tracy Clayton, "A Black Girl's History with Southern Frat Racism," www.buzzfeednews.com/article/tracyclayton/a-black-girls-history-with-southern-frat-racism; Amy Harmon, "Fraternity That Reveres Robert E. Lee Revolt over Racism," *New York Times*, www.nytimes.com/2020/10/19/us/kappa-alpha-robert-e-lee.html.

15. "NAACP Wants U. Ga.'s Knapp to Suspend Frat," *Athens Daily News*, Oct. 8, 1992.

16. Robert Cohen, "Driving Jim Crow off Frat Row: The Struggle against Discrimination in UC Berkeley's Fraternities and Sororities, 1946–1967," unpublished paper, 1987, in author's possession.

17. Robert Cohen to Charles Knapp, Sept. 30, 1992, copy in author's possession.

18. Cohen to Knapp.

19. Cohen to Knapp; on racial segregation in UGA's fraternity system, see Russ Bynum and Theresa Walsh, "Slur Spurs Reactions to Racial Split of Greeks," *Red and Black*, Sept. 29, 1992.

20. Cohen to Knapp.

21. Cohen to Knapp.

22. Charles Knapp to Robert Cohen, Oct. 8, 1992, copy in author's possession.

23. Cohen, "Driving Jim Crow."

24. After the author of the pledge pamphlet was asked by a fraternity interview committee composed of two members of the fraternity's administrative office and fifteen alumni of the fraternity chapter to leave Pi Kappa Phi, he resigned from the organization. But rather than suspend the fraternity itself, Pi Kappa Phi got off with a slap on the wrist, as an oversight committee staffed by six alumni of the fraternity was formed and would meet every three weeks to oversee the fraternity chapter's activities. See Russ Bynum, "Author of Racist Remark Resigns from Frat," *Red and Black*, Sept. 29, 1992; Russ Bynum, "Black Frats Question Pi Kappa's Apology," *Red and Black*, Sept. 30, 1992.

25. Bryan Pietsch, "Fraternity at University of Georgia Is Suspended After Racist Messages Are Exposed," *New York Times*, Sept. 22, 2020.

26. On this Klan–outside agitator argument and the actual KKK role in the riot see the evidence from the FBI investigation of the riot in chapter 3.

27. On the student role in leading the riot, see the discussion of the FBI investigation of the riot in chapter 3.

28. Charles Payne, *I've Got the Light of Freedom: The Organizing Tradition and the Mississippi Freedom Movement* (Berkeley: University of California Press, 2007), 418–19.

29. Frank Redwine III to Robert Cohen, Feb. 20, 1998, copy in author's possession.

30. Robert Cohen to Frank Redwine III, Mar. 2, 1998, copy in author's possession.

31. Cathryn Stout and Thomas Wilburn, "CRT Map: Efforts to Restrict Teaching Racism and Bias Have Multiplied Across the US," *Chalkbeat*, Feb. 1, 2022, www.chalkbeat.org/22525983/map-critical-race-theory-legislation-teaching-racism.

32. This cartoon was by the *Baltimore Sun*'s famed cartoonist Richard Q. Yardley. It was published in the *Baltimore Sun* on Jan. 13, 1961, and reprinted in Robert Cohen, "'Two, Four, Six, Eight, We Don't Want to Integrate': White Student Attitudes toward the University of Georgia's Desegregation," *Georgia Historical Quarterly* 80, no. 3 (Fall 1996), 641. It is reprinted in the photo section of this book.

33. Robert D. Heslep to Dean Russell Yeany, Feb. 13, 1998, copy in author's possession.

34. Heslep to Yeany. Yeany responded to this complaint by acknowledging that Heslep was "entitled" to his "opinion and perspective on any academic issue" but that he thought Heslep had overreacted in his "action to resign" from the multicultural task force. The dean also wrote that "the issues you raised should have been discussed with Professor Cohen," and "I still encourage you to discuss the issue directly with Robby," which he never did. (Russell H. Yeany to Robert D. Heslep, Feb. 20, 1998, copy in author's possession).

35. Robert Cohen to Dean Russell Yeany, Feb. 18, 1998, copy in author's possession.
36. Cohen to Yeany.
37. Phil Campbell interview with the author, May 29, 1997.
38. Campbell interview.
39. J. A. Williams, UGA dean of students, to O. C. Aderhold, Jan. 24, 1961, President O. C. Aderhold Papers, University Archives, Hargrett Rare Book and Manuscript Library, University of Georgia Libraries.
40. On the University of Alabama's resistance to integration, see E. Culpepper Clark, *The Schoolhouse Door: Segregation's Last Stand at the University of Alabama* (New York: Oxford University Press, 1993). On the University of Mississippi's resistance to integration, see Charles W. Eagles, *The Price of Defiance: James Meredith and the Integration of Ole Miss* (Chapel Hill: University of North Carolina Press, 2009).
41. Calvin Trillin, *Education in Georgia*; Robert A. Pratt, *We Shall Not Be Moved: The Desegregation of the University of Georgia* (Athens: University of Georgia Press, 2002); Maurice C. Daniels, *Horace T. Ward: Desegregation of the University of Georgia, Civil Rights Advocacy, and Jurisprudence* (Atlanta: Clark Atlanta University Press, 2001); Maurice C. Daniels, *Saving the Soul of Georgia: Donald L. Hollowell and the Struggle for Civil Rights* (Athens: University of Georgia Press, 2013); Charlayne Hunter-Gault, *In My Place* (New York: Farrar, Straus and Giroux, 1992); Mary Frances Early, *The Quiet Trailblazer: My Journey as the First Black Graduate of the University of Georgia* (Athens: University of Georgia Press, 2021).
42. Foot Soldier Project documentary films produced by Maurice Daniels: *Hamilton Earl Holmes: The Legacy Continues* (2004); *Foot Soldier for Equal Justice: Donald Hollowell* (2012).
43. "Holmes/Hunter Academic Building," Historical Marker Database, revised July 16, 2018, www.hmdb.org/m.asp?m=11699; and Heather Skyler, "UGA College of Education Named for Mary Frances Early," Feb. 26, 2020, https://news.uga.edu/college-education-named-for-mary-frances-early/.
44. William Anderson, *The Wild Man from Sugar Creek: The Political Career of Eugene Talmadge* (Baton Rouge: Louisiana State University Press, 1975), 10–12, 21–23, 205, 210; Scott E. Buchanan, "Herman Talmadge, 1913–2002," *New Georgia Encyclopedia*, updated Aug. 14, 2020, www.georgiaencyclopedia.org/articles/arts-culture/herman-talmadge-1913-2002/; Herman Talmadge, *You and Segregation* (Birmingham, AL: Vulcan Press, 1955); Christopher Allen Huff, "Roy V. Harris: 1895–1985," *New Georgia Encyclopedia*, updated Apr. 14, 2021, www.georgiaencyclopedia.org/articles/history-archaeology/roy-v-harris-1895-1985/; Gilbert C. Fite, *Richard B. Russell Jr., Senator from Georgia* (Chapel Hill: University of North Carolina Press, 1991), 74–75, 145, 229–32, 416, 428; and John Kyle Day, *The Southern Manifesto: Massive Resistance and the Fight to Preserve Segregation* (Jackson: University of Mississippi Press, 2015), 82–96.
45. John David Smith and John C. Inscoe, eds., *Ulrich Bonnell Phillips: A Southern Historian and His Critics* (Athens: University of Georgia Press, 1990), 1–14.
46. Fred Arthur Bailey, "E. Merton Coulter, the *Georgia Historical Quarterly*, and the Struggle over Southern History," *Georgia Historical Quarterly* 101, no. 3 (2017): 176–97.
47. Leslie M. Harris, James T. Campbell, and Alfred L. Brophy, eds., *Slavery and the University: Histories and Legacies* (Athens: University of Georgia Press, 2019).
48. Harris, Campbell, and Brophy, *Slavery and the University*, 1–10; *President's Commission on Slavery and the University* (Charlottesville: University of Virginia, 2018), 15–16, 25–28,

https://slavery.virginia.edu/wp-content/uploads/2021/03/PCSU-Report-FINAL_July-2018.pdf. Accessed January 19, 2024; Louis P. Nelson and James Zahmer, "Slavery and Construction," in *Educated in Tyranny: Slavery at Thomas Jefferson's University*, eds. Maurie D. McInnis and Louis P. Nelson, (Charlottesville: University of Virgina Press, 2019), 27–41.

49. In Thomas Dyer's otherwise insightful bicentennial history of the University of Georgia, for example, slavery is mentioned very briefly and on only five pages. See Thomas G. Dyer, *The University of Georgia: A Bicentennial History, 1785–1985* (Athens: University of Georgia Press, 1985), 63, 64–65, 109–10.

50. Alfred L. Brophy, "Pro-Slavery Political Thought in the Southern Academy, 1832–1861," in *Slavery and the University: Histories and Legacies*, eds. Leslie M. Harris, et. al. (Athens: University of Georgia Press), 65–83.

51. Robert Mickey, *Paths Out of Dixie: The Democratization of Authoritarian Enclaves in America's Deep South* (Princeton, NJ: Princeton University Press, 2015); Kimberly Johnson, review of *Paths Out of Dixie: The Democratization of Authoritarian Enclaves in America's Deep South, 1944–1972*, by Robert Mickey, *Journal of Politics* 79, no. 1 (Jan. 2017): e31–32, www.journals.uchicago.edu/doi/full/10.1086/689938.

52. Watson W. Jennison, *Cultivating Race: The Expansion of Slavery in Georgia, 1750–1860* (Lexington: University Press of Kentucky, 2012), 290–306; "Joseph Henry Lumpkin, 1799–1867," *New Georgia Encyclopedia*, Sept. 5, 2002, www.georgiaencyclopedia.org/articles/history-archaeology/joseph-henry-lumpkin-1799-1867/.

53. Jennison, *Cultivating Race*, 293–94; Thomas R. R. Cobb, *An Inquiry into the Law of Negro Slavery in the United States to Which Is Prefixed an Historical Sketch of Slavery* (1858; reprint, Carlisle, MA: Applewood Press, 2009); "Thomas R. R. Cobb, 1823–1862," *New Georgia Encyclopedia*, Mar. 18, 2005, www.georgiaencyclopedia.org/articles/history-archaeology/thomas-r-r-cobb-1823-1862/.

54. Alexander Stephens, "Cornerstone Speech," Savannah, GA, Mar. 21, 1861, www.battlefields.org/learn/primary-sources/cornerstone-speech.

55. Stephanie McCurry, *Confederate Reckoning: Power and Politics in the Civil War South* (Cambridge, MA: Harvard University Press, 2010), 1–2.

56. Chana Kai Lee, "A Fraught Reckoning: Exploring the History of Slavery at the University of Georgia," *Public Historian* 42, no. 4 (Nov. 2020): 12–27; Scott Nesbit, "History of Slavery at the University of Georgia Symposium," May 19, 2021, symposium session recording, 1 hr. 23 min., www.youtube.com/watch?v=2hGwdnBzNW8.

57. *Slavery and Justice Report*, Brown University Steering Committee on Slavery and Justice (2006), https://slaveryandjustice.brown.edu/report. Accessed May 26, 2023

58. Lee, "Fraught Reckoning," 12–27.

59. I helped organize such a commemorative event when, as part of a faculty initiative launched by UGA history professors William McFeely, Robert Pratt, and John Inscoe, I wrote UGA President Charles Knapp on behalf of the conference organizers asking him to personally welcome Horace Ward, the first African American to apply to UGA, back to the UGA campus, which he had not set foot on in decades (Ward's application to UGA's law school in 1950 had been blocked by the UGA administration's enforcement of the Jim Crow color line). Judge Ward accepted our invitation and addressed the conference we had organized, Civil Rights in Small Places in 1996, and was welcomed back to the campus by

President Knapp. See Pratt, *We Shall Not Be Moved*, 187n41. I was also a panelist at UGA's fiftieth anniversary commemoration of desegregation.

60. James Baldwin, "A Talk to Teachers," *Saturday Review* (Dec. 1963), reprinted in *James Baldwin: Collected Essays* (New York: Library of America, 1998), 686–87.

61. Walter Stovall interview with the author, Apr. 1, 2011, New York City, tape in author's possession.

Chapter One

1. Holmes v. Danner, 191 F. Supp. 394 (M.D. Ga. 1961).
2. *Holmes*, 191 F. Supp. at 394.
3. Calvin Trillin, *An Education in Georgia: Charlayne Hunter, Hamilton Holmes and the Integration of the University of Georgia* (1964; reprint, Athens: University of Georgia Press, 1993), 37.
4. Trillin, *Education in Georgia*, 38.
5. Trillin, *Education in Georgia*, 38; *Holmes*, 191 F. Supp. at 394.
6. *Holmes*, 191 F. Supp. at 394.
7. Trillin, *Education in Georgia*, 38.
8. *Holmes*, 191 F. Supp. at 394.
9. *Holmes*, 191 F. Supp. at 394.
10. *Holmes*, 191 F. Supp. at 394.
11. *Holmes*, 191 F. Supp. at 394. In a 1975 oral history interview, Walter Danner, UGA's registrar in 1961, apparently embarrassed about the inappropriate sexual questions asked of Holmes in the Georgia admissions process, sought to shift the blame for them to the university's lawyers, since as Danner put it "legal counsel told us to go into everything and find something to turn them [Holmes and Hunter] down" for admission to UGA. But this evades the queston of why Danner (a UGA graduate) and other Georgia officials proved so willing to engage in such unethical behavor to maintain the color line. See Walter Danner interview with John C Belcher, July 2, 1975, Charlyane Hunter-Gault papers, Richard Russell Library, UGA.
12. *Holmes*, 191 F. Supp. at 394; on the Ward interview, see J. Alton Hosch to O. C. Aderhold, Sept. 13, 1951, O. C. Aderhold Papers, University Archives, Hargrett Rare Book and Manuscript Library, University of Georgia Libraries.
13. *Holmes*, 191 F. Supp. at 394.
14. Trillin, *Education in Georgia*, 40.
15. Trillin, *Education in Georgia*, 41. Danner's disingenuous testimony about UGA, his claim that the university had no policies against admitting Black students, came as a shock to Winston Stephens, a UGA student, who was a member of the same (all-white) Athens church in which Danner was a deacon; he had been her Sunday school teacher. Witnessing his false testimony, she "felt like I'd been struck by lighting. He's lying! On the witness stand. How could he do that?" This was, she recalled, "a pivotal moment for me" (UGA Goin' Back Oral History interview with Joan Zitzelman and Winston Stephens, Aug. 16, 2017, Athens, GA, https://kaltura.uga.edu/media/t/1_u104dkq6). Harold Black, on the other hand, as a member of the first class of UGA Black students to succeed Holmes and Hunter, was not surprised by Danner's dishonesty, as Danner was, in Black's words, "the

most racist person I ever met in all my life" (Harold Black, Mary Diallo, and Kerry Rushin Miller, UGA Goin' Back Oral History interview with Charlayne Hunter-Gault, Jan. 12, 2017, Athens, GA, https://kaltura.uga.edu/media/t/1_kgtkhrp7/73671191).

16. Trillin, *Education in Georgia*, 42.

17. "Historical Note," Aderhold Papers, https://sclfind.libs.uga.edu/sclfind/view?docId =ead/UA10-110.xml;query=;brand=default; Robert A. Pratt, *We Shall Not Be Moved: The Desegregation of the University of Georgia* (Athens: University of Georgia Press, 2002), 12, 14, 18; Maurice C. Daniels, *Horace T. Ward: Desegregation of the University of Georgia, Civil Rights Advocacy, and Jurisprudence* (Atlanta: Clark Atlanta University Press, 2001), 100.

18. "University Policy Stable After Segregation Ruling," *Red and Black*, May 20, 1954.

19. Dean William Tate interview with John C. Belcher, Aug. 5, 1976, Charlayne Hunter-Gault Papers, Richard B. Russell Library, UGA.

20. Tate interview with Belcher. Tate also noted that in terms of resources, Aderhold understood that segregation in some respects hurt UGA, as when it caused Georgia to lose its chance to attain $50 million in federal funds for an agricultural research center, which went instead to a northern university. The implication was that though he would not say so publicly, privately he was aware that integration could bring benefits to UGA. Tate was trying here, a decade after UGA integrated, to show that Aderhold was smart enough to realize that integration, contrary to segregationist politicians, was the wave of the future for Southern higher education. But this revelation also can be read as attesting to the repressive power of the Jim Crow regime since it kept even the president of the university from speaking out publicly in any positive way about the connection between racial integration and the advance of higher education in Georgia.

21. Tate interview with Belcher.

22. "Russell Group Urges Support for President," *Red and Black*, Feb. 29, 1952.

23. Robert O. Arnold to J. Alton Hosch, Feb. 25, 1952, J. Alton Hosch Papers, University Archives, Hargrett Rare Book and Manuscript Library, University of Georgia Libraries.

24. Daniels, *Horace T. Ward*, 197–226.

25. Hosch to Aderhold, Sept. 13, 1951, Aderhold Papers.

26. " 'The Way I See It' . . . Students Turn Thumbs Down on Negro Seeking Entrance," *Red and Black*, Feb. 22, 1952.

27. "Students Turn Thumbs Down"; Arnold to Hosch, Feb. 25, 1952, Aderhold Papers.

28. Arnold to Hosch.

29. Arnold to Hosch.

30. Arnold to Hosch.

31. Charlayne Hunter-Gault, *In My Place* (New York: Farrar, Straus and Giroux, 1992), 237.

32. Hunter-Gault, *In My Place*, 237.

33. Harold Paulk Henderson, *Ernest Vandiver: Governor of Georgia* (Athens: University of Georgia, 2000), 128.

34. "Students Turn Thumbs Down."

35. "Students Turn Thumbs Down."

36. "Students Turn Thumbs Down." Segregationist sentiment was strong in UGA's law school. So when a group of UGA law students read this *Red and Black* story reporting overwhelming student opposition to Ward's admission to the university, they wrote in complaining

that the article had neglected them and their segregationist views. These law students were eager to express their own opposition to Ward's admission, some citing their opposition to social equality, others objecting to forced integration and that "time not force will lead to Negroes' acceptance." Of the seven of these law students, all but one was from Georgia, and the racist northerner among them. A Chicagoan who had done his undergraduate work at the University of Illinois, he "said that" at Illinois he "had attended classes with Negroes and had come to Georgia to avoid mixing in classes with them" ("Lawyers Affirm Segregation," *Red and Black*, Mar. 7, 1952).

37. "African Antics," *Red and Black*, Nov. 10, 1950; *Pandora* (Athens: University of Georgia, 1932), 10; *Pandora* (Athens: University of Georgia), 1914; Quimby Melton Jr., "Racial Equality Poster Found on University Bulletin Board," *Red and Black*, Oct. 10, 1941.

38. Karl Shapiro, "University," *Selected Poems* (New York: Library of America, 2003; reprinted, Poetry Foundation), www.poetryfoundation.org/poetrymagazine/poems/22722/university. Accessed May 30, 2023.

39. John C. Belcher, "Integration Issue," July 2, 1976, Hunter-Gault Papers.

40. Robert Dince interview with John C. Belcher, June 6, 1975, Hunter-Gault Papers.

41. Dince interview with Belcher.

42. Robert Ayers interview with John C. Belcher, May 20, 1975, Hunter-Gault Papers.

43. Paul Pfuetze to Lillian Smith, July 27, 1955, Lillian Smith Papers, Hargrett Library, UGA, https://crdl.usg.edu/record/guan_1283_021-044?canvas=0&x=1159&y=1763&w=12862.

44. Robert Ayers, *Memoirs of a Southern Liberal* (Athens, GA: Bilbo Press, 2017), 83–88.

45. Ayers interview with Belcher.

46. Ayers interview with Belcher.

47. Pete Range interview with John C. Belcher, June 20, 1975, Hunter-Gault Papers.

48. Range interview with Belcher.

49. Range interview with Belcher.

50. Range interview with Belcher.

51. Chappelle Matthews interview with John C. Belcher, 1976, Hunter-Gault Papers.

52. Roger Thomas interview with John C. Belcher, May 30, 1975, Hunter-Gault Papers.

53. For additional evidence suggesting that UGA faculty in the Jim Crow era did not dare directly challenge in their classes the white supremacists' assumptions of their students, see "Petition Presented to Governor," *Red and Black*, Oct. 17, 1941, where students assert that racial equality was not taught at UGA. On the lack of teaching about segregation and integration at UGA even on the eve of desegregation at the dawn of the 1960s, see UGA alumnus Pete McCommons's statement quoted in chapter 2 (n32), and in the same chapter, American Association of University Professors leader Thomas Brahana's statement on how the UGA faculty were too fearful to discuss desegregation (n33). Though this did not involve teaching, one can get a sense of how rare it was, and how difficult, for a UGA faculty member to dissent against Jim Crow from the case of James Lenoir, a law professor who in the early 1950s was the UGA law school's lone dissenter against that school's new admission standards, which had been revised specifically to keep Horace Ward from being admitted as UGA's first Black law student—requiring letters of recommendation from two UGA alumni and a judge that no Black applicant would be able to attain. As historian Robert Pratt's excellent account makes clear, once Lenoir took a public position against this "subterfuge," it

simply became untenable for him to remain on a law school faculty that had refused even to acknowledge the bad faith and racially discriminatory purpose of the new admissions requirements, and whose dean had designed those new requirements. So in 1953 Lenoir resigned and left UGA for Indiana University, much to the relief of UGA president Aderhold and law school dean Hosch, who had been concerned that Lenoir "might embarrass the university and the Board of Regents on this matter" (Robert A. Pratt, *We Shall Not Be Moved*, 18–19). At the University of Mississippi a decade later, historian James Silver met with a similar fate after his own scholarship critical of Jim Crow on campus and off generated so much heat that he left for Notre Dame University. See James W. Silver, *Running Scared: Silver in Mississippi* (Jackson: University of Mississippi Press, 1984). It would not be until well into the UGA integration crisis of January 1961 that Georgia's faculty finally, belatedly, stood up en masse to racism at UGA when hundreds of professors signed a statement condemning the segregationist riot and demanding the reinstatement of Hunter and Holmes. See the discussion of this faculty action in the postscript to chapter 2.

54. *Pandora* (Athens: University of Georgia, 1935), 132, 142, 161, 167, Georgiana page; *Pandora* (Athens: University of Georgia, 1934), 64, 109, 118, 178; *Pandora* (Athens: University of Georgia, 1912), "Slams" cartoon.

55. See front page photo of "Kapppa Sigma House Boy," *Red and Black*, Jan. 30, 1958.

56. Henderson, *Ernest Vandiver*, 10.

57. Henderson, 7. Vandiver would literally become family to Richard Russell, when he married Russell's niece, Sybil Elizabeth "Betty" Russell.

58. James F. Cook, "Eugene Talmadge, 1884–1946," *New Georgia Encyclopedia*, updated Sept. 9, 2019, www.georgiaencyclopedia.org/articles/government-politics/eugene-talmadge-1884-1946/.

59. Thomas G. Dyer, *The University of Georgia, A Bicentennial History, 1785–1985* (Athens: University of Georgia Press, 1985), 225.

60. William Anderson, *The Wild Man from Sugar Creek: The Political Career of Eugene Talmadge* (Baton Rouge: Louisiana State University Press, 1975), 205.

61. Anderson, *Wild Man*, 196–211.

62. Henderson, *Ernest Vandiver*, 36–82.

63. Martin Luther King Jr., "The Purpose of Education," Morehouse *Maroon Tiger* (Atlanta; reprinted, Martin Luther King Jr. Research and Education Institute, Stanford University), Jan.–Feb. 1947, https://kinginstitute.stanford.edu/king-papers/documents/purpose-education. Accessed June 3, 2023.

64. Henderson, *Ernest Vandiver*, 127.

65. Henderson, 82. In a speech before a large audience at UGA's chapel, Vandiver, as lieutenant governor, characterized the *Brown* decision as "a conspiracy to destroy traditions of 40 million people in this part of the country" ("Vandiver Lashes Court," *Red and Black* [Athens], Nov. 14, 1957).

66. Harvard Sitkoff, *A New Deal for Blacks: The Emergence of Civil Rights as a National Issue; The Depression Decade* (New York: Oxford University Press), 146.

67. Henderson, *Ernest Vandiver*, 83.

68. Henderson, 131.

69. Henderson, 81.

70. Henderson, 95.

71. Henderson, 142–50.

72. Henderson, 142–50; Reg Murphy, "Governor Blasts Bootle's Decision," *Atlanta Constitution*, Jan. 11, 1961; "Text of Vandiver's Wire to Judge: 'Must Register Strongest Protest'," *Atlanta Constitution*, Jan. 11, 1961; "Governor Wants New 'Anti-Mixing" Laws Enacted," *Augusta Chronicle*, Jan. 10, 1961; Gene Britton, "Vandiver to Ask Broad Changes in School Setup, *Macon Telegraph*, Jan. 18, 1961.

73. Herman E. Talmadge, *You and Segregation* (Birmingham, AL: Vulcan Press, 1955).

74. Paul Mayhew, "The Talmadge Story," *New Republic*, July 23, 1956, https://newrepublic.com/article/90769/the-talmadge-story.

75. Mayhew, "Talmadge Story."

76. Talmadge, *You and Segregation*, viii.

77. Louis Brandeis, "The Brandeis Brief in Its Entirety," https://louisville.edu/law/library/special-collections/the-louis-d.-brandeis-collection/the-brandeis-brief-in-its-entirety.

78. Talmadge, *You and Segregation*, 70–74.

79. Talmadge, vii–viii.

80. Talmadge, 42–49.

81. Talmadge, 44.

82. Talmadge, 45

83. Talmadge, 43.

84. "Loving v. Virginia," History, A&E Television Networks, Nov. 17, 2017, www.history.com/topics/civil-rights-movement/loving-v-virginia.

85. John Kyle Day, *The Southern Manifesto: Massive Resistance and the Fight to Preserve Segregation* (Jackson: University of Mississippi, 2000), 82–96.

86. "Southern Manifesto," https://content.csbs.utah.edu/~dlevin/federalism/southern_manifesto.html.

87. Gilbert C. Fite, *Richard B. Russell, Jr., Senator from Georgia* (Chapel Hill: University of North Carolina Press, 2002), 30.

88. Bruce Bartlett, *Wrong on Race: The Democratic Party's Buried Past* (New York: Palgrave Macmillan, 2009), 73.

89. Bartlett, *Wrong on Race*, 73.

90. Fite, *Richard B. Russell*, 74–75.

91. Harold Davenport to Richard Russell, Nov. 5, 1958, Richard B. Russell Papers, Richard B. Russell Library, University of Georgia Libraries.

92. Jenkins, High School Eleventh Grade English Class to Richard Russell, Oct. 31, 1958, Russell Papers.

93. Jenkins, High School Eleventh Grade English Class to Richard Russell, Russell Papers.

94. Richard B. Russell to Jenkins High School Eleventh Grade English Class, Nov. 10, 1958, Russell Papers.

95. Russell to Jenkins High School Eleventh Grade English Class.

96. Russell to Jenkins High School Eleventh Grade English Class.

97. David B. Parker, "The Soldier, the Son, and the Lost Cause: Georgia Textbook Authors and the Lost Cause," *49th Parallel*, no. 33 (Winter 2014), 1–18, https://fortyninthparalleljournal.files.wordpress.com/2014/07/2-parkerwinter-the-solder-the-son.pdf; William Percy,

"Georgia History Textbooks," *New Georgia Encyclopedia*, updated Aug. 21, 2013, www.georgiaencyclopedia.org/articles/education/georgia-history-textbooks; "Charles Henry Smith, 'Bill Arp'—Great American Humorist/Writer," Etowah Valley Historical Society, https://evhsonline.org/bartow-history/people/charles-henry-smith-bill-arp-great-american-humorist-writer. Accessed June 5, 2023.

98. Fred Arthur Bailey, "E. Merton Coulter, the *Georgia Historical Quarterly*, and the Struggle over Southern History," *Georgia Historical Quarterly* 101, no. 3 (2017): 176–97; E. Merton Coulter, *History of Georgia* (New York: American Book Company, 1954); E. Merton Coulter, *The South During Reconstruction, 1865–1877* (Baton Rouge: LSU Press, 1947), 47–69; E. Merton Coulter, *Negro Legislators in Georgia During the Reconstruction Period* (Athens: Georgia Historical Quarterly, 1968), 177–180; John David Smith and John Inscoe, *Ulrich Bonnell Phillips: A Southern Historian and His Critics* (Athens: University of Georgia Press, 1993), 1–6.

99. Dyer, *The University of Georgia: A Bicentennial History*, 225–40; James F. Cook, "The Eugene Talmadge-Walter Cocking Controversy," *Phylon* (2nd quarter, 1974): 181–92.

100. Dyer, *University of Georgia*, 225–40; Cook, "Talmadge-Cocking Controversy," 181–92; Anderson, *Wild Man*, 210; Kate Dahlstrand, "The Cocking Affair: UGA's Commitment to White Supremacy," *Activist History Review* (Nov. 2019), https://activisthistory.com/2019/11/27/the-cocking-affair-ugas-commitment-to-white-supremacy/.

101. "Petition Presented to Governor," *Red and Black*, Oct. 17, 1941.

102. W. E. B. Du Bois, "The Talmadge-Cocking Affair," July 16, 1941, W. E. B. Du Bois Papers, Special Collections and University Archives, University of Massachusetts, Amherst Libraries, https://credo.library.umass.edu/view/full/mums312-b213-i058.

103. Christopher Huff, "Roy V. Harris, 1895–1985," *New Georgia Encyclopedia*, updated Apr. 14, 2021, www.georgiaencyclopedia.org/articles/history-archaeology/roy-v-harris-1895-1985/. Harris's intolerance of dissent against the Jim Crow social order was also prominently displayed in one of his campus visits. In 1958 Harris spoke to the UGA campus chapter of the militantly segregationist States Rights Council, which he presided over as its president. When one student dissented from his racist views, Harris accused this dissenter of being "a Judas Iscariot to the South" ("Harris Speaks at Rights Meet," *Red and Black* [Athens], Apr. 7, 1958).

104. Pratt, *We Shall Not Be Moved*, 30–39.

105. John Keasler, "Jazz Society Cancels Brubeck Appearance for Campus Concert," *Red and Black*, Feb. 26, 1959.

106. Dave Cleghorn, "No Help Wanted," *Red and Black*, Apr. 9, 1959. As the title of Cleghorn's column suggests, this student resented Gleason's criticism of UGA for cancelling Brubeck. Brubeck termed UGA's ban on interracial bands "unconstitutional and ridiculous" ("Jazz Unit Rebuffed: Racial Policy Cancels Brubeck Quartet Show at Georgia University," *New York Times*, Feb. 25, 1959). Asked whether he would consider finding a white substitute for Eugene Wright at UGA, Brubeck responded, "Not for a million dollars" (John Keasler, "Jazz Society Cancels Brubeck Appearance at Campus Concert," *Red and Black* [Athens], Feb. 26, 1959).

107. "Council Discusses Jazz Club Petition," *Red and Black*, Apr. 16, 1959. The same passivity can be seen when random UGA students were asked by the student newspaper for their views of the ban on interracial bands. Not one suggested defying the ban, even though

some students disagreed with such racial restrictions on the arts. See John Stephens, "Campus Poll: Students Express Petition Opinions," *Red and Black*, Apr. 9, 1959. To its credit the student newspaper did publish one sarcastic student letter that mocked the Brubeck cancellation. (Robert Ingram, "Letter to the editor," *Red and Black* [Athens], Feb. 26, 1959). UGA's cancellation of Brubeck looks even worse when viewed in comparison to East Carolina University, which after nearly cancelling his quartet, in 1958, had its president call North Carolina's governor, and obtained authorization to allow Brubeck's campus concert to occur. See Kelsey A.K. Klotz, "Dave Brubeck's Southern Strategy," *Daedalus* (Spring 2019), https://www.amacad.org/publication/dave-brubecks-southern-strategy.

108. Pratt, *We Shall Not Be Moved*, 115.

109. Hunter-Gault, *In My Place*, 227–29.

110. Report of interviews of Center-Myers Hall residents on Jan. 14, 1961, Dean of Women Records, Edith Stallings Papers, University Archives, Hargrett Rare Book and Manuscript Library, University of Georgia Libraries.

111. Report of interviews of Center-Myers Hall residents.

112. Trillin, *Education in Georgia*, 64, 67.

113. Charles H. Martin, "Hold That Color Line! Black Exclusion and Southeastern Conference Football," in *Higher Education and the Civil Rights Movement: White Supremacy, Black Southerners, and College Campuses*, ed. Peter Wallenstein (Gainesville: University of Florida Press, 2008) 184–85.

114. Mary Frances Early, *The Quiet Trailblazer: My Journey as the First Black Graduate of the University of Georgia* (Athens: University of Georgia Press, 2021), 60.

115. Walter Danner interview with John C. Belcher, July 2, 1975, Hunter-Gault Papers.

116. Robert Mickey, *Paths Out of Dixie: The Democratization of Authoritarian Enclaves in America's Deep South* (Princeton, NJ: Princeton University Press, 2015), xi–xii, 13–14, 33–48; Kimberly Johnson, review of *Paths Out of Dixie*, *Journal of Politics* 79, no. 1 (Jan. 2017), e31–32, www.journals.uchicago.edu/doi/full/10.1086/689938.

Chapter Two

1. Garroway's comments were reprinted in the *Athens Banner-Herald*, Jan. 15, 1961.

2. *Atlanta Constitution*, Jan. 11, 1961; *Red and Black*, Jan. 5, 1961; *Columbus Ledger*, Jan. 11, 1961.

3. *Atlanta Constitution*, Jan. 7, 1961; *Athens Banner-Herald*, Jan. 10, 1961; *Red and Black*, Jan. 10, 1961.

4. *New York Times*, Jan. 12, 1961; "Shame in Georgia," *Time*, Jan. 20, 1961, 44; *Atlanta Journal*, Jan. 12, 1961; Calvin Trillin, *An Education in Georgia: Charlayne Hunter, Hamilton Holmes, and the Integration of the University of Georgia* (New York: Viking Press, 1964), 52. Although the evidence is not definitive, a number of reports indicate that a coalition of segregationist law students and undergraduates centered in UGA's reactionary debating society, the Demosthenians, was the driving force behind the riot. On the mindset of the Demosthenians' segregationist wing, see Robert C. Owen, "A Collage of Counterrevolution: Debate on the Race Question in the Demosthenian Literary Society, 1950–1964" (unpublished honors thesis, University of Georgia, 1984); Minutes of the Demosthenian Hall, Sept. 24, 1958, 158, and Jan. 22, 1956, 31, University Archives, Hargrett Rare Book and Manu-

script Library, University of Georgia Libraries (hereinafter cited as UGA Archives); Robert A. Pratt, "The Rhetoric of Hate: The Demosthenian Literary Society and Its Opposition to the Desegregation of the University of Georgia, 1950–1964," *Georgia Historical Quarterly* 90, no. 2 (Summer 2006), 236–59.

5. By suspending Holmes and Hunter first, UGA administrators did look as if they had caved in to the mob by punishing the targets rather than the perpetrators of the riot. But in the riot's aftermath, the administration suspended four riot leaders and placed eighteen on disciplinary probation. See J. A. Williams to O. C. Aderhold, Jan. 24, 1961, President O. C. Aderhold Papers, University Archives, Hargrett Rare Book and Manuscript Library, University of Georgia Libraries. One of the Associated Press photographs of Charlayne Hunter being escorted off campus can be found in her memoirs, along with the syndicated photo of UGA rioters hoisting their racist banner. See Charlayne Hunter-Gault, *In My Place* (New York: Farrar, Straus and Giroux, 1992). The racist banner photo also appears in the photo gallery of *Confronting Jim Crow*.

6. E. Culpepper Clark, *The Schoolhouse Door: Segregation's Last Stand at the University of Alabama* (New York: Oxford University Press, 1993), 71–90.

7. *Macon Telegraph*, Jan. 13, 1961.

8. Russell H. Barret, *Integration at Ole Miss* (Chicago: Quadrangle, 1965), 163–95; Charles W. Eagles, *The Price of Defiance: James Meredith and the Integration of Ole Miss* (Chapel Hill: University of North Carolina Press, 2009), 340–70.

9. Thomas G. Dyer, *The University of Georgia: A Bicentennial History, 1785–1985* (Athens: University of Georgia Press, 1986), 303–34; David G. Sansing, *Making Haste Slowly: The Troubled History of Higher Education in Mississippi* (Jackson: University Press of Mississippi, 1990), 156–95; Clark, *The Schoolhouse Door*.

10. It is curious that most, if not all, historical narratives portraying the desegregation of universities—institutions that are, at least theoretically, centers of intellectual discourse—say so little about ideas. In these studies we never see the students in classes or learn much about how the university addressed (or failed to address) issues relating to segregation, race, and desegregation. A more complete portrait of desegregating universities requires a merging of political and intellectual history and an understanding of the relationship between ideas and actions, and of the connections between the university as a political battleground and the university as a center of teaching and learning.

11. Telephone interview with Thomas Brahana by the author, Athens, GA, Feb. 13, 1995.

12. UGA students demonstrated their willingness to play up to TV cameras and reporters most memorably in an incident involving CBS News. After a CBS News team missed a segregationist campus demonstration, the students—apparently at the request of a CBS News employee—reenacted the demonstration for the TV cameras so they could appear on television. See Hunter-Gault, *In My Place*, 179.

13. On the faculty movement that condemned the riot and demanded the reinstatement of Holmes and Hunter, and on Brahana's role in this movement, see Kenneth Coleman and Horace Montgomery narratives, RG-43, Integration Box, UGA Archives; *Atlanta Journal Constitution*, Jan. 23, 1961. After Hunter and Holmes's reinstatement, Brahana was part of a volunteer faculty group from the campus chapter of the American Association of University Professors that—in coordination with the Athens police department—patrolled at night to prevent further racist violence and called the police when armed men were found

near Hunter's dormitory. See Amy Bellew, "U. Profs. Talk about 1961 Racial Unrest," *Red and Black*, April 8, 1988. Since Math 254 was a calculus (and not a social science or humanities) class, possibly student fears of offending their professor or jeopardizing their grade would have been mitigated by their knowledge that ultimately their mathematical skills, as opposed to their political views, would determine their grades. A handful of students did not sign their essays, but the signed rather than unsigned essays were the most ardently segregationist. Brahana never read most of the essays. Instead, he deposited them in the library and labeled them "results of an appropriate peaceful demonstration" of student opinion. Brahana interview; cover envelope of Math 254 essays, Student Essays on Integration—Dr. Thomas Brahana's Math 254 Class, 1961, Walter Danner Papers, UA97-116, Desegregation files, box 2, folder 6, UGA Archives.

14. University Guidance Center, *Report of the Freshman Class of 1961*, April 1962, RG-4, SG3M Integration Box, UGA Archives.

15. TT, Student Essays on Integration—Dr. Thomas Brahana's Math 254 Class, 1961, Walter Danner Papers. Since the students wrote these essays for an academic course, with an assumption of confidentiality, this seemed reason enough to consider keeping their names out of the narrative. And since their ideas rather than their individual identities are historically significant, I could find no compelling reason to disclose their names. Thus their names are not included in the text, and the notes will refer to them by initials only (or if the essay was unsigned, by the order in which they appeared in the archival folder).

16. C.C.H,, Math 254 Essays, Danner Papers.

17. G.B., Math 254 Essays.

18. S.L., Math 254 Essays.

19. Essay 12, Math 254 Essays.

20. R.C., H.G., Essay 15, Math 254 Essays.

21. P.C., Math 254 Essays.

22. Essay 2, Math 254 Essays.

23. Essay 2, T.T.; also see D.W., Math 254 Essays.

24. M.H.C., Math 254 Essays.

25. A.S., Math 254 Essays.

26. For a memoir that illuminates the way small Southern towns taught their white youths about race, see Melton McLaurin, *Separate Pasts: Growing Up White in the Segregated South* (Athens: University of Georgia Press, 1987). Also see, Jennifer Ritterhouse, *Growing Up Jim Crow: How Black and White Southern Children Learned Race* (Chapel Hill: University of North Carolina Press, 2006); Leann. G. Reynolds, *Maintaining Segregation: Children and Racial Instruction in the South, 1920–1955* (Baton Rouge: LSU Press, 2017).

27. Essay 2, J.A., Math 254 Essays.

28. J.B., H.S,, Essay 12, Math 254 Essays.

29. Essay 12, Math 254 Essays.

30. Essay 16, Math 254 Essays.

31. J.A., MHC, Math 254 Essays.

32. Peter McCommons interview with the author, Apr. 4, 1994, Athens, GA. Southern academics tended to avoid controversial civil rights issues not only in teaching but also in their research. Thus in 1954 no Southern university would accept the Fund for the Advancement of Education's offer to finance a study of the South's segregated school system.

This project would be headed by Arkansas journalist Harry Ashmore rather than by a professor since, in Ashmore's words, "the subject was considered too hot for any southern university to handle." See Numan Bartley, *The New South, 1945–1980* (Baton Rouge: Louisiana State University Press, 1995), 152.

33. Brahana interview. Brahana was referring to governor Eugene Talmadge's firing of UGA College of Education dean Walter D. Cocking. The firing was sparked not, as Brahana implies, by Cocking's advocacy of integration (that was a bogus charge made by those who wanted him fired), but by his removal of a UGA employee who was a Talmadge supporter, and by Cocking's authorship of a report that showed that Georgia spent less than any Southern state except Arkansas on Black higher education. See Dyer, *University of Georgia*, 225–40; and James F. Cook, "Politics and Education in the Talmadge Era: The Controversy over the University System of Georgia, 1941–1942," (PhD diss., University of Georgia, 1972), 46–61.

34. Eliot Wigginton, *Sometimes a Shining Moment: The Foxfire Experience* (Garden City, NY: Anchor, 1986), 309.

35. Albert. B. Saye, *Georgia: Government and History* (Evanston, IL: Row, Peterson, 1957), 310–14.

36. Bruce M. Galphin, "The University Leads the Way: Georgia Rejoins the Union," *Nation*, Feb. 11, 1961, 118. Finally departing from their historic timidity in the struggle for racial equality, UGA faculty played a pivotal role in promoting peaceful integration in 1961 (most notably *after* the riot). Progressive faculty members privately encouraged moderate students to organize against the state government's threat to close UGA rather than submit to court-ordered integration. The faculty petition condemning the riot and demanding the reinstatement of Holmes and Hunter was the first major public stance of UGA's professoriate on behalf of Holmes and Hunter; it helped turn campus opinion and the UGA administration away from further resistance to integration; Brahana interview; McCommons interview; Horace Montgomery interview with the author, May 3, 1995, Athens, GA.

37. For useful summaries of social science scholarship that from the 1930s through the 1950s had refuted white supremacist notions about Blacks, see Richard Kluger, *Simple Justice: The History of Brown v. Board of Education and Black America's Struggle for Equality* (New York: Vintage, 1975), 309–13; Harvard Sitkoff: *A New Deal for Blacks: The Depression Decade* (New York: Oxford University Press, 1978), 190–215.

38. Essay 35, Math 254 Essays.

39. JA II, Math 254 Essays.

40. DC, Math 254 Essays.

41. *Atlanta Constitution*, Jan. 9, 1961; *Atlanta Journal*, Jan. 9, 1961; Terry Hazelwood, "Your Responsibility," *Red and Black*, Jan. 9, 1961; "Campus Leaders Ask Students to Follow Non-Violence Course," *Red and Black*, Jan. 10, 1961.

42. Despite their differences over tactics, the unity that moderate and extremist students displayed in their shared preference for segregation at times made it difficult to distinguish between the two groups. Indeed, through the early stages of the integration crisis, moderate and extremist students had no difficulty working together politically. This occurred in the petition drive requesting that UGA be kept open, and in the segregationist street demonstrations on the night of Jan. 9. See *Macon Telegraph*, Jan. 10 and 13, 1961; McCommons interview; *Atlanta Constitution*, Jan. 10, 1961.

43. The student enrollment figure is from the start of the 1960–61 academic year. See the *Red and Black*, Sept. 30, 1960.

44. *Athens Banner-Herald*, Jan. 12, 1961; *Savannah Evening Press*, Jan. 14, 1961; James A. Dunlap to O. C. Aderhold, Jan. 13, 1961, Aderhold Papers; the *Atlanta Journal* estimated that the mob besieging Center-Myers was 500 strong, the *New York Times*, 600; Calvin Trillin, who covered the riot for *Time*, estimated 1,000 as did the UGA student paper, the *Red and Black*. Highest was the *Atlanta Constitution*, which reported that "nearly 2,000 students" rioted. See *Atlanta Journal*, Jan. 12, 1961; *New York Times*, Jan. 12, 1961; Terry Hazelwood, "Your Responsibility," *Red and Black*, Jan. 11, 1961; *Atlanta Constitution*, Jan. 12, 1961; Trillin, *Education in Georgia*, 52.

45. FBI files, 72–39, interviews with Athens police officers, Jan. 13, 1961, Athens, GA, 4, 42, 44, 48, 51, 59, 61; FBI files, 72–39, SAC Atlanta to FBI Director, Jan. 13, 1961. Copies of these FBI files are in the author's possession. The FBI investigation of the riot will be discussed in chapter 3; Trillin, *Education in Georgia*, 52–53.

46. Tom Johnson remarks at fortieth anniversary commemoration of UGA's desegregation, January 2001, Athens, GA, https://bmac.libs.uga.edu/index.php/Detail/objects/45388.

47. PC, Math 254 Essays.

48. Essay 12, Math 254 Essays.

49. CC, Essay 21, Math 254 Essays. This realism about the futility of further segregationist violence also reflected the hard line the students encountered after the January 11 riot as UGA officials banned segregationist demonstrations, an Athens grand jury drew up indictments against several rioters, the FBI came to Athens to investigate the riot, and the state patrol—which had done nothing to quell the riot—sent additional officers to Athens to discourage further violence. See Williams to Aderhold, Jan. 24, 1961, and Williams to students, Jan. 14, 1961, Aderhold Papers; *Athens Banner-Herald*, Jan. 13, 1961; Tom Blalcock, "Legislature Asks Return For Suspended Students; State, FBI Conduct Probes," *Red and Black*, Jan. 19, 1961.

50. *Atlanta Journal*, Jan. 12, 1961; "Prank, Riot, and Shock on Georgia Campus," *Life*, Jan. 20, 1961, 24; *Macon Telegraph*, Jan. 13, 15, 1961; *Athens Banner-Herald*, Jan. 15, 1961; *San Francisco Chronicle*, Jan. 12, 1961. UGA students were probably influenced as much by the Georgia press criticism of the riot as they were by the blasts from the national media. For examples of this Georgia criticism see *Marietta Daily Journal*, Jan. 13, 1961; *Columbus Enquirer*, Jan. 13 and 14, 1961; *Savannah Morning News*, Jan. 13, 1961; *Savannah Evening Press*, Jan. 12, 1961; *Brunswick News*, Jan. 12, 1961; *Gainesville Daily Times*, Jan. 12, 1961; *Waycross Journal Herald*, Jan. 16, 1961; *Rome News Tribune*, Jan. 15, 1961; *Thomaston Daily Times*, Jan. 15 1961; *Thomaston Free Press*, Jan. 17, 1961; *Dalton News*, Jan. 18, 1961; *Moultrie Observer*, Jan. 16, 1961; *Walker County Messenger*, Jan. 18, 1961; *DeKalb New Era*, Jan. 19, 1961; *Fitzgerald Leader and Enterprise*, Jan. 19, 1961; *Emory Wheel*, Jan. 19, 1961; *Thomasville Times-Enterprise*, Jan. 14, 1961.

51. Brahana interview; Essay 12, T.T., Math 254 Essays.

52. J.A., Math 254 Essays.

53. J.B., Math 254 Essays.

54. C.C. (emphasis added); Essay 12, Math 254 Essays.

55. Hunter-Gault, *In My Place*, 172.

56. J.M., Math 254 Essays.

57. Trillin, *Education in Georgia*, 74; Charlayne Hunter-Gault notes in her memoir that UGA students denounced Marcia Powell "openly and loudly" as a "nigger lover" because this white student had befriended her. See *In My Place*, 207; Caroline Ridlehuber recalled that her sorority ostracized her in 1961 in retaliation for merely walking Charlayne Hunter across campus (Ridlehuber speech at the Civil Rights in Small Places conference, UGA, Athens, GA, Apr. 15, 1996).

58. Report on interviews of Center-Myers Hall residents, Jan. 14, 1961, Edith Stallings, Dean of Women Papers, UGA Archives. This unfriendly posture toward Hunter and Holmes on the part of white students had considerable staying power. Both Hunter and Holmes told Calvin Trillin that they had "underestimated how long the unfriendliness would last." Indeed, as late as March 1963, as his graduation neared, Holmes complained about the coldness of his white classmates. See Trillin, *Education in Georgia*, 121; *Atlanta Journal*, March 20, 1963.

59. *Athens Observer*, Jan. 30, 1992.

60. Brahana interview.

61. *Athens Observer*, Jan. 30, 1992. Exceptions to McCommons's depressing conclusion about his classmates included the following: the few students who welcomed Hamilton Holmes and Charlayne Hunter to campus (some of whom were associated with Students for Constructive Action, a small group—based in the Westminster House, the campus Presbyterian facility—that advocated applying the golden rule to UGA's first Black students); five students who wrote in to the *Red and Black* rebutting a nasty column it had run attacking Holmes as an "alien"; and most notably, Walter Stovall, whose friendship with Hunter, as we shall detail in chapter 5, culminated in their marriage in 1963 (UGA's first interracial marriage), an event that aroused a storm of denunciation from racists across the state of Georgia. See Hunter-Gault, *In My Place*, 207, 227, 233, 235–37; Trillin, *Education in Georgia*, 175–78; SCA Golden Rule flyer (n.d.), Aderhold Papers; *Savannah Morning News*, Sept. 4, 1963; *Atlanta Inquirer*, Sept. 14, 1961.

Postscript to Chapter Two

1. Trillin, *An Education in Georgia: Charlayne Hunter, Hamilton Holmes, and the Integration of the University of Georgia* (1964; reprint, Athens: University of Georgia Press, 1992), 60; also see Zitzelman's discussion of Westminster House in UGA Goin' Back Oral History interview with Joan Zitzelman and Winston Stephens, Aug. 16, 2017, Athens, GA; Hunter-Gault also singled out a group of Jewish UGA students, who though not publicly outspoken, told her that since Jews had been the target of bigotry, they identified with her. And they expressed this solidarity by coming to her dorm suite and cooking dinner for them all to share (Charlayne Hunter-Gault remarks via Zoom at the author's 1960s class session at NYU, Sept. 19, 2022).

2. Trillin, *Education in Georgia*, 140.

3. Joan Zitzelman, "A Supporting Role: A Student's Recollections of Desegregation at the University of Georgia" (written in 1988, prompted by Charlayne Hunter-Gault's Commencement Address at UGA in 1988, updated in 2001), 1–2, unpublished mss., copy in author's possession.

4. Zitzelman, "Supporting Role," 2–4, 6.

5. Trillin, *Education in Georgia*, 140.

6. Trillin, 139–44.

7. Trillin, 87.

8. Hunter-Gault, *In My Place*, 227–29.

9. David L. Chappell, *A Stone of Hope: Prophetic Religion and the Death of Jim Crow* (Chapel Hill: University of North Carolina Press, 2004), 120–45.

10. Chappell, *Stone of Hope*, 120–23

11. *Macon Telegraph*, Jan. 13, 1961.

12. Peter McCommons interview with the author, Apr. 9, 1994.

13. *Atlanta Constitution*, Jan. 10, 1961; *Macon Telegraph*, Jan. 10, 1961.

14. "Campus Leaders Ask Students to Follow a Non-Violent Course," *Red and Black*, Jan. 9, 1961.

15. "Campus Leaders Ask Students."

16. *Atlanta Journal-Constitution*, Jan. 22, 1961.

17. On the way that fear kept most professors from taking a stand against the segregationist resistance during the Mississippi integration crisis, see Charles Eagles, *The Price of Defiance: James Meredith and the Integration of Ole Miss*, 332–33. But Ole Miss's small American Association of University Professors chapter did pass a resolution condemning their campus's segregationist violence. See James W. Silver, *Mississippi: The Closed Society*, 168–69.

18. Faculty Resolutions, Jan. 13, 1961, John C. Belcher, "Introduction: Integration Issues" (1974–75), Charlayne Hunter-Gault Papers, Richard B. Russell Library, UGA.

19. George Abney interview with John C. Belcher, June 10, 1975, Hunter-Gault Papers.

20. Kenneth Coleman interview with John C. Belcher, Aug. 5, 1975, Hunter-Gault Papers. It is revealing that even though the faculty were rallying behind the university and its administration in insisting that it stay open, President Aderhold made no public statement supporting the resolutions and made no comment at all even privately when Coleman called him to inform him that these resolutions had been adopted by the faculty. Aderhold's low profile and few public statements during the desegregation crisis—even as UGA was threatened with closure—mystified students and some faculty, who in a play on the first initials in Aderhold's name, O. C., mocked him for his silence by reversing the start of the national anthem, so instead of "O say can you see" it was "O. C. can you say?" Other faculty credited Aderhold for not antagonizing the powerful segregationist political leaders of the state, even arguing that his discretion and silence was wise and helped prevent those leaders from closing the university.

21. Nick Beadles and George Abney interview with John C. Belcher, Oct. 8, 1975, Hunter-Gault Papers.

22. Roger Thomas interview with John C. Belcher, May 30, 1975, Hunter-Gault Papers.

23. James E. Popovich interview with John C. Belcher, Nov. 5, 1975, Hunter-Gault Papers.

24. Popovich interview with Belcher.

25. Popovich interview with Belcher.

26. Popovich interview with Belcher.

27. Popovich interview with Belcher.

28. Robert Ayers, *Memoirs of a Southern Liberal* (Athens, GA: Bilbo Books, 2016), ix. Since the faculty patrol was focused on campus after dark, it was most involved in safeguarding Charlayne Hunter, since she lived on campus, rather than Hamilton Holmes, who lived with a Black family that was armed and so did not need faculty protection at night. Nonetheless, Ayers was not technically incorrect, for if the patrol intercepted a white supremacist bent on violence, that would aid in Holmes's protection too. Ayers's characterization of "a few" faculty liberals being involved in the patrol seems understated in light of documentation indicating that about fifty faculty were a part of this patrol. While there is no way of knowing how many of them had seen themselves as liberals in the past, the fact that they volunteered for the potentially risky task of guarding the campus against white supremacist terrorists after the riot does suggest that likely a substantial share of these fifty faculty constituted the core of UGA's relatively small group of liberal faculty, who in the midst of the integration crisis of 1961 had embraced an activist role. See "Report of the Faculty Patrol" in the John C. Belcher oral history materials, Hunter-Gault Papers; and Brahana's remarks in *Red and Black*, Apr. 8, 1988.

29. Charlayne Hunter-Gault, "Taunts, Tear Gas, and Other College Memories," *New Yorker*, Nov. 13, 2015, www.newyorker.com/news/news-desk/taunts-tear-gas-and-other-college-memories.

30. Hunter-Gault, *In My Place*, 226–27.

31. Pete Range interview with John C. Belcher, June 20, 1975, Hunter-Gault Papers.

32. Range interview with Belcher.

33. Range interview with Belcher.

34. Range interview with Belcher.

35. Range interview with Belcher.

Chapter Three

1. *Atlanta Journal*, Jan. 12, 1961; *Atlanta Constitution*, Jan. 12, 1961; *New York Times*, Jan. 12, 1961; *New York Herald Tribune*, Jan. 13, 1961; Calvin Trillin, *An Education in Georgia: Charlayne Hunter, Hamilton Holmes, and the Integration of the University of Georgia* (1964; reprint, Athens: University of Georgia Press, 1991), 52–54; Charlayne Hunter-Gault, *In My Place* (New York: Farrar, Straus and Giroux, 1992), 180–91; *Athens Banner-Herald*, Jan. 13, 1961; Department of Justice news release on investigation of the University of Georgia, Jan. 12, 1961, FBI document obtained under a Freedom of Information Act request. Copies of all FBI and justice department documents cited here and below are in author's possession.

2. On FBI and justice department reluctance to involve themselves in civil rights investigations and prosecutions during the Eisenhower era, see Michael R. Belknap, *Federal Law and Southern Order: Racial Violence and Constitutional Conflict in the Post-Brown South*, rev. ed. (Athens: University of Georgia Press, 1995), ix–xxv, 27–69; E. Frederick Morrow, *Black Man in the White House: A Diary of the Eisenhower Years by the Administrative Officer for Special Projects, the White House, 1955–1961* (New York: Coward-McCann, 1963), 28–31, 47–51, 56–58, 160–68; also see Daniel M. Berman, *A Bill Becomes a Law: The Civil Rights Act of 1960* (New York: MacMillian, 1962).

3. Harold R. Tyler to the author, Jan. 16, 1996; Kenneth O'Reilly, *"Racial Matters": The FBI's Secret File on Black America, 1960–1972* (New York: Free Press, 1989), 52; also see FBI

file 72-39, A. Rosen to Mr. Parsons, Jan. 12, 1961. The justice department files in the National Archives offer no clues as to why Rogers initiated the FBI probe at UGA. In contrast to the extensive FBI files on that probe, there are only a few pages of justice department documents on UGA's segregationist riot. This paucity of justice department files and the inaccessibility of the FBI files (which took more than a year to acquire) may explain why Eisenhower biographers and even experts on the Eisenhower civil rights record have ignored his response to the UGA desegregation crisis. See Belknap, *Federal Law and Southern Order*, and Robert Frederick Burk, *The Eisenhower Administration and Black Civil Rights* (Knoxville: University of Tennessee Press, 1984), for leading assessments of the Eisenhower civil rights record, which never even mention the FBI probe that Eisenhower's attorney general initiated following the segregationist riot at UGA.

4. When the earlier version of this chapter came out as an article published by the *Georgia Historical Quarterly* in the fall of 1999, it was the first to analyze the FBI's investigation of UGA's segregationist riot. Unfortunately, no historian (or lawyer) has followed up on my initial work declassifying the files of this FBI investigation, so we still do not have access to the segments of those files deleted by the FBI—deletions which in 1999 seemed excessive to me, and which appear even more so today considering that the investigation and riot occurred more than six decades ago.

5. David J. Garrow, *The FBI and Martin Luther King, Jr.* (New York: Norton, 1981); O'Reilly, *Racial Matters*, 61; Athan G. Theoharis and John Stuart Cox, *The Boss: Edgar Hoover and The Great American Inquisition* (Philadelphia: Temple University Press, 1988), 354–61; Richard C. Powers, *Secrecy and Power: The Life of Edgar Hoover* (New York: Free Press, 1987), 367–83, 410–11.

6. O'Reilly, *Racial Matters*, 4.

7. O'Reilly, 58.

8. On movement criticism of the FBI's unwillingness to protect the freedom riders from the racist violence directed against them beginning in spring 1961, see Howell Raines, *My Soul Is Rested: The Story of the Civil Rights Movement in the Deep South* (New York: Penguin, 1977), 230–31, 244, 379; also see O'Reilly, *Racial Matters*, 81–96; on the FBI's record with regard to protecting Deep South voter registration workers, which varied from mediocre to dismal and quite incompetent, see John Doar and Dorothy Landsberg, "Performance of the FBI in Investigating Violations of Federal Law Protecting the Right to Vote, 1960–1967," Senate Select Committee to Study Government Operations on US Intelligence Agencies and Operations, S-91, 1976; FBI hostility to the civil rights movement became a big national news story in November 1962, when Martin Luther King Jr. complained to the *New York Times* that in the recent civil rights struggle in Albany, Georgia, FBI agents sided with the segregationist establishment and racist police against the freedom movement. These (accurate) remarks infuriated FBI director J. Edgar Hoover, paving the way for his nasty public slandering of Dr. King as "the most notorious liar" in the United States. See Garrow, *The FBI and Martin Luther King, Jr.*, 54–55, 78–100. Hoover's loathing of King would lead the FBI to engage in extensive spying and harassment of the civil rights leader, which would not become public knowledge until 1975. See Beverly Gage, *G-Man: J. Edgar Hoover and the Making of the American Century* (New York: Viking, 2022), 723–24. In fact, even the first, limited public glimpse of the FBI's spying on King did not occur until the *New York Times* ran a story on this FBI spying in 1966. See James Reston, "Was This Done for Reasons?" *New York Times*, Dec. 14, 1966.

9. O'Reilly, *Racial Matters*, 58.

10. *Richmond Afro-American*, Jan. 21, 1961.

11. *Red and Black*, Jan. 19, 1961.

12. *Atlanta Journal*, Jan. 15, 1961; *Macon Telegraph*, Jan. 14, 1961; Joseph P. Williams, memorandum to students, Jan. 14, 1961, President O. C. Aderhold Papers, University Archives, Hargrett Rare Book and Manuscript Library, University of Georgia Libraries.

13. FBI file 72-39, Athens, GA, Jan. 13, 1961, 42. On the failure of the state patrol to show up at the riot scene, see Athens mayor Ralph M. Snow's critical remarks in the *Athens Banner-Herald*, Jan. 12, 1961. On the governor's disingenuous denial of the patrol's failure, see the *Augusta Chronicle*, Jan. 13, 1961.

14. *Athens Banner Herald*, Jan. 13, 1961.

15. FBI file 72-39, Athens, GA, Jan. 13, 1961, 101, 104–5, 109, 111, 122; Tom Blalock, "Legislature Asks Return for Suspended Students, State, FBI Conduct Probes," *Red and Black* Jan. 19, 1961.

16. Harold R. Tyler Jr. to the author, Jan. 16, 1996.

17. FBI file 72-39, J. Edgar Hoover to SAC, Atlanta, Jan. 12, 1961.

18. Tyler Jr. to the author.

19. Doar and Landsberg, "Performance of the FBI," 902–3.

20. FBI file 72-39, John Doar to FBI, Feb. 13, 1961; Hoover to SAC, Atlanta, March 3, 1961.

21. FBI file 72-39, Athens, GA, Jan. 13, 1961, 108, 142, and Feb. 17, 1961, 6–7. The FBI also found out that state officials had helped fund the drive of segregationist students to send anti-integration telegrams to legislators. See FBI file 72-39, Athens, GA, Jan. 14, 1961, 128.

22. FBI file 72-39, Athens, GA, Jan. 13, 1961, 117. An FBI source noted that "Cochran and this other individual are two of the leaders of the student demonstrations," and he identified Cochran as the "son of a man who has been a close friend of Lieutenant Governor Garland Byrd for many years" (FBI, Atlanta, Jan. 14, 1961, "School Desegregation University of Georgia, Athens, Georgia, Obstruction of Court Order," 2).

23. Phil Campbell interview with the author, May 29, 1997. In Campbell's defense it should be noted that another student protester told the FBI that Campbell counseled him "to refrain from violence," FBI file 72-39, Athens, GA, Jan. 15, 1961, 131. The closest public acknowledgment of collusion between Georgia officials and UGA rioters came in the riot's aftermath as Roy Harris, the arch-segregationist member of the Georgia Board of Regents, told the press that "'it was people holding high official positions in the Capitol' who encouraged last Wednesday night's rioting. He said that he would not name the officials now but would at a later time if any white students are expelled from the university" for their part in the riot. These officials "encouraged some of the students and now have run out on them." Harris said they "figured the governor would remove the Negro students in his role of preservator of peace if things got unpeaceful enough on campus" (*Atlanta Journal*, Jan. 16, 1961).

24. For a sampling of other editorial cartoons that denounced the University of Georgia and its segregationist riot, see *Cleveland* (OH) *Plain Dealer*, Jan. 13, 1961; *Louisville* (GA) *Courier Journal*, Jan. 11 and 13, 1961; *Baltimore Sun*, Jan. 13, 1961; *Los Angeles Times*, Jan. 13, 1961; *Chicago Defender*, Jan. 12, 1961; reprint of *Chicago Sun-Times* cartoon in *Marietta* (GA) *Daily Journal*, Jan. 12, 1961; *Knoxville* (TN) *News Sentinel*, Jan. 16, 1961; *Macon Telegraph*, Jan. 13, 1961. On the negative magazine coverage of UGA during the desegregation crisis,

306 Notes to Chapter Three

see "Shame in Georgia," *Time*, Jan. 20, 1961, 44; "Prank, Riot, and Shock on Georgia Campus," *Life*, Jan. 20, 1961, 24; "Nothing Was Lost but Georgia's Pride: Too Much for Governor Vandiver," *New Republic*, Jan. 23, 1961, 6–7. On national TV's criticism of the riot, see *Athens Banner-Herald*, Jan. 15, 1961. Although initially it was true that the UGA administration had punished the innocent (by suspending Holmes and Hunter, supposedly for their own safety) and failed to discipline the guilty (the rioters), by the end of the desegregation crisis the situation had been reversed. Hunter and Holmes were reinstated via a federal court order, while four rioters were suspended and eighteen others placed on disciplinary probation (J. A. Williams to O. C. Aderhold, Jan. 24, 1961, Aderhold Papers).

25. FBI file 72-39, 46, 57–58. Note that the controversy over the Klan is not only about whether they played any role in planning the riot but also over whether the Klansmen at the riot scene themselves engaged in violence. For varying accounts, see Claude Sitton's report on the riot for the *New York Times*, Jan. 12, 1961; and Trillin, *Education in Georgia*, 59. On this tendency to blame "outside agitators" and the Klan for having "masterminded" the riot, and the corresponding refusal to believe that UGA students "on their own initiative" would stoop to organizing such violence, see *Athens Banner-Herald*, Jan. 12, l961; *Savannah Evening Press*, Jan. 14, 1961; and Trillin, *Education in Georgia*, 58–59.

26. FBI file 72-29, SAC, Atlanta to Director, FBI, Jan. 13, 1961.

27. This Klansman in the fraternity house report is vague; it came from someone in the UGA community (probably an administrator, though the name of the person making this claim was deleted by an FBI censor), FBI file 72-39, 28. Even if we accept this report's validity, there is nothing in it that indicates this KKK connection went beyond this single fraternity, and nothing that even suggests that this adult white supremacist was involved in any of the campus-wide planning meetings.

28. FBI file 72-39, 112, 118, 125, 148. Literature from Lester Maddox's white supremacist group, "Georgians Unwilling to Surrender," was also distributed in the campus area (see SAC, Atlanta to Director, FBI, Jan. 19, 1961; SAC, Atlanta, Jan. 19, 1961, "School Desegregation, University of Georgia, Obstruction of Court Order," 4, 7).

29. FBI file 72-39, Athens, GA, Jan. 17, 1961, 2. The FBI interviews also make it evident that segregationist students at UGA were not some disorganized mass needing outside leadership but were instead a well-organized group of militants with a well-known leadership cadre (FBI file 72-39, Athens, GA, Jan. 13, 1961, 26–27, 29, 144; SAC, Atlanta, Jan. 18, 1961, "School Desegregation, University of Georgia, Obstruction of Court Order," 1–2; FBI file 72-1295, Atlanta, Feb. 22, 1961, 6).

30. *Atlanta Journal*, Jan. 13, 1961.

31. FBI file 72-80, Miami, FL, Feb. 2, 1961, 2. The FBI received one report that at a Jacksonville, Florida, KKK meeting, "Georgia Klan members had been instructed to do something about the Athens situation. However no specific information regarding what form the Klan intervention would take was known." FBI informants were not able, however, to confirm that the Florida KKK acted upon these instructions (see FBI file 72-39, Athens, GA, Jan. 13, 1961, 36; SAC, Atlanta, Jan. 19, 1961, "School Desegregation, University of Georgia, Obstruction of Court Order," 1, 10). Note that, as Craig's words suggest, when the KKK in the Athens area engaged unilaterally in racial violence during the desegregation era of the early 1960s, the results were far bloodier than the student riot at UGA. In 1964 Lemuel Penn, a Black reservist in the US Army, was murdered by Klansmen, who began to tail his

car on the street adjacent to the historic archway at the entrance of UGA. See Bill Shipp, *Murder at Broad River Bridge: The Slaying of Lemuel Penn by Members of the Ku Klux Klan* (Atlanta: Peachtree Publishers, 1981).

32. Frank H. Redwine III to the author, Feb. 20, 1996. Actually this alumnus's recounting of the basketball loss was not quite accurate. Kaiser's shot at the end of regulation did not win the game for Tech; it tied the game and forced the contest into overtime. And anger over his shot was fueled by the fact that "the throw-in and Roger Kaiser's game tying shot took about four seconds—but the buzzer, not synchronized with the clock, failed to sound until two seconds late. By then Kaiser's long jump shot was on its way—and hit." As infuriating as this bad officiating was, Georgia did get another chance to win in overtime and the crowd had some time to cool off. So the notion that a heartbreakingly close, last-second loss had set off the riot is groundless. In fact, UGA faded in overtime, and Kaiser got hot, so that the final score, 89–80 for Tech, was not even close. See United Press International's story on the game by David M. Moffit in the *Alabama Journal* (Montgomery), Jan. 11, 1961.

33. *Atlanta Journal*, Jan. 12, 1961.

34. FBI file 72-39, Athens, GA, Jan. 15, 1961, 128, 124, and FBI interviews with Athens police officer, 4; Trillin, *Education in Georgia*, 52. Another sign of the advanced planning for the riot was the "anonymous telephone calls to dormitories and fraternity and sorority houses [that] summoned [their] membership" to the segregationist protest scheduled to begin at 9 P.M. See *Atlanta Journal*, Jan. 11, 1961.

35. *Macon Telegraph*, Jan. 10, 1961; *Atlanta Journal*, Jan. 10, 1961; *New York Times*, Jan. 11, 1961.

36. In linking up with athletics crowds, the Georgia segregationists followed a pattern similar to that at the University of Alabama in 1956, where the first violent campus crowd rallying against integration began to coalesce after a basketball game (coincidentally also against Georgia Tech, but in this case since Tech lost no one could argue that athletic anger produced the racial violence). See E. Culpepper Clark, *The Schoolhouse Door: Segregation's Last Stand at the University of Alabama* (New York: Oxford University Press, 1993), 66; *Alabama Journal* (Montgomery), Jan. 12, 1961.

37. Campbell interview; EFN 203 student interviews with parent, class of 1962, UGA, Winter Quarter 1997; author interviews with UGA alumni, October 1996; FBI file 72-39, Athens, GA, 141.

38. Trillin, *Education in Georgia*, 53

39. Dyer, *University of Georgia*, 332.

40. FBI file 72-39, interviews with Athens police officers, Athens, GA, Jan. 13, 1961, 44–46, 51–52, 54, 57, 62, and interview with demonstrator, 111. Press accounts confirm the police reports (and not Trillin's contrary view) of "several attempts by groups in the crowd to rush the dormitory," which were foiled because "university officials and Athens police barred the way. A rush was made at the back door [of the dormitory] but police stopped it again by pushing them back and making more arrests and setting off another smoke screen of tear gas," *Macon Telegraph*, Jan. 11, 1961; *Augusta Chronicle*, Jan. 12, 1961.

41. FBI file 72-39, letter [author's name deleted by FBI censor] to FBI director of personnel, Jan. 13, 1961. A full assessment of the riot's violence must take into account more than just police injuries. Newspeople were also targets of the mob's rage "and had to dodge firecrackers and rocks all during the demonstration." A newsman's camera was a casualty when

a group damaged it while he was attempting to use a flash attachment. A reporter for the student newspaper was injured after being "struck in the leg by a brick-sized rock," *Macon Telegraph*, Jan. 11 and 12, 1961.

42. FBI file 72-39, interviews with Athens police officers, Athens, GA, Jan. 13, 1961, 4, 42, 44, 48, 51, 59, 61. The UGA administration does not come off well here in comparison with the police, since the police urged the cancellation of the basketball game, and university officials failed to follow this wise advice. The local police performance at the riot scene was not flawless: an Athens police officer threatened to kill a United Press International photographer if he did not "quit making those pictures," *Macon Telegraph*, Jan. 12, 1961.

43. An Alabama reporter who had covered the racist mob violence that had driven Autherine Lucy from the University of Alabama in 1956 was struck by the contrasting police roles in Alabama and Georgia desegregation crises: "In Athens, police have moved briskly and firmly against the mobs. In Tuscaloosa, resistance was almost passive. This was not the fault of the police officials involved. The [Alabama] officers had orders not to manhandle the University students. Powerless to remove the ringleaders, they couldn't stop the growth of the mob feeling," *Alabama Journal* (Montgomery), Jan. 12, 1961.

44. FBI file 72-39, interviews with Athens police, 5, 6, 38. The police interviews by the FBI also reflect a final irony with respect to the state patrol. When at 12:15 A.M. the state patrol finally did dispatch five squad cars to remove the now suspended African American students, ostensibly for their own safety, they were no longer in danger as the riot had ended.

45. Trillin, *Education in Georgia*, 45–46.

46. Trillin, 79–82.

47. FBI file 72-39, 123, 132.

48. *Macon Telegraph*, Jan. 13, 1961. Cochran may have thrown the agent off by claiming that he was opposed to violent protests. The question, of course, was how such claims could be squared with his emulation of an Alabama model that was violent. Additionally, one needs to ask whether Cochran thought it possible to keep nonviolent an anti-integration protest by angry white students outside the dormitory of UGA's first Black student—or why a demonstration designed to be nonviolent should be held under the cover of nightfall. The Alabama model, moreover, may have been significant regarding the *intent* and *level* of the violence deployed by the UGA rioters. Since Autherine Lucy had been driven off the Alabama campus in 1956 by a racist mob that had threatened but did not actually hurt or kill her (followed by her subsequent expulsion), the Georgia rioters may have thought they could do the same and with the same result. In other words, the Alabama precedent suggested that deadly violence was not needed to keep the university white; all that was needed was a riot tumultuous and threatening enough to convince Hunter, Holmes, and the authorities that the student body would not accept integration, and so no Black student would dare attempt to matriculate at UGA. See John C. Belcher, "Introduction: Integration Issue," 1974–75, Charlayne Hunter-Gault Papers, Richard B. Russell Library, UGA.

49. Clark, *Schoolhouse Door*, 71–90.

50. O'Reilly's position on the FBI's record may actually be more confused and contradictory than flat out wrong. He opens his book by asserting that "to describe one of these [poor FBI civil rights] investigations is to provide a sense of them all.... Federal agents

stood ... with the enemies of black people." But then only a few pages later, O'Reilly goes on to contradict this first overstatement by conceding that "a case-by-case examination of the FBI record does in fact reveal a bewildering collage, with Hoover and his men appearing to stand with the movement one day and with the resistance the next," *Racial Matters*, 4, 7–8. The Athens case conforms more closely to this second and more careful assessment.

Postscript to Chapter Three

1. The cartoon, showing FBI agents snooping on UGA students, was first published in *Red and Black*, Jan. 19, 1961.

2. James Barrow interview with John C. Belcher, Feb. 24, 1976, Charlayne Hunter-Gault Papers, Richard B. Russell Library, UGA. Snow, in turn, warned university officials.

3. "Hamilton Holmes: The Doctor Who Integrated the University of Georgia," *Athens Observer*, Jan. 20, 1977. Note, however, that Judge Barrow's oral history indicated that it was the Georgia Bureau of Investigation (the GBI) that offered Holmes personal protection during those first tense weeks, after the segregationist riot, at UGA. So it is possible that Holmes retrospectively confused the FBI with the GBI. For Barrow's account, see Barrow interview with Belcher, Feb. 24, 1976.

4. Robert A. Pratt, *We Shall Not Be Moved: The Desegregation of the University of Georgia* (Athens: University of Georgia Press, 2002), 9–66.

5. Thomas G. Dyer, *The University of Georgia: A Bicentennial History, 1785–1985* (Athens: University of Georgia Press, 2002), 303–34.

6. *Atlanta Constitution*, Jan. 7, 1961; *Athens Banner Herald*, Jan. 10, 1961; for the comparison to the University of Alabama's desegregation crisis of 1956, I am indebted to the fine reporting of Phil Smith of the *Atlanta Journal*, who had covered that crisis, and at the time of the segregationist protests and riot at UGA was on hand to publish an insightful comparative analysis of the UGA and Alabama segregationist resistances to integration. See *Atlanta Journal*, Jan. 12, 1961; on Autherine Lucy and the Alabama desegregation crisis, see E. Culpepper Clark, *The Schoolhouse Door: Segregation's Last Stand at the University of Alabama* (New York: Oxford University Press, 1993), 53–113.

7. "Non-Violence Urged by Dean of Students in Campus Meeting," *Red and Black*, Jan. 9, 1961.

8. Calvin Trillin, *An Education in Georgia: Charlayne Hunter, Hamilton Holmes, and the Integration of the University of Georgia* (1964; reprint, Athens: University of Georgia Press, 1992), 52; FBI file 72-39, SA Atlanta, "School Desegregation, University of Georgia," Jan. 15, 1961.

9. Trillin, *Education in Georgia*, 54.

10. Barrow interview with Belcher.

11. Trillin, *Education in Georgia*, 52.

12. Note, however, that Vandiver did not say he ordered the suspension of Hunter and Holmes, only that he "ordered the state patrol to remove them from the dormitories and take them to the safety of their own homes." Vandiver said he ordered this action after Aderhold told him that "he believed the black students were in danger." It is difficult to know how much credence to give Vandiver's memoir on this, first, because Hunter and Holmes were suspended after the riot had been quelled; second, because Vandiver did not

even offer here an explanation of why the state patrol failed to show up to suppress the rioters; and third, because Holmes did not reside in a campus dormitory but lived with a Black family off campus and was never endangered by the riot on campus. S. Ernest Vandiver, "Vandiver Takes the Middle Road," in *Georgia Governors in an Age of Change: From Ellis Arnall to George Busbee*, ed. Harold P. Henderson and Gary L. Roberts (Athens: University of Georgia Press, 1988), 160.

13. Pratt, *We Shall Not Be Moved*, 99.

14. Joseph Williams interview with John C. Belcher, Aug. 6, 1975, Hunter-Gault Papers.

15. William Tate interview with John C. Belcher, Aug. 5, 1976, Hunter-Gault Papers. Tate also said that Aderhold thought that students after a basketball game would be hungry and so, inclined to go eat rather than riot, an absurd argument given the widely known advance preparations that had been made for a riot.

16. Owen V. Whitman to Herman E. Talmadge, Jan. 31, 1961, O. C. Aderhold Papers, University of Georgia Archives, Hargrett Rare Book and Manuscript Library, University of Georgia Libraries.

17. UPI-67 (with Integration), Jan. 15, 1961, FBI file 72-1295, Jan. 25, 1961.

18. UPI-67 (with Integration).

19. J. A. Williams to O. C. Aderhold, Jan. 24, 1961, Aderhold Papers.

20. FBI Investigation, University of Georgia, Athens, GA, Obstruction of Court Order, FBI file 72-39, Athens, GA, Jan. 13, 1961, 108, 142, and Feb. 17, 1961, 6–7.

21. Joseph P. Williams Memorandum to Students, Jan. 14, 1961, Aderhold Papers.

22. On these segregationist politicians' complaints about the UGA administration's suppression of anti-integration student organizing in the weeks following the January 11 riot, see *Post-Searchlight* (Bainbridge, GA), Jan. 26, 1961. Critics of these politicians pointed out, however, that Georgia's segregationist establishment had so poor a record on free speech—including suppression of student dissident writing against segregation—that their waving the banner of free speech for segregationist students was hypocritical and self-serving. See *Red and Black*, Feb. 2, 1961. The most prominent critic of the UGA administration's handling of the desegregation crisis was the state's leading white supremacist politician and state board of regents member Roy Harris, who made the ridiculous claim that President Aderhold had "brainwashed" UGA into accepting Black students, and he vowed to get Aderhold removed from office ("Shame in Georgia," *Time*, Jan. 20, 1961, https://content.time.com/time/subscriber/article/0,33009,871979,00.html); in a subsequent oral history interview, Harris claimed, "I knew what I was talking about" in denouncing Aderhold in this way, that UGA's president had for years been a covert advocate of integrating the university, a ludicrous claim for which there is no evidence and which is contradicted by Aderhold's public record and private correspondence. See Roy Harris interview with John C. Belcher, Sept. 26, 1975, Hunter-Gault Papers.

23. Dyer, *University of Georgia*, 333.

24. Homer C. Eberhardt to O. C. Aderhold, Jan. 14, 1961, Aderhold Papers.

25. Eberhardt to Aderhold.

26. Trillin, *Education in Georgia*, 44–45

27. Vandiver, "Vandiver Takes the Middle Road," 161.

28. Charlayne Hunter-Gault, *In My Place* (New York: Farrar, Straus and Giroux, 1992), 176–77.

29. William Tate interview with John C. Belcher, Dec. 27, 1974, Hunter Gault Papers. Tate gave as good as he got, knocking the teeth out of the student who assaulted him and a police officer.

30. Tate interview with Belcher.

31. Pratt, *We Shall Overcome*, 95.

32. Hunter-Gault, *In My Place*, 176.

33. William Tate to Douglas Jeter, Apr. 6, 1961, Dean of Men William Tate Papers, University of Georgia Archives, Hargrett Rare Book and Manuscript Library, University of Georgia Libraries.

34. The most the UGA administration would do is see to it that further violence did not occur in violation of the federal court order that had brought about the admission of Holmes and Hunter. As dean of students Joe Williams put it in an oral history interview with John C. Belcher, "Our stand and belief [was] that whatever the law of the land was, that was what we would support, whether we personally believed in integration or segregation or not, that couldn't be a factor in our actions. We had to take action in terms of what the court orders were," to which Belcher responded, "So no one [in UGA's administration] stood up and said integration is a good thing." Agreeing, Williams replied, "That is right. No one got up and championed integration" (Williams interview with Belcher).

35. That one female reporter was Kathryn Johnson. See her remarks at the journalists panel, 40th Anniversary Commemoration of UGA's Desegregation, Jan. 9, 2001, Athens, GA, https://bmac.libs.uga.edu/index.php/Detail/objects/47433.

36. Trillin, *Education in Georgia*, 52.

37. FBI file 72-39, Jan. 14, 1961.

38. "Taunted by Jeering Students," Associated Press wire photo, Jan. 9, 1961.

39. Report of interviews of Center-Myers Hall residents, Jan. 14, 1961, Dean Edith Stallings Papers, University Archives, Hargrett Rare Book and Manuscript Library, University of Georgia Libraries.

40. Williams interview with Belcher.

41. *Atlanta Constitution*, Jan. 13, 1961.

42. *Atlanta Constitution*, Jan. 13, 1961.

43. *Atlanta Constitution*, Jan. 13, 1961.

44. Hunter-Gault, *In My Place*, 182.

45. Hunter-Gault, 183.

46. Hunter-Gault, 183.

47. Tom Johnson remarks at the journalists' panel, 40th Anniversary Commemoration of UGA's Desegregation, Jan. 9, 2001, Athens, GA, https://bmac.libs.uga.edu/index.php/Detail/objects/47433).

48. Johnson remarks at the journalists' panel.

49. Hunter-Gault, *In My Place*, 184.

50. SAC, Atlanta to Director of FBI, Jan. 13, 1961, FBI file 72-1295-19.

51. FBI Investigation, University of Georgia, Athens, GA, Obstruction of Court Order, FBI file 72-39, SAC Atlanta, Jan. 15, 1961, 102, 112, 119.

52. FBI Investigation, University of Georgia, Athens, GA, Obstruction of Court Order, FBI file 72-39, SAC Atlanta, Jan. 15, 1961, 62, 104, 106, 125.

312 Notes to Chapter Four

53. FBI Investigation, University of Georgia, Athens, GA, Obstruction of Court Order, FBI file 72-39, SAC Atlanta, Jan. 15, 1961, 62, 106, 136.

54. *Macon Telegraph*, Jan. 13, 1961; FBI Investigation, University of Georgia, Athens, GA, Obstruction of Court Order, FBI file 72-39, SAC Atlanta, 113.

55. *Macon Telegraph*, Jan. 13, 1961; FBI Investigation, University of Georgia, Athens, GA, Obstruction of Court Order, FBI file 72-39, SAC Atlanta, 113.

56. FBI Investigation, University of Georgia, Athens, GA, Obstruction of Court Order, FBI file 72-39, SAC Atlanta, 26, 42, 142, 144; "School Desegregation University of Georgia, Athens, GA, Obstruction of Court Order," FBI file 72-39, 72-1295, SAC Atlanta. Feb. 22, 1961, 6; Athens city attorney Judge Barrow recalled that the students who organized the riot "had been receiving calls from Atlanta . . . legislators in the main, who were prominent university alumni, and some of them, I know were egging the students on: just make the campus too unpleasant for them [Hunter and Holmes] to stay there. We don't want 'em killed or hurt; just put them in coventry" (Barrow interview with Belcher).

57. FBI Investigation, University of Georgia, Athens, GA, Obstruction of Court Order, FBI file 72-39, SAC Atlanta, 107.

58. FBI Investigation, University of Georgia, Athens, GA, Obstruction of Court Order, FBI file 72-39, SAC Atlanta, 38.

59. Williams interview with Belcher.

60. Journalist panel, 40th Anniversary Commemoration of UGA's Desegregation, Jan. 9, 2001, tape three, Walter J. Brown Media Archive and Peabody Awards Collection, https://bmac.libs.uga.edu/index.php/Detail/objects/45388.

61. Robert Dince interview with John C. Belcher, June 6, 1975, Hunter-Gault Papers. Note, however, that Athens city attorney Judge Barrow denied that any shots were fired during the riot. See Barrow interview with Belcher.

62. Thomas Brahana interview with the author, Feb. 13, 1995.

63. Peter McCommons interview with John C. Belcher, Sept. 2, 1975, Hunter-Gault Papers.

Chapter Four

1. A striking consequence of this lack of a UGA archive devoted to the university's desegregation is that the materials of the one UGA professor who did any research on UGA's desegregation, the oral history interviews by sociologist John C. Belcher (with UGA administrators and faculty) completed in the 1970s, did not find their way to the university library until 2011, when they went to the Russell Library as part of the Charlayne Hunter-Gault Papers, which opened that year. See https://sclfind.libs.uga.edu/sclfind/view?docId=ead/RBRL043CHG.xml.

2. Calvin Trillin interview with the author, Jan. 28, 2011, tape in author's possession; for more on the depth of his reportage on Black Atlanta in *An Education in Georgia*, see Robert Cohen, "Reporting Across the Color Line: A Retrospective on Calvin Trillin's *An Education in Georgia*," *Reviews in American History* 39, no. 4 (Dec. 2011): 575–82.

3. Robert A. Pratt, *We Shall Not Be Moved: The Desegregation of the University of Georgia* (Athens: University of Georgia Press, 2002); Maurice C. Daniels, *Horace T. Ward: Desegregation of the University of Georgia, Civil Rights Advocacy, and Jurisprudence* (Atlanta:

Clark Atlanta University Press, 2001); in terms of public history, Holmes's story reached the most people via Maurice Daniels's documentary film *Hamilton Earl Holmes: The Legacy Continues* that aired on Georgia Public Television in 2004. See Deepika Rao, "Documentary Focuses on the Life of Hamilton Earl Holmes," *Red and Black*, Jan. 23, 2004.

4. Jim Dodson, "For Charlayne Hunter-Gault Life Is Calm 17 Years After the Storm," *Atlanta Journal Constitution Magazine*, Aug. 20, 1978, 9.

5. Charlayne Hunter-Gault, *In My Place* (New York: Farrar, Straus and Giroux, 1992), 3–129.

6. Hunter-Gault, *In My Place*, 2, 109.
7. Hunter-Gault, 97.
8. Hunter-Gaul, 2.
9. Hunter-Gault, 59.
10. Hunter-Gault, 114.
11. Hunter-Gault, 126.
12. Hunter-Gault, 146.
13. Hunter-Gault, 169.
14. Hunter-Gault, 172.
15. Hunter-Gaul, 174.
16. Hunter-Gault, 172.
17. Hunter-Gault, 171.
18. Hunter-Gault, 171.
19. Hunter-Gault, 171.
20. Hunter-Gault, 184.
21. Hunter-Gault, 190.
22. Hunter-Gault, 182.
23. Hunter-Gault, 183.
24. Hunter-Gault, 190.
25. Hunter-Gault, 190.
26. Hunter-Gault, 192.
27. Hunter-Gault, 196–97.
28. Hunter-Gault, 203.
29. Hunter-Gault, 203.

30. Charlayne Hunter-Gault, "Taunts, Tear Gas, and Other College Memories," *New Yorker*, Nov. 12, 2015, www.newyorker.com/news/news-desk/taunts-tear-gas-and-other-college-memories.

31. Hunter-Gault, *In My Place*, 186–88.

32. Hunter-Gault, *In My Place*, 248–57.

33. Calvin Trillin, *An Education in Georgia: Charlayne Hunter, Hamilton Holmes, and the Integration of the University of Georgia* (New York: Viking, 1964), 15.

34. "Hamilton Holmes: The Doctor Who Integrated the University of Georgia," *Athens Observer*, Jan. 20, 1977.

35. Hunter-Gault, *In My Place*, 126–27.

36. Trillin, *Education in Georgia*, 31. And in fact Holmes's academic success did generate attention from white Georgians. His election to Phi Beta Kappa in 1963 was the topic of a

political cartoon (included in this book's photo gallery) by Clifford "Baldy" Baldowsi, the *Atlanta Constitution*'s famed political cartoonist.

37. "Hamilton Holmes."
38. Trillin, *Education in Georgia*, 30.
39. Trillin, 102–3
40. Trillin, 100.
41. Trillin, 100
42. Trillin, 69.
43. "Hamilton Holmes: The Doctor Who Integrated the University of Georgia," In this same interview Holmes said that he never attended a UGA basketball game because the games were played in old Woodruff Hall, which was dark, and so seemed unsafe for him.
44. Trillin, *Education in Georgia*, 89.
45. "Hamilton Holmes."
46. Trillin, *Education in Georgia*, 83.
47. Trillin, 90.
48. Ben Chester, "Negro Medical Graduate: Emory's Hamilton Holmes Starts New Life in Month," *Atlanta Journal*, May 23, 1967.
49. Randy Loftis, "To Aid Black Goals Holmes Urges Education," *Red and Black*, Jan. 18, 1977.
50. Keith Graham, "Color Barrier One of Many Doctor Broke, "*Atlanta Journal*, Aug. 25, 1983.
51. "Hamilton Holmes."
52. "Hamilton Holmes."
53. In his memoir, Jordan devoted a little under seven pages to UGA's desegregation. See Vernon E. Jordan Jr. with Annette Gordon Reed, *Vernon Can Read!* (New York: Public Affairs, 2001), 137–43.
54. Jordan, *Vernon Can Read!*, 126.
55. Jordan, 130; see the informative biography by Maurice C. Daniels, *Saving the Soul of Georgia: Donald Hollowell and the Struggle for Civil Rights* (Athens: University of Georgia Press, 2013).
56. Charlayne Hunter-Gault, remarks at the author's NYU class session, Sept. 19, 2022; Tomiko Brown-Nagin, *Civil Rights Queen: Constance Baker Motley and the Struggle for Equality* (New York: Pantheon, 2022), 116.
57. Jordan, *Vernon Can Read!*, 130–36.
58. Jordan, 131–33.
59. Jordan, 133–34.
60. Jordan, 127.
61. Jordan, 135.
62. Jordan, 141.
63. Jordan, 141.
64. Baker Motley did write a memoir, but she had so many of her civil rights cases and victories to recount that she devoted only three paragraphs to the UGA desegregation struggle. See Constance Baker Motley, *Equal Justice Under Law* (New York: Farrar, Straus and Giroux, 1998), 137–38. Her work in the UGA case is discussed at greater length in Brown-Nagin, *Civil Rights Queen*, 115–24.

65. Jordan, *Vernon Can Read!*, 140.
66. Jordan, 139.
67. Jordan, 137.
68. Pratt, *We Shall Overcome*, 82.
69. Hunter-Gault, *In My Place*, 164.
70. Jordan, *Vernon Can Read!*, 142.
71. Jordan, 142.
72. Jordan, 142, 143.
73. Jordan, 142, 143.
74. Mary Frances Early, *The Quiet Trailblazer: My Journey as the First Black Graduate of the University of Georgia* (Athens: University of Georgia Press, 2021), 52.
75. Early, *Quiet Trailblazer*, 55–56.
76. Early, 60.
77. Early, 60.
78. Early, 60–61.
79. Early, 66.
80. Early, 67–68.
81. Early, 68–69.
82. Early, 71.
83. Early, 71.
84. Early, 73–74.
85. Early, 85–86.
86. Early, 100.
87. Maurice C. Daniels, foreword, in Early, *Quiet Trailblazer*, x.
88. Early, *Quiet Trailblazer*, 138–67.
89. Early, caption in photo gallery.
90. Trillin, *Education in Georgia*, 114.
91. This neglect of Black Athens's history has begun to be recticified thanks to an ambitious oral history project launched by UGA in 2014. See https://sclfind.libs.uga.edu/sclfind/view?docId=ead/RBRL361AOHP.xml;brand=default.
92. Trillin, *Education in Georgia*, 114–18.
93. Trillin, 117.
94. Trillin, 115.
95. Trillin, 116.
96. "Mary Blackwell Diallo," *UGA Today* (Aug. 9, 2022), video of Blackwell Diallo's remarks made at a ceremony in which a UGA dorm was named for her and her classmates Harold Black and Kerry Miller, who were the first Black undergraduates to attend UGA for all four years, having come in as freshman—unlike Hunter and Holmes who came to UGA as transfer students after matriculating at other universities while their court case was litigated.
97. Mary Blackwell Diallo, "Fear Was Rampant," *University of Georgia Magazine* 90, no. 2 (Mar. 2011): 21; "Mary Blackwell Diallo," *UGA Today*, Aug. 9, 2022, video of Blackwell Diallo's remarks.
98. *UGA Today*, Aug. 9, 2022, video of Blackwell Diallo's remarks; Blackwell Diallo, "Fear Was Rampant."

99. Trillin, *Education in Georgia*, 117. Trillin also found that students in Athens's Black high school were 50 to 150 points behind their white counterparts on the college boards, which he attributed to these educational inequities in Jim Crow Georgia.

100. Clarke County School District, "Public School Review," www.publicschoolreview.com/georgia/clarke-county-school-district/1301170-school-district; Demographics, Athens–Clarke Unified County Government, updated May 15, 2023, www.accgov.com/105/Demographics; "Athens: Addressing Upward Mobility," *Red and Black*, Apr. 12, 2018.

101. "Athens: Addressing Upward Mobility."

102. Paul Thomas Zenki, "When Athens GA Burned Black Homes for UGA," *An Injustice*, Feb. 21, 2022, https://aninjusticemag.com/when-athens-ga-burned-black-owned-homes-for-uga-c7dc25f3b2b6; Char Adams, "Georgia Destroyed a Black Neighborhood. Now Former Residents Want Justice," NBC News, Dec. 2, 2021, www.nbcnews.com/news/georgia-destroyed-black-neighborhood-now-former-residents-want-justice-rcna7148.

See also Audra D. S. Burch, "A New Front in Reparations: Seeking the Return of Lost Family Land," *New York Times*, June 8, 2023, www.nytimes.com/2023/06/08/us/black-americans-family-land-reparations.html.

103. Robert A. Pratt, "The Long Journey from LaGrange to Atlanta: Horace Ward and the Desegregation of the University of Georgia," in *Higher Education and the Civil Rights Movement: White Supremacy, Black Southerners, and College Campuses*, ed. Peter Wallenstein (Gainesville: University Press of Florida, 2009), 92–115.

104. Robert A. Pratt, "Horace T. Ward, 1927–2016," *New Georgia Encyclopedia*, updated May 4, 2021, www.georgiaencyclopedia.org/articles/history-archaeology/horace-t-ward-1927-2016/.

105. Pratt, "Horace T. Ward"; Daniels, *Horace T. Ward*, 49–142; Pratt, *We Shall Not Be Moved*, 10–26.

106. Pratt, "Horace T. Ward"; Daniels, *Horace T. Ward*, 49–142; Pratt, *We Shall Not Be Moved*, 10–26.

107. Horace T. Ward, foreword, in Daniels, *Horace T. Ward*, x.

108. Ward, foreword, xi.

109. Ward, foreword, xi

110. Pratt, "Long Journey," 111.

111. Memorandum of the interview by the committee with Horace T. Ward, Sept. 8, 1951, J. Alton Hosch Papers, Hargrett Rare Book and Manuscript Library, University of Georgia Libraries.

112. Pratt, "Long Journey," 111.

113. Daniels, *Horace T. Ward*, 211.

Chapter Five

1. "Negro Student Eats Meal at University Cafeteria," *Macon Telegraph*, Mar. 21, 1961.

2. Bruce Galphin, "Dining Hall Opened to 2 Negroes," *Atlanta Constitution*, Mar. 10, 1961; Charlayne Hunter-Gault, *In My Place* (New York: Farrar, Straus and Giroux, 1992), 177–78.

3. Hunter-Gault, *In My Place*, 206.

4. "Negro May Delay Dining Hall Use," *Atlanta Journal*, Mar. 10, 1961; "Bootle Spells Out University Decree: Judge Says All School Facilities Must Be Extended to Negro Students," *Macon News*, Mar. 10, 1961.

5. "Negro Student Eats Meal."

6. Hunter-Gault, *In My Place*, 207.

7. Village Voice Staff, "James Baldwin: The Last Interviews, *Village Voice*, Feb. 24, 2017, https://www.villagevoice.com/james-baldwin-the-last-interviews/.

8. Martin Arnold, "Charlayne Hunter Discloses Marriage to Student She Met at U. of Georgia," *New York Times*, Sept. 3, 1963; "Wed to White Georgian, Charlayne Hunter Reveals," *Atlanta Journal*, Sept. 3, 1963.

9. "Georgia Calls Negro Co-Ed's Wedding Illegal: Bars Any Return by Couple—University President Is 'Shocked' at Marriage," *New York Times*, Sept. 4, 1963.

10. Roscoe C. to O. C. [Aderhold] (Sept. 1963), President O. C. Aderhold Papers, University Archives, Hargrett Rare Book and Manuscript Library, University of Georgia Libraries.

11. Cartoon attached to Roscoe C. to Aderhold, Aderhold Papers.

12. Anon. to Aderhold, (Winter Haven, FL), Sept. 4, 1963, Aderhold Papers.

13. Young H. Fraser to Aderhold, Sept. 4, 1963, Aderhold Papers.

14. Calvin Trillin, *An Education in Georgia: Charlayne Hunter, Hamilton Holmes, and the Integration of the University of Georgia* (Athens: University of Georgia Press, 1992), 40.

15. O. C. Aderhold to Young Fraser, Sept. 7, 1963, Aderhold Papers.

16. University of Georgia News Bureau to Associated Press, United Press International, Sept. 3, 1963, Aderhold Papers.

17. Memo to Aderhold on secret marriages [Sept. 1963], emphasis added, Aderhold Papers.

18. "Sanders Says Stovall Marriage a Disgrace," *Savannah Morning News*, Sept. 6, 1963.

19. "Stovall Marriage a Disgrace."

20. "State May Void Negro's Diploma," *LaGrange Daily News*, Sept. 4, 1963; "The Stovall Story," *Augusta Chronicle*, Sept. 8, 1963.

21. Sid Williams, "Segregationists Happy Over Mixed Nuptials," *Ellaville Sun*, Sept. 11, 1963.

22. Marvin Griffin, "Some Georgians Have Acted as if Chrissie Keeler Had Come," *Post Searchlight* (Bainbridge), Sept. 12, 1963; Marvin Griffin, "Those Who Sow the Wind Must Reap the Whirlwind," *Post Searchlight* (Bainbridge), Sept. 5, 1963; Roy V. Harris, "Strictly Personal," *Augusta Courier*, Sept. 23, 1963; also see "A Shocking Incident," *Dawson News*, Sept. 5. 1963; *Augusta Herald*, Sept. 7, 1963; *North Georgia Tribune*, Sept. 5, 1963; *Daily Times* (Gainesville, GA), Sept. 5, 1963; *Swainsboro Forest-Blade*, Sept. 11, 1963; *Oglethorpe Echo*, Sept. 12, 1963; *Thomasville Times-Enterprise*, Sept. 9, 1963.

23. Trillin, *Education in Georgia*; Robert Pratt, *We Shall Not Be Moved: The Desegregation of the University of Georgia* (Athens: University of Georgia Press, 2006).

24. Walter Stovall interview with the author, Apr. 1, 2011, New York City, tape in author's possession.

25. Stovall interview.

26. Stovall interview.

27. Stovall interview.
28. Stovall interview.
29. Stovall interview.
30. Stovall interview; Vanderbilt's undergraduates were still overwhelmingly opposed to integration in 1962 when the university's undergraduate school was finally desegregated. See Melissa Kean, *Desegregating Higher Education in the South: Duke, Emory, Rice, and Vanderbilt* (Baton Rouge: Louisiana State University Press, 2008), 206–7.
31. Stovall interview.
32. Stovall interview.
33. Stovall interview.
34. Stovall interview.
35. Stovall interview.
36. Pratt, *We Shall Not Be Moved*, 115; also see Joan Zitzelman, "A Supporting Role: A Student's Recollections of Desegregation at the University of Georgia" (unpublished manuscript), Hargrett Rare Book and Manuscript Library, University of Georgia Libraries, 9–10.
37. Stovall interview.
38. Stovall interview.
39. Stovall interview.
40. Stovall interview.
41. Hunter-Gault, *In My Place*, 233.
42. Stovall interview.
43. Hunter-Gault, *In My Place*, 237.
44. Hunter-Gault, 238.
45. Charlayne Hunter-Gault interview with the author, Jan. 11, 2011, Athens, GA.
46. Stovall interview.
47. Paul R. Spickard, *Mixed Blood: Intermarriage and Ethnic Identity in Twentieth Century America* (Madison: University of Wisconsin, 1989), 292–93; Sidney Portier, *The Measure of a Man: A Spiritual Autobiography* (New York: Pocket Books, 2001), 119–21.
48. Hunter-Gault, *In My Place*, 241.
49. Hunter-Gault, 242.
50. Hunter-Gault, 253.
51. Stovall interview.
52. Stovall interview; note that in Hunter-Gault's memoir *In My Place* (242) the "don't rock the boat" phrase is attributed to Dean Tate, not Dean Stallings. Stovall, however, told me it was Stallings who spoke those words to him. But these two deans met together with Stovall in part because, as Stovall put it, Tate "mumbled," and Stallings was there to "translate for him, really," so even though it was her words it was also Tate's sentiment she was conveying.
53. Trillin, *Education in Georgia*, 178; Hunter-Gault, *In My Place*, 239.
54. Trillin, 177–78.
55. Hunter-Gault, *In My Place*, 239.
56. Jonathan Zimmerman, "Crossing Oceans, Crossing Color: Black Peace Corps Volunteers and Interracial Love in Africa, 1961–1971," in *Sex, Love, Race: Crossing Boundaries in North American History*, ed. Martha Hodes (New York: New York University Press, 1999), 516.

57. Trillin, *Education in Georgia*, 176.

58. Peggy Pascoe, *What Comes Naturally: Miscegenation Law and the Making of Race in America* (New York: Oxford University Press, 2009), 203–4.

59. *Atlanta Daily World*, Sept. 5, 1963.

60. Hunter-Gault interview.

61. Hunter-Gault interview.

62. Pratt, *We Shall Not Be Moved*, 73–89.

63. Hunter-Gault interview; on white students' response to UGA's desegregation crisis in January 1961, see chapter 2.

64. John H. Britton, "She's Not Talking But Nation's Tongues Are Furiously Wagging: Charlayne's Secret Marriage to Georgia White Man," *Jet*, Sept. 19, 1963, 18–19, 23.

65. Britton, "She's Not Talking," 24–25.

66. Britton, 24.

67. Stovall interview.

68. Stovall interview.

69. Hunter-Gault, *In My Place*, 252.

70. Mary Frances Early telephone interview with the author, Jan. 11, 2011, tape in author's possession.

71. Stovall interview.

72. "The Charlayne Stovall News," *Atlanta Inquirer*, Sept. 7, 1963.

73. "A Calm Reflection: What Would They Tell Them," *Atlanta Inquirer*, Sept. 21, 1963.

74. Hunter-Gault, *In My Place*, 242.

75. Hunter-Gault interview; Stovall interview; on *Loving v. Virginia*, see Peter Wallenstein, *Tell the Court I Love My Wife: Race, Marriage, and the Law—An American History* (New York: Palgrave, 2002), 215–30. Note that the case was litigated not by the NAACP but by the American Civil Liberties Union—again reflecting the reluctance of the civil rights movement to take on the intermarriage issue. See Pascoe, *What Comes Naturally*, 275–84.

76. Stovall interview.

77. Stovall interview.

78. Stovall interview.

79. Sara Evans, *Personal Politics: The Roots of Women's Liberation in the Civil Rights Movement and the New Left* (New York: Vintage, 1980), 78–82; Doug McAdam, *Freedom Summer* (New York: Oxford University Press, 1998), 93–96.

80. On this isolation, Stovall recalled that at the University of Georgia in 1963 there were so few people committed to racial equality and supportive of Hunter and Holmes that you could fit this group into a small "room and they wouldn't be bumping into each other" (Stovall interview).

81. Transcript of CBS News interview with Charlayne Hunter and Walter Stovall, Sept. 3, 1963.

82. "Charlayne Gets Her Man," *Albany Herald*, Sept. 8, 1963; "Charlayne Sought License in Ohio," *Atlanta Journal*, Sept. 5, 1963.

83. Stovall interview.

84. "Wed to White Georgian, Charlayne Hunter Reveals," *Atlanta Journal*, Sept. 3, 1963.

85. Transcript of CBS News interview with Hunter and Stovall.

320 Notes to Chapter Five

86. Stovall interview.

87. Stovall interview.

88. Transcript of CBS News interview with Hunter and Stovall.

89. Cronkite commentary and reporter prediction made on CBS News, Sept. 3, 1963. See CBS News interview with Hunter and Stovall.

90. Hunter-Gault interview.

91. Stovall interview; Martha Stovall to George Stovall, May 11, 1963, Walter Stovall Papers, Richard B. Russell Library, University of Georgia Libraries.

92. M. Stovall to G. Stovall, Stovall Papers.

93. Lynn Stovall Cass telephone interview with the author, Sept. 7, 2011, tape in author's possession; William Tate to Lynn Stovall, Aug. 1 and 18, 1963, Stovall Papers; William Tate to Walter Stovall, Aug. 21, 1963, Stovall Papers.

94. Walter Stovall to Lynn Stovall, July 28, 1963, Stovall Papers.

95. W. Stovall to L. Stovall, Stovall Papers.

96. W. Stovall to L. Stovall.

97. W. Stovall to L. Stovall.

98. Stovall Cass interview.

99. Stovall Cass interview.

100. Evelyn M. Dickerson to Martha Stovall, Dec. 4, 1963; G. H. Mingledorff to George and Martha Stovall, Sept. 6, 1963; J. B. Oliff to George Stovall, Sept. 3, 1963; Margarett Middlebrook to Martha and George Stovall, Sept. 4, 1963; Elizabeth Person to Martha and George Stovall, Sept. 5, 1963; Mrs. John Wolf Jr. to Martha and George Stovall, Sept. 9, 1963, all in Stovall Papers.

101. Stovall Cass interview.

102. Stovall Cass interview; Stovall interview.

103. J. E. Stovall to George and Martha Stovall, Oct. 5, 1963, Stovall Papers.

104. Stovall Cass interview.

105. Stovall Cass interview.

106. Stovall Cass interview.

107. Robbi Blanton, "Peers Hassle Interracial Couples," *Red and Black*, Apr. 21, 1972. Note that the article did not include interviews with white female students or gay students, so the article, illuminating as it is, offers an incomplete picture of interracial relationships.

108. Blanton, "Peers Hassle Interracial Couples."

109. Blanton.

110. Blanton.

111. Blanton.

112. Blanton.

113. Pascoe, *What Comes Naturally*, 290, 385n14.

114. Hunter-Gault and Stovall interviews; https://www.mvartsandideas.com/2014/07/suesan-stovall/

115. On the honoring of Hunter-Gault and Holmes, see *Celebrating Courage: 50th Anniversary of Desegregation at UGA* (Athens: University of Georgia, 2011), copy in author's possession.

116. Hunter-Gault interview.

Chapter Six

1. See Robert Cohen, "Reporting Across the Color Line: A Retrospective on Calvin Trillin's *An Education in Georgia*," *Reviews in American History* 39, no. 4 (Dec. 2011): 575–82.

2. There has yet to be a published study on the desegregation of downtown Athens's restaurants and other businesses. But see the University of Georgia Oral History Collection, oral histories of Homer Wilson: https://georgiaoralhistory.libs.uga.edu/RBRL361AOHP/RBRL361AOHP-001; Bennie McKinley: https://georgiaoralhistory.libs.uga.edu/RBRL361AOHP/RBRL361AOHP-002; Rev. Archibald Killian: https://georgiaoralhistory.libs.uga.edu/RBRL361AOHP/RBRL361AOHP-003; and the short documentary film by Nicole Taylor and Southern Foodways Alliance, *If We So Choose*, which explored the desegregation of the downtown Varsity, www.southernfoodways.org/film/if-we-so-choose/.

3. "Senator to Speak," *Red and Black* Jan. 21, 1964; "Negro Plans Pioneer Talk for Thursday," *Red and Black*, Feb. 4, 1964. The press of his legislative work forced Johnson to cancel his UGA talk at the last minute ("Negro Postpones Talk," *Red and Black* [Athens], Feb. 11, 1964). The Black Student Union, with its annual Black Awareness Week event and its commemoration of Martin Luther King Jr.'s birthday from the late 1960s onward, did the most to bring major African American speakers to UGA. But even earlier, in 1966, there were signs of a growing receptiveness to Black speakers at UGA. Most striking was the Phi Kappa literary society's action in not only hosting a campus talk by Julian Bond but voting to make this state legislator and former Student Nonviolent Coordinating Committee leader the first Black honorary member of Phi Kappa (see "Phi Kappa Selects Bond as First Negro Nominee, *Red and Black* [Athens], Oct. 13, 1966; "Phi Kappa Slates Picture on Bond," *Red and Black* [Athens], Oct. 18, 1966; "Membership Extended to Bond by Phi Kappa Literary Society," *Red and Black* [Athens], Oct. 20, 1966). Even the most reactionary student group on campus, the Demosthenians, which regularly hosted white supremacist speakers, was affected by this move toward speaker diversity, coming close to inviting Martin Luther King Jr. to campus, first voting to do so but then by a single vote (cast by its president) deciding not to invite King, while making a pledge to explore inviting some "civil rights worker" to speak at UGA in the future (Don Rhodes, "Society Says 'No' on King," *Red and Black* [Athens], Jan. 13, 1966).

4. "Class Officers Investigate Mixed Entertainment Ban," *Red and Black*, Feb. 22, 1962. There seems to have long been an awareness among UGA students that the racial restrictions on musicians often led to second rate entertainment. This can be seen in the way the student newspaper referred to Johnny "Scatt" Davis, who in 1946 was to play at a campus dance, as "the white Cab Calloway,"— someone whose claim to fame was a musical style that supposedly resembled a much more famous Black musician. "Scatt Davis Orchestra to Play," *Red and Black*, April 19, 1946. But since nobody at UGA back then dared to invite Cab Calloway himself to campus in defiance of the color line, they made due with a white imitator.

5. "Class Officers Investigate Mixed Entertainment Ban," *Red and Black*, Feb. 22, 1962; "Entertainment Censorship," *Red and Black*, Feb. 22, 1962.

6. "Beneke Music Sets Mood for Weekend of Festivity," *Red and Black*, Apr. 29, 1949; "Dorsey Music to Initiate Festive Weekend," *Red and Black*, Apr. 21, 1950, "Military Dance Set for Tonight," *Red and Black*, Mar. 2, 1951; "Dorsey to Play at Little Commencement," *Red*

and Black, Apr. 1, 1954; "IFC Engages Band for Dance at Homecoming," Red and Black, Oct. 4, 1956..

7. "Trumpet Artist to Lead Band at AO Pi Dance," Red and Black, Jan. 27, 1955, and "Little Commencement to Feature Ellington," Red and Black, Mar. 25, 1955.

8. Red and Black, May 19, 1955. The cartoon is reproduced in this book's photo gallery. Ellington's appearance was especially unusual because it was for a campus-wide event, which meant it featured a very large audience and was held on campus—a venue that had been rigidly restricted to white performers, whereas with off campus events—fraternity dances— the prohibition was not as sweeping, and so in the late Jim Crow era, in addition to Armstrong in 1955, Roy Hamilton played at a UGA fraternity dance in 1960 ("Popular Singer to Entertain at Chi Phi Fraternity Formal," Red and Black [Athens], April 7, 1960).

9. Earl Leonard, "Armstrong to Appear for Stegeman Dance: Tour through South to Continue Despite Dynamite Blast," Red and Black, Feb. 21, 1957; Laurence Bergreen, Louis Armstrong: An Extravagant Life (New York: Broadway Books, 1997), 470.

10. "Armstrong Packs Stegeman for Saturday Night Program," Red and Black, Feb. 28, 1957. In contrast to the IFC's political timidity, Red and Black columnist Lamar Gunter heatedly criticized the Georgia legislature for seeking to bar Black musicians from performing in the state, and was in this same memorable column scathing, in condemning as "asinine" the legislature's vote championing the impeachment of six US Supreme Court justices for their support of the Brown decision. See Lamar Gunter. "So Long Salons," and the accompanying political cartoon, Red and Black, Feb. 28, 1957.

11. "Martin, Crew Cuts Set for Dance Appearance," Red and Black, May 15, 1958; "Singer, Jazz Ensemble to Entertain Saturday at Campus-wide Dance," Red and Black, Apr. 15, 1959; "Banquet to Top 'Greek Week' Activities," Red and Black, May 11, 1961.

12. Dave Cleghorn, "Get The Picture" Red and Black, Feb. 26, 1959. Within the civil rights community, in fact, both Black entertainers and white, during the Jim Crow era, were criticized for even agreeing to play for whites-only audiences like UGA's. See Ingrid Monson, Freedom Sounds: Civil Rights Call Out of Jazz and Africa (New York: Oxford University Press, 2007), 58-65.

13. "Two Orchestras Planned for Formal at Sigma Nu," Red and Black, March 31, 1950; Chris Jones, "White Fraternities and Black Music in the Early 1960s, Boom Magazine (Oct. 1. 2023), https://boomathens.com/white-fraternities-and-black-music-in-the-early-60s/.

14. "McPhatter, Reed Star in Climax of Activities," Red and Black, Apr. 4, 1963.

15. Wilson Sings for Students," Red and Black, May 21, 1963

16. "Recording Star Clyde McPhatter to Entertain Friday at the IFC Street Fair," Red and Black, Apr. 28, 1964; "The Platters Quartet to Appear in Cultural Affairs Program," Red and Black, Apr. 22, 1965; "Greek Week Includes Brown and the Flames," Red and Black, Apr. 28, 1966; "Rhythm and Blues Singer Stirs Coliseum Audience," Red and Black, May 10, 1966; "Motown Swingers Wow 10,000 Fans," Red and Black, May 9, 1967.

17. Jackie Ross, "Civil Rights Act Affects Greeks," Red and Black June 24, 1965.

18. William Tate interview with John Belcher, Aug. 5, 1976.

19. Tate interview with Belcher.

20. Tate interview with Belcher.

21. Tate interview with Belcher.

22. Tate interview with Belcher.

23. Tate interview with Belcher.

24. Dr. Ben Rucker interview by Ashley Carter, July 25, 2019, UGA Black Alumni Oral History Project, https://kaltura.uga.edu/media/t/1_2fogiqyv/157116721l; Nawanna Lewis Miller interview by Ashley Carter, June 30, 2019, UGA Black Alumni Oral History Project, https://kaltura.uga.edu/media/t/1_2fogiqyv/157116721.

25. John Belcher, "Integration Issue," unpublished manuscript, 1974–75, 1–2, Charlayne Hunter-Gault Papers, Richard B. Russell Library, UGA.

26. Charlayne Hunter, "After Nine Years: A Homecoming for the First Black Girl at the University of Georgia," *New York Times Magazine*, Jan. 25, 1970.

27. Hunter, "After Nine Years."

28. Hunter.

29. Hunter.

30. Hunter.

31. Hunter.

32. Hunter.

33. Hunter.

34. The BSU at UGA was a Georgia manifestation of a nationwide Black Power–oriented student movement among African American undergraduates, graduate students, and even high school students in the mid and late 1960s. See Martha Biondi, *The Black Revolution on Campus* (Berkeley: University of California Press, 2012).

35. O. Suthern Sims to George Parthemos, Jan. 11, 1969, President Frederick C. Davison Papers, University Archives, Hargrett Rare Book and Manuscript Library, University of Georgia Libraries.

36. Hunter, "After Nine Years."

37. A. Levert Hood to Fred Davison, Feb. 21, 1971, Davison Papers.

38. Robinette Kennedy and Myra Black, "All Men Are Created Equal," *Impression* (May 1969), 46. Not all UGA administrators were dismissive of BSU demands. O. Suthern Sims, the acting dean of student affairs, privately noted that he found their demands "reasonable and justifiable" and thought the administration "would be wise to not only discuss them but to act" upon them. See Sims to Parthemos, Davison Papers.

39. Ken Dious interview with Venus Jackson, UGA Black Alumni Oral History, Mar. 11, 2020, https://kaltura.uga.edu/media/t/1_x4uz8xno/157116721.

40. "Dr. Fred C. Davison: An Interview with the President," *Impression* (May 1969), 9.

41. Chuck Cooper, "Demands of Black Students Answered," *Athens Banner-Herald*, Mar. 10, 1969; Philip Gailey, "Davison Tells of Demands by Students," *Atlanta Constitution*, Mar. 11, 1969; see also "Black Recruitment: The Black Demands," *Red and Black*, May 13, 1971; Deborah Blum, "Students Force End to Shockley Speech," *Red and Black*, Mar. 6, 1974; and Brian O'Shea, "Continuity Said BSU Problem," *Red and Black*, May 9, 1978.

42. Christopher A. Huff, "Conservative Student Activism at the University of Georgia," in *Rebellion in Black and White: Southern Student Activism in the 1960s*, ed. Robert Cohen and David J. Snyder (Baltimore: Johns Hopkins University Press, 2013), 179–87.

43. "Davison Tells of Demands by Students," *Atlanta Constitution*, Mar. 11, 1969;; "Demands of Black Students Answered." *Athens Banner-Herald*, Mar. 10, 1969.

44. Nawanna Lewis Miller interview with Ashley Carter, Nov. 14, 2019, UGA Black Alumni Oral History Project, https://kaltura.uga.edu/media/t/1_2fogiqyv/157116721.

45. Miller interview with Carter.

46. Miller interview with Carter.

47. "Racial Signs Down after Athens Row," *Atlanta Constitution*, Jan. 21, 1968; "Black Student Union Protests Segregation," *Red and Black*, Jan. 23, 1968.

48. "Racial Signs Down"; Felicia Bowens, "Advisor Says BSU Necessary," *Red and Black*, Apr. 17, 1974; Dious interview with Jackson.

49. Hunter, "After Nine Years."

50. "Black Students Increased Number, Influence over Last Nine Years" (1970). This article, which included excerpts from a telephone interview with Charlayne Hunter, was in the clippings file of the UGA archives, which cited it as having been published in the *Red and Black*, Jan. 13, 1970. The article did not appear in the *Red and Black* on that date, but the interview was clearly done with Hunter in 1970.

51. Kathryn Johnson, "Blacks at U. Ga. Want Action on Demands in the Fall," *Atlanta Journal and Constitution*, June 20, 1971.

52. "Black Students Increased Number."

53. "Black Students Increased Number." For a firsthand account of the first Black student in the 1960s who tried to join UGA's Jim Crow football team but was kept off the team by its racist coach, see Dious interview with Jackson; Bill Clark, "Negro Gridder Out at UGA," *Atlanta Constitution*, Apr. 7, 1966.

54. "U. Ga. Mix in Sports Discussed," *Athens Banner-Herald*, Apr. 5, 1967.

55. "U. Ga. Mix."

56. Charles H. Martin, "Hold that (Color) Line! Black Exclusion and Southeastern College Football," in *Higher Education and the Civil Rights Movement: White Supremacy, Black Southerners, and College Campuses*, ed. Peter Wallerstein (Gainesville: University of Florida, 2008), 184–85. Internal UGA administration correspondence attests that this pressure from the federal government was crucial in forcing the segregationists in UGA's athletic department to end their Jim Crow practices and finally give scholarships to talented Black athletes. See O. C. Aderhold to Joel Eaves, Apr. 8, 1967, Aderhold Papers, University Archives, Hargrett Rare Book and Manuscript Library, University of Georgia Libraries.

57. Robert Ayers, *Memories of a Southern Liberal* (Athens, GA: Bilbo Press, 2016), 115.

58. Sally Lofton, "HEW Rejects State Deseg Plan," *Athens Daily News*, Nov. 14, 1973.

59. Sharon Fell, "State, University Fall Short on Black Ratios," *Athens Banner-Herald*, Jan. 3, 1975.

60. Nelson D. Ross, "25 Years After Brown Decision—University Still Has a Long Way to Go," *Red and Black*, May 17, 1979; also see Justin Gillis, "Opinions Differ on the Present State of Racism," and Ben Fugitt, "BSU Grows through Stormy History," both in *Red and Black*, May 17, 1979.

61. Susan Laccetti, "Recruit Blacks Better BSU Will Urge," *Red and Black*, Apr. 8, 1983.

62. "25 Years After Brown Decision."

63. "Recruit Blacks Better."

64. Mark Sheftall, "University Hires Black Faculty as Part of Minority Recruitment," *Red and Black*, Oct. 18, 1988.

65. Randall H. Harber, "Black Recruitment Lags at 'Liberal' Minded U. Ga." *Athens Daily News*, May 27, 1971; Also see Penny Mickelbury, "Know Your Neighbor: Benjamin Colbert," *Athens Banner-Herald*, Sept. 17, 1970.

66. Harber, "Black Recruitment Lags."

67. Harber.

68. Hunter, "After Nine Years."

69. Hunter.

70. Phil Gailey, "500 Whites Look on: Blacks List Demands in University Rally," *Atlanta Constitution*, Apr. 18, 1969; also see "Black Student Union Holds Grievance Rally Thursday," *Red and Black*, Apr. 22, 1969.

71. Gailey, "500 Whites Look on: "Blacks List Demands."

72. Gailey.

73. Gailey.

74. Gailey.

75. Gailey.

76. Gailey.

77. Ronnie Feinberg, "Aired Grievances a Progressive Step," *Red and Black*, Apr. 29, 1969.

78. Feinberg, "Aired Grievances."

79. "The Wall, 1969," *Red and Black*, May 8, 1969. This political cartoon is reprinted in the photo gallery of this book.

80. *Atlanta Journal*, Mar. 6, 1974.

81. *Atlanta Journal*, Mar. 6, 1974 and Apr. 24, 1974; "President Apologizes to Shockley," *Red and Black*, Mar. 7, 1974; William K. Broker, "Protesters Attack Free Speech," *Red and Black*, Mar. 7, 1974; "Shockley Has a Right to His Ideas," *Red and Black*, Mar. 7, 1974; on Shockley's ideas, see Southern Poverty Law Center, "William Shockley," www.splcenter.org/fighting-hate/extremist-files/individual/william-shockley. The UGA debate was later held, transcribed, and published.

82. *Atlanta Journal*, Mar. 6, 1974.

83. *Atlanta Journal*, Mar. 6, 1974.

84. Hunter, "After Nine Years."

85. Hunter.

86. Hunter; Robert Benham, who as a UGA law student was a BSU leader and whose house was used for the initial BSU meetings, later became the Georgia Supreme Court's first Black chief justice.

87. Levert Hood interview with Steven Armour, July 15, 2022, UGA Black Alumni Oral History Project, https://kaltura.uga.edu/media/t/1_zn37rmsi.

88. Hunter, "After Nine Years."

89. *Atlanta Constitution*, Mar. 14, 1970; Charles Crowe, draft letter to the American Historical Association's Academic Freedom Committee (also known as the Hackney Committee, named for its chair Sheldon Hackney), Mar. 1970, copy in author's possession.

90. Will Holmes telephone interview with the author, May 16, 2022, tape in author's possession. Note that though much of the UGA faculty was too timid to speak up during the trial and registration of Holmes and Hunter, the faculty found its voice shortly after the riot—some two-thirds of the faculty (405 out of a total faculty of about 600) signed a resolution condemning the segregationist violence and calling for the reinstatement of Hunter and Holmes. See *Atlanta Journal Constitution*, Jan. 22, 1961.

91. Holmes interview; Robert Griffith, "Georgia's Compatibility Oath," *Change* 3, no. 6 (Oct. 1971): 16–17; Rebecca Leet, "History Fracas: Academic Power Struggle," *Red and

Black, Mar. 31, 1970; Rebecca Leet, "Professor Says About Half of History Faculty May Leave," Red and Black, Mar. 31, 1970; Ronnie Feinberg, "Faculty Argue Compatibility Issue," Red and Black, Apr. 2, 1970.

92. Griffith, "Georgia's Compatibility Oath."
93. Griffith.
94. Griffith.
95. Griffith.
96. Griffith; Holmes interview.
97. Charles Crowe to Al Young, June 4, 1972, American Historical Association's Academic Freedom Committee Papers, copy in author's possession; Holmes interview.
98. Holmes interview.
99. Crowe, draft letter.
100. Griffith, "Georgia's Compatibility Oath."
101. Crowe to Young, Academic Freedom Committee Papers.
102. Charles Crowe to George L. Simpson Jr., Sept. 7, 1969, American Historical Association's Academic Freedom Committee Papers, copy in author's possession.
103. Holmes interview. Though this loss of talent and progressive faculty was substantial, this setback did not leave UGA's history department barren of talented and racially egalitarian faculty. Thomas Dyer, who had been a graduate student in the department during the 1970s, recalled that "there was an amazing group of graduate students (Jim Cobb, Clarence Mohr, Theda Perdue, Tennant McWilliams, and Hardy Jackson, among others) and a tremendous amount of work going on focused on race and intolerance in the South and in the nation. Charles Crowe, Numan Bartley, F. N. Boney, Robert Griffith, Will Holmes . . . all approached race and Southern history in ways that were innovative and intellectually liberating. In the end, I think all of us were inspired by the civil rights movement" (Thomas Dyer to Robert Cohen, Mar. 23, 2011, copy in author's possession).
104. Harrell Rodgers to President Davison, Mar. 11, 1969, Davison Papers.
105. Brett W. Hawkins to Raymond Payne, Mar. 14, 1969, Davison papers.
106. On the Black faculty and staff organization of UGA, see www.facebook.com/BFSOUGA/.
107. Robinette Kennedy and Myra Black, "All Men Are Created Equal," Impression, May 1969, 46.
108. Christopher A. Huff, "Conservative Student Activism at the University of Georgia," in Rebellion in Black and White: Southern Student Activism in the 1960s, ed. Robert Cohen and David J. Snyder (Baltimore: Johns Hopkins University Press, 2013), 171–91.
109. Nick Curry to George Parthemos, Jan. 14, 1970, Davison Papers.
110. Rebecca Leet, "Black Students' March Encounters Little Reaction," Red and Black, Jan. 20, 1970.
111. Harber, "Black Recruitment Lags."
112. Harber.
113. John Toon, "Black Student Protest," Athens Banner-Herald, Feb. 27, 1974; Bob Massey, "Blacks Tell Davison About Grievances," Red and Black, Feb. 27, 1974; Buddy Walker, "Two Fraternities Put on Probation" and "Black Policy Group Formed," Red and Black, Feb. 28, 1974.
114. Massey, "Blacks Tell Davison." Red and Black, Feb. 27, 1974; Davison's improved handling of Black student protests by this time seems connected to the fact that by the

1970s there were several African Americans in mid-level administration positions at UGA who served as informal advisors to the BSU and as liaisons between the Black students and the Davison administration. See Levert Hood interview with Steven Armour, July 15, 2022, UGA Black Alumni Oral History Project, https://kaltura.uga.edu/media/t/1_zn37rmsi.

115. Mary Hill, "Grievance List Long Overdue," *Red and Black*, Feb. 28, 1974.

116. Gail Hall, "King's Birthday Remembered," *Red and Black*, Jan. 16, 1975.

117. Beth Slaughter, "Three Hundred Attend Freedom Rally," *Red and Black*, Jan. 16, 1979.

118. Nelson D. Ross, "BSU Rallies at Memorial for King, Black Solidarity," *Red and Black*, Jan. 16, 1980. The MLK birthday events were so central to Black student culture and politics that they offer a unique window into Black perspectives on life at UGA. One impressive aspect of these events was their tendency toward gender equity in that both African American male and female students played important roles in these events. But on the issue of sexuality there was some division. Gay Black students complained of being mocked by homophobic marchers when they participated under a gay and lesbian rights organizational banner in the 1992 King birthday event. See Terrance Heath, "King Holiday Isn't a Celebration for Just a Few," *Red and Black*, Jan. 23, 1992.

119. "Athens Calm: More May Come," *Red and Black*, May 19, 1970; Sharyn Kane, "Did Brutality Exist Here?" *Red and Black*, May 26, 1970. In an earlier expression of interracial solidarity, the main New Left organization at UGA, the campus chapter of Students for a Democratic Society, joined with Black students in protesting at the Rail, a bar in downtown Athens that as late as 1967 was refusing to allow African Americans to drink there. See Hayes McGlaun, "SDS Members Assist Local Bar Integration," *Red and Black*, May 16, 1967.

120. Kent Hannon, "Lectureship to Honor 1st Blacks at UGA," *Atlanta Journal*, June 20, 1985.

121. Charles H. Martin, "Hold that (Color) Line!" 185.

122. Dyer to Cohen.

123. Hannon, "Lectureship to Honor," *Atlanta Journal*, June 20, 1985.

124. As late as 1977 when Hamilton Holmes was the featured speaker at the Black student–organized King day event at UGA, no university official had come out to greet or introduce him (Randy Loftis, "Holmes Urges Education to Aid Black Goals," *Red and Black* [Athens], Jan. 18, 1977).

125. Hannon, "Lectureship to Honor."

126. Todd Holcomb, "Black Student Leaders to Meet with UGA Administrators," *Red and Black*, Feb. 24, 1983; Jim Barber, "Officials Explain Why So Few Blacks Enroll," *Red and Black*, Apr. 7, 1983; Susan Laccetti, "Recruit Blacks Better, BSU," *Red and Black*, Apr. 8, 1983; Clarice Makemson, "Blacks to Protest Recruitment Today," *Red and Black*, Apr. 12, 1983, Clarice Makemson, "Black Leaders Allege 'Hidden Racism,'" *Red and Black*, Apr. 13, 1983; *Atlanta Constitution*, Apr. 14, 1983.

127. Robert Cohen, "Race, History, and the Holmes-Hunter Lectures," UGA *Columns*, Oct. 30, 1995.

128. Cohen, "Race, History."

129. Hannon, "Lectureship to Honor."

130. Cohen, "Race, History."

131. Grace Elizabeth Hale, *Cool Town: How Athens, Georgia Launched Alternative Music and Changed American Culture* (Chapel Hill: University of North Carolina Press, 2020): 200–202.

132. Sarah Hawk, "University Has Difficulty Retaining Black Students," *Red and Black*, Feb. 18, 1988.

133. Steven M. Sears, "Blacks at UGA, THEN and NOW, 1961–1991," *Athens Daily News*, Sept. 30, 1991.

134. Merrill Morris, "A Question of Racism?" *Athens Observer*, Apr. 21, 1983. On an earlier and more widely disseminated application of the term "culture shock" to the Black student experience at UGA, see Joe Lamia, "'Culture Shock': Black Student Guide Says Life May Be Rough at UGA," *Red and Black*, Oct. 21, 1982.

135. Christopher Grimes, "Holmes Tells Marchers to Fight for Civil Rights," *Red and Black*, Jan. 12, 1990. Note that by 1990 the role that the BSU had played since 1967 representing Black students was now being played by the Black Affairs Council. See Mara Holmes, "New BAC President Is Young—and Very Busy," *Red and Black*, June 6, 1990.

136. Mark Sheftall, "University Housing Not Harmonious," *Red and Black*, Oct. 20, 1988.

137. Robert Todd, "Two Myers Residents Formally Apologize for Racial Incident," *Red and Black*, Dec. 2, 1988.

138. As of May 1990, there were twenty-four white fraternities and eighteen white sororities at UGA. There were no Black members of any of these UGA sororities. UGA's sorority adviser claimed that "other minorities, such as Orientals and American Indians were represented in the traditionally white sororities" but offered no statistics or names of sororities to support this claim. The UGA fraternity advisor claimed that there were "one or two black members of the white fraternities on campus, although he wouldn't say which fraternities." It was also reported that one Black student in the fall quarter of 1986 affiliated with the Kappa Alpha Theta sorority but had since graduated. UGA had four Black fraternities and four Black sororities (Marla Edwards, "UGA Greeks Remain Segregated," *Red and Black* [Athens], May 8, 1990).

139. Mark Sheftall, Johann Van der Wal, and Jack Stenger, "Black Greeks at UGA," *Red and Black*, Oct. 21, 1988; also see Clarice Makemson, "Black Fraternities Wary of Joining IFC," *Red and Black*, Mar. 1, 1983.

140. Edwards, "UGA Greeks Remain Segregated."

141. John Stenger, "KA Defends Flag Flying," *Red and Black*, June 1, 1988.

142. "KA Defends Flag Flying"; for a brilliant account of the way this kind of romanticized view of the Confederacy and its symbols has promoted racism and intolerance on Southern campuses, see Stephen M. Monroe, *Heritage and Hate: Old South Rhetoric at Southern Universities* (Tuscaloosa: University of Alabama Press, 2021).

143. "KA Defends Flag Flying." The Confederate battle flag (the stars and bars) would also be deployed to racially harass an Asian student at UGA, who in 1990 had eggs thrown at his dorm window and the rebel flag hung outside his room inscribed with racial slurs, which was condemned by the student newspaper. See Anne-Marie Fanguy, "Asian Student Is Target in Racial Incident," *Red and Black*, May 15, 1990. Unlike the Jim Crow era, by 1990 there was considerable public UGA student opposition to such Confederate remnants. That opposition was centered in a group, Students Against the Confederate Symbol, which pointed out that the Confederate battle flag was a symbol of slavery and racism that offended one-third of Georgians, who were Black. UGA historian F. Boney noted that the stars and bars had been placed on the Georgia state flag in 1956 as a symbol of resistance to racial integration. That image would not be removed from the state flag until 2001. See Mira

Shah, "Young Democrats Meeting Turns into Fiery Georgia Flag Debate," *Red and Black*, May 18, 1990; AJC staff, "A History of Georgia's State Flag," *Atlanta Journal-Constitution*, Oct. 23, 2018, www.ajc.com/news/local/history-georgia-state-flag-things-know/rQoDK2 QtuSP13EStbLC5iK/.

144. "Portrait Initiated Move to UGA Black Cultural Center," *Athens Daily News*, June 4, 1989; Luke Boggs, "Cultural Center: Racial Bridge or Barrier," *Red and Black*, June 22, 1989; Mocking the idea of a Black cultural center, a *Red and Black* political cartoon suggested that such a center would lead to UGA president Knapp being subject to demands for separate cultural centers not only by Asian and Hispanic students but even by the campus's rodents. The cartoon shows a harried Knapp being presented with the rats' petition: "They want a cultural center too," *Red and Black*, May 25, 1989. A related image a few weeks later suggested that the UGA student government would dub a basketball court the African American cultural center, *Red and Black*, June 9, 1989 (reprinted in gallery of images).

145. John Dowling to Fred C. Davison, April 26, 1984, Davison Papers.

146. University of Georgia, "Steps Toward Diversity: Timeline of African American Achievements and Milestones at the University of Georgia, 1960–2022" (2022), https://fanda.uga.edu/Diversity/Milestones-in-UGA-history-FINAL.pdf; Dyer to Cohen; Walter Colt, "Hiring Minority Faculty Getting More Difficult Despite UGA Efforts." *Red and Black*, Feb. 21, 1990.

147. Andrew Kennedy, "UGA Black Faculty Double in Two Years," *Red and Black*, June 7, 1989. As of October 1991 there were still only 49 Black faculty out of the 1,835 UGA faculty members. See Stephen M. Sears, "Georgia Black Faculty: Tale of Two Universities," *Athens Daily News*, Oct. 1, 1991.

148. Sears, "Tale of Two Universities."

149. Jill Corson, "Today 30th Anniversary of Desegregation Decision," *Red and Black*, May 17, 1984. Holmes also noted that despite *Brown*, prevailing over UGA's segregationist leaders had been quite a struggle and that it took more than one Supreme Court decision to change America: across the South, and beyond, Blacks had to engage in mass protest to win their rights. See Susan Laccetti, "Segregation Still Exists Says UGA Grad," *Red and Black*, May 19, 1984.

150. Robert A. Pratt, *We Shall Not Be Moved: The Desegregation of the University of Georgia* (Athens: University of Georgia Press, 2002), 159.

151. Pratt, *We Shall Not Be Moved*, 156.

152. Hannon, "Lectureship to Honor."

153. "Georgia Gov. Kemp Signs Bill into Law That Limits Discussion of Race in the Classroom," CNN, Apr. 28, 2022.

Chapter Seven

1. This quote and all quoted students below were enrolled in my UGA educational foundations/history class (EFN 203) in the 1997 and 1998 academic years. The quoted materials are from the essays they submitted for this class. To preserve their privacy, I will only identify the students via their initials or a student number I assign them. This first quote is from TM (EFN 203); this and all essays cited below are in author's possession.

2. TM (EFN 203).

3. EH (EFN 203).
4. KH (EFN 203).
5. NS (EFN 203).
6. *Red and Black,* Jan. 12, 1990.
7. *University of Georgia Fact Book* (Athens: UGA Institutional Research and Planning, 1997), 57; and 1998, 57.
8. TM (EFN 203).
9. AY (EFN 203).
10. GK (EFN 203).
11. GK (EFN 203).
12. JD (EFN 203).
13. NS (EFN203).
14. SA (EFN 203).
15. SA (EFN 203).
16. MM (EFN 203).
17. MM (EFN 203).
18. BA (EFN 203).
19. BA (EFN 203).
20. BA (EFN 203).
21. LB (EFN 203).
22. LB (EFN 203).
23. KH (EFN 203).
24. KH (EFN 203).
25. KH (EFN 203).
26. KH (EFN 203).
27. KH (EFN 203).
28. JA (EFN 203).
29. KJ (EFN 203).
30. JS (EFN 203).
31. CM (EFN 203).
32. KN (EFN 203).
33. SA (EFN 203).
34. SA (EFN 203).
35. AM (EFN 203)
36. AM (EFN 203).
37. CM (EFN 203).
38. CM (EFN 203).
39. AO (EFN 203).
40. TO (EFN 203).
41. VS (EFN 203).
42. VS (EFN 203).
43. TT (EFN 203).
44. SS (EFN 203).
45. MSk (EFN 203).

46. TC (EFN 203).
47. TCa (EFN 203).
48. TC (EFN 203).
49. NE (EFN 203).
50. NE (EFN 203).
51. NE (EFN 203).
52. Student 2 (EFN 203).
53. MS (EFN 203).
54. LL (EFN 203).
55. AC (EFN 203).
56. AM (EFN 203).
57. B (EFN 203).
58. B (EFN 203).
59. JA (EFN 203).
60. Sherry Liang, "UGA Fraternity Self-Suspends after Racist, Offensive Messages Released," *Red and Black*, Sept. 20, 2020 (updated Apr. 30, 2021), www.redandblack.com/uganews/uga-fraternity-self-suspends-after-racist-offensive-messages-released/article_7c7faf6e-fb7b-11ea-9fb9ef3e1f4bf3bc.html#:~:text=The%20University%20of%20Georgia%20chapter,Interfraternity%20Council%20President%20Brennan%20Cox.
61. AW (EFN 203).
62. The photo of the UGA student with the lynched Black puppet appeared in a *Life* magazine story on the segregationist race riot but not on the magazine's cover. This photo appears in the photo gallery of this book.
63. AW (EFN 203).
64. Hunter-Gault, *In My Place* (New York: Farrar, Straus and Giroux, 1992), 251.
65. Hunter-Gault, *In My Place*, 251.
66. Hunter-Gault, 249.
67. Hunter-Gault, 249–50.
68. Hunter-Gault, 254.
69. Hunter-Gault, 254–55.
70. Hunter-Gault, 252.
71. Hunter-Gault, 255.
72. Hunter-Gault, 256.
73. Thomas G. Dyer to Charlayne Hunter-Gault, May 27, 1988, copy in author's possession.
74. Dyer to Hunter-Gault.
75. KB (EFN 203).
76. Jim Farmer, "Hunter-Gault: 'All Have Failed in Responsibility to University,'" *Red and Black*, June 16, 1988.
77. Farmer, "Hunter-Gault: 'All Have Failed.'"
78. "Coming Full Circle," *Red and Black*, June 16, 1988.
79. "Coming Full Circle."
80. *University of Georgia Fact Book* (Athens: UGA Office of Institutional Research, 2013), 21.

Coda

1. Fortieth Anniversary Commemoration of UGA's Desegregation, Jan. 9, 2001, tape one, Walter J. Brown Media Archive and Peabody Awards Collection, https://bmac.libs.uga.edu/index.php/Detail/objects/47431; for the tapes of UGA's fiftieth anniversary of desegregation, see Walter J. Brown Media Archive and Peabody Awards Collection, https://bmac.libs.uga.edu/index.php/Detail/objects/373823; George T. Smith, who had been speaker of the house in Georgia's legislature during the UGA integration crisis, also served as a panelist at the fortieth anniversary commemoration; his remarks echoed those of Vandiver and Sanders.

2. Hunter-Gault keynote speech, Fortieth Anniversary Commemoration, https://bmac.libs.uga.edu/index.php/Detail/objects/47431.

3. Vandiver remarks at panel discussion, Fortieth Anniversary Commemoration, https://bmac.libs.uga.edu/index.php/Detail/objects/47431.

4. Actually, there was considerable public support in Georgia for recognizing political reality that, as the Little Rock school crisis had shown, defying federal court orders for educational segregation was a losing strategy, so that it was absurd and self-destructive—damaging to youth, education, and the state's future—to close public schools or state universities rather than integrate them. Thus, newspapers across Georgia ran editorials against closing UGA. See the quotes from many of the state's newspapers urging repeal of the massive resistance law and keeping UGA open in *Atlanta Constitution*, Jan. 13, 1961. Also see Ashton G. Ellett, "Not Another Little Rock: Massive Resistance, Desegregation, and the Athens Business Establishment, 1960–61," *Georgia Historical Quarterly* 97, no. 2 (Summer 2013): 176–216; Jeff Roche, *Restructured Resistance: The Sibley Commission and the Politics of Desegregation in Georgia* (Athens, University of Georgia Press, 1998).

5. Constance Baker Motley remarks in panel discussion, Fortieth Anniversary Commemoration, https://bmac.libs.uga.edu/index.php/Detail/objects/47431.

6. Reg Murphy, "Governor Blasts Bootle's Decision," *Atlanta Constitution*, Jan. 11, 1961; "Text of Vandiver's Wire to Judge: 'Must Register the Strongest Protest,'" *Atlanta Constitution*, Jan. 11, 1961.

7. Murphy, "Governor Blasts Bootle's Decision."

8. Murphy; Gene Britton, "Vandiver to Ask Broad Changes in School Setup," *Macon Telegraph*, Jan. 18, 1961. The main thrust of Vandiver's culminating speech on education (given on Jan. 18, 1961) in the wake of the UGA's desegregation crisis was that with good reason the majority of Georgians remained loyal to their traditional, racially segregated educational system. He agreed with that assessment and claimed that segregation was the best way to preserve amicable race relations, but that since the old massive-resistance laws failed in court to preserve segregated schools, those laws must be replaced in order to preserve the right of Georgians to segregated education. For the text of this Vandiver speech, see https://vault.georgiaarchives.org/digital/collection/adhoc/id/383.

9. Murphy, "Governor Blasts Bootle's Decision"; Governor Ernest Vandiver's Public Education Address, Georgia Archives, University System of Georgia, https://vault.georgiaarchives.org/digital/collection/adhoc/id/383. Accessed July 1, 2023.

10. Governor Ernest Vandiver press conference, WSB TV, July 30, 1962, https://crdl.usg.edu/record/ugabma_wsbn_wsbn42712.

11. William Yardley, "Carl Sanders, 89, Dies, Led Georgia in '60s," *New York Times*, Nov. 18, 2014.

12. All the remarks discussed and quoted below from Hollowell, Baker Motley, and Ward are from the panel discussion, Fortieth Anniversary Commemoration, https://bmac.libs.uga.edu/index.php/Detail/objects/47431.

13. Maurice Daniels speech introducing Fortieth Anniversary Commemoration, https://bmac.libs.uga.edu/index.php/Detail/objects/47431.

14. This, and all Hunter-Gault's remarks discussed and quoted below, are from Hunter-Gault keynote speech, Fortieth Anniversary Commemoration, https://bmac.libs.uga.edu/index.php/Detail/objects/47431.

15. Kerrie Mayer, "Students Demand Commitment to Diversity," *Red and Black*, Jan. 11, 2001.

16. Mayer, "Students Demand Commitment to Diversity."

17. The original of the photo is available through Getty images; in it the crowd behind the car with Holmes and Hunter is clearly visible, not obscured as they were when the photo appeared in the poster for UGA's Fortieth Anniversary Commemoration of the university's integration. See Getty Images photo archive, "Charlayne Hunter-Gault," www.gettyimages.ca/photos/charlayne-hunter-gault. The smudged version of the photo appears in the photo gallery of this book, where the fortieth anniversary of desegregation commemorative poster is reprinted.

18. Angie Harrington, "Pictures Reflect Two Different Images," *Red and Black*, Dec. 7, 2000.

19. Harrington, "Pictures Reflect."

20. Harrington.

21. Jason Sokol to Robert Cohen, Oct. 23, 2022, email in author's possession.

22. This photo of students with this racist banner is reprinted in the photo gallery of this book.

23. This was also the case with the poster UGA produced in 2021 to commemorate the sixtieth anniversary of the university's desegregation; it included no photographs and no visual representation of racist student resistance to integration. Its only visuals were silhouettes of Holmes, Hunter-Gault, and Early. See https://news.uga.edu/new-page-commemorates-desegregation-anniversary/.

24. "Johnson v. Board of Regents of the University of Georgia," (2001) Casetext, https://casetext.com/case/johnson-v-board-of-regents-of-univ-of-ga. UGA's affirmative action policy in admissions that the court rejected was not a policy that impacted the vast majority of UGA applicants. It worked as follows: "About 90 percent of University students were admitted solely on their grade point average and SAT scores. Admission[s] for the remaining 10 percent were based on a scoring system called the Total Score Index (TSI). The TSI assigns students points based on four broad categories: academic, demographic, leadership activity and various other factors—including race and relations to alumni." With the district court ruling, UGA suspended the use of race in considering freshman applications (Greg Bluestein, "Race Based Admissions: Federal Judge Rules against University," *Red and Black* [Athens], Aug. 28, 2001).

25. *University of Georgia Fact Book, 2000* (Athens: UGA Institutional Research and Planning, 2000), 57.

26. Melanie Horton, "Court Case Hurts Black Enrollment," *Red and Black*, Aug. 20, 2001.

27. "Race Based Admissions: Federal Judge Rules Against University" *Red and Black*, Aug. 28, 2001).

28. Opinion of the Supreme Court, "Students for Fair Admissions vs. President and Fellows of Harvard College," 35, www.washingtonpost.com/documents/4ff078d7-f01b-4533-8edc-5a894fc82cde.pdf?itid=lk_inline_manual.

29. Justice Sonia Sotomayor, dissenting, "Students for Fair Admissions vs. President and Fellows of Harvard College and University of North Carolina," 600 US, June 29, 2023 (J Sotomayor dissenting, 23, www.washingtonpost.com/documents/4ff078d7-f01b-4533-8edc-5a894fc82cde.pdf?itid=lk_inline_manual_3).

30. Sotomayor dissenting, 17.

31. Greg Sargent and Paul Waldman, "A Georgia Teacher's Plight Exposes the Essence of Anti-Woke MAGA Fury," *Washington Post*, July 5, 2023, www.washingtonpost.com/opinions/2023/07/05/georgia-teacher-termination-gender-identity-maga-desantis-trump/.

Index

Abney, George, 79
Aderhold Hall, 2, 3, 9
Aderhold, O. C., 47, 53, 179, 292–93n53; alumni relations, 112–13, 178; athletics program, 110, 310n15; Holmes & Hunter admissions, 2, 22, 115, 309–10n12; perjury, 2, 21–22; relationship with legislature, 22, 30, 114, 302n20; segregation support, 3–4, 22–23, 24, 33, 41, 106, 113, 177–78, 291n20, 302n20, 310n22
affirmative action, 252–56, 276–79, 333n24
African American Cultural Center, 139, 238
Afro-American Choral Ensemble, 252
Alexander, Joseph, 237
Allen, Walter, 169
Americanism/anti-Americanism, 3, 56
anti-Black admissions policy, 2
anti-Black stereotypes, 24, 31, 35, 58–60, 178, 222–23
anti-Black thought, xvi, 6
anti-intellectualism, 33, 44
antiracism, xvii, 8, 15, 17, 31, 81, 82, 105, 106, 195, 203, 244, 285n1
anti-urbanism, 33
Armstrong, Louis, 207, 322n8
Arnold, Robert O., 23, 24, 25
Ayers, Robert, 28–29, 82, 218, 303n28

Baldwin, James, 17, 177
basketball, 314n43, 329n144; rioting, 7, 65, 97–99, 101, 108–110, 116, 122, 259, 307n36, 308n42, 310n15; segregation, 7, 65, 97–99, 101, 108–110, 116, 122, 217, 259, 308n42; UGA-Georgia Tech rivalry, 7, 65, 97–99, 101, 108–110, 116, 122, 217, 259, 307n32
Bassett, Tim, 203
Beadle, Ned, 79

Belcher, John: oral history work, 31, 82, 123, 312n1; UGA desegregation, 210, 311n34, 312n1
BESTeam, 252
B-52s (Indie rock band), 235
Bissett, Harry, 246
Black Affairs Council, 237
Black business ownership, 144
Black churches, 71, 74
Black community (Athens), 15, 156, 167–68, 169–70, 173, 232, 235, 260–61
Black community (Atlanta), 51, 143, 146, 147, 152, 154, 155, 159, 171, 216
Black Faculty and Staff Organization, 229
Black faculty, 158, 210, 212, 215, 219–20, 228–29, 234, 238–39, 254, 262–63
Black families, 144, 156, 175, 249, 303n28, 309–10n12
Black fraternities, 230, 237, 250, 328n138
Black Freedom movement, 74, 151, 190–91, 193, 205, 242, 262, 267, 276
Black historical agency, 45
Black History Month, 252
Black history, 141–42, 143, 226, 233
Black House, 224
Black integration leaders, xi, xii, xiii, xviii, 2, 5, 7, 10, 18, 19, 21, 48–50, 74, 84, 107, 129, 142; *see also* Early, Mary Frances; Holmes, Hamilton; Hunter-Gault, Charlayne; Lucy, Autherine; Meredith, James
Black Lives Matter, 3
Black memory, 163, 167, 170, 172, 174
Black musicians, 206–208
Black Panthers, 230
Black political power, 206
Black Power, 216, 221, 323n34
Black professional class, 147, 152, 160, 162, 269

Black schools, 45, 57–58, 61, 168–69, 316n99
Black servant trope, 32
Black sexuality, 20, 290n11
Black sororities, 230, 236–37, 250, 328n138
Black student alienation, 6, 138, 204, 222, 255–56, 258
Black student enrollment, 205, 212, 218–19, 254, 272, 277, 279
Black student protests, 218–19, 221, 231, 326–27n114, 327n119
Black student recruitment, xviii, 26, 157, 219, 220, 235, 238, 262, 277–78
Black Student Union (BSU), 136, 137, 213–14, 215, 216, 321n3, 323n34, 328n135
Black studies program, 213
Black voting rights, 12–13, 14, 34, 44, 105
Black, Harold, 73, 290–91n15
Black, Hugo, 107
Black-white campus relations, 17, 32, 90, 237–38, 245–59, 261–62, 315n91
Boas, Franz, 62
Bond, Julian, 321n3
Boney, F. N., 16, 326n103, 328–29n143
Bootle, W. A., 19–20, 49, 52, 75, 107, 147
Brahana, Thomas, 55, 60–61, 66, 67, 69–82, 123, 297n13, 299n33
Brown v. Board of Education (1954): Black emboldenment, 145, 219, 239, 272, 329n149; criticism of Supreme Court, 43, 44, 322n10; post-*Brown* resistance, 3, 35, 181, 270, 277; Southern political leadership responses, 12, 35, 40, 44, 146, 260, 266, 293n65; UGA response to, 2, 22, 239; white anxiety over, 37, 181
Brown, James, 208
Brubeck, Dave, 16, 47, 206, 295n106, 295–96n107
Byrd, Garland T., 121, 305n22

Calhoun, John C., 3
Campbell, Phil, 9, 94–95, 305n23
Canterbury House, 73, 81
capitalism, 50
Carter, Jimmy, 171, 258
Catholic students, 73

Catholicism, 145
Center-Myers Hall, ix, 48, 53, 67, 70, 117–18, 148, 209, 261, 300n44
Chappell, David L., 74
Christianity, 65, 162, 197–98, 266
Civil Rights Act of 1960, 86, 87
Civil Rights Act of 1964, xii, 208, 217, 231, 268
Clark Atlanta University, 167
Clark College, 163
Clark, E. Culpepper, 54
Clark, Kenneth B., 38, 62
CLASS program, 252
Cobb, Preston, 159
Cobb, Thomas R. R., 14
Cochran, Thomas, 53–54, 75, 94, 103–104, 120, 305n22, 308n48
Cocking, Walter D., 33, 45–46, 299n33
Colbert, Ben, 219, 220
Coleman, Kenneth, 79, 302n20
Commodores, the, 224
Communism, 50, 57
Confederacy, 14, 44, 237, 328n142
Confederate flag, 25, 52, 184; demands for its removal from campus, 222, 251, 328–29n143; hoisted by UGA students, 76, 134, 150, 237, 251, 255, 261, 328–29n143
conservatism: in Georgia, 16, 225; prevalence of, xvi; as political power play, 1, 276; racial politics, 7, 82; UGA administration, 206, 225–26; UGA faculty members, 27, 78, 79, 83, 224, 226–28; UGA students, 207, 221, 232, 247, 256; US Supreme Court, 278, 279
Cooper, Jeff, 235
cosmopolitanism, 16, 182, 183, 200, 247
Coulter, E. Merton, 12, 14, 45, 226
Craig, C. F., 97, 306–307n31
Critical Race Theory, xv, 3, 9
Crowe, Charles, 226, 227, 233, 326n103

Daniels, Eddie, 219
Daniels, Maurice, xvii, 11, 142, 167, 172, 173, 219, 270, 272, 312–13n3
Danner, Walter, 21, 49–50, 290n11, 290–91n15

Davis, Angela, 230
Davison, Frederick, 220, 233; Black student relations, 136, 137, 213–15, 223, 228, 230–31, 234, 326–27n114; recognition of Black students, 234, 240
Demosthenian Literary Society, 76
Diallo, Mary Blackwell, 168–69, 173, 315n96
Dince, Robert, 27–28, 286n11
dining hall, 156, 165, 175–76, 218
direct-action campaigns, 92, 191
Dixie (song), 163, 214–216, 230
Doar, John, 93–95, 104, 304n8
Dollard, John, 62
Dooley, Vince, 16
Du Bois, W. E. B., 16, 280; on despotic nature of Jim Crow Georgia, 46
Dyer, Thomas G., 33, 54, 99, 233–34, 262, 289n49, 326n103

Early, Mary Frances, xi, 11, 140, 156, 163, 166, 275; application/interview process, 49, 164, 173, 269; white community hostility toward, 165, 166, 174, 190; family background, 163, 164, 171; media coverage/celebrity, 163, 164
Earth, Wind, and Fire, 224
Eastland, James, xiv, 37
Eberhardt, Homer C., 113
Eisenhower, Dwight D., 35, 85–87, 92, 303–304n3
Elitism, 27, 28, 41, 181
Ellington, Duke, 128, 207, 322n8
Emory University, 20, 142, 157, 158, 199, 258
eugenics, 222
Eurocentrism, 221

faculty: bias against Black students, 215, 216; role in UGA integration crisis, 77–85
Faubus, Orval, 87
Federal Bureau of Investigation (FBI): civil rights leaders' files, xvi, 9, 88, 164; civil rights movement hostility, 88–89, 304n8, 308–309n50; racial violence investigations, 92; UGA riot investigation, 7, 9–10, 17, 65, 86–107, 112, 116–17, 119–23, 131, 132, 300n49, 303–304n3,4, 305n21,22,23, 306n29,31
Federalism, 62
Fiala, Rick, 273, 274
Fink, Conrad, 273
Fite, Gilbert C., 41
Floyd, George, 3
Foot Soldier Project, 11, 12
football, 16, 156. 178, 181 183–84, 230; integrated, 218, 232–33, 245 integration demanded, 213, 217–18, 221–22; segregated, 49, 155–56, 261
Forty Watt Club, 235
Frazier, E. Franklin, 38
Freedom Summer (1964), xviii, 193

Galphin, Bruce M., 62
Garroway, David J., 52, 88
gay liberation movement, 232, 320n107, 327n118
Geer, Peter Zack, 112, 121, 149, 267
gender roles, 116, 118–19, 202, 327n118
George, Mary Dean, 181
Georgia exceptionalism, 259
Georgia Historical Quarterly, xvii, 17, 71
Georgia Tech, 7, 65, 97–98, 152, 217, 259, 307n36
Gleason, Ralph, 47, 295n106
Golden Rule, 72, 74
Gotesky, Rubin, 28–29, 31
Graham, Richard, 212–13, 238
Gregory, Dick, 224
Griffin, Marvin, 180
Griffith, Robert, 225–26, 326n103

Hale, Grace Elizabeth, 235
Hall, Gail, 231
Hardy, E. E., 100, 102
Harris, Lamar, 25
Harris, Roy, 12, 14, 46–47, 79, 97, 121, 179–80, 225, 295n103, 305n23, 310n22
Hart, Garson, 16
Hawkins, Brett W., 228
Herskovits, Melville J., 62

History department (UGA): "compatibility" crisis, 225–28, 326n103; desegregation, 228
Hollowell, Donald, 2, 11, 142, 158–60, 167, 175, 265, 268–69
Holman, Carl, 151, 191
Holmes v. Danner (1961), xviii, 2, 19, 32, 50, 78, 83, 156, 158–62, 171, 205, 265, 270, 290n11, 290–91n15
Holmes, Alfred "Tup," 152
Holmes, Hamilton Mayo, 152
Holmes, Hamilton, Jr., 236
Holmes, Hamilton, vi, xi, 1, 10, 11, 12, 20–21,141–42, 163, 173, 177, 180, 236, 272, 309n3, 333n17; academic performance, 152, 153, 154, 155, 157, 313–14n36; admission/interview, 19–21, 22, 48, 49–50, 76, 107, 161, 164, 186, 210–11, 269, 290n11, 311n34, 319n80; campus segregation challenges, 175, 176, 182; community hostility toward, 4, 10, 52–56, 66, 68–70, 72–73, 86, 108, 129, 133, 139, 146, 154–56, 158, 213, 217, 254, 273–74, 301n58,61, 303n28, 308n48, 312n56, 329n149; desegregates Emory University medical school, 157; desegregation commemoration, *140*, 204, 233–34; faculty support for, 78, 79–80, 81–82, 84–85, 299n36, 325n90; football, 49, 155, 217; media coverage/celebrity, 146, 188, 312–13n3; medical practice, 142, 146, 157, 258; named lecture series, 234, 240, 262; suspension/reinstatement, 10, 55, 62, 66, 77, 78–79, 83, 90, 103, 106, 108–11, 149–50, 163, 270–71, 292–93n53, 297n5, 297–98n13, 305–306n24, 309–10n12; see also *Holmes v. Danner* (1961)
Holmes, Isabella, 152
Holmes, Will, 226, 326n103
Holmes-Hunter Academic Building, 265
Hood, A. Levert, 137, 214, 217
Hoover, J. Edgar: civil rights movement hostility, 88, 89, 92, 93, 105, 308–309n50; Martin Luther King Jr. feud, 89, 105, 304n8; UGA riot investigation, 89, 91–94, 104

Hosch, J. Alton, 23–24, 25, 292–93n53
Humphrey, Hubert, 180
Hunter, C. S. H., 144, 189, 209
Hunter-Gault, Charlayne, 11, 12, 68, 114, 145, 232, 240–41, 260–64, 272, 277, 301n1; admission/interview, 146, 147, 148, 258; campus segregation challenges, 150, 151, 153–54, 173–74, 190; commencement speech (1988), 151, 185–86, 239, 260–61, 272; community hostility toward, xviii, 48, 118, 145, 146, 149, 260, 270–71, 274–77, 301n57; desegregation commemoration, *140*, 204, 233–34, 265–66, 267; faculty relationships, 83, 262; home life, 143, 144, 145, 146, 163; *In My Place*, 24–25, 48, 118, 142–44, 146, 147–49, 184–87, 249, 274, 301n57, 318n52; interracial marriage, 176–77, 186–87, 188–89, 191–94; professional life, 167, 185, 200; *Red and Black*, vi, 150, 151; suspension/reinstatement, 53, 66, 79, 83, 103, 108–11, 148, 179, 211, 309–10n12

Inscoe, John, xvii
interracial bands, 207, 295n106, 295–96n107
interracial dating, 201, 202, 203
interracial friendships, 69, 73–74, 249, 255
interracial marriage, 16, 18, 35, 39, 43, 176, 178–80, 185–87, 189, 192, 203; see also Hunter-Gault, Charlayne: marriage; *Loving v. Virginia* (1967)
interracial sex, 39, 58, 180, 191, 193

Javits, Jacob, 180
Jazz Club, 47–48, 206, 295n106
Jenkins, Bryndis Roberts, 238
Johnson v. Board of Regents of the University System of Georgia (2000), 277, 333n24
Johnson, Leroy B., 206
Johnson, Lyndon B., xii, 268
Johnson, Nathaniel, 159
Johnson, Tom, 118
Jordan, Vernon, 158–63, 167, 234, 269, 314n53

Kappa Alpha fraternity, xii, xiv, 134, 150, 213, 215, 222, 237, 245
Kemp, Brian, 1, 15
Kennedy, John F., xiii, xv, 89, 92, 93, 95
Kennedy, Robert "Bobby," 180
Kennedy, William, 221
Keppel, Francis, 208
Kerr, Clark, 6
Killian, Archibald, 168
King, B. B., 224
King, Corky, 73, 165
King, Martin Luther, Jr., 16, 42, 71, 159, 175, 187, 229, 271; critique of Eugene Talmadge, 34; FBI investigation/sabotage efforts, 88, 89–90, 105, 304n8; hostility toward, 27, 267; memorial events, 157, 244, 321n3, 327n118,124; national holiday, 230, 231, 232
Klineberg, Otto, 35, 62
Knapp, Charles: African American Cultural Center, 238, 329n144; Black faculty hiring, 238, 262; Black student recruitment/support, 238, 289–90n59; Pi Kappa Phi fraternity racism, 5, 6
Ku Klux Klan (KKK), 247, 306n27; FBI investigation of, 65, 96; racial violence, 105; UGA riot presence, 7, 8, 96–97, 101, 119, 306–307n31

Lee, Chana Kai, 15
Lee, Donald, 26
Lenoir, James, 292–293n53
Lester, Leonard, 222
Leverett, Jack, 25
liberalism, 37, 85, 196, 199, 200, 268, 279; Athens community, 16, 235; journalists, 72, 180, 184–85; religion, 29, 65, 71, 73; UGA administration, 6, 112, 225; UGA faculty, 64, 78, 79–80, 82, 84, 224, 225–26, 228, 303n28; UGA students, 73, 177, 250
Linnentown, 170
Liston, Joan, 168
Litwack, Leon, xviii
Lost Cause myth, 44
Lott, Trent, xiv, xv

Loving v. Virginia (1967), 39, 192, 194, 203, 319n75
Lucy, Autherine, 53–54, 78, 85, 86, 103–104, 108, 109, 308n43,48
Lumpkin, John Henry, 14
Lumpkin, Ola, 168
Lundy, Walter A., 47
lynching, 4, 5, 40, 67, 129, 145, 270, 286n11, 331n62

Maddox, Lester, 214, 225, 306n28
Martin Charles H., 232
Mary Frances Early College of Education, 12, 167, 204
mass mobilizations, 40, 65, 92
Matthews, Chappelle, 30
Mayhew, Paul, 37
McBee, Louise, 208
McCarthy, Joseph, 37, 57, 225
McCommons, Pete, 60, 69–70, 75, 123–24, 292–93n53, 301n61
McFeely, William S., xvii, 289–90n59
McGill, Ralph, 52, 72, 180, 185
McPhatter, Clyde, 208
McPherson, Robert G., 226, 227
Meek, Edwin, xiii
Meredith, James, xi, xii, xiv–xv, 21, 54, 70, 78
Mickey, Robert, 14
microaggressions, xi, 151, 156
Miller, Nawanna Lewis, 216
Minter, Jim, 234
Mitchell, Sidna Brower, xii, xiii, xiv
Montgomery, Horace, 82
Morehouse College, 34, 152, 167
Morrow, John, 239
Motley, Constance Baker, 2, 21–22, 158, 160–61, 265–66, 268–70, 272, 314n64
Mullendore, Richard, 272
Myrdal, Gunnar, 38, 62

National Association for the Advancement of Colored People (NAACP), 72, 118, 149, 172, 188; lawyers, 21, 158, 160; leadership, 57, 187; school integration,

National Association for the Advancement of Colored People (NAACP) (cont.) 20, 58, 66; white responses to, 32, 35, 38–39, 57–58, 66, 69, 115; *see also* Hollowell, Donald; Motley, Constance Baker; Wilkins, Roy
New Left, 85, 232, 327n119
Nesbit, Scott, 15
Nixon, Richard M., 85
nonviolence: philosophy of, 146, 216; white leaders' calls for, 64, 75, 76, 80, 308n48

Office of Minority Services and Programs, 238, 277
O'Reilly, Kenneth, 88–89, 91–92, 93, 104, 308–309n50
outside (UGA) influence, xvi, 6, 50–51, 65, 96, 103, 108, 117, 220, 226, 267, 306n25

Paine College, 29, 72
pan-Africanism, 211
Pandora (student yearbook), 26, 32
Parks, Joseph, 80
parochialism, xii, 13, 26–27, 37, 40, 43, 46, 148, 183, 225, 237, 243, 255
Pascoe, Peggy, 187
Pfuetze, Paul, 28–30, 31
Phi Delta Theta fraternity, 124
Phillips, U. B., 45
Pi Kappa Phi fraternity, 5, 6, 287n24
Platters, the, 208
police brutality, 232
political cartoons: antiracism, 8, 67, 130, 131, 135, 222, 287n32, 305–306n24, 313–14n36; FBI investigation, 90, 105, 309n1; racism, 26, 32, 95, 133, 177–78, 207, 322n8, 329n144
political correctness, 244
poll taxes, 40
Popovich, James, 81, 164
poverty, 168, 170, 197
Powell, Adam Clayton, 28
Powell, Lewis, 278
Powell, Marcia, 176, 301n57
Pratt, Robert A., xvii, 11, 115, 142, 161, 172, 239, 289–90n59, 292–93n53

Presbyterian students, 72, 73, 301n61
Protect Students First Act, 1, 279–80
public history, xvii, 3, 312–13n3

racial education, 31, 59, 62, 144
racial egalitarianism, 24, 27, 31, 73, 144, 176, 190–91, 193, 201, 268
racism: expression of (racial slurs/caricatures), ix, 4–5, 26, 31, 32, 68, 129, 146, 147, 162, 214, 229–30, 232, 243, 248, 286n12, 297n5; fraternity/ sorority systems, xiv, xviii, 4–5, 6, 50, 213, 215, 222, 237, 245, 301n57, 328n143, 333n22; militantism, xiv, 162, 229; prevalence in South, xiv, xvii, xix, 26–27, 35, 60, 171; UGA administration, 15, 20–21, 23, 28, 169, 170–71, 208; UGA faculty, xvii, 15, 27, 215, 224; UGA students, ix, xi, xiii, xiv, xix, 7, 10, 26, 32, 53–54, 68, 72, 73–74, 240, 244; University of Alabama, xvii, 11, 104, 308n43,48; University of Mississippi, xv, xvi–xvii, 11; violence, xiv, xv, xvii, 8, 11, 35, 52, 66, 75, 82–83, 149, 164, 220, 243, 304n8, 306–307n31; whitewashing of, 1, 2–3, 7, 9; *see also* antiracism; Critical Race Theory; eugenics; interracial bands; interracial dating; interracial marriage; interracial sex; riot University of Georgia; Kappa Alpha; Ku Klux Klan (KKK) microaggressions; Phi Delta Theta; Talmadge, Eugene; Talmadge, Herman; Thurmond, J. Strom; Wallace, George; Vandiver, Ernest; white racial resentment
Range, Pete, 30, 31, 84
Reconstruction, 12, 26, 34, 44, 45, 206
Red and Black (student newspaper), 23, 238; desegregation coverage, 25–26, 32–33, 37, 90, 105, 219, 222, 230, 236, 291–92n36, 301n61; editorial support for desegregation, 47, 52, 64, 76, 222, 263; interracial dating coverage, 201, 202, 203; *see also* Hunter-Gault, Charlayne: *Red and Black*
Reeves, Linda, 1

regionalism, 81
religious students: role in UGA integration crisis, 71–74
R.E.M. (Indie rock band), 235
riot (anti-integration): University of Alabama, xi, 53–54, 103–104
riot (anti-integration): University of Georgia, 11, 69, 82, 292–93n53, 296–97n4, 299n36, 303n28, 307n34, 307–308n41, 308n48, 310n15, 325n90; anti-integration roots, xiii, 53–54, 65–66, 75–77, 83, 85, 86, 90, 98–99, 154, 229, 267, 275; criticism of, xii, 55, 62; FBI investigation, xv, 7, 9, 17, 65, 86–96, 98–107, 116, 117, 119–23, 132, 300n49, 303–304n3, 304n4, 312n56; fraternity role, 4, 102, 123–24; Georgia government leaders' encouragement, 9, 10, 93–94, 121, 149, 305n23; KKK involvement, 8, 65, 96–97, 106, 119–20, 149, 240, 306n25, 306–307n31; lawlessness of, xii, 79–80; media coverage, 4, 6–7, 8, 52–53, 67, 99, 116–17, 123, 130, 131, 148–49, 234, 300n44,50, 309n6; photo-documentation of, xiii, 117, 129, 331n62; police response, 99–102, 109, 122, 308n42; reputational damage, 68, 74, 80, 90, 110; UGA administration role/response, 10, 29, 36, 83, 108, 110, 111–12, 115, 297n5, 310n22; *see also* Cochran, John Thomas; Holmes, Hamilton: suspension/reinstatement; Hunter-Gault, Charlayne: suspension/reinstatement
riot (anti-integration): University of Mississippi, xi–xvii, 70
Rodgers, Harrell, 228
Rogers, William P., 86–7, 303–304n3
Roosevelt, Theodore, 234
Rosenwald Fund, 26
Russell, Richard B., 23, 40, 44, 260; filibustering, 12, 41; segregation support, xvii, 12, 14, 23, 33, 41–43; UGA education, 114, 148; *see also* Southern Manifesto, The

Sanders, Carl, 114, 179, 265–68, 332n1
Savio, Mario, xviii

Saye, Alfred B., 61
Scarlet, Francis, 159
Scherschel, Joe, 4–5, *129*
second-wave feminism, 118, 190, 232
Shapiro, Karl, 26
Shaw, Eleanor, 168
Shipp, Bill, 47
Shockley, William, 222, 223
Silver, James, xv, 293n53
Simmons, Ruth, 15
Simpson, George L., Jr., 227
Sims, O. Suthern, 212, 323n38
Smith, Charles Henry, 44
Smith, Lillian, 29, 72
Smith, Vanessa, 277
Snow, Ralph, 100, 101, 102, 106, 309n2
socialism, 38, 62
Sotomayor, Sonia, 279–80
Southern Christian Leadership Conference (SCLC), 230
Southern exceptionalism, 259
Southern Manifesto, The, 12, 40
Southern populism, 33, 233
Southern strategy, 85
Stallings, Edith, 186, 318n52
Stephens, Alexander, 14
Stovall, Edwin, 199
Stovall, George, 193–94, 195–96, 200
Stovall, Lynn, 196, 201, 202
Stovall, Martha, 196, 200
Stovall, Walter, III: antiracism, 17, 25, 176, 183–86, 193, 204; US Army, 181, 182, 183, 184; early life, 181–82; marriage to Charlayne Hunter, 16, 25, 149, 176–77, 179, 183, 185–201, 203, 301n61; reaction to Hunter marriage, 179–80, 188, 190, 193–95, 198, 200–201, 204, 268, 318n58, 319n80
Student Nonviolent Coordinating Committee (SNCC), 151, 188, 191
Students for Constructive Action, 72, 301n61
Students for Fair Admissions Inc. v. President and Fellows of Harvard College and the University of North Carolina (2023), 278, 279

Talmadge, Eugene: higher education meddling, 30, 33, 45–46, 61, 299n33; racist demagoguery, 12, 14, 33–34, 39
Talmadge, Herman, 34, 47; public school integration fight, 35, 36, 38; red-baiting, 37, 38; white supremacy, 12, 14, 37; *You and Segregation*, 37, 38–39, 40, 44
Tate, William: January 11 riot, 53, 102, 110, 115, 122, 310n15, 311n29; Hunter-Stovall relationship, 186, 196, 318n52; segregationist views, 22–23, 110; UGA integration, 114–15, 116, 209, 274, 291n20
Tau Kappa Epsilon fraternity, 237
Temptations, The, 208
Theoharis, Athan, 88, 105
Thomas, Roger, 31, 80
Thurmond, J. Strom, xiv
Till, Emmett, 145
Tillich, Paul, 29
tokenism, 68, 83, 180, 206, 253, 279
Trillin, Calvin: Black academic performance, 168, 169, 316n99; Black student community acceptance/safety, 72, 73, 114; Charlayne Hunter-Gault coverage, 186, 205, 301n58; desegregation coverage, 141–42, 205; *Education in Georgia*, 1, 11, 99, 123, 142, 151–52, 168, 206; Hamilton Holmes coverage, 153, 156, 205, 301n58; *Holmes v. Danner*, 2, 21–22, 205; January 11 riot coverage, 100, 116, 148–49, 307n40; *New Yorker* articles, 133, 156, 205–206
Trump, Donald, xv, 1, 85
Tyler, Harold R., Jr., 87, 92–93

US Army, 3, 144, 181–82; integration of, 170, 182, 183, 184, 185, 201; racism, 268, 269

Vandiver, Ernest, 293n57; January 11 riot, 95, 102, 109; public school desegregation, 10, 11, 35, 265–66, 293n65; UGA desegregation, 33, 35–36, 76, 265–67, 268, 309–10n12, 332n8; white supremacy, 33, 34, 41, 114
Voting Rights Act of 1965, xii

Walker, Herschel, 232
Wallace, George, 11, 85
Ward, Horace: as first Black UGA applicant, xvii–xviii, 11, 23–24, 47, 82, 107, 161, 171–73, 258, 289–90n59, 291–92n36, 292–93n53; UGA admission interview, 20, 22, 164; UGA desegregation battle, 142, 170, 265, 268–69
Warren, Earl, 37, 38, 43–44, 232
Westminster House, 72, 73, 301n61; *see also* King, Corky; Presbyterian students
white nationalism, 64, 276
white racial resentment, xv, 36, 70, 82, 85, 154, 247, 260, 263, 278
White, Walter, 39
Wigginton, Eliot, 61
Wilkie, Curtis, xiii
Wilkins, Roy, 187
Williams, Joseph: criticism of Georgia state patrol, 122; mixed-race entertainers controversy, 206, 208; January 11 riot, 91, 109–10, 112, 117; UGA desegregation, 108, 311n34
Wilson, Jackie, 208
wokeism, 3
Wonder, Stevie, 208
Woodruff Hall, 97, 314n43

Yeany, Russell, 8, 287n34

Zitzelman, Joan, 72, 73